Thomas Sobchack
The University of Utah

Vivian C. Sobchack
The University of California, Santa Cruz

An Introduction to
FILM

Second Edition

D0209175

Scott, Foresman and Company
Glenview, Illinois   Boston   London

Library of Congress Cataloging-in-Publication Data

Sobchack, Thomas.
   An introduction to film.

   Bibliography: p. 467
   Includes index.
   1. Moving-pictures.   I. Sobchack, Vivian Carol.
II. Title.
PN1994.S6118   1987   791.43   86-15220
   ISBN 0-673-39302-X

Copyright © 1987 by Thomas Sobchack and Vivian C. Sobchack
All Rights Reserved.
Printed in the United States of America.

789101112131415-WKK-999897969594939291

ACKNOWLEDGMENTS

Material on manuscript preparation is adapted by permission from Sylvan Barnet, *A Short Guide to Writing About Literature*, 4th ed. Copyright © 1979 by Little, Brown and Company.

"Sound and Silence in Citizen Kane" is used by permission of the author, Kenneth E. Neff. Copyright © 1985 by Kenneth E. Neff.

"The Detective Genre" is used by permission of the author, J. Dan Broadhead. Copyright © 1980 by J. Dan Broadhead.

"The Changing Role of the Cult Film" is used by permission of the author, William Bedford. Copyright © 1985 by William Bedford.

Portions of *A Glossary of Film Terms*, John Mercer, compiler (Journal of the University Film Association, Monograph No. 2), are reprinted by permission of John Mercer and the editor of the Journal of the University Film Association. Copyright © 1978.

Text and cover photographs are from The Lester R. Glassner Collection and are reprinted by permission.

PREFACE

The movies are part of my culture, and it seems to me that their special power has something to do with their being a kind of "pure" culture, a little like fishing or drinking or playing baseball — a cultural fact, that is, which has not yet fallen altogether under the discipline of art.

Robert Warshow, *The Immediate Experience*

There has long been a popular assumption that movies encourage mindless escapism, that they divert us from our ordinary experiences by entertaining us. Many movies, however, do more than provide us with light entertainment; as well as diverting us, they enlighten us. Chaplin's *City Lights* and Coppola's *The Godfather*, for example, are highly entertaining and widely popular movies. Yet both are also films which make us recognize human relationships, social inequities, and their own artistry. A knowledgeable filmgoer, then, enters the theater receptive, open to the possibilities of both entertainment and enlightenment, realizing that a film can be experienced from a variety of perspectives — cultural, ideological, and aesthetic.

An Introduction to Film assumes that familiarity with these perspectives and others will increase the viewer's understanding and will also add to the pleasures of the commonplace moviegoing experience. A grasp of the basics of filmmaking and the context of film production will develop a respect for the complicated choices made by the artists and artisans responsible for a completed work. An awareness of the variety of cultural and theoretical approaches to the film will help a person appreciate a range of films wider than those usually shown at local movie theaters and on television. And a sense of film history will connect each individual film, not only with other films, but also with the growth, development, and change in technology and culture during the twentieth century. A basic understanding of these aspects of film and filmmaking cannot help but create a more conscious and visually knowledgable viewer, a viewer who is able to respond fully to the array of images that present themselves on theater and television screens throughout a lifetime. *An Introduction to Film*, in short, seeks to help the general student of the humanities, the fine arts, and the sciences to become an active rather than a passive film viewer.

An Introduction to Film is divided into five parts. Part I (The Production of Film) reveals the film as a product created by the culture through an industry. Part II (The Elements of Film), by considering space, time, and sound, discusses basic film aesthetics. Part III (Mainstream Narrative Film) and Part IV (Alternative Film) discuss a variety of film types, film movements, and filmmakers, with an emphasis on the cognitive rather than sensuous experience of film viewing. Finally, Part V (A Guide to Film Analysis and Criticism), beginning with the development of the varied critical and theoretical approaches to film, goes on to consider the problems faced by the student writer (illustrated with examples of student writing). Each of the five parts of the text includes Historical Overviews, which supply the reader with a connected, chronological account of relevant technological and cultural events so that discussions of film form and content will not occur in a historical vacuum. Finally, the text concludes with a bibliography designed to help the student find published source materials and a glossary of terms boldfaced in the text. Although the text can be read straight through as presented, chapters can also be assigned selectively without a loss of coherence. Each chapter is self-contained, and the numerous headings within chapters will even enable instructors to assign only portions of chapters if they wish. Because each part of *An Introduction to Film* is independent, there is necessarily some repetition of key material. Certain films, filmmakers, and historic events are referred to more often than others. Such repetition or emphasis is justified, we believe, by the acknowledged aesthetic or historic importance of the film, filmmaker, or event. It has been our consistent intent to refer to films that students will most likely have the opportunity to see, and to balance citations of classic films with contemporary films, foreign-language films with English-language films, and esoteric films with popular films.

Still photographs are another form of cinematic citation used in the text. Although stills cannot duplicate or even approximate the temporal and changing nature of the film experience, they can provide an image that jogs the memory of that experience or whets the appetite for it. Certainly, it is impossible to demonstrate what a tracking shot is or does with a group of selected stills; even if every frame of the shot were represented, the illusion of continuous time and space and motion would be shattered into separate photographs on the page. Nevertheless, it is true that the discussion of tracking shots is made clearer for the reader when some photographs are included. And stills can effectively illustrate cinematic elements such as lighting and composition. Some of the photographs in *An Introduction to Film* are studio stills (that is, publicity photographs taken on the set during filming, many of them posed or shot under ideal lighting conditions and that therefore have only a tangential relationship to comparable images in the released film). Others are frame enlargements from the films themselves. Frame enlargements are preferred, of course, since what one sees in the photograph is what one sees (for a split second) in the film; yet frame enlargements often do not reproduce very well and, in some instances, are simply not available. Although the text uses both studio stills and frame enlargements, the captions indicate (either directly or indirectly) whether a particular image actually appeared as shown in a given film. Unless credited otherwise, all the pictures are from The Lester R. Glassner Collection. To illustrate the text further, various filmmakers and artisans are quoted in appropriate sections. These quotations clarify our discussion and provide provocative statements that may occasion thought and spark discussion. They have been chosen as much for their liveliness as for their appropriateness in prefacing a specific section of the text.

Many people must be thanked for their help and guidance in the writing of this book. Sylvan Barnet's incisive editing made this a more concise, readable text. Lester Glassner's sensitive and indefatigable efforts in locating stills cannot be adequately measured. Jim Schwenterly was ready to provide an elusive film title or release date on a moment's notice. Suggestions and recommendations for this new edition were offered by Robert Appleman, Indiana University; David Bastian, the University of Cincinnati; E. Ann Kaplan, Rutgers; and Gerry K. Veeder, North Texas State University. The enthusiasm and support of Little, Brown editors Joseph Opiela, Nancy DeCubellis, and Cynthia Chapin saw the book through to completion. Throughout the many revisions, Karen Anastasopoulos, Sharan Bennett, Karen Donahue, Lisa Hancock, and Pat Tiemans typed and retyped the manuscript; their efforts are most appreciated. Special mention must be made of the generosity of the University of California, Santa Cruz; a substantial Faculty Research Grant helped support this second edition. And finally, we must thank our students. We extend particular gratitude to Ken Neff, J. Dan Broadhead, and William Bedford, who kindly consented to let us use their class papers, and we also are indebted to our students at the University of California at Los Angeles and Santa Cruz, the University of Vermont, and the University of Utah, who helped create this text from their insights, questions, problems, and interest. Without them, this book would have neither substance nor relevance.

Thomas Sobchack
Vivian C. Sobchack

CONTENTS

PART I
THE PRODUCTION OF FILM

PART II
THE ELEMENTS OF FILM

PART III
MAINSTREAM NARRATIVE FILM

PART V
A GUIDE TO FILM ANALYSIS
AND CRITICISM

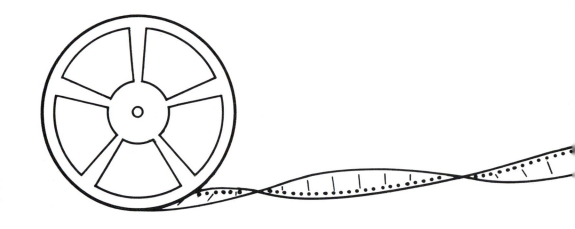

PART I
THE
PRODUCTION
OF FILM

1

THE HOLLYWOOD STANDARD

"Classical Hollywood cinema" has come to mean different things to different people, and above all, it has aroused different emotions — from misty-eyed nostalgia for the days of the studio system to frustrated fury at the multiheaded monster that is the Hollywood movie business, forever devouring its competitors and critics.

Thomas Elsaesser [1]

This book announces itself as an introduction to film. From the outset, however, what is meant by film is problematic. When we speak of film as an object of study, we are speaking of many things. **Film** is the term we use to describe a particular material and medium of communication that has certain specific properties governed by certain physical laws. *Film* is also the term we use to describe both a single work and an entire body of works produced through this material and in this medium. Film is not only its material and medium, but also their use to produce particular communicative texts that formulate particular fields of symbolic meaning and effects, and meet particular sets of criteria that give them particular value. The meanings, effects, functions, and cultural value of a film shot from a plane for reconnaissance purposes or by a bank surveillance camera are clearly different from those of an epic narrative like *Ran* (Akira Kurosawa, 1985), a feminist documentary like *The Life and Times of Rosie the Riveter* (Connie Field, 1980), or a popular blockbuster comedy/thriller like *Ghostbusters* (Ivan Reitman, 1984). Thus, the term *film* can be perceived as variously associated with the communication of information, with personal expression as art, with the argumentative power of rhetoric, and, of course, with the undemanding pleasure of entertainment.

We must not forget, however, that *film* is also a term used to describe a commercial product made in the context of American capitalism. The material, medium, and texts we call *film* are nearly always produced as commodities whose form, content, and function in our culture are economically determined. When we speak about film, we implicate an industry of mass production dependent upon mass consumption. Like the automobile industry, the film industry is primarily concerned with profit and with the cost-effectiveness of standardizing and regulating not only the modes of film production, distribution, and exhibition, but also the desires, tastes, and habits of film consumers. As a result of this economic emphasis, American film culture has become highly institutionalized. Both in our country and around the world, this standardization, regulation, and institutionalization of the film industry and film culture has become associated with Hollywood: that place where film production first concentrated itself into a major American industry and expanded its economic influence and aesthetic norms to set what has become a world-wide standard. It is, indeed, in relation to and against this Hollywood standard that alternative and oppositional kinds of cinema have emerged, struggled, and identified their practices. Always marginalized by their alternative forms and functions, and by the economic constraints on their means of production, distribution, and exhibition, American avant-garde films, for example, or Third World films or most documentaries will never make it to our local shopping mall fourplex theaters. On the other hand, whether made in Hollywood or elsewhere, films reproducing the Hollywood standard — or not straying too far from it — will.

Illusionism

It is important to recognize the implications of what we here call the *Hollywood standard*. Standards or general rules and conventions of visual and aural representation tend, over time, to become normative. That is, standardized film practices (of both production and viewing) can become so dominant and pervasive that they seem not only normal, but soon also natural (Figure 1-1). In the context of these standardized practices, it becomes increasingly difficult to imagine or understand alternative practices. Eventually, standard practices are so taken for granted that they become, in a sense, invisible to their practitioners. Rules and conventions become treated as natural law, determining the limits of what a film is and what it might be. Hypothetically, any form of representation can set the standard against which others are understood and judged. We might, for example, imagine a not too distant future in which nonnarrative rock videos have become so culturally dominant

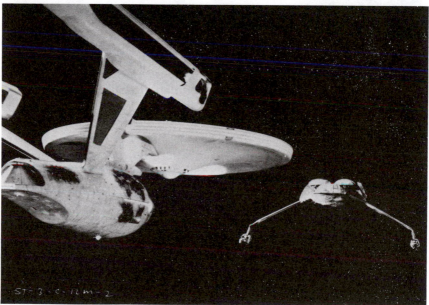

1-1 Even with the demise of the studio system, the Hollywood standard exists. The audience understands the terms of the basic illusionism of narrative films. In *Star Trek III: The Search for Spock* (Leonard Nimoy, 1984), for example, we accept the actors in make-up and costume as Klingons and the small models as space ships in some far off galaxy as long as the filmmakers have done their part to disguise these illusions by not indicating the technology and labor used in their production.

that narrative "story" films seem really strange, "old-fashioned," and possibly even difficult for the general viewer to understand.

Whatever we might hypothesize for the future, however, is countered by the present domination of the *Hollywood standard* — a changing but contained and regulated set of film production practices which emerged around 1917 and lasted until the 1960s. (This is when the monolithic studio structure broke down, and production processes were reformulated and relocated in response to new economic conditions in a world of multinational capital and corporate control).[2] Now often referred to as *classical* Hollywood cinema, the films produced during these years have greatly influenced our present expectations of what makes for a *satisfying* film experience and a *good* film. Certainly, over the years, the Hollywood standard has stretched to accommodate a range of technological, technical, and aesthetic innovations. These innovations, however, have been put to the service and maintenance of two constant, intimately related, normative practices: the production of narrative (or story) films, and the rejection from these narrative films of all signs which might indicate the technology and labor used in their production. That is, the Hollywood standard has promoted our engagement with and concentration on the cinematic product, which is the story. And, correlatively, it has diverted our attention away from the cinematic processes and labor involved in producing that story (Figure 1-2).

In one sense, this dual aim is not particularly surprising in the context of American industrial and consumer practices. Certainly, we seldom think about the processes and labor involved in the production of our manufactured goods: we concentrate on the final product and how effectively it functions. We want the toaster to work, the car to run well, the dress to be aesthetically pleasing. The manufacturer covers up the toaster's mechanisms with a bright metal shell, the car body's separate pieces with a unifying paint job, the dress's untidy seams and joinings by specifying them as the *inside* of the garment. And the consumer, focused on these finished products, does not usually think about who decided to make them; what the properties of their raw materials are; how their production was standardized and regulated not only for quality, but also for profit; how they were assembled, packaged, advertised, wholesaled, and finally retailed. The Hollywood standard, then, seems similar in its general practices and goals to other American industrial standards.

In another sense, however, despite its industrial context, film is quite different from a toaster, a car, or a dress. Unlike these products, film is a medium dependent upon a basic illusion, an illusion seen as necessary to its very existence as a *motion* picture. The car, for example, will still function as transportation even if its engine is exposed, and the dress

1-2 This still photo was taken on the set of *Silverado* (1985); the man with modern spectacles and sweater is the director, Lawrence Kasdan, talking with his actors. Notice the reflector in the background behind his head. Such images of the labor and the cinematic processes required to produce a narrative film are never shown within the film itself in a Hollywood standard movie. It would break our concentration on the story, break the spell of illusion.

does not have to hide its cloth, and would still be functional even if its seams were outwardly apparent. From the first, however, the motion picture must cover up its origins to function, to constitute the illusion of apparent motion. The celluloid moving through the camera and the projector moves discontinuously as single frames and still pictures (24 frames per second for normal sound film). Thus, discontinuous and intermittent motion is absolutely necessary to what we perceive and understand as the continuous and smooth motion of moving pictures, and this stop-and-go process must disguise itself in order to produce its product. In other words, it is generally argued that to function as a moving picture, the moving picture must hide its materials and processes of production at its most basic operational level.

Films produced according to the Hollywood standard, then, are doubly involved in drawing our attention away from their origins in material, technology, industry, and labor. They do so at their most elemental and technological level and in their further dominant function of showing and telling seamless stories (Figure 1-3). To absorb spectators in the film narratives that are the major commodity produced under the Hollywood standard, most feature films disguise not only the operation of

1-3 The illusionism of the Hollywood standard comes in many forms. The obviously posed and romantically lit publicity still of Michael Douglas and Kathleen Turner released as part of the campaign to sell *Romancing the Stone* (Robert Zemeckis, 1984) creates an aura of glamour for the performers. The image from the film showing them as people in desperate straits in a jungle downpour creates an image of authenticity. Both images are equally false, since Turner and Douglas are neither the romantic couple of the one image, nor the desperate couple of the other, but performers pretending to be both.

their technology, but also the constructed nature of their narratives. Our spectator's attention is diverted away from the fact that the story is shaped through the materials of the medium, and that the events and characters we see and the way we see them could be other than they naturally appear to us. According to the Hollywood standard, the primary pleasure of narrative is its capacity to absorb us. Thus, a good film is seen as the one best able to take us in, to create the conditions that most appeal to our credulity — to our willingness to believe in the visible, in what we see, as true. In effect, if we and the film together are to make-believe successfully, if we are to invest fully our care in the fictional world created on the screen, the ways in which that illusion is created and the fact that the narrative is being narrated must not be made visible. If they are, the illusion will be destroyed; the spectator absorbed by the story will awaken and become distanced from it — possibly to question the nature and function of the story, to examine what kind of desire it is expressing and generating, to recognize the story as not his or her own, and to imagine radically other ways of telling and imaging.

Standard Hollywood practice has been to make the construction and production of its fictions as transparent and invisible as possible. This

1-4 Though the terms of narrative film are always exaggerated and contrived — they are, of course, *fictions* — comedies are more obviously so.
Nevertheless, the audience is meant to follow the circumstances of the fictional characters as if they were real rather than representations constructed
for us by others. Michael Keaton, playing the businessman turned housewife in *Mr. Mom* (Stan Dragoti, 1985) defies common sense in his response
to his new duties, and yet his actions are taken as plausible.

practice has a dual function: it provides the general audience with the
visual pleasure of engaging with a certain form of narrative, and it
enables the cinematic institution to maintain stability and continuity in
its production of both its product and consumer desire for it. Thus, the
Hollywood standard and classical Hollywood cinema have promoted
and extended the illusionism of the cinema's basic mechanisms to the
secondary level of narrative, and have generated a dynamic history of
rules and conventions aimed at hiding both narrative construction and
the cinematic apparatus. We are meant to experience cinematic events as
directly as possible, to follow the circumstances of fictional characters as
if they were real rather than representations constructed for us by others
(Figure 1-4).

Rules and conventions of editing have been established to divert our
attention away from the individual shots and splices, which together
construct dramatic scenes and sequences — and finally the whole story.
Such editorial techniques as matching action, cutting on an action, or
taking advantage of characters' sight lines are part of the Hollywood
standard, constituting the staple editorial conventions of classical cine-

ma — and all are used to engage us with the story and disengage us from the way it is being produced. Films not observing these conventions tend to be seen by general audiences as particularly arty or as poorly edited. Thus, not only do we have certain expectations about the content of the films we are likely to see, but also we expect the film's narrative or story to unfold in certain invisible and seamless ways. And, as spectators of the film, we expect to be situated in relation to the narrative in equally invisible ways. We expect, are given, and enjoy the special privilege and pleasure of being able to look into a parallel space and time without our own presence being acknowledged.

Thus, except under special circumstances, the Hollywood standard dictates that performers not look directly into the camera — for if they do, their gaze will seem to acknowledge our space and recognize our position as spectators and, in effect, destroy the fictitious wholeness of the narrative world their characters inhabit. The beginning of a foreign narrative film like *Colonel Redl* (Istvan Szabo, 1985) is very unsettling in this regard, and its exceptional practice serves both to prove the rule of more conventional practice and the expectations we have that this rule will be observed by our fictions. Initially, several characters in this period film (set before World War I) turn their heads to look directly at the camera. They seem to recognize and smile at *us* — acknowledging our presence and consciously inviting us into their world. Soon, we understand from dialogue and action that their gaze is directed toward a yet unseen child. Until we actually see the child, however, and see the gaze of characters exchanged in screen space (or between screen spaces), the cinematic space of the film's world disturbingly extends into our own, and we are somehow implicated in the narrative (and with the unseen character) in ways that challenge our habitual and safe position as spectators and also make us actively work to interpret the meaning of what we see.

The conventional containment of the fictional world of the narrative and the rule that characters should not transgress screen space to engage the spectator are more comically challenged in *Purple Rose of Cairo* (Woody Allen, 1985). Characters do not only address the film's fictional film audience. (We, the real audience, are thus safe and feel amused rather than threatened.) One of the characters also actually steps down off the screen into the real world of that fictional audience. Both the film's plot and humor emerge from this violation of the rules of classical cinematic narrative. The film-within-the-film's characters and its audience restlessly argue with each other as they await the return of the hero whose absence has stopped the screen story. But the romantic and clean-living hero delights us as his behavior in the film's real world

1-5 Parody is generally the only cinematic form in which the Hollywood standard admits its own existence, exposing both its illusionism and our acceptance of that illusionism as natural. In *Airplane!* (Jim Abrahams, 1980), Lloyd Bridges and Robert Stack comically portrayed the same roles they had played seriously in airport disaster films, counting on the audience's awareness of the make-believe inherent in the straight versions of this subgenre.

both fulfills our expectations of romantic heroes constructed by the Hollywood standard and also subverts them — as we (and he) are comically reminded how that standard has constructed and constricted his possibilities for action and knowledge.

Indeed, comedy — particularly parody — is generally the only cinematic form in which the Hollywood standard admits its own existence, exposing both its illusionism and our acceptance of that illusionism as natural (Figure 1-5). The technological apparatus, for example, used in producing the story we are seeing is never supposed to appear on screen. A boom microphone hanging into the scene, the tracks that the camera rolls on, cables and electrical equipment — if these were apparent to us, they would destroy the illusion that what we see is not constructed, but somehow just there: a real world we literally and psychologically buy into and to which we have privileged access. As a parodist, Mel Brooks takes particular delight in exposing the cinematic apparatus at unexpected moments and making us laugh at the extent of our absorption in cinematic illusions. In *High Anxiety* (1977), Brooks not only pokes fun at and pays tribute to Alfred Hitchcock's suspense thrillers, but also exaggerates and exposes the construction of knowledge and suspense by the cinematic apparatus. Two people sit around a glass coffee table, and we become aware of the camera's position and our privileged (if suddenly ridiculous) access to them from *under* the table — for the characters start obscuring this privileged view by placing so many cups and saucers on the table that finally the camera (and we) can see nothing. In another sequence, we and the camera are invisibly positioned outside some French windows during a suspenseful scene, but begin slowly and intensely to move closer and closer to the action inside the room. Such a sequence in a Hitchcock film would magically take us through the closed windows and we would be so involved with the story and the smoothness of the intensifying vision we had of the scene that we would never think about the camera or how it got through a set of closed windows. Brooks, however, breaks both the illusionism of the scene and the windows — for at the moment of most intense suspense, the camera is exposed, visibly crashing through the glass in its effort to get inside, comically emphasizing both its finite power and its concrete presence.

Despite its accommodation of parody, however, the Hollywood standard and the classical cinema are primarily devoted to the production of seamless narratives that are cinematically transparent and illusionistic. And this devotion is shared by the general audience. It would be quite unfair to suggest that the primacy of narrative film and cinematic illusionism was simply the film industry's doing. Spectators are also part of the institution of cinema, and they help to shape and maintain its dominant aesthetic values as much as those values also help to shape and maintain spectators as appreciative consumers. In other words, we are complicit in the institutionalization of cinema, in the creation and maintenance of the Hollywood standard. We tend to want to buy narratives of a certain kind. And we generally want to be able to engage them in a certain way. We want to appropriate the narrative as if it were produced by our own imagination rather than imaged by others through technology and the processes of mass production. Certainly, in our role as spectators, we know what we are watching is only a movie — that the story is a fictional construct, that we are watching images and not real people, that those are performers up there, stuntmen, special effects, bits and pieces of time and space all glued together to make a seamless whole. But our conventional role as spectators also determines that we forget. And when we do, we have the sense that we are looking through a transparent window onto a real (if parallel) world.

Film Culture

It should be clear at this point that an introduction to film implicates more than the materials and medium which constitute the cinema, more than the single film texts we see and talk about. An introduction to film

1-6 While contemporary audiences might have difficulty accepting the stylization of a silent film like Murnau's *Sunrise* (1927), they have no difficulty understanding a stylized modern film like *American Graffiti* (George Lucas, 1973). The way in which films produce their meanings is both historically grounded and dynamic, responding to changes in film culture and the culture at large.

recognizes film culture — the body of films we see, the manner in which these films are constructed, and the ways in which they work to teach us to see, understand, and desire other films. It also recognizes film culture as specific and relative, as both historically grounded and dynamic. Across cultures and history, films produce their meanings in a variety of ways and in a variety of contexts — some seeming particularly natural and familiar to a given spectator at a given cultural moment, others unnatural and strange.

While most contemporary American spectators, for example, would have little difficulty in understanding a stylized modern film like *American Graffiti* (George Lucas, 1973), a stylized silent film like *Sunrise* (F. W. Murnau, 1927) is less immediately accessible to us. We do not really question the temporally concentrated and melodramatic action of *American Graffiti*, or its stereotypical characters, or its highly stylized settings (Figure 1-6). Nonetheless, a similar concentration of action and melodrama in *Sunrise* is difficult for the contemporary audience to deal with — as are its archetypal characters and its highly stylized settings. Both films are extremely complex in structure and visual design: *Sunrise* cannot be dismissed as a primitive cinematic artifact, nor can *American Graffiti* be celebrated as a technically and aesthetically superior work. Rather, both films derive from and most easily speak to different moments in American film culture. This same cultural relativity accounts for the formation and regulation of editorial expectations and preferences for a certain type of cinematic rhythm. Used to the fast pacing and rapid editing of American action films whether light entertainment like *Romancing the Stone* (Robert Zemeckis, 1984) or more substantial fare like *The Killing Fields* (Roland Joffe, 1984), it is not particularly surprising that American audiences might find it hard to sit through or appreciate the meticulous editorial detailing and slow rhythms of the Bengali film, *The Home and the World* (Satyajit Ray, 1985).

The study of film allows us to open a space in which we can begin to understand, appreciate, and even imagine other cinematic possibilities than the ones we were born into. It introduces us to the diversity of film cultures and to the various ways and contexts in which films produce and acquire their meanings for and from their spectators. And, most importantly, it makes us aware that film culture is something we *learn*, and that what we learn is both dependent upon our personal experience of the individual films we see and upon what our culture legitimates and promotes as the correct ways to make films, see them, and understand them. (In this regard, it is important to recognize that the book you are now reading contributes to this cultural legitimation and promotion of particular film cultures — even as it will attempt to make explicit their specific, constructed, and relative nature.)

Initially, learning to see what film is and how to understand it is as effortless (and as complex) as learning to speak and understand our natural language. This learning process is so effortless and occurs so early in our lives that it is usually experienced as invisible. Surrounded by moving images, we are immersed in a film (and video) culture from infancy. Indeed, it is hard to even imagine the experience of a culture without moving images. It is hard to believe reports that the first film audiences were terrified that the train they saw arriving at Ciotat Station was going to chug off the screen into the theater — or that a young woman watching a film comedy for the first time did not understand it or film editing, and saw nothing funny about the mutilation of human bodies accomplished by closeups and editorial cuts from one shot to the next. And yet, all of us were born into our moving image culture unable to identify and understand moving pictures as more than a random play of light and shadow and color. As with spoken language, it was in the actual practice of seeing moving pictures in a particular society that we learned to understand moving pictures were representations and meaningful. We also learned how to take and make their specific meanings. Thus, the natural activity of seeing (and understanding) films is hardly natural — even though it is utterly familiar. It is, rather, a cultural activity we learn. Our historicized, ideological, and social instruction both sets what seem the natural boundaries of what we think of as cinematically possible and limits the range of our cinematic desires, expectations, taste, and knowledge.

Our literacy, freedom, and possibilities for personal growth and social change would seem to depend upon an ability to denaturalize what seems natural and test those boundaries that limit our cinematic experience and choices. This ability, however, is not won easily. It only emerges through a secondary form of learning that is more difficult and self-conscious than our first engagement with film culture — in our case, the dominant Hollywood standard. Thus, the study of film provides us with a context for denaturalizing our seemingly natural relations with moving pictures. It allows us the critical distance from which to see how our own dominant film culture is produced, how our cinematic expectations and criteria of what constitutes a meaningful cinematic experience are formed and regulated, and how that experience might be broadened and transformed. An introduction to film, then, is an introduction to the analysis of film culture. Its primary focus is on the ways and means by which films construct their meanings for us, the contexts in which they do so, and on the various kinds of films that represent both the dominant cinema associated with Hollywood and those cinemas alternative to or opposed to the dominant cinema and its institutionalized standards. It is to the institutionalization and standardization of cinematic practice that we now turn — for the Hollywood standard has so dominated cinematic production that it is the primary context in which all film culture emerges.

The Film Industry

The production of cinema always has been both a commercial and collaborative enterprise involving many people with various skills, interests, and motives informing their participation. When Thomas Edison first made movies in the late nineteenth century, he had William Dickson assisting him. Later, various divisions of labor became necessary. Some people operated the camera, others devised the scenarios, others directed the action. Still others manufactured and processed the film and made it ready for viewing. The completed films would then have to be delivered to a place where the public could gain access to them — first the Kinetoscope parlor and then the nickelodeon, both of which were managed by yet other people invested in the successful marketing of the new medium. Each of these people were early collaborators in the industrialization and institutionalization of the cinema. Each connected to the others in a system of economic exchange — some as entrepreneurs or owners, some as investors, some as wage-earning employees, most as paying consumers. After a very brief period in which the cinema was regarded by its inventors as a scientific curiosity or a mere toy, it became the product of a mass entertainment industry organized so as to facilitate and control its production, distribution, and exhibition. There were, however, some major differences between the industrial practices of Edison's time and industrial practices in today's Hollywood. What began as small studio market capitalism in the early 1900s turned into the major studio monopoly capitalism of the 1920s to the 1960s, and now has become the multinational capitalism of an industry financially concentrated and yet geographically dispersed.

In the early 1900s, the first film producers sold copies of their films outright to exhibitors who projected them over and over until they fell apart or their audiences no longer wanted to see them. Very soon, however, it became apparent to exhibitors that the same print of a film could be seen by many different audiences over a period of time if the films were circulated from one theater to another — and no single exhibitor need purchase a film that would quickly exhaust its box office value. Exhibitors set up film exchanges in order to reduce their costs and maximize their profits. As might be expected, the exchanges were initially opposed by the people making the films for it meant a major loss in revenue. Eventually, however, film producers gained control of the exchanges and film distribution became a separate tier of the emerging industry's operation. Exhibitors no longer bought films; they simply rented them from the distributor who charged a flat fee for the period of the rental or contracted for a percentage of the ticket sales.

During this period, many small companies had formed to make moving pictures. These companies were called *studios* rather than factories but, nevertheless, they were similar to other American businesses. They had overhead costs: rentals for production space, cameras, lights, and so on. They hired both the creative personnel and the technicians to make the film products to which they owned the rights. They were also fiercely competitive and all sorts of pirating went on. To protect its films from being sold by others as their own, a growing company like the Biograph Studio, for example, made sure that its corporate insignia was built into the movie's set design so that it actually appeared on screen and in the background of most of the action. Until all the major patents on motion picture technology were registered and copyright procedures for the new medium determined, small production companies fiercely — and often violently — competed to gain control over the medium and the marketplace.

In the midteens, however, the industry began to settle down. During that time, Thomas H. Ince created the first studio in which efficient and cost-effective assembly line methods were used. Film production was organized and patterned after the practices of any big business. Separate units worked on the scenarios and scripts. (Ince was the first actually to require that these be written down and available prior to shooting.) Other units handled the production process: set design and construction, lighting, editing, and so on. The small business film production company found it increasingly difficult to match the output and technical quality of the films produced by larger companies. They also suffered as these larger companies gained major control of the film exchanges, economically coercing them not to accept and distribute films made by independents. Slowly, the smaller businesses went out of business, or were bought up by larger ones. The market capitalism of the early industry gave way to the monopoly capitalism of the 1920s — a transformation humorously and aptly noted in *Silent Movie* (Mel Brooks, 1976), which displays the name "Engulf and Devour" on the door of a major silent studio's office suite.

By the 1920s, Ince's industrial model prevailed, and his organizational principles and assembly-line processes were ubiquitous. Studios divided into the majors (MGM, for example) and the minors (Warner Brothers, for example), but even the minors were a far cry from the fly-by-night independents of earlier years. Making and selling movies was truly big business, requiring stable production practices and standardized products that appealed to a mass audience. In an enterprise that involved massive capital outlay, the need for effective cost control, for organizational stability, for the standardization of practices and products, was apparent. While strengthening the industry, however, this institutionalization of the cinema also diminished the power of individual producers, writers, directors, and performers to make unique and unconventional films. The studio heads now controlled both the figurative and literal shape and dimensions of the film product.

Because standardization was cost-effective, the studios (particularly the ones making large profits) tended to resist change and innovation. Not only did an innovation in technology or production practice cost money, but also change in one part of the industry generally caused change in other parts. This was true even in the early days of the studios. One of the reasons D. W. Griffith left the employ of Biograph was their resistance to his production of films that were longer than one or two reels. While Griffith felt that such short films limited the kind and complexity of the stories he was able to tell, Biograph felt that longer films would mean less customer turnover at the box office — and less profit. An innovation in production was perceived as having an adverse effect on exhibition. Generally, then, studios responsible for meeting overhead costs and making a profit could not afford to let individual artists experiment. And yet, paradoxically, they also looked to novelty as a way of gaining preeminence for their products. An uneasy reciprocity between invention and convention arose (and still exists) — a result of the industry's need for the marketable differentness of technological and aesthetic novelty and its opposing desire for the cost-effective sameness of technological and aesthetic stability.

Usually, however, convention holds the upper hand in this tense relationship. When director Erich von Stroheim delivered his forty-two reels (7 hours of film already edited by the director from $9\frac{1}{2}$!) of *Greed* (1924) to Metro-Goldwyn-Mayer (MGM) , the studio ordered it cut to ten reels or $2\frac{1}{2}$ hours. As one scholar of the film put it: "For the first time in its history, Hollywood had mutilated a prototype without any consideration for its historic importance and its artistic value because the film didn't fit in with the accepted norms of picture-making."[3] MGM did not believe they could sell a theatrical film running 7 hours to a mass audience, and they were probably right. (Now, such an epic work might, indeed, turn a profit and gain a large audience — but only restructured as a television miniseries and accommodating commercial interruptions.) With little exception, the outlook of the financially successful studios was essentially conservative and focused on turning out a homogenized product for what was perceived as a homogeneous audience. They organized pools of trained and specialized labor to make the product. They created a publicity machine to create a desire for the product, a distribution system to get it to market, and, for a while, even financially controlled the theaters where the product was exhibited and consumed. In a powerful and profitable structure, the Hollywood film industry had extended its control over the marketplace through a three-tiered vertical organization: manufacturing (film production), wholesaling (film distribution), and retailing (film exhibition).

The relatively monolithic and monopoly-oriented industrial and business practices, which established and maintained the Hollywood standard, remained unchallenged until the late 1940s. In 1948, an antitrust suit decision held that studios could not control film exhibition; those studios that owned theater chains were ordered to sell them. Other judicial rulings also weakened studio control over distributors and exhibitors. By the 1950s, television had become more than a novelty and, despite its small screen and lack of color, soon became an integral part of nearly every American home. The industry responded with its own attempts at novelty: various wide-screen processes, 3-D movies, more mature and explicit subject matter. Nonetheless, profits declined and it was clear that the movies no longer dominated the entertainment market. And, although movie attendance was down, the costs of film production rose. Studio sound stages and back lots, once teeming with activity, were emptied as production units went abroad to film; it was less expensive to make movies with foreign crews. As well, foreign capital was readily available for financing. Formerly in the shadow of American cinema, which set a production standard difficult to match, foreign film producers saw coproduction as a way of economically animating their own cinemas at home and breaking into the United States distribution and exhibition circuit. International coproductions became commonplace by the 1960s.

During the 1960s, changes in American culture and the American economy (both entailed with changes in technology) radically altered the film industry. The movies no longer enjoyed dominant status as mass entertainment, and so no longer could assume a relatively unselective and homogeneous audience. Once the studios' major productions were made for and sold to the whole family (presumed to be white, Anglo, working, and middle-class). By the mid-60s, audiences seemed to be evolving into special interest groups. Younger and older generations divided over civil rights (relating not only to racial discrimination, but also to sexual preference), over the Vietnam war and its aftermath, and over feminist issues. Increased fragmentation of the traditional family also fragmented the homogeneity of the audience. So did a growing recognition of economic and class differences — emphasized by rising ticket prices. (When it costs $5.00 per person to see a film, going to the movies becomes more than casual entertainment for the entire family or the working-class family, particularly when television offers its moving images for free.) In sum, there was no longer (if, indeed, there ever had been) a single ideologically stable mass audience who could be counted upon to consume happily all the films the American film industry produced.

The Hollywood studios found themselves in deepening financial trouble. Some went out of business. Others were bought up by multinational corporations who could absorb (and even make a profit from) possible financial loss. Some changed their major emphasis to television production. Others began to rent their space and equipment to *in-*

1-7 One way to insure making a film today is to organize a package of bankable personnel. *Prizzi's Honor* (1985) fielded a known actor and actress, Jack Nicholson and Kathleen Turner, as well as a successful director, John Huston, in order to get financing for what proved to be an off-beat film.

dependent producers who had put together their own production packages of script, bankable stars, director, distribution deals, and the like (Figure 1-7). Many of the largest studios had to let most of their employees go and auction off their inventory of equipment, sets, costumes and props — including Dorothy's ruby red slippers from *The Wizard of Oz* (Victor Fleming, 1939) and the "Rosebud" sled from *Citizen Kane* (Orson Welles, 1941), the latter most appropriately bought by the financial wonder of the new Hollywood, Steven Spielberg. The sale of these items and the nostalgia generated by their auction publically signaled the end of the monopoly system under which American film production had flourished. By the beginning of the 1970s, the traditional Hollywood studio with its large physical plant and stable of trained employees doing assembly line work to produce films for a homogenized mass audience was no more. Many of the names are still there: MGM, Twentieth Century Fox, Columbia. But these studios no longer make movies the way they used to: originating stories from a script department, casting from a group of players under contract, financing the entire production, and ultimately distributing for exhibition to the public.

Hollywood as *the* place where movies come from now exists more as a state of mind and a set of technical and narrative conventions than it does as the real geographical center of Hollywood filmmaking. Certainly, most of the film industry's laboratories and postproduction facilities are still there, but both the filmmaking and its financing have become increasingly decentralized and dispersed. Fewer theatrical films are made in connection with the studios, and most of them are tightly concentrated packages whose contents are controlled by business interests external to the studios. The financial and aesthetic power of the monopolistic Hollywood studio system has been dispersed, absorbed, and reconcentrated in the capital and power of today's multinational corporation. Nonetheless, the basis of the Hollywood standard — the regulated and cost-efficient production of filmed stories — still informs nearly all current cinematic practice even if the financial and industrial mechanisms of that practice have changed.

The Film Process

Although there are all sorts of exceptions (particularly in the case of experimental film production, much documentary film production, and certain third world and politically oriented film production), the complex process of producing, distributing, and exhibiting contemporary films follows a general pattern derived from the Hollywood standard. The aim is to produce a technically high-quality but cost-efficient narrative film that will be sold to the largest possible audience for the greatest possible profit. Let us trace the current process through its various phases from the inception of a film's production to its commercial exhibition on our local theater screens.

THE SCREENPLAY

Someone, of course, must initiate the idea for any given narrative film. That idea may be for an original story, or it may be for an adaptation of narrative and dramatic material from other media (most often, from literature and theater) (Figure 1-8). Whichever the case, the idea for the film must be prepared in such a way that it can be submitted for consideration for production. This submission (almost always through an agent) may be to a studio, to a major performer able to get financing or to insist that the film be made, or to an independent producer. If the person with the idea is already in the film industry in some relevant

1-8 Screenplays adapted from literature have always been popular in Hollywood, at least in part because of the presumption that the audience will recognize the title and be more likely to attend. David Lean wrote the screenplay and directed *A Passage to India* (1984) based on E. M. Forster's classic novel.

capacity, a production deal may be made on the basis of a brief and very general account of the narrative's basic plot action and characters. This short and compressed summary, which contains no breakdown of actual scenes and no dialogue, is called the **treatment.** The treatment is usually a combination of short story and expository report. It avoids screenwriting terminology, tells the film's story, and gives the reader a clear idea of both the content and emotional appeal of the finished film. The treatment may range from a few pages to perhaps thirty pages, and is meant to allow evaluation and discussion of the proposed project by people less interested in the techniques of filmmaking than in the characters, plot, settings, and potential cost of the production. The person who is already an industry professional may sell the treatment outright for someone else to develop into a screenplay, or may contract to continue with the project and write the screenplay. If the person is an industry unknown, however, more than a treatment is usually necessary if the film idea is to be seriously considered as a production possibility. Thus, in most cases, the person with an idea for a film will write a treatment as a preliminary summary and guide to further writing, but will also go on and actually write a complete screenplay before contacting an agent.

The screenplay is written in a conventional film script format, and its purpose is twofold. Certainly, it is the writer's attempt to communicate a story through dramatic action and dialogue, to construct a pre-text, which will act as the structural scaffold for creating the eventual text that is not written, but is dramatized and filmed. But the screenplay is also the primary means by which the film idea is sold to people who have particular interests and limited time. It will undoubtedly be read by a variety of people looking at it from different perspectives: performers looking for a strong role to play, directors looking for an interesting and complex narrative to film, producers looking for a generic category into which the story can be pigeonholed and easily sold and at the potential cost of its production. Thus, although the screenplay must be dramatically written, and must be detailed enough to convey a unified vision throughout a complex process of collaboration, it must also be easy to read — uncluttered by the writer's ideas about its potential visual realization. This screenplay, then, is quite different from those eventually published for a general (rather than scholarly) readership. The latter are usually continuity scripts — written after the fact of the film's production and from a viewing of the completed film, and containing brief descriptions of cinematic techniques meant to enhance the reader's visual memory of a film already seen.

The screenplay that the screenwriter commits to paper does not have the details found either in the continuity script or the shooting script the director will use on the set and in postproduction work. Its emphasis is on dialogue and action. Although its format may be variable, the primary purpose of the screenplay is to structure the key elements of the dramatic scenes which will constitute the narrative of the completed film. Of necessity, the screenplay will include some descriptive prose — most detailed when it introduces characters or settings for the first time and least detailed when it indicates place and time and peripheral action or camera movements or angles. For the sake of brevity (and the script's sales potential), a description of a character may invoke a known (and bankable) performer who plays certain kinds of roles, has a certain look, and conveys certain values (for example, "John is a Harrison Ford-type wise guy: cynical with a heart"). Scene descriptions of place, time, and situation will be less than elaborate (for example, "Barn, interior. Night. The Vet inspects the horse while John and Susan watch."). The screen-

1-9 Susan Alexander works on one of her puzzles in Xanadu in *Citizen Kane* (Orson Welles, 1941). Did the idea of the puzzle — "What is Rosebud?" — come from the director or from the screenwriter? The shooting script of the film was published in *The Citizen Kane Book,* which also contains an essay by Pauline Kael that discusses the issue of film authorship.

play's emphasis will tend to be on the character's dialogue, with prose descriptions of action included where necessary (for example, "She angrily walks to her car." or "He begins to sob."). The screenwriter will not indicate camera setups, particular lighting effects, or other cinematic elements, which are the director's responsibility when the scene is actually shot. The only usual exception is when a particular camera movement or cinematic element needs to be specified because it forwards the plot, or creates the suspense of the scene, or reveals something special about the character (for example, "The camera slowly moves forward from a long shot of the crowded room to the bandstand and into a close-up of the drummer's twitching eye." or "The camera pulls back to reveal that Dave is sitting in a wheelchair."). In sum, the initial screenplay is written less in terms of its final appearance on the screen than in terms of its clear narrative and dramatic potential — particularly as that potential can be easily and quickly communicated to agents, actors, producers, directors, and investors, all of whom have specialized interests and criteria in selecting one film idea over others (Figure 1-9). Hundreds of screenplays circulate regularly in Hollywood, but only a few get sold and even fewer are actually realized on the screen.

FINANCING AND PACKAGING
Creativity and quality are not necessarily the criteria upon which film financing is based. Indeed, in most instances, financial backers prefer conventional stories, plot structures, and characterizations —

screenplays that basically imitate past box office successes. That is why there are films like *Friday the 13th — The Final Chapter* (Joseph Zito, 1984) and *Rocky IV* (Sylvester Stallone, 1985). At the same time, however, originality and novelty sometimes prove to have commodity value. An off-beat screenplay may be difficult to sell, but the occasional commercial (and critical) success of an eccentric film like *Terms of Endearment* (James L. Brooks, 1983) means that the unconventional screenplay is at least potentially worth a reading. Agents, then, are necessary not only to forestall law suits between screenwriters and producers, but also to find people in a position of power willing to read a particular kind of screenplay.

The move from getting a reading to getting financing is likely more dependent upon luck and salesmanship than it is upon the inherent quality of the screenplay under consideration. Someone with administrative and/or financial power has to step forward and say (for whatever reasons): "I want to make this film." This person and his or her associates have to convince the banks that the projected film is worth financing. They first might have to secure the interest of bankable stars (like Barbra Streisand or Robert Redford), or, in some cases, of a director (like Steven Spielberg). The film might be offered to a number of creative personnel to form a package, which in its totality will seem like a good investment to financial backers. Here is where the deals are made, and where they fall through. Ultimately, no one is assured of financing, and many creative filmmakers have been denied backing for particular projects. (Both Robert Altman and Francis Ford Coppola have attempted to initiate alternative structures for financing and producing their often extremely unconventional films, but with little success) (Figure 1-10).

The production package (the screenplay only a small — if crucial — part of the whole) is put together with maximum profit as its goal. How much money will be necessary to make the film is projected against possible returns on the investment. Thus, in general, it will be much more difficult to secure financing for an original film musical or for a Civil War epic with a cast of thousands than for a tight action drama or a light comedy with a relatively small cast. To realize the Civil War screenplay as a film might cost 30–50 million dollars (1985 figures), whereas the light comedy might cost only 4–5 million. (The average cost of a feature film is currently around 10 million dollars.) Given these major production costs, the package also will usually include an agreement with a distributor. Here is where studios like Twentieth Century Fox and MGM/UA get back into business. Not only may they agree to finance the distribution of a given film after its completion, but they may also invest in the film up front or help arrange for financing. At this point, the package is also enhanced if contractual arrangements have

1-10 Robert Altman who directed the film version of David Rabe's play *Streamers* (1983) has attempted to initiate alternative structures for financing of such unconventional films. Though the money was secured for this and other projects, no one can ultimately be assured of financing. Altman's recent films, for example, though critically acclaimed, have not been big box office hits.

been made for other sources of revenue: foreign distribution, cable and network television rights, video cassettes, subsidiary merchandising rights for products like toys. Many of these deals can be made so that money is secured in advance, and basic production costs are covered before even a foot of film is shot. Sometimes, however, the money invested up front may barely cover the cost of a completed release print. (This is particularly descriptive of small independent productions put together on shoestring budgets by regional filmmakers, for example.)

If the initial package does not include a guaranteed distribution arrangement, the film may never be made. Tom Selleck (considered a reasonably bankable star because of his popularity on television's "Magnum P.I." series) had an option on a screenplay he liked and in which he wanted to star. Distribution was secured for the project — provided that

Selleck's then current release made a profit. It did not. Despite the popularity of science fiction movies, *Runaway* (Michael Crichton, 1984) played poorly. As a result, the distribution company withdrew its support for Selleck's next project and the package deal fell apart. It still seems a truism in Hollywood (and on Wall Street) that "You're only as good as your last picture." Even when producers are able to secure financing actually to make the film, without a distributor the completed work may never be seen by the general public in commercial theaters. Thus, without commercial distribution secured in advance, major investors see little chance of a return on their money, and so will refuse to participate financially in the project.

In most cases today, the decision to finance the production of a particular film is made by a lot of people who have nothing to do with the actual art and craft of making movies. Bankers, corporate officials, and investment firms have nothing invested in film production but money. Although they were also primarily businessmen, the old studio moguls were thoroughly engaged in the production process, and they took a certain amount of pride in the products that carried their names and sometimes secured them a reputation for quality entertainment. On occasion, they would even risk losing money on a given production — not only in hopes of enhancing the studio's name, but also because (given the studio structure) they could absorb the loss in the profits made by their many other films. Today's bankers have nothing to gain or to lose but their financial investment in relation to each particular and isolated film package. Their names do not appear on the screen, nor do they think in terms of critically acclaimed loss leaders as good business practice since they have no studios to promote. All that matters is that the projected profits have a good chance of being realized. The nature and quality of the film product is, to a great degree, irrelevant.

PREPRODUCTION

If a package deal is signed and sufficient financial backing secured, then the producers begin to prepare financially and physically for the actual production of the film. Time is money in the film industry, and so a budget and production schedule are prepared meticulously to plan the most cost-efficient use of craft labor, materials, locations, and performers. Casting performers, selecting production crews, deciding on locations, renting studio space and technical equipment, securing transportation, lodgings, catering services — all this and more must be done in advance of shooting the film, and at a cost that is in line with the film's total budget and scheduled production time. The production schedule and budget — and adherence to both during actual production and postproduction work — are the producer's responsibility. And while the production schedule will meticulously project and detail the expenditure of time, the budget will meticulously project and detail the expenditure of money. It will indicate both above-the-line costs (how much of the invested money will be spent on payroll and material costs to complete a print of the film) and below-the-line costs (how much will be spent on making release prints for theatrical distribution, and on publicity and advertising). It is important to note that in today's cinematic economy, below-the-line costs usually far exceed above-the-line costs, as usually much more money is spent on advertising a film than on its actual production.

Before shooting begins, the person chosen to direct the film is also at work. In consultation with the production's other contracted creative personnel (the screenwriter, the director of cinematography, the art director, and so on), the director's initial task is *literally* to envision the film in its realized narrative unity. That is, the director must turn the original screenplay into a shooting script, which will serve as both a technical and aesthetic guide to getting the story from its written form to its filmed form. The screenplay (which may have already been rewritten several times at this point) usually comes to the director in one of two formats: the dialogue and brief visual descriptions of scenes alternate down the page, or the dialogue and other aural elements like music and sound effects and the visual description are divided, the former running down the left side of the page and the latter down the right. In both formats, however, scenes are numbered in chronological order as they shift in their locales and dramatic action. Thus, one of the director's major preproduction tasks is to break down screenplay scenes into specific shots (also numbered so as to correspond with the scenic numbering). Each separate shot that might be used to constitute a given dramatic scene will be noted. Camera distance from the action will be indicated — as will be camera angle and movement, movement of the performers, particular lighting instructions, and special effects. Sometimes, in concert with this work on the shooting script, an actual pictorialization of the desired shots and their sequence may be drawn as what is called a **storyboard.** The storyboard consists of individual drawings, which together, rather like a comic book, give a sense of the finished film's visual continuity: the actual way in which shots, scenes, and sequences are to look and cohere as a unified narrative. (Many directors use storyboards — not only those who came from a previous art background as did Alfred Hitchcock and Satyajit Ray, but also those like George Lucas who use a great many special effects, which cannot be literally visualized until the film is nearly completed.)

1-11 Director David Lean is shown here on location in India while shooting *A Passage to India* (1984). In addition to writing the screenplay, Lean had to write a shooting script, consult with his technicians, and rehearse the performers as part of the preproduction work involved with bringing the film to the screen.

It is at this time that the director begins to put a personal imprint upon the film's narrative vision, selecting and shaping the visual and aural elements of the cinema in a singular way, literalizing an attitude toward the story and its characters by planning the camera's physical point-of-view. Although they are usually only available for study in film archives or special library collections, actual shooting scripts complete with the director's marginal notations (on lighting, set details, performance, camera movement, and so on) can reveal much about the process through which the written screenplay (or pre-text) is transformed into the visual and aural complex of the final film text. In actual production, the director may alter the vision that is detailed in the shooting script, but it is during this preproduction period that the director's basic vision is formed, articulated, and discussed with the film's other creative collaborators. Part of this discussion may occur in conference, but part of it also occurs in rehearsal with both the performers and technicians (Figure 1-11). The director's other major preproduction task is rehearsal for the actual production. It is in the immediate and contingent situation of rehearsal that practical problems and their solutions emerge —

sometimes limiting, sometimes enhancing, but always to some extent altering the director's originally planned interpretation of the script.

PRODUCTION

The actual production begins, finally. To reduce costs, film scenes are usually shot out of their chronological sequence in the screenplay and narrative. They are grouped together for shooting on the basis of their similar location, their use of a particular performer (who may be available only for a few days of the production), their need for a particular piece of rented equipment. Contingency plans for shooting are also prepared to accommodate uncontrollable elements like the weather or illness. This scheduling is the producer's responsibility — as is sending out the various production assistants to make last minute arrangements with local police or to buy extra rolls of electrical tape from a hardware store. Before principal creative personnel like the director, the cinematographer, or the star performers arrive for the day's work, things are made ready according to the production schedule. Trucks arrive with equipment. A small army of expert technicians (whose union regulations specify they may perform only a given set of functions) place the lights, reflectors, sound equipment, camera tracks, cranes, dollies, lenses, and camera as they are required of the scene to be shot. The set (in a studio or on location) has been dressed and props are in place. Performers and extras have been costumed and made-up.

All is finally ready for the given scene to be shot. That scene may be simple or complex — filmed continuously as a single shot with the camera in a stationary position or moving in relation to the action, or filmed discontinuously in many separate shots taken from various camera set-ups, which require the technical crew to move various equipment or to change lenses and focus. Time, money, technical talent, and directorial vision determine the kind and number of shots that will eventually provide the material from which the editor constructs the finished scene. Nonetheless, the Hollywood standard has generally set a conventional procedure meant to secure the broadest coverage of the scene for the director and editor (and, in the studio days, for the producer and studio head who had final say about the final version of the film). This procedure involves shooting what is called a **master shot** of the whole scene: the scene is played through and shot continuously from a relatively distant position so that the whole action will be visible. Next, medium shots of dominant action in the same scene are filmed from various camera set-ups and points-of-view; this will mean delays on the set as set-ups, lenses, and lights are changed, as performers are directed to reenact their previous performance but to do certain things

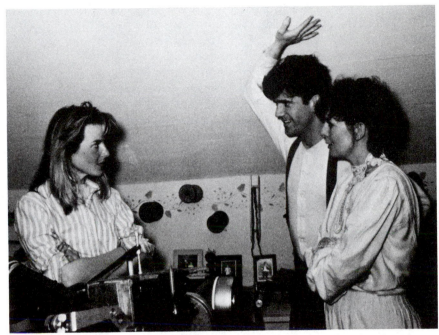

1-12 The Australian director, Gillian Armstrong, prepares for the shooting of a scene from *Mrs. Soffel* (1984), her first film made in America, with performers Diane Keaton and Mel Gibson.

that will be visible only in medium shot. For extra coverage and a wide selection of shots in the editing room, action may be repeated again and again with the camera recording first the action of one character, next the reaction of another, and again the reaction of a third. (Which image of which character will actually be used in the finished film is not yet determined.) Then close-ups are made — as are insert shots of potentially significant props or items in the decor. During the actual filming, the director (usually with the producer and sometimes with the editor) will also be looking at the rushes or dailies — the film rushed to the lab for processing so the previous day's shooting can be screened and necessary retakes scheduled.

The process of shooting a film not only requires that action be repeated again and again, but it also requires a great deal of time be spent on changing set-ups. While technicians move cables and tracks, or change lights or lenses, or readjust apertures, the performers and the rest of the production crew wait (Figure 1-12). Shooting a single scene can be extraordinarily time-consuming even when things do not go wrong. And much of the time, it is a very boring process for those not immediately concerned with the particular procedure in progress. And, if not boring, it can be frustrating. The director and cinematographer may have to contend with unexpected material problems: the light is not quite right; a bulb burns out and must be replaced; a horse refuses to behave; a costume rips; a performance is uneven. The Hollywood standard of illusionism, however, has extended to the general public's notion of filmmaking as glamorous. (This has been one way the industry has been able to sell performers as stars, and advertise the high costs of production as part of the Hollywood fantasy of luxury and excess.) For most of the people involved, however, filmmaking is difficult, tiring, and often dangerous work. It involves a small army of people who must communicate and collaborate with each other whatever their individual vision or temperment, and who must work under the pressure of limited time and budgetary constraint.

Those tedious and exasperating aspects of filmmaking are themselves often the stuff of which both fictional and documentary movies are made (even if the process is still ultimately glamorized in most cases). *Day for Night* (François Truffaut, 1973) is a rather loving dramatization of the problems of making a feature film — its director, Truffaut, acting out the exasperation and passion of his own narrative's fictional director. And, although dominated by the presence of Peter O'Toole playing a demonic director, *The Stunt Man* (Richard Rush, 1980) emphasizes the complex, dangerous, and somewhat crazed nature of the production process from rehearsals of both stunts and dramatic action, to shooting (out of sequence), to looking at dailies. There have also been many inside documentary looks at the production of particular films like *Raiders of the Lost Ark* (Steven Spielberg, 1981). Perhaps one of the most fascinating of these (because it is a complex film in its own right) is *Burden of Dreams* (Les Blank, 1982), which documents German filmmaker Werner Herzog shooting *Fitzcarraldo* (1982) in the Peruvian Amazon — and reveals not only the battles the director had with the natural and cultural world of his chosen landscape, but also his near-crazed obsession about his film and its completion (Figure 1-13).

POSTPRODUCTION

After the filming is completed, the long, complex, and relatively dispersed postproduction period begins. First, the director and editor work together to edit the film from rough cut (a crude assembly of selected shots and sound structured in narrative order) to fine cut (an extremely refined and highly structured assembly, which constitutes not only the narrative, but also the film's rhythm and pacing) to final cut (the form in

1-13   One of the most fascinating inside documentary looks at the making of a film is Les Blank's *Burden of Dreams* (1982) which follows German film-maker Werner Herzog shooting *Fitzcarraldo* (1982) in the Peruvian Amazon. This film reveals not only the battles the director had with the natural and cultural world of his chosen landscape, but also his obsession with the completion of the film. Les Blank is shown above on location.

which the film will be commercially released). The producers may also get involved in the editorial process, and may, in fact, have the right to decide what constitutes the final cut. It is also during this editorial phase that if the film needs optical effects (freeze frames, for example), they are added through special optical printing processes in specialized laboratories contracted to do such work.

Once the film is in its final visual form, various aspects of its sound track will be adjusted or added. Special sound effects will be added to the sound mix of dialogue tracks and other sound recorded at the time of shooting. The mix itself will be fine-tuned. At this point, musical scoring and recording will also occur — for even if a composer has been contracted early on, only broad themes (or original songs) have been completed. The film needs to be projected in its final form before background music can be paced and played in a manner appropriate to the work as a whole. Title sequences and credits are also part of the postproduction process, and sometimes the former are done by specialists who have had no previous connection with the film. The same is true for the film's previews (sometimes called "trailers"). When all this work is done, then many commercial release prints are made from the original negative and the film is ready to distribute and exhibit. The entire postproduction process involves an enormous number of people — many more than those who worked on the actual filming. These people, however, hardly constitute a centered or close-knit group. Some may be isolated in laboratories, or before computer terminals, others may form very small groups to make sound effects, and a small proportion may literally band together — to form the orchestra that will record the film's music. Amid such a dispersion of labor, both the director and the producer must keep track of the film's progress and keep in mind its original vision.

MARKETING: DISTRIBUTION AND EXHIBITION

Long before a film's general release date has been set, it will have been announced and described to the public in some way. Entertainment columns in general newspapers, announcements and progress reports in trade papers like *Variety*, articles in monthly magazines, interviews with directors and performers in both written and televised form (as on the very successful "Entertainment Tonight") — all inform both the industry and the public of various phases of production from the film's inception to its release. This, of course, functions as a preliminary marketing of the film; that is, it constitutes a way of informing people of the availability of the product and also creates an anticipatory context of desire for the product. The distributor who has been involved with the production as part of the initial package deal will have been lining up exhibitors — preferably large chains like General Cinema Corporation or the American Multi-Cinema Corporation who each have more than 500 theaters around the country. Smaller regional chains and independent theater owners will be contacted too and, in fact, may be more appropriate exhibitors for certain kinds of films appealing to specialized audiences. Over the last several years, the major distributors have been the big studios. No longer producing many of their own films for theatrical release, companies like MGM/UA, Twentieth Century Fox, and Columbia Pictures have made a major business distributing films produced by package deal. In this regard, small independent producers who have not secured a distribution deal in advance with one of these studios or their subsidiaries will have a hard time getting their films exhibited. Usually the strategy is to get the film accepted for screening at various national and international film festivals in the hopes it will be seen by or brought to the attention of a distributor who now will recognize its commercial potential. If this does not work, the independent filmmaker will go door-to-door, showing the film to small distributors. Finally (and usually as a last resort because they require an outright sale of the film), the filmmaker will attempt to sell the film to cable television or for home video distribution. Independent producers and filmmakers who have not been able to secure advance distribution, particularly with the major studios, have a hard time getting their films advertised, marketed, and exhibited.

The studios are also highly concerned with marketing and advertising strategies since they now concentrate so heavily on distribution. Sometimes, however, these strategies backfire — particularly when the marketing campaign and the film seem to have little to do with each other, when the ads celebrate a particular aspect of a film so as to appeal to a particular audience that may, in fact, not be the audience appropriate to the film. Ad campaigns are designed to reach into specific markets. Teenagers, for example, were presumed to be the target audience for *Desperately Seeking Susan* (Susan Seidelman, 1985) because the popular rock star Madonna had a part in the film. This eccentric film, however, was about a New Jersey housewife seeking her identity in a world of ephemeral relationships and casual sex, and was directed more towards a sophisticated adult audience than it was to teenagers who, perhaps, were expecting another *Flashdance* (Adrian Lyne, 1983) or *The Breakfast Club* (John Hughes, 1985). Until the ad campaign was altered, the film foundered — desperately seeking an appropriate and appreciative audience. There are, of course, other marketing strategies: sneak previews, which get people into the theater and, it is hoped, spread advance word about how good the film is. Often benefit screenings usually held the day before the film's regular release will be offered to community groups. Or local radio stations will give away free tickets, advertising the film over the air as they do so. And more contemporary marketing of films has tied in with ancillary products — toys, tee shirts, and particularly records and tapes.

Most first-run movies seen today open simultaneously across the country in 200–500 theaters. In larger cities, there may be many screens running the same film. Sometimes, however, even in a large market area, a single theater may have exclusive rights to exhibit a particular film. Whether a single chain has exclusive rights to exhibit a given title depends upon negotiations and contracts between the distributor and exhibitor. Exactly how much the film will cost to book into the theater and how long the run will last are also negotiable. Some of these negotiations may occur through a bidding process by which various chains and exhibitors located in certain regional areas bid for the right to show the film, and the distributor takes the best deal offered (whether it is the highest flat rental fee or the highest percentage of the box office gross). Sometimes exhibitors get a chance in trade previews actually to see the product before bidding on it. Sometimes, however, the exhibitors in a particular area must engage in blind bidding, and will not have an opportunity to see the product before they negotiate for exhibition rights. This process, of course, puts a burden on the exhibitor — particularly if the unseen film turns out to be a box office bomb. In such a case, the exhibitor may take a heavy loss. The business is, indeed, so risky that the exhibitor has found the theater concessions (the candy counter and popcorn machine) the most stable source of income — hence the outrageous price of refreshments helps cover losses at the box office.

It might be useful to trace just what happens to the money you pay for a ticket to see a first-run feature film. The exhibitor's deal with the distributor usually includes a guarantee of a flat minimum sum versus a percentage of the gross ticket sales (whichever is highest). Thus a deal might be struck for a $50,000 minimum versus 35% of the total ticket sales. If the film does not play very well, the exhibitor may have to give up 60% or more of ticket sales to meet the minimum guarantee. If, however, the film pays well, the exhibitor will get to keep 65% of each ticket sold. From this gross profit, the exhibitor must pay overhead costs such as employee salaries, theater maintenance, and local advertising. In one way or another, the flow of money slowly moves backward from the spectator/consumer to the film's producers. The distributor gets the amount agreed upon from the exhibitor as the film plays and then, in turn, passes a percentage on to the producers according to the original terms of a contract (which may have been made at the film's inception as part of the original production package, or may have been made, as in the case of small independent films, after the film's completion). While variable, the distributor's percentage will be sufficient to make a net profit after paying for distribution expenses: the cost of multiple release prints, shipping, bookkeeping, the collection of rental monies, national advertising, and so on. The expenses of distribution and exhibition run so high that in many cases even a box office hit may take an extremely long time before its producers and initial investors will realize a profit. In this regard, the gross ticket sales figured in the trade papers and general press are deceptive.

Filmmaking is a risky business venture for all concerned. Thus, the industry is essentially conservative; neither Hollywood filmmakers nor Wall Street bankers encourage risk, and policymakers from both quarters do everything possible to safeguard their investments. The profits of a hit movie can be enormous — *Ghostbusters* presumably made enough to keep Columbia from filing for bankruptcy in 1984 — but the odds are against it. Audiences are both fickle and fragmented. Even when a film is planned to appeal to what demographic studies say is the major theatrical film audience (currently, teenagers), no single film can

1-14 Audiences today are both fickle and fragmented; no single film can be programmed for success. *Raiders of the Lost Ark* (Steven Spielberg, 1981), though a comparatively expensive production, turned out to be a far greater hit than anyone at the Lucasfilm organization imagined.

be programmed for success (Figure 1-14). Audiences also no longer have to pay the high price of a ticket if they want to see a film. The booming home entertainment market provides a cheaper and more convenient alternative to theatrical exhibition. Taking this market into account, today's motion picture producers figure cable, cassette, and network television sales as part of their potential return. The film industry has had to change its business practices in response to changing technology and its alteration of American cultural practices. Going to the movies today is not the same kind of cultural activity as it was in the 1940s. And the business of making movies today has had to change accordingly.

THE CREDITS

It may be a cliché to say that making a film is a collaborative enterprise, but it is also true. As indicated above, the industry practice of assembly line production requires an enormous number of people to make a single film. These workers can be divided into two groups: those whose names appear in the film's credits and those whose names do not. The uncredited group are as much responsible for the film we see as those who do receive screen credit for what we normally think of as filmmaking. As we might expect, the uncredited group includes little and unsung film workers like the individuals who work in the optical lab (the lab itself will be listed in the credits), but it also includes some of the most powerful people connected with the film's production. The people who put the production package together will not normally get screen credit unless they are also considered the film's executive producers. Similarly, the major investors (bankers, managers of mutual funds, organized companies that specialize in film financing, and so on) will not get screen credit. And, finally, agents representing both screenwriters and performers do not get screen credit (although casting agencies do). These people are not engaged in the material production of the film, but today — in the absence of the studio system — they are the most responsible for getting the necessary capital and personnel together so that the material work can begin and a film can be produced.

The following people literally do the labor required to make a particular film and are given principal or secondary credit on the screen. (There are others who also get screen credit, but space does not permit inclusion of their titles and functions.) The principal credits are those that either precede the beginning of the narrative or are superimposed over its initial scenes. Secondary credits appear after the narrative is over and tend to roll by unattended by patrons in the process of leaving the theater.

PRINCIPAL CREDITS

Executive Producer/Producer

These are the people assigned by the investors to oversee the production. Their primary concern is physically organizing and coordinating all the materials and personnel needed to make the film within the confines of the budget. The executive producer may have little direct contact with the production; the producer, on the other hand, is directly involved with the day-to-day work of making the film.

Performers

These are the dramatic players. First credited are the stars whose presence is crucial to the sale of the movie to consumers. Smaller credits list supporting performers. Sometimes special arrangements are made to indicate featured performers who are singled out (either graphically or with a solitary credit) to distinguish them from supporting performers.

Screenwriter

One or more persons is credited with writing the screenplay. Often, a story credit will also be given to distinguish the person who originated the idea (and the treatment) from the person who actually wrote the screenplay. Credit may also be given to a novelist, short story writer, or dramatist if the screenplay is an adaptation of a previous work.

Director of Cinematography
The person chiefly responsible for the film's visual character, the director of cinematography directs camera operators, lighting technicians, and other personnel to achieve the desired image.

Art Director
This person is primarily responsible for designing and decorating the film's sets — usually in close collaboration with the director, the cinematographer, and the costume designer. Sometimes the credit may be listed as *visual consultant* when the person designs a whole concept — as did Syd Mead for *Blade Runner* (Ridley Scott, 1982).

Musical Director
Credit is given to the composer of the film's score if it is original. If a potential hit single song has been written and recorded by a popular artist, both the song and singer may also get credit at this point.

Director
Usually emphasized as the last of the principal credits, the director is creatively in charge of the entire production and works with all personnel to realize a finished film with a unified vision. More specifically, the director creates a working schematic from the screenplay, directs performers and cinematographers during filming, and finally oversees the postproduction assembly of the film. (There are other directorial positions such as second unit directors who shoot supplementary or specific location footage and assistant directors, but these functions are credited at the end of the film.)

SECONDARY CREDITS
Editor
Although some editors have special arrangements with specific directors and receive principal screen credit, most are credited at the end of the film. The editor is in charge of the film's final assembly, working closely with the director to realize the screenplay in the most effective way possible. This person may literally splice film or use computerized editing, but most of the actual physical work is done by assistants, only some of whom receive screen credit.

Sound Recording
The person credited here manages the recording of the sound taken during shooting as well as the recording of any other sound effects added in postproduction.

Sound Editor/Mixer
This is the person (or persons) responsible for editing and mixing all of the separate sound tracks — dialogue, music, sound effects — into a final and composite sound track. (Again, there are many people involved in this process, only some receive screen credit.)

Camera Operators
Supervised by the director of cinematography, these are the people who actually operate the cameras, doing the actual shooting, changing lenses, and so on.

Grips and Gaffers
These are the people who actually do the physical work of moving the lights, cables, and various heavy equipment used during production. The key grip supervises the various work crews.

Costume Designer
This person designs and/or selects the clothing the performers will wear. If the film's costuming is especially elaborate (as for a historical drama or a musical), or if the designer is well known (as, for example, was Edith Head), then the designer may get principal credit. Design or costume credit may also be given individually for the person dealing with the clothing worn by a single star performer.

Property Master
This person is in charge of securing and having on hand for shooting the various objects used on a set or on location.

Make-Up
This person makes-up performers for both the special needs of the character and the screenplay and the particular kind of illumination that will used in the shooting. Recently, individual credit has been given to make-up designers who specialize in horror and science fiction films.

Hair Stylists
These people not only design and realize hair styles for the film, but are also responsible for attending to performers' hair so that it does not seem to change from shot to shot.

Continuity
This person records what happened in each shot taken so that the exact position of the performers and props are known so as to ensure the continuity of space and time in a dramatic scene. Their work makes possible the matching of various shots filmed from different angles and out of sequence.

Casting
Usually credited to an agency rather than to individuals, these people are responsible for casting the film's secondary roles and extras after the production has been financed. (The principal performers usually are involved in the initial package.)

Special Effects
These credits may refer to individuals or to specialized companies (such as Industrial Light and Magic) who are responsible for out-of-the-ordinary (and out-of-the-camera) visual or auditory effects. Most often, these credits are prominent in film genres like horror, science fiction, and fantasy films.

Second Unit
Usually providing a whole credit list in itself, the second unit is constituted by a director, a group of camera operators and relevant technicians, sound operators, and so on, who are responsible for the filming of certain sequences in the production that do not involve major performers or major action. If, for example, the film needs a shot of an airplane landing as a transition between two other scenes, the second unit will be sent to shoot it. Certain location shooting (when it is used as background for the principal action) is also done by the second unit.

Although it may seem so, this is not an exhaustive list of the functions and individuals who receive screen credit. The next time you see a film, read the credits closely and you will appreciate how many people and businesses are involved in the collaborative process of making a movie. Also remember all those other people and businesses who are not credited but who are responsible for that movie's exhibition and distribution: the publicists, ad writers, theater owners, projectionists, ticket takers, and concession operators. The film you see on the screen is the product of an enormous amount of labor.

This chapter has been a short and somewhat cursory look at the complexity of film as a cultural institution, a billion-dollar industry, and a standardized product made as a commodity in a capitalist system of production and consumption. Understanding that this system exists and how it works can only help us to comprehend more fully the cultural signs and symbols and conventions that industry and system produce. However much we tend to forget the fact, films are not images produced through our immediate and direct contact with the world. Rather, films are *mediated* visions of the world. They provide us an indirect vision, one which is filtered through the lens not just of a camera, but also of someone else who has a particular interest in seeing the world in a particular way. That interest may be merely aesthetic. It may be highly moral. It may be purely economic. It will surely be, to some measure, political and social. Whatever that interest is, however, it informs the films we see. No film is innocent of the conditions and practices that went into its making. Thus, it becomes important that we understand those conditions and practices as the ground upon which films are both technically and aesthetically constructed and seen as culturally significant.

NOTES

[1] Thomas Elsaesser, "What Makes Hollywood Run?" *American Film* 10, no. 7 (May 1985): 52.

[2] These dates are derived from the most current and definitive study of Hollywood cinema: David Bordwell, Janet Staiger, and Kristin Thompson, *The Classical Hollywood Cinema: Film Style and Mode of Production to 1960* (New York: Columbia University Press, 1985).

[3] Herman G. Weinberg, *The Complete* Greed *of Erich von Stroheim* (New York: E. P. Dutton, 1972).

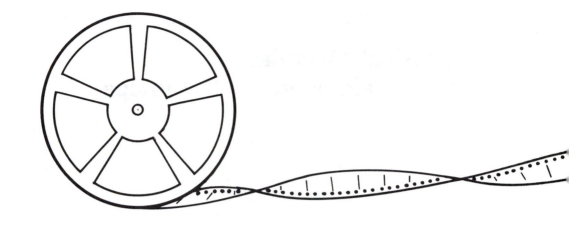

PART II
THE
ELEMENTS
OF FILM

Historical Overview:
The Development of the Image

EARLY MECHANISMS

The invention of photography in the early part of the nineteenth century by Joseph Niepce and Louis Daguerre in France was the first step toward capturing the moving image of reality, a dream held by artists and philosophers for thousands of years. Once still photography had been achieved, attempts to invent *moving* photographic pictures began. There already were mechanical devices that gave motion to *drawn* figures, ancestors of our animated films (Figure 1). There were also experiments that attempted to use the photographic process to give motion to images of real figures; a series of still photographs taken by Eadweard Muybridge in the 1870s with a battery of twenty-four cameras so as to capture increments of motion in a racehorse was projected on a screen in rapid succession to give the illusion of movement. But the final stages of the development of a practical motion picture camera and projection system had to wait until the perfection of a flexible film that could replace glass photographic plates. Soon after a celluloid film base was discovered by an amateur inventor, the first roll film was marketed by George Eastman in 1888.

It was the team of William Dickson and Thomas Edison, however, who used the flexible film for cinematography rather than still photographs. By 1889, the rudimentary problems with regulating the movement of the celluloid strips through the camera had been solved, and Edison shortly marketed a box device into which a single viewer could peer to see the unprojected images in motion. The kinetoscope, as it was called, was a great success. By 1894 there were peep-show parlors all across the country and around the world as well.

Within a year inventors from every industrial nation came out with their own versions of cameras that could take moving pictures, and it was only a short step to adapt the mechanism for projection on a large screen. For ex-

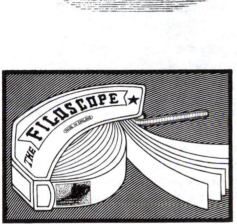

1 Throughout the nineteenth century, inventors tried to solve the problem of creating the illusion of motion. Based on Roget's theories about the "persistence of vision," these parlor toys were the first steps toward the motion picture. The movements drawn in individual pictures blend together to give the impression of continuous motion when the machines are revolved. The key to the illusion is that each of the little pictures must be seen separately and distinctly. The Zoëtrope (top left) uses slits to isolate each increment of motion; the motion picture process uses a shutter.

ample, Auguste and Louis Lumière devised their Cinématographe, which took, printed, and projected the films they made; their contribution to the development of an effective projection system was their invention of a clawlike device that regulated the movement of the film in front of the source of light. They projected their first set of films in Paris in 1895 (Figure 2).

2 Although the Lumière brothers chiefly produced short films of everyday occurrences, their first program of publicly projected films included fictional narratives. This scene comes from *The Hoser Hosed,* a slapstick physical comedy from 1895.

The first films, lasting only about a minute, simply showed anything that moved: scenes from ordinary daily life (people walking, a train entering a station, workers taking lunch) alternated with the extraordinary, such as staged performances of jugglers, acrobats, and clowns. From the beginnings of film there were filmmakers who wanted to capture images of real life on the screen and filmmakers who wanted to create an imaginary or fictional world on the screen. Even the Lumière brothers, who were primarily interested in photographing daily life and objects, made a few short films that had a little narrative action: a practical joke being played on a gardener, a card game which ends with the classic accusation of cheating and the upended table and scuffle.

The narrative powers of the motion picture began to emerge as a function of longer lengths of film just as viewers were becoming jaded and bored. Seeing a film of the world in motion was no longer enough to sustain viewer interest. After all, one could look around one and see the world in motion. Georges Méliès, a professional theatrical magician in France, became fascinated with his discovery that the camera could not only record tricks and illusions, but also perform them. In short pantomime films, Méliès used the camera mechanism to create mysterious disappearances and reappearances of his characters, to dissolve one image into another, to duplicate images in the same frame through masking, double exposures, and superimpositions, and to tell fantastic stories like *A Trip to the Moon* (1902). Yet another Frenchman, Ferdinand Zecca, employed fast motion and slow motion in his fantasy films, usually culminating in a comic chase. Filmmakers now had the mechanical equipment and the imagination to alter reality if they chose, to defy gravity, to play games with time and space. The two greatest assets of the film medium had been discovered — its ability to *record* and its ability to *create*.

THE MOBILE CAMERA

In all these films, however, the camera never moved from its firmly rooted position on a tripod, no matter whether the subject was recorded or created. All of the action and all of the bodies of the players were visible in the frame. The frame was treated almost as a stage and the camera like the eyes of the theatergoer who had the best orchestra seat. Although it seems like the simplest of ideas in retrospect, someone had to think of moving the camera. To do so, one would have to be thinking cinematically, not theatrically. The physical limitations of the stage were not relevant to this new and mechanical medium.

Working for Biograph Studios between 1908 and 1912, D. W. Griffith began changing the position of the camera within scenes as well as between them, attempting to create more dynamic angles from which to view the action. For example, in *The Lonely Villa* (1909) the camera is placed so that the diagonal movement of the robbers is emphasized as they enter; this is more visually dynamic than if the camera had viewed their entrance straight on. Griffith composed his actors into groupings, using cinematic space more dramatically than it had been used before. For example, the farmers in *A Corner in Wheat* (1910) are not found simply in the center of the frame (Figure 3, Figure 4). Their asymmetrical arrangements and movements emphasize their relationship to their environment in visually significant images. Griffith also experimented with the use of shadows and highlights. By the time he made *The Birth of a Nation* (1915), Griffith had liberated the camera from its fixed position during individual shots so it could follow and participate in the action. In short, Griffith's greatest contribution to the art of film was to make the motion picture camera almost as important as human actors in developing a narrative through exposition and drama; the camera no longer merely recorded a story — it structured, interpreted, and narrated the story through its shifting perspectives, movements, and visual emphases.

FURTHER EXPRESSIVE TECHNIQUES

In Germany, filmmakers explored ways in which the camera could express psychological subjectivity through lighting, highly stylized and artificial sets and acting. Robert Wiene's *The Cabinet of Dr. Caligari* (1919) used angular sets and heavy shadows to develop a macabre and horrific atmosphere for its tale of

3 In this scene from *A Corner in Wheat* (1910) D. W. Griffith broke with the tradition of placing the actors in the center of the frame.

Don't blame us
the
rise in wheat
responsible

Owing to the
advance in the
price of flour
the usual 5ᶜᵗ loaf
will be 10 ᶜᵗ's

4 Griffith displays composition in depth in this shot from *A Corner in Wheat*.

murder and madness; although in many ways visually unique, the film was also typical of the early German cinema's preoccupation with nightmarish themes conveyed by subjective and expressive images — what was to become conventionalized as the horror film. There were also German filmmakers who dealt with more realistic subjects but who did so expressively. In *The Last Laugh* (1924), F. W. Murnau dispensed with the common practice of using **titles** between shots and relied primarily on his images to communicate the narrative. He used a **subjective camera** at times: the audience sees the scene as the leading character does, for example, in an intoxicated blur. He took his camera on location into the street and moved it down alleys and into buildings, through

crowded apartments. In Murnau's hands, the camera became a mobile spectator of the action; special cranes, dollies, and elevators were built so that the
camera seemed to have unlimited mobility. The point of view shifts instantaneously from that of one character to another and then to the third person, the
dispassionate bystander.

Although the German film in the 1920s contributed much to the development
of the *image* within the frame, other countries' contributions should not be overlooked. The Russians, too, were bent on conveying meaning without the use of
a great many titles to explain the action; in many films, the way in which the
images were composed created dynamic and dramatic tension and the **high**
or **low angles** from which they were shot told the audience how to regard the
characters and situations. France also contributed to the growing sophistication
of silent cinema. Paralleling changes in the other arts, French cinema was often
highly experimental. The film frame was used as a canvas for cinematic **surrealism, abstraction, cubism.** The fluidity of the film images seemed perfectly suited
to the rejection of realism and to the espousal of dream logic that characterized
the surrealists. Additionally, Abel Gance was attempting to expand the limits of
the film image; he experimented with projection on a screen that completely
surrounded the viewers and made films that used **split screen** images and multiple screens, the forerunner of modern wide screens and **Cinerama.**

Film technology both preceded and followed the constantly increasing sophistication and artistry of the camera work of the silent cinema. One example of
how technology influenced the quality of the image, and therefore its artistry,
involves **film speed.** Most of the silent **film stock** was relatively **slow-speed** (the
slower the speed of the emulsion, the more light is needed to capture an image), and particularly indoors it required **lens apertures** to be larger, more wide
open, to record an image at all. By 1933, however, Eastman Kodak had come
out with their Plus X film, which was faster than previous stock. Thus, smaller
apertures could be used, which meant that more of the background in a given
image could be kept in as clear a focus as was the subject in the foreground.
The filmmakers of the late 1930s, then, through **deep-focus cinematography**
were able to convey more complex spatial relationships between characters and
objects than was possible before.

Perhaps the most important technological advance that influenced the film
image was the addition of sound to the cinema around 1927. Initially, that influence was not a positive one and many critics and filmmakers felt that motion
pictures had taken a giant step backward. Because the earliest microphones
were extremely inefficient, requiring actors to stay within close range of a mike
hidden on the set, the once fluid and mobile camera of the late silent period
became rooted to one spot. Then, too, camera noise presented another technical problem, which was at first solved by placing the camera in a bulky soundproof booth, further curtailing the camera's mobility. The very novelty of sound
itself robbed the image of its expressive possibilities: the emphasis was on dia-

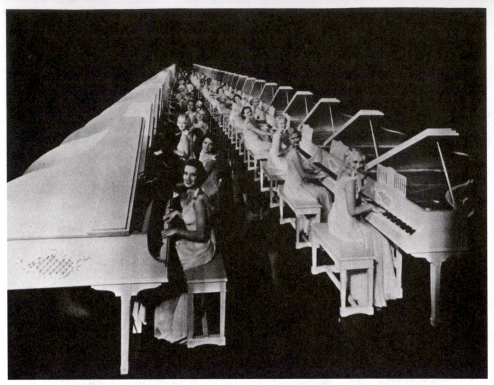

5 Busby Berkeley's most significant contribution to the musical film was his original use of cinematic space for the staging of dance numbers. Even when a dance appeared to begin on a stage in a theater, it would soon expand through a change in camera position to some huge area which could only exist on a sound stage. There, the camera could provide everything from underwater shots to bird's-eye views of the figures in the dance. In this number from *Gold Diggers of 1935* (Busby Berkeley, 1935), white grand pianos move about in a black space to form geometric patterns which are viewed from a variety of angles.

logue, talk, on lips moving synchronously with the words on the sound track. Eventually, however, wheels were added to the sound booths, allowing for limited camera movement. And, in 1931, a soundproof housing (a **blimp**) for the camera alone was perfected and the camera was once again free to move about. By that year, the image on the screen became as flexible in the hands of artists like René Clair in France and Ernst Lubitsch and Rouben Mamoulian in the United States as it had been before 1927 (Figure 5).

The next major addition to making the screen image both more expressive and more realistic was color. Although some films were colored as early as 1908, the means available were so clumsy as to have little commercial impact. At first, films were actually hand-painted, frame by frame. Then films were printed on tinted stock; certain specific colors came to have conventional meanings: red was used for violent or passionate scenes, blue for night sequences, yellow for daylight. Technicolor in its original state was developed in 1916 and 1917; at that time it was a two-color (red and green) process, hindered in its commercial use by the fact that it was extremely expensive. The perfected three-color Technicolor process, in which three reels (one each of red, blue, and green film stock) were synchronized in the same camera, photographing the same subject at the same time, was available by 1932. Although a few features were made in Technicolor well before 1939, it was the release of Victor Fleming's *Gone with the Wind* and *The Wizard of Oz* in that year which brought the process full public and industrial approval. From this point on, it became a matter of artistic as well as of commercial choice whether to make a film in color or not. Color was still considerably more expensive than black-and-white stock, and it was still difficult to modulate the **color saturation** so that it was artistically in agreement with a particular film's mood and tone. For these reasons, during the 1940s and early 1950s, color was primarily used in star vehicles and in lavish musicals where rich color values seemed important and appropriate. Today, of course, it is black-and-white film that is a novelty and is generally used for very specific atmospheric reasons. Since the 1960s, color has been accepted as the norm for films dealing with all sorts of subject matter; it is used not merely as a means of dressing up the film image so that it is pretty, but as a powerful visual element capable of creating meaning.

Although Abel Gance had experimented with the use of three screens to enlarge his epic film *Napoleon* in 1926, it took the onslaught of television (a huge threat to the Hollywood box office by 1950) to bring about the development and use of various wide-screen processes. If television was smaller, then movies would be bigger. Cinerama was introduced in 1952, but the process required a special theater and equipment. It did, however, animate the flagging film industry into investigating other ways in which the screen could be widened (Figure 6). The development of the **anamorphic lens** (which squeezed the image during shooting but widened it during the projection process) led to **Cinema-Scope** in 1953 and subsequent variations. Three-dimensional film (3-D) was attempted as well, but the audience and theater owners soon tired of the gimmick; it was necessary to wear special glasses to unify the two projected images into one image, giving the illusion of three dimensions. A third kind of wide-screen process was developed in 1955; the process simply used wider film, 65 or 75 millimeter instead of the traditional 35 millimeter. All of these processes were designed to lure television viewers away from the tiny image in their living rooms, but they also caused filmmakers aesthetic headaches. Composing images and moving the camera for the wide screen was not like composing images and moving the camera for the smaller screen. The space had to be filled differently and movement had to be adjusted as well.

Today the standard screen size is approximately 1 unit high to 1.85 units wide, considerably wider in proportion to its height than it had been up to the early 1950s. Most films, however, still keep the action in the center of the frame so that subsequent showings on television will be less of a problem. Most

6 The aspect ratio (the relationship between the height and width of the motion picture image) of early silent films was nearly 1 to 1. To expand the width and create a more epic vista, Abel Gance experimented with a triple screen (top) for his film *Napoleon* (1926). But it was not until the fifties that the wider image became commonplace. Systems such as Cinerama (middle, *How the West Was Won*, 1962), CinemaScope, Todd-AO, and 70mm film have given way to the current standard, approximately 1.85 to 1 (bottom, *Back to the Future*, 1985), considerably wider than the 1.33 to 1 used during the thirties and forties.

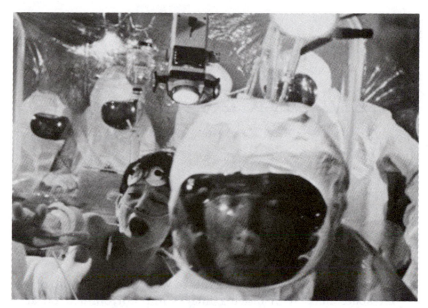

7 With today's technology, special effects can be used to create whatever effect the filmmaker desires. *E.T.* (Steven Spielberg, 1982) even allowed the kids from the neighborhood to fulfill a childhood fantasy by flying on their bicycles.

Cinerama theaters have converted to regular screens and 3-D has been resurrected on occasion. Incredible advances in special effects cinematography have been made since *2001: A Space Odyssey* (1968). A film like *Koyaanisqatsi* (1984) is composed almost entirely of such images. The invention of the Steady-Cam and the Louma crane (basically gyroscopic devices that hold the camera steady while it is in the hands of a moving camera operator) have allowed unprecedented mobility for moving camera shots, which are now possible without using a conventional dolly or track system.

   The historical development of the mechanisms and techniques used to create the image and present it to the viewer has given filmmakers nearly total control over how the image will look. The range of camera movement, lighting, film stocks and lenses is quite extensive. Filmmakers do have a choice and can, depending on their degree of independence or skill, create the precise effects they wish to convey (Figure 7).

2

FILM SPACE

Belement-frame

If we were asked to describe a movie we might first think of a rectangular space filled with moving images and surrounded on all sides by darkness. Although sounds are an essential part of the cinematic experience, the projected picture seems paramount. What we see tends to dominate our perception — whether it is a representation of actual objects (houses, trees, people, animals) or abstract forms (colors, textures, lines) or a combination of the two. The first element of cinematic space, then, is the **frame**: that rectangular area that is bounded on all sides by darkness and contains the projected screen image. In certain abstract or nonrepresentational films, which chiefly represent visual patterns, this space is used as a two-dimensional canvas; the image has length and breadth, but there is often no attempt to achieve the illusion of depth or a sense of off-screen space. In documentary films and most narrative films, however, this space is used to represent not only length and breadth, but also the depth we associate with our everyday existence in the world. In the abstract film we tend to look *at* the space and what is happening in and on it; the frame functions like the frame of a painting, *separating* and making us aware of the space it bounds as of a different order or logical type from the space we mundanely inhabit. In the documentary and classical narrative film, we tend to look *through* the frame as if it were transparent; the frame functions like a window, *connecting* us with a space that seems to continue beyond the frame's boundaries and extend itself into our own. Despite these differences, however, the space of all motion pictures is a *represented* space — a space that gains its meaning precisely because it is selected and manipulated and projected as a finite field of vision. This is the cinematic space to be discussed in Chapter 2.

⊛   # The Image

> There is no short cut to photographic skill; to master it requires not only
> theory but intensive practice. Lens, light, material, subject, composition,
> angle, and the pattern of movement provide a thousand and one pit-
> falls for the unwary. The ablest painter, sensitive as he is to a single can-
> vas, is helpless to control the ever-shifting, mobile canvas of the motion
> picture.
> Josef von Sternberg [1]

THE LIVED WORLD AND THE FILMED WORLD

Everyday life brings us into constant visual encounter with people,
animals, and objects in spatial and temporal movement. This movement
is initiated by the viewed objects themselves, and by us as we shift the
attention of our gaze or physically move our bodies in relation to them.
In its most familiar forms, the cinema seems to provide us with a similar
visual experience of the world. Thus, we often take cinematic vision as
much for granted as we take our own. Like our own vision, cinematic
vision is always interpretive — interested and invested in what it
chooses to look at and actively determining the meaning of what it sees.
Also like our own, cinematic vision seems invisible; that is, it is much
more directed toward *what* it sees than to *how* it sees.

Most of the time, we do the same — and this similarity between
cinematic vision and our own is one of the reasons we often relate to
cinematic vision as if it were transparent. That is, we tend to see *through*
it rather than look *at* it. To a great degree, we forget that the images we
see projected on the screen are not directly and *immediately* our own, but
are indirectly given to us to see — first *mediated* by the combined mechanical and human vision of others. Indeed, this tendency to appropriate and trust film images as if they were our own, to lose sight of their
external origin and to identify subjectively with their source, gives the
cinema much of its special power to engage us so thoroughly. Our
complicity in the cinema's **illusionism** also gives the cinema license to
fool us, to confuse us, to surprise and delight us, to play with and take
advantage of our perceptual complacence and certainty.

Sometimes, however, the cinema exposes its illusionism and reminds
us that our visual encounter with the filmed world is quite different from
our encounter with the lived world. In various ways and to varying
degrees, certain films reveal and dramatize the mediated nature of
cinematic vision. These **reflexive films** make us aware of cinematic
technology and technique and also of the perceptual psychology that
governs our usual complicity with dominant forms of cinematic illusionism. Such films also often subvert and point to the various perceptual
expectations we have formed as interpretive habits from our past

moviegoing experience. A particularly flamboyant example in narrative form is *The Stunt Man* (Richard Rush, 1980). The film concerns a young fugitive who finds himself in a perceptually ambiguous and disturbing situation: his real lived world and the fictional filmed world of a movie he has been hired to stunt at first overlap and then become inextricably confused. He finds that he cannot trust that his perceptions, his vision of the world, are truly his own — and that, in fact, they have not been first constructed, mediated, and directed by the godlike filmmaker who oversees and seems to determine his every action.

The character, however, is not the only one fooled and often mistaken about what he sees or whose experience he is suffering or enjoying. Our vision as spectators is also mediated and manipulated — revealed to be no less subject to the filmmaker's tricks and illusions than the vision of the film's protagonist. Our vision, like the stunt man's, has been *set up*. It has been set up by the camera's physical placement and narrational point-of-view, by the angles from which actions were filmed, by what has been included and excluded from the framed images *chosen* for us to see. Unlike most conventional narrative films following the Hollywood standard (films that work to keep their manipulation of our vision hidden and transparent), *The Stunt Man* does more than merely take advantage of our tendency to believe in the truthfulness of the cinematic image; it goes on to reveal the cinema's power to lie and distort and trick us if we complacently accept its vision as our own. As the film progresses, we become as self-conscious and wary of the naturalness of the images we see as the stunt man becomes paranoid about the origin of his perceptual experience. We come to realize that taking cinematic vision for granted always puts us at risk — even as it also provides us the basis for much of our narrative pleasure.

The Stunt Man and other reflexive films remind us of what we may have forgotten because of our familiarity with the cinema and our cultural immersion in its dominant conventions for representing vision. They remind us that those images we see upon the screen are not our own, and that the lived world and the filmed world exist as different orders of experience. That difference has first to do with the difference between human vision and mechanical vision. But it also has to do with the difference between what we perceive as our direct and immediate visual experience of the world and that experience which comes to us indirectly — mediated and filtered through the perceptions and expressions of others. Even though we make mistaken judgements about it, even though our own direct engagement with it is always informed and shaped by our cultural situation, our lived world is experienced as visually *present* to us. The filmed world, however much we may believe in it or be moved by it, is experienced as a visual *representation*. Thus, our

2-1 Though most films present an illusion of a lived world, a space that looks and feels like the one the audience inhabits, there are films that use the same photographic mechanisms to destroy that illusion. The space represented above in *Monty Python's The Meaning of Life* (Terry Jones, 1983) is clearly the work of the prop and art departments; the characters' bizarre costumes and make-up, their making eye contact with the viewer, all announce the recognition of film as artifice.

experience of space and time in the lived world is not the same as our experience of space and time in the filmed world — even though they converge when we find ourselves present at that representation, which is the film.

In sum, the dog we see trotting down the street in the filmed world bears only a resemblance to the dog we see in the lived world. We and the dog no longer share the same mode of being, nor the same space and time. Our being has different substance and dimensions than the image of the dog on the screen; it is a two-dimensional projection of light and shadow, while we are solid in our theater seats and occupy space not only in terms of height and width, but also of breadth. As well, the dog we see on the screen may be walking and doing its doggy business on what appears before us as a street on a sunny day — but we are seeing the street as we sit in a theater and visually experiencing the sunny day in the midevening. The filmed world may appeal to our sense of the real, but its seemingly truthful resemblance and representation to the lived world (what could be called its *verisimilitude*) is one of the many illusions the cinema can create (and also deny or destroy) (Figure 2-1).

The lived world and the filmed world also provoke our attention in different ways. While our bodies are relaxed in a seat in a darkened theater (or on a couch in the living room), our consciousness is set free from the wide-ranging distractions of the lived world or from our narrow focus on the progress of our own lives. Perhaps for the very reason that we are spatially and temporally differentiated from the events before us and that they are not directly present *to* us but represented *for* us, these events take on greater significance than they might were we to see them in the context of the lived world. That dog, the likes of which we may have seen hundreds of times in our daily lives and casually dismissed, becomes an object of our visual attention when it is represented on the screen. It takes on significance, potential importance. Where is the dog going? Why is it stopping just there? Is it not an amusing/ugly/dirty/friendly/shaggy dog! Why are we being shown this dog now in just this way and from just this point-of-view? What does this shaggy dog image mean and how does it connect to the images that came before it and to those that will come after it? Our intellect and our emotions are excited into activity — not because we have seen a dog, but because we have seen a dog visually represented to us in an image, and we take its representation to mean something, to have a particular significance.

The filmed world is a transformation of our lived world. It selects and represents elements of the lived world and gives them new meaning as it takes a point-of-view toward them, manipulates, alters, and combines them into a new form of experience. Even in its most basic form, the filmed world gives these elements from the lived world special significance merely by virtue of their selection and projection on the screen. The Lumière brothers in 1895 set their camera on a tripod and pointed it at the workers leaving their factory at the end of the day, or at a train coming into a station and halting to allow passengers to get on and off. The camera remained stationary for these *actualitiés*, as they were called; the entire scene was shot in one continuous 60-second movement of the film through the camera. There was no **editing,** no reshooting. Simple as they were, however, these brief bits of film, when projected on the screen, amazed audiences with their faithful and even frightening representation of the movement of people and objects in the lived world and gave these people and objects and their ordinary action new and extraordinary significance.

Even an attempt to deny or reject the significance that cinema adds to the lived world in transforming it to the filmed world becomes itself significant as a cinematic representation. Andy Warhol, the noted pop artist, made a film called *Sleep* (1963), which was what experimental filmmakers call, appropriately enough, a **minimal film.** Lasting 6 hours, *Sleep* represented a man sleeping for 6 hours; the film's only visible movement was the subject's shifting in his sleep. Even less movement was visible in Warhol's *Empire* — an 8-hour film that appears as a single shot of the Empire State building. These minimal films, nonetheless, still transform the lived world to the filmed world and alter the significance of the sleeper and the Empire State building — for both now exist in the cinematic statement of films that have selected and used them to challenge the spectator's conventional expectations of what constitutes cinematic action and drama. Thus, the very act of positioning the camera, pressing the button, and recording an image on film inevitably makes that image significant as something other than (if, indeed, something like) an image directly constituted by our own vision.

THE EYE AND THE CAMERA

Let us, then, first take a look at the physical process of getting an image on film. Although materially and chemically complex, a basic description of what occurs can be simply stated. Passing through a lens, light strikes a light-sensitive emulsion that selectively coats a strip of flexible celluloid and divides it into a series of individual **frames.** In most cases, the emulsion on that celluloid strip chemically reacts so that the light and dark values of the filmed object are reversed and register a negative impression when the film is processed. A further strip of celluloid, therefore, must be exposed and processed in relation to this negative so as to produce a positive print, which registers the original light values of the object. It is this positive print that is projected.

Through a complicated but ordinary perceptual phenomenon described in some detail by psychologists, the human eye is capable of constituting an illusion of continuous motion from these series of still images if they are intermittently projected on a screen under certain conditions of illumination and within a certain range of projection speed. (Too little light in relation to a certain rate of intermittent projection and a flicker will begin to appear, making the motion seem discontinuous and jerky.) The mechanisms of the cinema technically depend upon this human tendency — under the appropriate conditions — to constitute motion perceptually where, in fact, there is none. This tendency is referred to as the *phi phenomenon*[2]. Both motion picture cameras and projectors are mechanically constructed so as to activate the phi phenomenon in the spectator. That is, the aim of both is to work in such a way as to transform still images in intermittent motion into the illusion of apparent and continuous motion.

Each image on the celluloid strip is recorded when the film (though not necessarily the object) is motionless. Otherwise the object would register on the emulsion as a blur. Each single frame (or individual image) on the film strip is held momentarily still as it records the image in the camera and as the image is later projected. If during projection, for example, the film slips off the sprockets, which regulate its intermittent advance, and it begins to move continuously through the gate, we will see a blur on the screen. Both camera and projector have mechanisms that regulate the film and its advancement: stopping each frame for an instant, opening a **shutter** to admit light, closing the shutter to cut off the light, and advancing the next frame into position. The movement of the images we see on the screen seems, in most cases, continuous and smooth — though, in fact, twenty-four separate images are being projected each second (that is, for sound film: silent film speed varied). Although we do not usually see it (except as a flicker when the projection speed is too slow in relation to the speed of the camera that recorded the images), the screen is totally dark and imageless when the shutter comes down as each individual frame moves into or out of position.

The ability of the eye to blend together specific instances of stopped motion into the appearance of fluid motion can be demonstrated with a cartoon flip book (Figure 2-2). Here a series of drawings represents the movement of the limbs or face or body of the character. Because each drawing differs slightly from the one before and after it, when the pages of the book are flipped one at a time at a fairly rapid pace, the eye will see continuous movement. A deck of cards held in one hand and thumbed with the numbers and faces toward the eye will also show this effect; the spots will appear to move. The series of drawings in a cartoon flip book, by the way, is similar to the series of drawings used to produce animated films. Each increment of change in a facial expression, or in the movement of a body, must be represented in a separate drawing. Then each of these drawings is photographed by a movie camera that has been adjusted to photograph one frame at a time rather

2-2   The cartoon flip book illustrates the illusion of motion which makes the motion picture possible. Separate still pictures showing increments of a continuous motion are viewed by the eye individually just as with any still picture, if one flips the cartoon book very slowly to see each frame separately. When the still pictures follow each other more rapidly, however, the eye cannot distinguish the separateness; if one flips the book rapidly, the motion appears continuous.

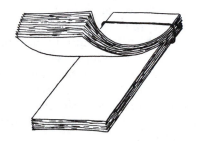

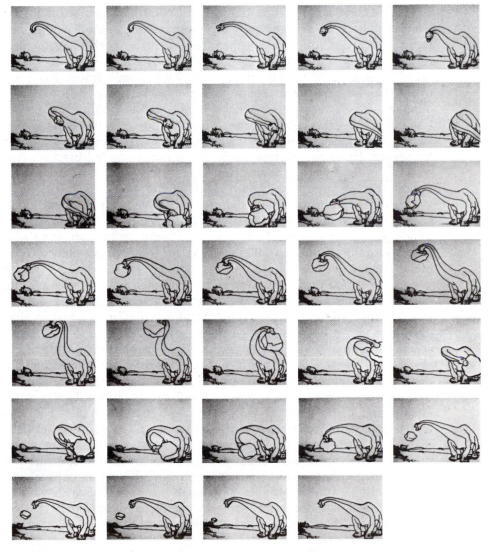

than to mechanically shoot twenty-four frames per second. But the rate of projection stays the same, twenty-four frames per second, and so the series of pictures conveys movement. On the other hand, in ordinary — or live-action — shooting, as long as the button is depressed, the movie camera photographs its individual still pictures at the rate of twenty-four frames per second. The end result for animated or live film is the same: no matter at what rate those thousands of small still photos were recorded on their strips of celluloid, projected at twenty-four frames per second they will present the illusion of motion.

There is one exception to this general condition, which might be mentioned here: the **freeze frame.** Although the processes of cinematography and projection occur as previously described, the illusion that results from the projected image is of its nonmovement. Such an effect is called a *freeze frame* because it appears that a single frame has been frozen in place in the projector and motion has stopped. Actually, although the viewer perceives a lack of movement, the film is nonetheless still moving through the projector at the rate of twenty-four frames per second. It does not seem that way because each of those twenty-four frames (or, let us say, forty-eight frames if the image is frozen for two seconds) is exactly alike, having been duplicated in the laboratory in an optical printing process.

One other important point ought to be touched upon in any discussion of the relation between the eye and the camera. The camera is an optical device, a mechanical construction. Unlike the human being who is born into the world with a limited range of biological possibilities (one of the reasons we make tools), the basic optics of the camera might have been quite different than they are. Many film theorists interested in the nature of film and in the camera's capacity for representation point out that the cinematic apparatus is constructed in imitation of a certain kind of human vision of the world — one based on Renaissance painting's schematic representation of perspective. Renaissance perspective represents a 3-D space on a two-dimensional plane by schematizing a distant vanishing point within the plane, depicting objects in relation to that point as larger in the foreground and smaller in the background, and by organizing both the vanishing point and the depicted objects in relation to the centered vision of an unseen viewer — a position assumed by the painting's spectator. This system of representation privileges the individual human being as the absolute center around which the painting's world is organized — and thus it implicates a whole notion of social and cultural relations not necessarily shared by the pre-Renaissance world nor by some contemporary cultures. Nonetheless, this system of representation has become dominant in our culture and greatly influenced first the development of camera optics, and later the conventions for using them to represent only a single view of reality.

Tone

> A director may often say to a lighting cameraman that he didn't much care for yesterday's rushes, and that he thought the mood of the lighting was a bit *too* gay or *too* sinister. But he can only talk in general terms like that and he can only talk about the past. He can't make criticism of the moment because the moment is unintelligible to everyone on the floor except the lighting cameraman. It's even unintelligible to the camera operator or another cameraman coming on the set, because he doesn't have in his head all the technical facts of film stock and aperture and he hasn't seen each of the lights coming on in turn.
> Douglas Slocombe[3]

Given the present machinery, the mechanical process of capturing the image is quite simple. Artistically, however, it is extremely complicated. The cinematographer must try to photograph not only the physical objects indicated by the director, but also try to construct the particular emotional effect or atmosphere appropriate to the narrative. We, the viewers, not only see images, but we feel, say, pity or terror or joy. This aspect of the images we see on the screen can, perhaps, cumulatively be called the **tone** of the film. The tone of a film relates physically — visually — to the tones or shadings of the actual images we see. The images in a musical, for example, are almost always bright, the images in a horror film generally dark. These distinctions, of course, are extremely broad; as we shall see, tone is usually a subtle accumulation of various elements, dictated much more by the overall effect produced by the quality of the image than by any one element in the image. A film's tone emerges from what we see and hear in the total film (Figure 2-3). With the proper combination of, for instance, film stock and lighting, a sense of anxiety can be produced with color images such as appear in Michelangelo Antonioni's *Blow-Up* (1966), Ingmar Bergman's *Cries and Whispers* (1972), and Robert Altman's *Three Women* (1976). On the other hand, a sense of dreamy romance can be depicted in the cool, quiet, dark images of Ingmar Bergman's *Smiles of a Summer Night* (1955). A musical comedy can keep its lightness though shot in dark, somber, or muted color as in Joshua Logan's *Paint Your Wagon* (1969) or it can seem cynical and depressing if its dark images are duplicated by the narrative and characterizations as in *Pennies from Heaven* (Herbert Ross, 1981). And, as Mel Brooks showed in *Young Frankenstein* (1974), even a sense of

[handwritten margin note: TONE - Always in musical - bright " " horror - generally dark *]*

2-3 The tone of a film like *The Third Man* (Carol Reed, 1950) is dark and brooding. Most of the action takes place at night, in darkened interiors, on mist-laden streets, or in the depths of the sewers. The strange and dank atmosphere is created as much by the expressive use of light and shadow as by the nature of the place. Lit from behind, figures in the tunnels of the sewer cast ominous shadows.

uproarious comedy can be conveyed through the use of black-and-white film, which parodies the dark vision of expressionist lighting. The choices that the cinematographer must make to visualize concretely the director's vision are almost infinite.

FILM STOCK

First the filmmaker must decide whether to shoot the film with black-and-white or color stock. The effect of using one or the other will be important to the final and cumulative tone of the film. Until the late 1950s, color was used primarily for musicals and historical films. At that time it might have seemed tonally inappropriate to use color stock for a film dealing with serious subject matter simply because past usage had caused the viewer conventionally to associate color with frivolous and lavish spectacles. Today, of course, color is used for most films — whether serious, thought-provoking films like *Seven Beauties* (Lina Wertmüller, 1975), murder mysteries like *Farewell My Lovely* (Dick Richards, 1975), or grim films about contemporary problems such as *Taxi Driver* (Martin Scorsese, 1976), *The Verdict* (Sidney Lumet, 1982), and *Silkwood* (Mike Nichols, 1983). To be sure, the actual physical tone of the color in these films is carefully controlled and modulated so that it can be used in a variety of ways that were not possible years ago.

Michelangelo Antonioni used color in his *Red Desert* (1964) to express not only the emotional state of his main character but also to communicate the incongruities inherent in modern industrial society. In this, his first color film, Antonioni put his characters in drab clothing, which blends into background walls and fog and landscapes of industrial waste, while factory vats, pipes, and industrial paraphernalia are vividly painted in primary colors. The contrast between the drab and the colorful suggests the ascendance of machinery over man, of object over subject.

This same growth of aesthetic sophistication resulting from advances in technology and tools can be seen in the way contrasting film stocks have been used in the same film. As early as 1939, in Victor Fleming's *The Wizard of Oz*, black-and-white film stock was contrasted with color for specific aesthetic reasons. Although the contrast is certainly not subtle, it is totally effective in communicating visually the difference between Dorothy's drab Kansas and the world she finds "over the rainbow," a world filled with witches and magic slippers and Munchkins and a trio of improbable friends. More subtle in its aesthetic effects, yet equally powerful, is *Butch Cassidy and the Sundance Kid* (George Roy Hill, 1969), which moves between color and monochromatic sepia-tinted stock. The color sequences, contemporary in mood and tone, involve us with the characters on an immediate emotional level that convinces us to join the characters in their — and the film's — present tense. Conversely, the sepia sections (which are often combined with freeze frames) remove us from the characters and remind us of old photographs in old picture albums, daguerreotypes dusty with time, their subjects long dead. This tension between our immediate engagement and our sense of nostalgia is created, to a large degree, by the shift in color stock; a technical element that might not seem important to the average spectator bent on following the story nonetheless creates emotional responses to the film. Most recently, both *Sophie's Choice* (Alan Pakula, 1982) and *Kiss of the Spider Woman* (Hector Babenco, 1985) also use contrasting film stock. The flashbacks to the concentration camp that reveal Sophie's life-shattering choice are shown in dark and somber tones while her present life is in bright and delicate color. And the highly stylized movie narrated by Molina as an imaginative escape from prison is eccentrically colored in comparison to the normal color used for the daily reality of his incarceration.

The cinematographer (usually working in collaboration with the director) must also make choices about black-and-white film. For instance, a **high-speed,** or **fast, film** (one which needs less light to capture an image) will produce a **grainy, high-contrast** image: the blacks will be very black and the whites very white, with very few shades of gray in between. Because such film is — or has been — used by newsreel cameramen to record the events of the day in on-the-spot coverage, it

2-4 The choice of black-and-white film stock affects the tone of the image. In order to match the look of authentic newsreels from the first half of this century, Woody Allen used high-speed, high-grain, black-and-white film stock for his *Zelig* (1983). Ingmar Bergman used a similar stock in *Wild Strawberries* (1957) for the old professor's nightmare, but switched to a fine grain, low-contrast stock for the old man's memories of his adolescence.

produces a newsreel effect — that is, our sense of the actuality of the image is heightened. Although the association between fast black-and-white film stock and immediate reality may be weakening because movie theaters no longer show newsreels, and because color film and videotape bring us immediate events clearly and on television, modern filmmakers may still choose to authenticate their content and their images by using such a stock. Even if the viewer has never seen old, grainy newsreels, the grain and contrast in the stock still has a link with the grainy photos that daily appear in newspapers, and has served as a traditional code or convention for signifying the real (Figure 2-4).

An interesting example is *The Battle of Algiers* (Gillo Pontecorvo, 1966). The film begins with a printed message, informing the audience that the film they are about to see is fiction. None of the footage is compiled from newsreels. Yet within a minute or so after the beginning of the movie, we have forgotten the message because the film uses many of the visual codes and conventions associated with documentary film. What we see before us looks like a newsreel, like film shot hastily by a reporter whose life might be in danger and who had no time for composing his shots carefully. The images we see in the film are grainy and high-contrast; the camera is frequently hand-held; there are no known actors. We *feel* we are watching a documentary filmed on the spot during an actual historical event, even though we recall somewhere in the back of our minds the printed disclaimer at the movie's beginning, even though we *know* we are watching a fiction film. Such is the power of the images we see as the action unfolds — and some of that power is attributable to the choice of film stock.

Just as contrasting film stock can be used in sophisticated ways within the same color film, contrasting black-and-white stocks within the same film can heighten drama and show two distinct temporal or spatial worlds. Time and space, for example, are fluid in *Wild Strawberries* (Ingmar Bergman, 1957), a film whose central character is an elderly man who, though functioning in the present, has nightmares and fantasies and who visits his past through memory. If the filmmaker had to tell us verbally of each change in time and space, the film would bog down. Instead, Bergman uses different film stocks to signal to the viewer that the elderly man is no longer in the present, but in a dream or a memory. High contrast for the nightmare sequence makes us aware that we are in a dream, and it also helps us to feel the terror of the protagonist. An image rich in light, full of details communicated in infinite gradations from very black to very white and all shades of gray in between, illuminates (literally and figuratively) the scenes of the protagonist's past. A moderate, though somewhat somber, contrast is used to depict his melancholy, pedantic, and empty present. In *Wild Strawberries* the choice of film stock is the starting point for the effects which the viewer will recognize in the finished film.

Robert Enrico also combined different black-and-white film stocks in his short film *An Occurrence at Owl Creek Bridge* (1961). In the opening sequence a man is being prepared for a military execution at dawn. The film stock is **low-contrast,** and the scene has the look and feel of late autumn. The texture and grain of the images are somewhat reminiscent of old Civil War photographs taken by Matthew Brady — and this is appropriate, for the film takes place during that period. In the film's next sequence, in which the man appears to have escaped his captors, Enrico uses a richer, fuller film stock, a slow-speed film that captures the image with exactitude and clarity. This sequence has bright highlights, sparkles with a feeling of life, and has the look and feel of warm spring with summer approaching. The extreme clarity of the image in this sequence somehow makes the man's escape seem much more real than the earlier, less sharply defined imagery of the military sequence. Near the end of the film we perceive that the escaping man only lived the escape in his mind in the instant before he died. We see him hanging, and we are abruptly jerked back to reality — partly by the film stock, which is that of the beginning of the film, with its hazy November mood. The evocation of tone, as well as the credibility of the various segments, is created in great part by the choice of film stocks.

LIGHTING

Having made a selection of film stock, the cinematographer's next expressive tool for producing the tone of the final image is **light.** The amount and kind of light used will depend upon the particular film stock chosen and, of course, the effect the director wants the film to have. The original properties for which the film stock was chosen will be amplified or subdued by the appropriate selection of light. In *The Battle of Algiers,* for example, the extremely bright quality of the Mediterranean sun brings out the high contrast inherent in the film stock. The light of the Swedish sun in the outdoor scenes of *Wild Strawberries,* however, is less intense, therefore moderating the tone of the final image.

Obviously the use of outdoor light imposes certain restrictions upon the filmmaker who must wait upon the weather and the time of day. If long shadows are desired, shooting can only occur in the morning or late afternoon. If the day is too overcast, shooting may not occur at all, unless **floodlights, reflectors, filters,** or **sunscreens** are used in order to alter the available natural light.

In interiors, however, modification of the final image through effective lighting takes place most strikingly. Films designed to strike terror create their chilling, spine-tingling atmosphere with selective lighting. Two small **pin spots** focused on the eyes of Count Dracula make us believe in the intensity of his hypnotic strength and sensuality. Flickering shadows playing on the dungeon wall as Fritz, the hunchback, threatens Frankenstein's monster with a torch, are purposefully eerie. Alfred Hitchcock uses the harsh light from a naked light bulb to add to the terror of the dénouement in *Psycho* (1960) (Figure 2-5). A lone

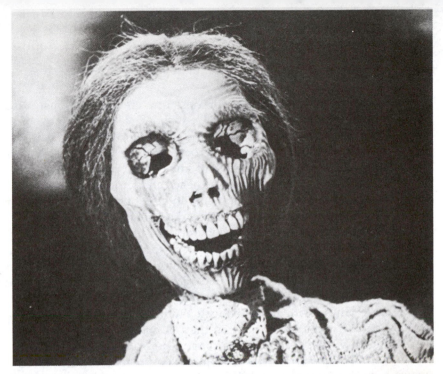

2-5 Shadows and harsh lighting create the emotional response associated with horror films. This scene (above) from Alfred Hitchcock's *Psycho* (1960) was lit by a single bare bulb which swayed back and forth, throwing light and dark alternately on the mummified figure. A color film like *Blade Runner* (Ridley Scott, 1982) also creates a sense of urban nightmare with shadows and harsh lighting.

woman descends into the darkness of a creepy old house's fruit cellar and turns on a single light bulb, which reveals the figure of a woman sitting in a chair, her back to the camera. When the chair is wheeled around, we and the female protagonist are looking at a mummified body. The woman screams and knocks the overhanging light bulb so that it swings crazily about overhead, changing the direction of the light source from moment to moment, an effect that is in sympathy with the situation and is disorienting and disquieting to the viewer.

The effect of light in the horror film is obvious to all observers. But in other films it is perhaps more difficult to spot the subtle effects produced by what might be called *normal* lighting. We see a scene in a living room: sofas, chairs, tables, a couple of lamps, people talking or reading the newspaper. Everything is clearly visible. Somehow we feel that the two table lamps with their 100-watt bulbs are the actual source of illumination for the scene, just as they would be in our own living room. Actually, just out of camera range, there are **spotlights** and floodlights with thousands of watts of illuminating power carefully placed — above or below, in front or behind, obliquely — so as to produce the illusion of normal room lighting. Even lighting this comparatively simple scene requires great skill and knowledge. Imagine, then, the more difficult lighting assignments: creating the effect of early morning or late afternoon on the set when, indeed, actual sunlight may be unavailable; making a room look as though it is lit by candles, gaslight, crystal chandeliers — or a single naked light bulb; lighting the face of an actor or actress to emphasize those physical characteristics that complement the character he or she is playing. Or, in fact, actually using gaslight or candlelight or firelight to illuminate the set sufficiently well to capture the image with the control usually made available by artificial lighting (Figure 2-6).

Though the interplay between light and shadow is most noticeable in black-and-white films, it is also crucial to color films. Whether filmed in black and white or color, a romantic heroine is often **backlit** to create a halo effect on her hair. Filters and gauzes, placed before the camera, soften and diffuse light so that what appears on the screen seems hazy, distant, soft, and muted. In *Vertigo* (Alfred Hitchcock, 1958), the mysterious Madeleine seems ghostly, romantic, and ephemeral because of the way light is used (both indoors and out) to soften and diffuse her appearance. In *Bonnie and Clyde* (Arthur Penn, 1967), there is a marked difference in tone when the film shows the Barrow gang returning to Bonnie Parker's home to visit her mother; because the light in the scene is diffused by lenses, filters, and gauze, the interlude seems like a dream, unreal, thereby foreshadowing the impossibility that the Bar-

2-6 To capture a photographic image, enough light must strike the emulsion to effect a chemical change. Low light conditions, as in this scene from
Barry Lyndon (Stanley Kubrick, 1975) where candlelight is the only illumination, are extremely difficult assignments for the cinematographer. In such
cases the film stock must be overdeveloped or "forced" in the laboratory to
reveal a visible image.

rows will ever escape their present lives. And in *Blade Runner* (Ridley
Scott, 1982), dark shadows contrast with glittering, sputtering neon to
convey the nightmarish qualities of urban life in the future. Scenes in
Detective Deckard's apartment also use the contrast between the muted
colors revealed by a few table lamps and the shadowy edges of the
rooms to suggest the emotional bleakness of his existence as a hunter
and destroyer of replicants.

In color films, light can also be effectively controlled within the
camera itself or in the laboratory when the print is developed. Overexposed or underexposed color film (too much or too little light reaching
the film stock) can guide the viewer's response to the image. If a
filmmaker wants us to feel the heat and dryness and blinding sun of a
desert, the film in the camera may be overexposed so that it looks
bleached, washed-out, and parched. In the laboratory development
process, many cinematic tricks can be performed with light. Using

black-and-white film in 1922, F. W. Murnau, for example, wanted to produce a ghostly image in his horror film *Nosferatu*; to convey the eerie quality of a phantom coach, he not only used speeded up motion but also a **negative image,** which was inserted in the film amidst all the positive footage. We can see the fascinating effects of color negative images in a film like *2001: A Space Odyssey* (Stanley Kubrick, 1968), but more often these effects are found in experimental film and video.

The specifically selected use of light can add, then, to the meanings of an image; it can cause us to respond emotionally and physiologically. Soft or harsh lighting can manipulate the viewer's attitude toward a setting or a character. In *Tom Jones* (Tony Richardson, 1963), for example, the scenes of English eighteenth-century country life on Squire Allworthy's estate seem to glow with warmth and a languorous richness; they are softly lit and diffused enough to make the green countryside seem almost dewy. On the other hand, when Tom is evicted from these idyllic surroundings and forced to make his way in a hostile London, the scenes of that city are harshly lit and the images appear cooler, either more forbidding or more brittle. The color, then, helps the viewer subconsciously to equate the country with warmth, honesty, and natural vitality, and the city with coldness, corruption, and artificial gaiety.

This kind of contrast in lighting works just as well in black and white. *Dr. Strangelove; or, How I Learned to Stop Worrying and Love the Bomb* (Stanley Kubrick, 1964) is a classic example. Because of the differences in the lighting in the various locations of the film, the characters seem to inhabit different worlds, and the possibility of their communicating with each other is virtually nil. The maddest characters in the film — the psychotic General Jack D. Ripper and the totalitarian paraplegic Dr. Strangelove — are lit as if they inhabited an old 1930s Universal Studio horror film; their faces, made grotesque by shadows, emerge from blackness. On the other hand, the military base from which the general issues his insane commands and the interior of the B–52 bomber, which is attempting to carry out his attack plan on Russia, are both lit with the flat and gray style reminiscent of 1950s war movies. The disparity in lighting styles visually underscores the impossibility of communication between the men in the B–52 bomber and the top brass in the War Room of the Pentagon. They exist in two separate worlds.

Of course, lighting effects need not be so obvious as a clear contrast in styles. The lighting of a character throughout a film may evolve slowly, shaping our responses. In *Citizen Kane* (Orson Welles, 1941), for example, the lighting of the central character changes slowly as the film progresses. The face of the youthful and idealistic Charles Foster Kane is fully and evenly lit so that it appears attractive, soft, without shadows.

2-7 The lighting in Orson Welles's *Citizen Kane* (1941) often undercuts or modifies the viewer's perceptions of a scene. Leaning over the table to ceremoniously sign the "Declaration of Principles," Kane's face slips into shadow, darkening the mood of exuberance associated with his pledge to help the downtrodden.

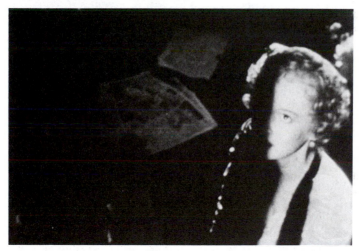

2-8 Shadows also complement the activity of the dialogue and action in *Citizen Kane*. When Kane silences Susan Alexander's protests about her career, his shadow moves across her face as though blotting out her personality.

At one moment in the early part of the film, however, Kane's change of character is literally foreshadowed. As he is writing a Declaration of Principles (which he will later betray), his face is in complete shadow while the faces of those watching him can be clearly seen (Figure 2-7). As Kane's idealism fades, and as he becomes a more complex and less comprehensible figure, his face is seen more and more frequently in partial shadow. As he becomes finally an enigmatic cipher, more inscrutable in his motives and actions, so does the light reveal less and less of him to the audience. (See Figure 2-8.)

⊛   Composition

> The camera is only an accessory to the human eye and serves principally to frame — to include and to exclude. Within the frame the artist collects that which he wishes us to share with him; beyond the frame is placed what he considers of no value to his thought.
> Josef von Sternberg [4]

Composition is the arrangement of people and objects within the space of the film frame. Even if the camera remains perfectly still, that rectangular space within the frame can be filled in many ways. It may show us people and things arranged in pleasing and harmonious relationships, or it may show discordant relationships. Objects and people (and the camera's relation to them) can be arranged so symmetrically that viewers are aware they are not watching real life, but a movie which has been artificially constructed — or they can be arranged so randomly and spontaneously that viewers almost forget they are watching a film and instead feel as though they were looking through a window into the real world. Composition, then, is a tool that helps the filmmaker to create and communicate meaning (Figure 2-9). Understanding a film's spatial relations is a way to understand its human relations and their meanings.

Indeed, one of the difficulties contained in the widespread use of movies on broadcast television or video cassettes is that the film image is transformed from the original. It is often cut off on both sides and its aspect ratio (height-to-width relation) is altered, distorting the chosen spatial composition. The film's narrative may remain the same, but it will have different nuances than originally conceived since spatial compositions tell us significant things about the characters' relation to their environment and each other. Extremely wide formats like CinemaScope suffer most when transferred to television or cassette. *Once Upon a Time in the West* (Sergio Leone, 1969) is an almost operatic western, dependent on its wide screen composition for both its mythic and exaggerated effects. On video the film hardly creates the same impact. Sometimes even more drastic changes occur when films are reproduced for television viewing. Images originally planned for the wider screens in theaters are scanned with an optical printer, a process that breaks down one wide shot of two characters, for example, into two separate shots. Again, this alters (however slightly it may seem), the characters' relation to each other — and our relation to them.

COMPOSITION IN THE FRAME

When Michelangelo Antonioni composes a shot, he frequently shows us the feelings his characters have toward each other not by the dialogue

2-9 Composition — the arrangement of objects in the frame — can indicate relationships between people and people, people and place. In the top picture from Antonioni's *Red Desert* (1964), the man and woman are separated from each other, and from the fruit vendor. Having the main subjects in the shot stretched across the top half of the frame heightens the sense of anxiety and dislocation. In the bottom photo, from John Ford's *Stagecoach* (1939), the human characters are dwarfed by the setting. They seem to be intruders in the wilderness.

2-10 The complex information contained in the visual images of a film is illustrated in this shot from François Truffaut's *400 Blows* (1959). Photographed through the wire grid, the reform school boy appears trapped, enclosed, locked up. At the same time he has locked out the observer: his folded arm position, his face half hidden by the sweater indicates that. The eyes, however, are not simply defiant, but full of anxiety. Thus both the subject and the way in which the subject is revealed by the composition combine to construct meaning.

they speak but through their position in the frame. In a scene in *Eclipse* (1961), a young, ambitious stockbroker is trying to locate his latest amour. She is clearly visible to us on one side of the screen, but a huge marble pillar stands between them so he cannot see her, a pillar that holds up the roof of the stock exchange in Milan. The lack of connection between these two people is visually suggested by their physical separation in the frame as well as by the specific representation of the world of finance.

John Ford is famous for spacious westerns, with scenes where the sky fills nearly two-thirds of the frame. Although Ford's essentially optimistic themes stress the positive aspects of taming the wilderness into a civilization, many of his **long shots** dwarf the characters and their creations, such as wagons or houses, showing them as small and inconsequential against the awesome breadth and power of nature. The vast landscape emphasizes the heroism and the fragility of their attempts to civilize the wilderness.

On the other hand, the *lack* of space and spaciousness can be used for aesthetic and thematic effect (Figure 2-10). In films as separated by history and theme as Carl Dreyer's *The Passion of Joan of Arc* (1928) and Ingmar Bergman's *Persona* (1966), close-up shots of faces are a major portion of the footage. The viewer, forced to observe in close-up the planes and angles, the hills and valleys, of the human face removed from context, becomes somewhat dislocated in space. The sudden strangeness of what we usually take for granted in real life helps to make

2-11 By placing objects in the foreground plane and having the characters in a background plane, in a sense Hitchcock has created a close-up within a medium shot. As long as both planes are in focus, the relationships between the two can be revealed. In the above shot from *The Lady Vanishes* (1938), tension results from this relationship because the viewer knows the glasses have been drugged but the prospective victims do not.

us receptive to the intense inner life of the character. *The Passion of Joan of Arc* deals with the mystery of saintliness, with the transfiguration of a peasant girl into a figure who will transcend time. It is, therefore, appropriate that Dreyer shoots so much in close-up, that he angles Joan's head in the frame so that it bears some resemblance to Christ's attitude on the cross, and that he lets us gaze for long periods of time at her eyes, the window to the soul. Bergman's *Persona* deals less with spiritual matters than it does with the mysteries of the psyche, with the ambiguous nature of madness and sanity. Bergman's decision to dislocate the viewer from an environment, to fill the frame with close-ups, causes the viewer to feel psychologically disoriented and disquieted, to feel the actual claustrophobia of being confined with one or two beings in an ill-defined but nonetheless restricting space.

The position of performers in the frame is only one aspect of composition; every object visible in the final shot will be part of the composition of that shot. Thus, the spatial relationships between objects and people and between objects and objects are extremely important. In *The Lady Vanishes* (Alfred Hitchcock, 1938), for example, the heroine and hero are on a train seated in the dining car with the film's villain. We know, but they do not, that the villain has filled the couple's after-dinner drinks with poison. We view much of this scene through the brandy glasses, which occupy the foreground of the frame. The liquor glasses, the largest objects in the frame because they are in the foreground, dominate the smaller figures, making clear the power of the poison and unnerving the viewer (Figure 2-11). The relationship of people to the objects that surround them and the relationship of objects to objects is, in fact, the very theme of Jacques Tati's amazing comedies. Using relationships within a single image, Tati communicates the complexities of human life with minimal dialogue. In his *Playtime* (1967), for example, a busload of tourists have come to Paris to see the marvelous city. What the audience directly sees of the city is all angular and modern, all chrome and steel and glass. One sees the old Parisian landmarks like the Eiffel Tower or Sacre Coeur only when they are reflected in the windows of the bus or in an occasional glass door. The implication is that romantic Paris can be experienced only in juxtaposition with modern transportation and modern architecture.

Certain contemporary films follow Tati's lead by filling the image with activity and visual relations that are dispersed all over the screen space rather than centered and emphasized in midscreen. Both *Airplane!* (Jim Abrahams, 1980) and *Repo Man* (Alex Cox, 1984) delight us with hidden comic bits, which are funny because we discover them and because they depend on their spatial placement. In *Airplane!*, for example, amidst the busy confusion of an airport control tower filled with people at circular radar screens, someone in the background opens the door of a circular laundramat washing machine and puts in his laundry. Alone, isolated in close-up, or centered in the screen, the activity would seem merely silly. Its humor and wit are utterly dependent upon its spatial relationship — to its proximity to similarly shaped objects and to its relegation to the background.

COMPOSITION OUT OF THE FRAME

It may seem strange, in considering cinematic composition, to discuss the space that exists offscreen, out of the frame. After all, because it is not part of the image we cannot see anything in it. And yet **offscreen space** does exist as part of many films, particularly those that, striving for verisimilitude, for realism, want viewers to feel not as though they are looking at a painting, a piece of art quite distinct from life, but rather as if they were peering through a window at life itself.

Since the seventeenth century, the proscenium arch has traditionally defined theatrical space in the live theater; the stage, framed by the arch, contains the play. Each member of the audience views entire actors from top to toe, from a singular vantage point, the seat she or he happens to be occupying. Of course actors or actresses exit to the wings, but we scarcely think of a world offstage unless it is evoked by an actor or actress onstage. The sense of space in film is different. Although it can show — in a long shot — the entire bodies of all the characters, it can also show in the frame, only parts of actors — heads only or feet

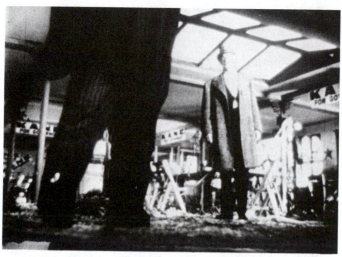

2-12   Offscreen space is created by nearly all shots in films. Since the camera can move left or right, up or down, any shot implies that the world viewed within the frame continues beyond the boundaries of the frame. This is particularly clear when only a portion of an object or person is included in the frame. Here in *Citizen Kane* (Orson Welles, 1941), Kane's leg is visible in the frame; we assume that his body continues outside the frame.

only, or an eye only — incomplete images, images that are not whole unless the viewer mentally or emotionally fills them in, using the offscreen space as a larger canvas. The incompleteness of the image *in* the frame causes the viewer to continue the image *out* of the frame into offscreen space. Although examples of this **extended image** occur as a matter of course in most films, a dramatic example exists in *Citizen Kane*. The scene begins in Kane's campaign headquarters after he has been defeated for a gubernatorial race because of his involvement in a scandal. In the background Kane's best friend and campaign manager, Jed Leland, stands surveying the wreckage of posters and confetti on the floor. We see Leland's entire figure, but suddenly, along the whole left side of the frame, a dark shape emerges. It is a trousered leg, but because it is in the foreground it is gigantic in comparison with Leland, who is in the background (Figure 2-12). A conversation occurs between Jed Leland and the owner of that leg. Obviously, it is quite ridiculous to think of a leg having a conversation; we know from his familiar voice that Charlie Kane is conversing and that the leg is merely part of him. Without really thinking about it, we fill in the rest of Kane; we know he continues as a physical body beyond the rectangular confines of the frame. If we acknowledge his spatial reality outside the frame we are also acknowledging that the world of the film continues beyond the frame. Such extended images can be used for aesthetic purposes, which complement the subject or theme of a film also. Akira Kurosawa's *Yojimbo* (1961) concerns an unemployed samurai who becomes involved in the petty larceny of two rival families in a small town. Each family attempts to employ him to destroy the other family. The samurai needs money, but he has no love for either of the families and does not trust them. He proceeds to manipulate both clans until they end up destroying each other. The samurai is viewed by the camera both as a down-at-heel, scruffy opportunist and also as a godlike man impatient with cruelty and pettiness. The characterizations developed in the film suggest that the samurai is both dynamically real and remarkable, whereas the members of the two families are like inconsequential puppets or scurrying insects. The composition of frames in *Yojimbo* helps create and then confirm these characterizations. In many scenes, the camera peers over the shoulder of the samurai, who fills the screen's foreground with half his head and half the upper part of his torso while he and the viewer look down the street to see the little figures of the warring families. The samurai's body extends out of the image, conferring on him a spatial reality that goes beyond the frame; the corrupt townspeople, contained within the frame, seem less real. Other scenes, too, show that the pettiness of the families and its full representation in screen space is no accident. While we again peer over the shoulder of this samurai whose vitality extends beyond the frame, we see as he does through an opening in a wall: in the building across the way, one of the families is placating a petty official from another town. It is as if we are actually watching a performance on a stage, so small are the figures and so contained in the rectangular opening in the wall.

Another and even more subtle way in which offscreen space can be created and communicated relates to certain kinds of composition within the frame. Robert Bresson's *The Diary of a Country Priest* (1950) concerns the anguish of a young priest who is in spiritual turmoil. The black-and-white film is extremely austere in the way it is lit, in the way the camera moves, and in its spare compositions. But the young priest seems consistently framed within the screen space by vertical planes (Figure 2-13). He is seen through the vertical bars of an iron gate, caught in the vertical darkness created by an open doorway, and so on. His face or his body, imprisoned by verticals, is discomfiting to watch. It seems almost as if we were trapped also, for it requires an effort of will to make our eyes move laterally across the screen. More often than not, our only release from the confines of the entire film frame is vertically oriented;

2-13 Objects within the frame can be used to isolate certain elements of the frame, by creating a change in the aspect ratio (the relation between the height and width of the image). Normally the rectangular shape of the frame emphasizes the horizontal, the horizon of the everyday world. In this scene from *Diary of a Country Priest* (1950), Robert Bresson has framed the priest in a doorway, emphasizing the vertical. In effect, he has modified the normal frame to create one which is higher than it is wide. Since the priest is concerned with the problems of salvation, heaven, and hell, using such framing often in this film makes the viewer sense that there is no horizontal escape for the young man.

we are made visually aware that escape lies upward or downward out of the frame. Since the film deals with the notion of religious grace and faith and humility, it is appropriate that our attention be directed upward or downward, that the space of some sort of heaven or hell be implied offscreen by what we see in the frame.

VIEWPOINTS

When we discuss **viewpoints** in a motion picture we are talking about several things: the apparent distance from which the camera records the subject, the angle from which the camera records the subject, and the literal attitude of the filmmaker toward the subject. Again, as with all cinematic elements, choice affects communication and meaning; from

2-14 The close-up limits the field of vision to a specific subject, forcing the audience to see what the filmmaker thinks is important. In addition, as in this still from Susan Seidelman's *Desperately Seeking Susan* (1985), the close-up will abstract the subject from a context.

2-15 Medium and long shots show a subject within a context. In this shot from *The Killing Fields* (Roland Joffe, 1983) the relationship between the characters and the war-torn ruins is made evident.

2-16 The extreme long shot emphasizes the background since the subject is usually seen from a distance. In such views the subject appears lost in the context, at the mercy of larger forces. In this scene from *The Killing Fields*, the world of war seems to swallow up all the characters.

what apparent distance and from what angle we see what we see determines part of our response to the subject being filmed and to our interpretation of its meanings.

The filmmaker can choose to move the camera closer to a subject in order to block out or mask material from the audience. Or the filmmaker can move the camera closer to the subject to concentrate our attention, focusing it more intently on the subject (Figure 2-14). We call this shot a close-up (for example, a shot of a face) or an **extreme close-up** (for example, a shot of an eye), depending on the distance between the camera and the subject. Reversing the process, the filmmaker can choose to place the camera far away from the principal subject, forcing the viewer to see the surroundings in which the subject is located and the relationship between that subject and its context (Figure 2-15). We call such a shot a long shot or an **extreme long shot** (Figure 2-16), depending on the distance between the camera and the subject. And, of course, somewhere in between is the **medium shot** (for example, showing the upper half of a figure), with the camera fixed so as to incorporate most of the subject and some of the subject's surroundings. These

2-17 The choice of lens will change the spatial relationships within the image. In a telephoto shot the background planes will be compressed and will appear closer to the camera. Any figure moving toward or away from the camera will appear to make little progress, as in these shots from *An Occurrence at Owl Creek Bridge* (Robert Enrico, 1961). Such shots emphasize the intense but futile effort of the figure as he moves toward the camera.

definitions of shots, however, are conventional. Whether we consider a shot a long shot or a medium shot or a close-up is finally relative and dependent upon the context of the shot and the object of our attention. An image of a human face (sometimes perceived as a close-up) might seem a medium shot or a long shot if the narrative context directed our attention to a tiny scar or the movement of an eyebrow.

The use of different lenses will also change the perspective of a shot. Although the camera may still be the same distance from the subject, the image it records will be altered depending on the lens in use (Figure 2-17). A **telephoto lens,** for example, is used to photograph Peyton Farquahr, the protagonist of *Occurrence at Owl Creek* (Robert Enrico, 1961), running toward his wife. We see him running toward the camera, but the telephoto lens distorts the perspective, foreshortens the image, and creates the impression of a treadmill. Farquahr is running as fast as he can but seems to be getting nowhere. A **wide-angle lens** will produce the opposite effect: the background will appear farther away, but the person moving towards the camera will grow in relative size more quickly than with a normal lens (Figure 2-18). In numerous scenes in *Citizen Kane*, Kane walks toward the camera from what appears to be the

2-18 The wide-angle lens, on the other hand, makes background planes appear to recede from the camera, to be farther away. Any figure moving toward or away from the camera will appear to cover the ground rapidly. In this scene from *Citizen Kane,* Orson Welles will dominate the group as he moves forcefully, in a stride or two, from the back of the room to the front. He appears to cover a relatively large distance with ease and agility.

far corner of a room. As he approaches the foreground he becomes so much larger, so quickly, that it is impossible not to feel the dominance of his physical being and therefore his character. In other words, the character of Kane is created not only by Orson Welles's performance but also by the cinematographer's choice of distance and lens.

The selective use of **focus** is another element of perspective and viewpoint (Figure 2-19). The camera may focus on a subject and record an image in which everything is clear and discernible, whether the subject is near or far in the frame; we say such a shot has a wide **depth of field** and is an example of deep-focus cinematography (Figure 2-20). The camera may, by changing its focus, blur an object in the foreground where our attention is normally placed, calling our attention to something clearly defined in the background of the frame; such a shifting of focus from foreground to background or vice versa is called *pulling focus* (once called *rack focus*). Or the camera may totally blur or distort our vision of the subject or it may present us with such clarity of vision that it seems we are looking through an incredibly powerful microscope.

A filmmaker will select these effects achieved by focus and **focal length** not only for their novelty or oddness but also for their expressiveness within the particular film. In *An Occurrence at Owl Creek Bridge*

 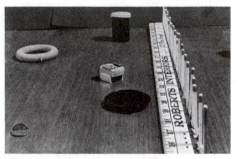

2-19 Depth of field describes the area in front of a camera lens within which objects are in focus. The depth of field in the shot on the left is relatively narrow: only the letters from "R" through "N" are clearly in focus. In the shot on the right, the depth of field is quite large: except for the first match every object from in front of the camera to the back wall is in focus. This is sometimes referred to as "deep focus." Generally, the more light available to film, the greater the possible depth of field. (Photos by Rob Wilkie)

2-20 The way in which "deep focus" or extended depth of field can show relationships between background and foreground planes is nowhere more evident than in this shot from *Citizen Kane*. While Mrs. Kane signs guardianship of her son over to Mr. Thatcher at a table in the foreground, and Charlie's father hovers ineffectually in the middle distance, young Charlie is visible through the window playing innocently in the snow. Thus the free-spirited boy is present in the viewer's consciousness as we see his mother put in motion the series of events which will deprive him of his innocence and freedom.

2-21 When the camera is tilted on its axis so that normally vertical lines in the image appear slanted either to the left or right, ordinary expectations of a stable world are frustrated. Such shots are often used in mystery and suspense films to create a sense of unease and disequilibrium in the viewer — as in Carol Reed's *The Third Man* (1950).

(1961), Jean Boffety photographs leaves and dewdrops and insects in extreme close-up and by pulling — or racking — focus so that the clarity of the image *emerges* before us, revealing not only the aesthetic beauty of nature and its patterns, but also conveying the intensity of the protagonist's attention to the world around him.

The angle from which the subject is photographed also dramatically affects the viewer's interpretation of the image's meaning (Figure 2-21). If the camera is placed about eye level with the subject, the viewer sees what seems essentially a neutral, objective — or, we might say, comfortably familiar — shot. If the camera looks down on its subject from above in what is called a **high-angle** shot, the subject is diminished physically and seems small and vulnerable. When the escaping protagonist of *An Occurrence at Owl Creek Bridge* is caught in the rapids of a river and carried downstream, the high-angle shot of him makes him seem particularly small and vulnerable. If, on the other hand, the camera looks up at its subject from below in what is called a **low-angle** shot, the power, stature and strength of that subject tends to be increased. Before the cattle drive begins in *Red River* (Howard Hawks, 1948), the camera photographs each of the major characters from a low angle as they sit astride their horses; they appear confident and powerful and we visually know that they are "tall in their saddles." A different use of this effect of the low angle occurs in *E.T.: The Extra-Terrestrial* (Steven Spielberg, 1982); here the low angle conveys a child's height and vulnerable position in the world — making the adults seen from this angle seem particularly threatening and anonymous.

2-22 A "normal" shooting angle is approximately eye level with the figures. High angles — looking down on a subject — tend to diminish the subject. On the other hand, low angles — looking at the subject from below — tend to emphasize the power and towering stature of the subject. In these shots from *Citizen Kane*, Welles looms large even though he has just lost an election, whereas Susan Alexander appears small, even though she is yelling aggressively at Kane.

By selecting a particular position in relation to the subject, the filmmaker allows the viewer to see the subject only in that particular way. In this sense, the camera's angle and position allow the filmmaker to function like the narrator of fiction who *tells us something about* the characters; the narrator is able to move freely in time and space, to observe anything and everything and, indeed, to editorialize or comment visually on the events and characters presented to the viewer. Camera angles also allow the filmmaker to convey to us how one character is seen by another character. In *Citizen Kane*, Susan Alexander is dominated by Kane until the moment when she finally decides to leave him. In almost every scene in which the two appear, Kane is photographed from below waist level, from a low angle. He appears taller, larger, more dominating because of the camera's stance. Susan Alexander is invariably photographed from above, the high angle revealing her own sense of weakness and subservience (Figure 2-22).

2-23 Alfred Hitchcock successfully involves the audience by making them identify with both the protagonist and antagonist. Here, in *Strangers on a Train* (1951), we see through the eyes of a murderer as he is transfixed by the reflection in a woman's glasses, the image recalling for him (and for us) the murder he has committed.

The filmmaker may thus use a **subjective viewpoint,** attempting to show a first-person point of view (the "I" of fiction) by photographing not only *what* a character sees, but also *how* the character sees it. Many images in *Downhill Racer* (Michael Ritchie, 1969) could be visible only from the skier's vantage point: visible in the lower foreground are the ski tips themselves; the image swoops around corners, leaps over bumps, skids across ice patches. We feel and see as though we *are* the skier, actually feeling what he feels as he plunges headlong down the steep race course. Similarly, shots taken from the driver's viewpoint in the fire engine chase sequence of *A View to a Kill* (1985) are often powerful and seem real enough to make the viewer lean in his or her seat as the fire engine careens around turns. Less spectacularly although more substantively, we share the vision of Travis Bickle as he — and we — look through the windshield of his cab in *Taxi Driver* (1976); thus, for various moments during the film, we are linked to, *become,* a psychotic and paranoid consciousness isolated in the protective interior of a taxicab. This kind of subjective viewpoint is often particularly successful in portraying a character's abnormal state: the effects of drugs, alcohol, visions, fantasies, and dreams. And, on occasion, the subjective viewpoint can be used to compound drama and suspense in novel ways (Figure 2-23). During the scenes in *Wolfen* (Michael Wadleigh, 1981), in which the creature hunts potential victims, subjective shots give us the wolfen's-eye view. We are torn between our natural inclination to sympathize with the potential victim of the attack and our enforced subjective viewpoint, which makes us see through the eyes of the wolfen. Our perceptions are physiologically linked with those of the villain, while at the same time our emotional concerns are for the human being

2-24   The subjective shot presents what is seen by a character, as if the camera lens were actually the person. *Lady in the Lake* (Robert Montgomery, 1946) made us see primarily through the eyes of the protagonist. Throughout most of the film we only saw him when he looked in a mirror. To force the viewer to see only from a first person perspective, however, undercuts the standard notion of the objectivity of the camera's view. The experiment has seldom been repeated.

he is ostensibly going to attack. The opening moments of *Halloween* (John Carpenter, 1978) are very unsettling not only for this reason, but also because the subjective vision with which we are forced to identify in order to see has not yet been seen and located in a character's body.

Subjective shots are used to some small degree in most films. But when the viewpoint is used for too great a length of time, it becomes obvious and gimmicky. One interesting attempt at creating a film told almost entirely in the first person, *Lady in the Lake* (Robert Montgomery, 1946), made us see primarily through the eyes of its protagonist. Throughout most of the film we saw him only when he looked in the mirror (Figure 2-24). (Perhaps the problem with such a filmic viewpoint is that if *we* see through the character's eyes, we *become* the character and should, therefore, see *ourselves* in the mirror.) Cinema's strength as a narrative medium frequently lies in its flexibility of viewpoint and perspective. That is perhaps why most films seem shot from the stance of an omniscient narrator, one who is able to move back and forth, in and out, over and under, to adapt quickly to any change in action, mood, or thought, to slip in and out of the minds of its various characters, all to the benefit of the total film.

Movement

> . . . this pursuit of the subject by the camera has brought me some of my most thrilling moments, both in my own films and in those of other directors. . . . Needless to say, if the technique is to be perfect it must be imperceptible — as is true of all techniques. The audience must not notice that the camera is positively dancing a ballet, subtly passing from one actor to another. A sequence of this kind, if it is to succeed, must be like an act in itself, and this without forgetting the background, which is particularly difficult to cover because the ground is littered with lighting material.
>
> Jean Renoir[5]

MOVEMENT IN THE FRAME (SUBJECT MOVEMENT)

The complexity of composing the image of the motion picture frame becomes clear when we realize that some or all of the objects being photographed can be in motion. This motion can be lateral (from right to left or left to right), vertical (up and down in the frame), directly toward or away from the camera, diagonal, or in any direction in between. And we are just speaking here of the movement of the subject, without considering the added complications of camera movement.

Ordinarily a still photograph will have the object of most interest toward the center of the frame, but whatever its position, its relationship to the other objects in the frame will always remain as they were when the photo was snapped. On the other hand, an object in a film image is in constantly changing relationships with other objects. For example, imagine an actress moving from her position in a chair in the center of the frame to the left, where she gazes at a portrait hanging over the fireplace. Her relationship with the objects in the room has changed. Moving physically closer to the portrait makes us feel she is emotionally closer to the portrait, or at the very least, more intensely engaged with observing the portrait. We have learned something about the character without words.

When there is more than a single moving object or person in an image, the direction of the movement of each in relation to the others can also convey information nonverbally. Do characters move together? Do they move in and out of the frame? Do they seem to be at odds in their movement? The more movement there is in an image, the more complex the image becomes. In *Traffic* (Jacques Tati, 1972) an auto accident becomes a comic ballet because of the related movements of the car hoods, people testing themselves for whiplash, and tires rolling and bouncing through the scene. And in the Russian *Hamlet* (Grigori Kozintsev, 1964), Hamlet's movements counterclockwise to the movement of

2-25 D. W. Griffith expressed the movement of the Ku Klux Klan riding to the rescue in *The Birth of a Nation* (1915) with a combination of static camera shots showing the horsemen riding obliquely toward the camera (above), pan shots as the horsemen ride past the camera, and trucking shots with the camera mounted on a truck moving down the road in front of the oncoming Klan (below). In the trucking shot the subject remains stationary relative to the frame as the background flows past in a blur at the edges of the frame.

the rest of the court literalizes his isolation and difference from those who surround him.

MOVEMENT OF THE FRAME (CAMERA MOVEMENT)

Most silent filmmakers moved the frame of the image by physically moving the camera *between* shots, but a few, like D. W. Griffith, experimented with moving the camera *during* the shot. In *The Birth of a Nation* (1915), he shot the ride of the Klansmen by mounting the camera on a truck moving just ahead of the oncoming horsemen. Consider the difference between an image produced by such a **trucking shot** and that produced by a fixed camera (Figure 2-25). With the trucking shot (more commonly called a **tracking shot**), the image of the horsemen appears continuous, relentless in the center of the frame, while at its edges surrounding objects slip by in a blur. With a fixed camera the objects at the edge of the frame would be constant while the horsemen would grow larger if they were headed straight for the camera, or they would speed past in a blur of motion if they were moving laterally. Each choice — to move the camera and thus the frame or to fix the camera and the frame — will produce its own effect. Griffith actually used both a static and a moving camera in his film, as well as subject movement in the directions cited, so as to give a composite impression of the Klan: they were relentless, speeding swiftly, and growing larger as they moved toward the rescue of the film's sympathetic principals.

The way in which the camera moves — in, out, across, and around — and the angle at which it photographs its subject — high, low, eye-level, tilted — is of paramount importance to the meaning the film will have to its audience (Figures 2-26, 2-27). When the camera moves in toward a stationary subject, the subject is intensified as it grows larger in the frame. In such a forward **dolly** or tracking shot, seeing through the eyes of the camera, we move toward the subject — sometimes against our will. The movement of the camera toward the subject can produce great anxiety, as we are dragged along to see something we would perhaps rather not see. The forward movement of the camera in Alain Resnais's *Night and Fog* (1956) impresses upon us the physical sense of numbers as it tracks forward in empty concentration camp dormitories and we sit in constant fear of what will be revealed to us next; the forward movement in *Psycho* (1960) takes us deeper and deeper into the terror of Norman Bates's home and psyche until we find the secret in the fruit cellar; and *Jaws* (Steven Spielberg, 1975) moves us unwillingly forward as the shark — and we — gain momentum toward our next victim.

Conversely, when the camera recedes from a subject, the subject becomes smaller, less significant in the frame (Figure 2-28). The camera itself can move backward in a tracking shot, or the camera may remain stationary and a **zoom lens** may be used. This movement away from the subject is a dominant practice of Stanley Kubrick's *Barry Lyndon* (1975). Starting with a close-up of various characters, with an emphasis on the film's nominal hero, Kubrick slowly zooms back to reveal the vast surroundings they inhabit. The movement ironically undercuts the romantic and beautiful images of lovely looking people involved in intense dramas of love and dueling and war, by showing, as it takes us away from them, how small individual human beings are in the context of the natural and social world.

The movement of the camera when it rotates, on the pivot point of the tripod, across the subject matter is called a **pan.** The pan can be graceful and leisurely, allowing us time to appreciate the subject it is moving across, or the pan can flash across the subject so rapidly (a **flash pan**) that the image blurs and creates in us the feeling of speed and dizziness. The wedding procession in *Shadows of Forgotten Ancestors* (Sergei Parajanov, 1964) employs a combination of slow and fast pans to create an almost drunken and celebratory rhythm. The movement of the camera on a dolly circling completely around a subject reveals all aspects of the subject; besides being a notable technical achievement (where do all the cables and equipment go?), it creates a sense of omniscience in the viewer.

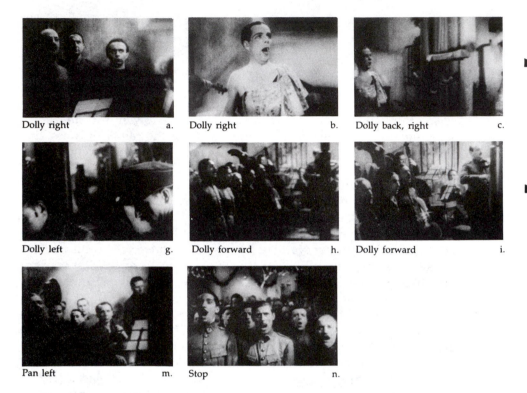

Dolly right   a.   Dolly right   b.   Dolly back, right   c.

Dolly left   g.   Dolly forward   h.   Dolly forward   i.

Pan left   m.   Stop   n.

2-26 Jean Renoir has been hailed as a master of mise-en-scène filmmaking. He himself has said, "Another of my preoccupations was, and still is, to avoid fragmentation. . . . A sequence of this kind, if it is to succeed, must be like an act in itself, and this without forgetting the background, which is particularly difficult to cover because the ground is littered with lighting material."[5] The establishment of an actual space and the creation of shifting relationships within that space during the course of a shot in which the camera continually moves is exemplified in this single shot from *Grand Illusion* (1937). In the middle of the Allied prisoners' Follies, it is announced that a French town lost to the Germans a few days earlier has been retaken by the French. A young British POW who has been acting the part of a girl removes his wig and begins to sing the French national anthem. The camera tracks backwards, panning slightly to the right to show the men on stage who are also now singing. As the camera continues to move back, Maréchal leans forward menacingly toward the pit. Continuing backwards, the camera picks up the object of his attention: two German guards, who begin to move left. The camera pans left with their exit for a moment. Then it picks up the first row of the men in the audience who have risen to sing. The camera then tracks along the first row of singers back to the pit orchestra. Then, panning slightly to the right, it picks up the British soldier for a moment (coming full circle both literally and figuratively). And, finally, it tracks back and pans left in order to frame the first row of singers, but from such a position that we see towards the back of the auditorium and take in the entire audience of Allied prisoners singing patriotically. The camera holds till the shot ends.

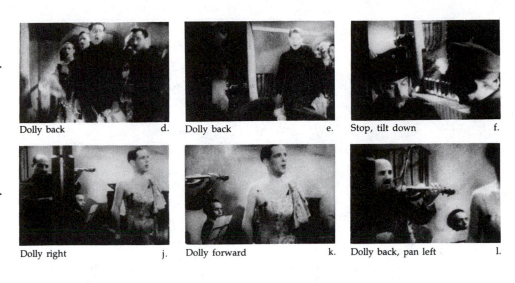

Dolly back   d.   Dolly back   e.   Stop, tilt down   f.

Dolly right   j.   Dolly forward   k.   Dolly back, pan left   l.

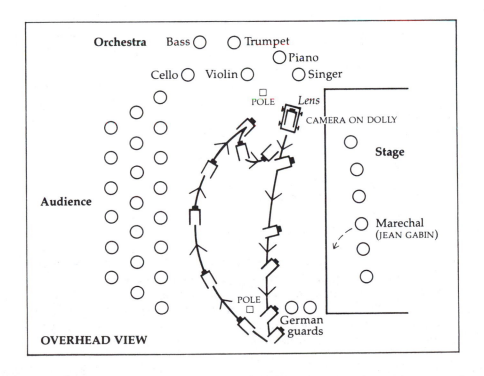

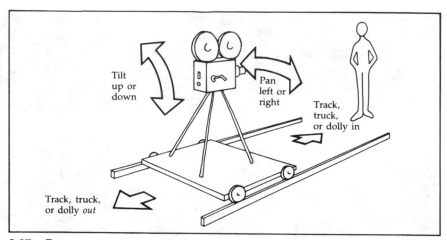

2-27 Camera movement will change the relationship between the subject and the background, discover new elements in a scene, add to the illusion of reality by moving about in a space, and affect the viewer's feelings by the speed of the movement. Slow movements tend toward the lyrical, melancholic, or the inexorable, while swift movements may seem comic, adventurous, exciting, or terrifying.

The speed of camera movement also influences the total image and the way we react to it. The camera can move slowly in or slowly out or it can move rapidly. A gradual dolly shot (the camera moving forward or backward on a wheeled platform) is not nearly so startling to the eye as is a quick zoom. If the filmmaker wishes to make camera movement relatively invisible, that is, not consciously noticed by the viewer, the movements will generally be smooth, unless they reflect the subjective viewpoint of the characters. Those films that wish to call attention as much to the process of filmmaking as to the film's subject, may choose then, quick and disorienting camera movements.

The speed at which the camera moves in relation to the speed and direction of a moving subject also contributes to the effect and meaning of the image. The camera can move in a direction parallel to the moving subject and at the same rate of speed; this parallel movement (a tracking shot) creates a great sense of motion without calling attention to the camera itself, as the background whizzes past the subject held securely in the frame. If the camera movement does not parallel the subject movement, our attention may be called to the camera itself. And such a shift in our attention may be artful. In *An Occurrence at Owl Creek Bridge* it is necessary that the audience's emotional identification with the protagonist be disengaged gradually, so that by the time spectators find out

2-28 Camera movement away from a subject tends to diminish the subject as its size relative to the frame grows smaller. In this scene from Stanley Kubrick's *Barry Lyndon*, the duel between Lyndon and the Captain becomes more and more meaningless as the camera pulls back away from the action. Movement towards the subject, on the other hand, tends to magnify the importance of the subject.

that the escape was all a fantasy and that the protagonist has really been hanged they will not feel tricked by the film. Thus, toward the beginning of the last part of the film, we are shown the escaped man running toward the camera. After a moment, the camera begins to track slowly backward. The man stumbles and falls, but the camera keeps tracking backward, a movement we do not notice until it stops about ten yards down the road from the man. Suddenly jolted, we are less conscious of the protagonist than we are of the camera. Suddenly, we become aware of a space that can be inhabited, that is three dimensional. If, for scene. The device is used to diminish our emotional identification with the hero and to start to prepare us subtly for his death.

Camera movements in general fortify our sense of actuality, our sense of a space that can be inhabited, that is, three dimensional. If, for instance, in the frame, we see a seated character who then stands up, walks to her left through a doorway and down a hall, and the camera follows her movements in a continuous shot, we are more likely to believe that the room and the hall are in a real house and not on a studio back lot.

One of the characters in Bernardo Bertolucci's *Before the Revolution* (1964) says, "A **360 degree pan** is truth in cinema." What he means is if a camera in the center of a room rotates on its tripod in a complete circle, we will see the entire room; all four walls will succeed themselves in our field of view and they will be physically connected, as real walls are. From pictures you may have seen of typical shooting sessions in operation, you will realize how difficult this particular illusion is to create. Somewhere behind every camera there are technicians, lights, reflectors, microphones, props, and cables. A director using a 360 degree pan is going all out to create the illusion of real space, allowing us to feel that we are invisible observers standing in the middle of a real room in the middle of someone's real world.

One does not *have* to go to such lengths, however, to create a sense of real space. Almost all camera movements inscribe cinematic space as having thickness and dimension. For example, take a character sitting at his table. He may be reading a newspaper and drinking a cup of coffee. If the camera moves away from him and pans to left or right to show us the objects that surround him and fill his life — his furniture, his walls, his ceiling, his floors — we get a sense of the world the character inhabits.

The screen world becomes a place to dwell in — attested to by the movement of the camera. Items that were outside the frame when we first see an actor or actress become visible as the camera moves, giving us the sensation that they were there all the time and there is a spatial continuity surrounding this figure we are watching. He or she inhabits, we are forcefully led to believe, a world similar to ours in this respect, and this belief reinforces the illusion that what we see on the screen is as real as the world we live in. We accept these mediated images as a reality, even when we know they are fictitious. The frame is stretched and extended by the continuous movement of the camera and it makes us see it more as a window than as a container.

But a filmmaker may wish to reverse this illusion of real space, to break the spell, to call the viewer's attention to the fact that watching a *film* of real life is not real life itself. In *Tout Va Bien* (Jean-Luc Godard, 1973), the camera tracks slowly and monotonously in a repeated set of movements back and forth across a supermarket. Eventually its movement in relation to events of various kinds going on before it seems utterly mechanical — disinterested — and the space of the market begins to seem flat and two dimensional. Whenever such devices are used, the filmmaker clearly wants to jar us out of our customary response to

2-29 Film space can sometimes bear no resemblance to any space in the real world. The interior of the spacecraft in *The Adventures of Buckaroo Banzai* (W. D. Richter, 1984) exists without well-defined borders either above, below, or beyond.

the images on the screen, to make us think about ourselves and our mediated relationship to the events, characters, and themes being presented in the film as well as our visual acceptance of the filmed image as immediate reality (Figure 2-29).

A filmmaker can effect another sort of break with the illusion of reality by varying the camera speed. We are all aware of the way some silent filmmakers used faster than normal motion to get extra laughs in chase sequences, but high-speed action has also been used to heighten suspense or to portray panic. In the silent version of *The Phantom of the Opera* (Rupert Julian, 1925), the frightened crowd disperses from the opera house in **fast motion.** The lyric and romantic quality of slow motion was amply demonstrated in *The Black Stallion* (Caroll Ballard, 1979). On the other hand, slow motion is not used for romance by Sam Peckinpah, who, in *The Wild Bunch* (1969), used it to amplify violent, grisly death. The paradoxical balletic grace only made the effect grislier and more ironic. Time lapse cinematography, which creates ultrafast motion on the screen, was used to show an eerie change in time as afternoon light fades too quickly to darkness in *Rumble Fish* (Francis Coppola, 1983). And *Koyaanisqatsi* (Godfrey Reggio, 1983), a cinematically fascinating nonnarrative film, uses all sorts of film speeds to show contemporary life as a life out of balance. At times, however, the effects are so beautiful or mesmerizing that the point is lost.

In addition to slow or fast motion, filmmakers have on occasion dispensed with motion altogether by freezing a single frame on the screen. There is possibly no finer example of a freeze frame than the last shot of François Truffaut's *The 400 Blows* (1959) in which the young boy running from his pursuers is stopped in midstride at the edge of the ocean. He is trapped in time between the sea and his pursuers. Because motion is so essential to the screen image, when the motion suddenly stops, the viewer is forced to reflect upon the lifeless, still image frozen there on the screen that only seconds before was full of life and movement.

Finally, how the camera is mounted will also affect the movement of the camera and thereby the image. In the early days of cinema, the camera did not move at all but was mounted on a tripod to hold it steady. Today, cameras can be mounted on almost anything to achieve special effects and yet still capture the image. A camera mounted on a track or **crane** or dolly (a low platform that rolls on casters) will capture a steady, fluid image. It would have been impossible, however, to use a dolly to follow Rocky up the steps of the Philadelphia Art Museum. The shot used a Steady Cam, one of a number of devices that strap the camera to the operator, but keep it from jiggling in response to the operator's movements. Hence fluid, smooth tracking shots can now be achieved without tracks or a dolly. If the filmmaker wants to create a sense of immediacy or of chaos, or the feeling that the viewer is directly participating in the action, the camera may still be hand-held; this produces a jerky, bouncing, unsteady image that seems to respond physically to the events around it. Similarly, a camera mounted on a car can give the viewer the sense of being the subject; we see what the driver sees as he careens around corners and through traffic.

It should be apparent by now that what we *see* on the screen, though it may seem simple and straightforward, is achieved only by a complex pattern of choices made by the filmmaker who controls cinematic space and uses it to construct material relationships, which, in turn, construct cinematic meaning. The filmmaker must combine the appropriate choices of each element (film stock, lighting, composition, movement, and camera angle) to produce the particular and unique image that will

2-30   Most camera movements are visible to the viewer. During a shot, the frame appears to move relative to the subject within the frame. This is clear even when the subject is moving. But another kind of movement is invisible. It takes place *between* shots, rather than within a shot. This movement is detected as an abrupt change in area covered by the frame. In the courtroom scene here, the area visible in each successive shot becomes dramatically smaller, and the subject correspondingly larger, as the camera is moved closer to the witness box between shots. Here camera movement becomes a function of editing when the separate shots are linked in a logical order.

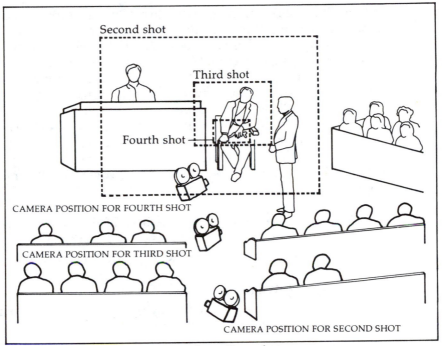

First shot—Long shot

Second shot—Medium shot

Third shot—Close-up

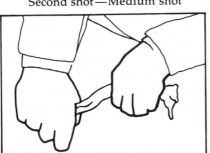

Fourth shot—Extreme Close-up

best contribute to the meaning or the story. One can learn the mechanics of making motion pictures in a day, but it takes an understanding and knowledge of space to produce beautiful and profound cinematic images that move an audience in the theater and linger in the memory long after the viewing experience is over. These images constitute and contribute to a significant vision of the world (or a world).

All of these filmic elements discussed thus far are visible to the viewer, taking place during a shot, imparting a certain style, character, and tone to the image. But another kind of movement is invisible. It takes place *between* shots rather than within them. We recognize this movement through the abrupt change in area covered by the frame. For example:

First shot:	Courtroom from the back of the room showing the judge, bench, witness stand, spectators (long shot)
Second shot:	View of bench, judge, witness stand, witness, attorney (medium shot)
Third shot:	Witness's face and chest (close-up)
Fourth shot:	Witness's hands playing with tear-soaked handkerchief (extreme close-up)

Camera movement took place *between* each of these shots (Figure 2-30), but this movement was not visible on the screen. This process of linking separate shots is called *editing*. The same group of shots could have been combined into one shot rather than being fragmented into four; a camera on a dolly could have begun the shot from the back of the room and slowly moved toward the witness stand until, in a single continuous shot, all the details of the scene would have slipped past the edges of the frame, leaving only the hands and handkerchief in close-up. Each of these ways of showing the same content would produce a slightly different effect. The single shot will appear smooth, slow, but steady (and perhaps relentless) as the setting surrounding the witness disappears. The four-shot sequence will compress time, providing information to the viewer quickly. Which will have the greater emotional impact? This will depend on how the shot or the editing strategy fits into the whole film, how it relates to the plot, the theme, and the rhythm of the other sequences. There is no rule that states that camera movement during a shot is better than the camera movement between shots, although theories of film art have been advanced emphasizing the primary importance of one or the other of these editing strategies.

NOTES

[1] *Fun in a Chinese Laundry* (New York: Macmillan, 1965), p. 322.

[2] Susan J. Lederman and Bill Nichols, "Flicker and Motion in Film," in Bill Nichols, *Ideology and the Image (Bloomington: Indiana University Press*, 1981), pp. 293–301.

[3] *Screen Education Yearbook*, 1967, p. 37.

[4] *Fun in a Chinese Laundry*, p. 310.

[5] *My Life and My Films* (New York: Atheneum, 1974), p. 157.

Historical Overview:
The Development of Editing

BEGINNINGS: MÉLIÈS, PORTER, AND GRIFFITH

In the earliest films, running time and screen time were identical. The film consisted of one shot, starting when the camera was turned on and ending several seconds or several minutes later when the camera was turned off. Time was continuous, unbroken from beginning to end; the film was projected as a single shot. In short, the first films of the Lumière brothers, Edison, and others made no use of the cinema's ability to manipulate time and space.

Even though Georges Méliès did not literally film a scene in segments, cut the segments apart, and glue them together again in some new kind of order and chronology, his films show his recognition of the relationship between running time and screen time. He was the originator of "in the camera" editing. He found that after filming the end of one scene, he could crank the film backward a number of frames and then begin shooting the new scene over the end of the old. He was able to create trick appearances and disappearances of objects and characters by stopping his camera in the middle of a scene, adding or removing the object or character while keeping the camera and setting exactly as it was, and then starting to film again: this technique, called _stop motion photography_ manipulated time for the audience watching the finished film. They saw what appeared to be continuous time even though Méliès, by stopping the camera for a moment and then starting it up again, had really cut a piece of time out of the film by not recording it. Despite his expertise with his cinematic tricks, Méliès never realized the implications such techniques had for the development of narrative cinema. His charming story films joined scenes in the camera chronologically.

Edwin S. Porter, an American who had become Edison's head of production, experimented with actually cutting up shot footage and reassembling it. In *The*

Life of an American Fireman (1903), he created the first **simultaneous time** in the cinema by telling the same story twice, once from outside the burning building and once from inside. For example, we get a shot of a fire truck arriving at the burning building and then a shot of a woman and child inside the building. The audience understands, of course, that the two scenes take place not one after the other, but at the same time (or nearly the same time).

Toward the end of 1903, Porter's *The Great Train Robbery* was released to popular acclaim. Again, Porter used simple **cuts,** simply splicing one piece of footage to the next. Each scene was photographed from a single camera position and was complete in itself. Porter manipulated three separate units of the action (the interior of a telegraph office, a dance hall, and a changing exterior) to create not only simultaneous time but also to structure suspense; each edited scene was not resolved immediately, but all moved to a climax of resolution in which a gun battle brought outlaws and posse together. *The Great Train Robbery* also ends with one of the first dramatic close-ups, an image of a gun aimed and discharged directly at the camera. But this close-up is used simply as a sort of cinematic punctuation mark, an exclamation point to finish the film. It is not an integral part of any scene and, in fact, the catalogue describing the film indicated that the shot could be used at the beginning or end of the film — or both!

Although Porter exploited editing, and in these films manipulated time so that running time and screen time were not identical, he seemed not to understand fully what he had done. His later films do not take advantage of some of his own discoveries. It took D. W. Griffith to sense the power and impact of both parallel editing and close-ups and to advance and refine their use.

Like many directors at the beginning of the twentieth century, Griffith did much of his own editing. During his stay at the American Biograph Company (1908–1913), turning out two or more pictures a week, he had ample opportunity to develop new ways of constructing scenes through the judicious use of long, medium, and close shots. Besides realizing that the camera was not cemented to a spot equivalent to a front-row center seat in a theater, at the editing table Griffith joined these various shots to create a dramatic and visually interesting scene. This kind of editing in the narrative film is relatively unobtrusive and has often been called **invisible editing** because the viewer, primarily involved with the narrative, is not aware of the process of editing. Griffith's breaking down of a scene into shots (inserting into the main action medium and close shots to heighten emotion or to show details that would be lost in a long shot) is the basis of most editing even today.

Griffith also discovered that the length of shots on the screen and the rapidity with which one shot replaces another created a sense of variety or heightened suspense. In *The Lonely Villa* (1909), for example, he crosscuts between three separate simultaneous actions (the bandits battering at the door outside the villa, the mother inside guarding her children, and the father speeding to the rescue from a distant point), but he added to what Porter had done previously by short-ening the length of each shot as the three dramatic units moved to convergence in a climax. By shortening the length of each shot as he cut back and forth among the three activities until the rescue occurred, Griffith accelerated the rhythm of the film, increasing the dramatic momentum. He used this same kind of editing at the climax of *The Birth of a Nation* (1915), where he went further, controlling the various elements of *two* last-minute rescues. In one, the Ku Klux Klan rides to the rescue of a family who are being attacked by the black militia; in the other the Klan arrives in the nick of time to save the horrified heroine. By 1916, when Griffith filmed *Intolerance,* he was no longer content to crosscut or parallel-edit two last-minute rescues together (with their respective single dramat-ic units combined and crosscut); in *Intolerance* he juggles four periods of history (ancient Babylon, Christ's Judea, Renaissance France, and early twentieth-century America), each using another as a **cutaway,** and each period having its own last-minute rescues created by internal parallel editing. Griffith also began in *Intolerance* to use the close-up *within* scenes to great dramatic effect, for in-stance, a close-up of a woman's hands distressedly clutching a handkerchief was cut into a courtroom scene to indicate the character's tension and anxiety.

Griffith also practiced the cutaway shot in an attempt to translate verbal metaphors into visual terms. For example, in *Way Down East* (1920), he cuts away from the heroine to a shot of two white doves billing and cooing. The doves obviously represent her unphotographable inner thoughts: she is in love. The Russians extended the range possible with this technique. Impressed with *Intolerance,* the Russians studied Griffith, theorized about the implications of his editing, and (lacking raw film stock) actually edited and reedited old pieces of film footage so as to explore the possible combinations of shots and their poten-tial meaning.

THE RUSSIANS AND MONTAGE

Perhaps the first theorist of editing was Lev Kuleshov, a young filmmaker who in 1920 established the Kuleshov Workshop. He assumed that editing was the pri-mary way in which the cinema communicated. Kuleshov's experiments are now famous; he intercut an actor's unchanging, expressionless face with a bowl of soup, a woman in a coffin, and a child with a toy — and audiences applauded the subtle changes in the actor's expression as he supposedly reacted to all three. Kuleshov thus demonstrated that the meaning of a shot was not inherent in that shot but stemmed from its juxtaposition with other shots. Editing freed the cinema from a dependence on real time and space and allowed it to create a new geography, new time, and impossible people. It could, for example, cre-ate a believable city from streets existing in several cities.

Three other Russian filmmakers and theorists went on to develop and use in their own films the editing principles Kuleshov had demonstrated: Dziga Vertov, Sergei Eisenstein, and V. I. Pudovkin. While Kuleshov was conducting his work-

1 These two shots from *Mother* (1925) illustrate how Pudovkin used montage. He linked the scene of the uprising of the workers to the breaking up of ice after a long, cold winter. What differentiates Pudovkin's "organic" montage from Eisenstein's montage of conflict, is that Pudovkin found his images within the context of his narrative. The workers' uprising is taking place in the spring, and the bridge under which the ice is breaking is the same bridge the workers must cross to free the political prisoners. Thus, the two images are connected in narrative time and space.

shops, Vertov was making **compilation films** of available footage, attempting various combinations of shots for various effects. He scorned the melodramatic, professionally acted story film, finding everyday life more exciting and truthful than contrived and acted drama, but despite this documentary approach he considered editing (the manipulation of time and space) and various other uniquely cinematic devices (like fast, slow, and **reverse motion**) crucial to film's ability to reveal life to the viewer. Vertov's imaginative use of the medium culminates in his *The Man with a Movie Camera* (1929), in which he uses photographed bits and pieces of everyday life — stores opening for business, people playing sports, machinery revolving, trolley cars moving — like phrases in a musical composition, editing them together according to mass, motion, and action to create a composite portrait of Russian society in the late 1920s.

Pudovkin, who after seeing Griffith's *Intolerance* abandoned his career as a chemist and entered Kuleshov's workshop, believed shots were like building blocks and that meaning resided in an accumulation of details that naturally arose out of the story. In *Mother* (1925), for example, Pudovkin juxtaposes shots of a crowd going to liberate political prisoners with a shot of the spring thaw's effect on a river of solid ice, the blocks of ice breaking off and churning in the water (Figure 1). Although the second image has a metaphorical value, referring to the crowd freeing the prisoners, it is also literally relevant since there is a river in the story and the season actually is spring.

Eisenstein, on the other hand, did not believe that narrative images were only building blocks or that their juxtaposition necessarily had a slow,

2 In the Odessa Steps sequence from *Potemkin* (1925), Eisenstein edits his material largely on the basis of changes in directional flow of the subjects. Above left, the movement of the soldiers is toward the lower right corner of the frame. Above right, the soldiers at the top are moving down in opposition to the woman at bottom center who is moving up. On the facing page, in the close-up of the woman carrying her child, the camera is tracking backward up the steps. At far right, the woman is moving diagonally toward the lower left corner of the frame (top), though in fact she is walking *up* the steps; and the camera tracks along with the baby carriage moving *down* the stairs (bottom) but *up* toward the upper left corner of the frame. Throughout the sequence Eisenstein alternates between directional flows to create the sense of confusion and terror in the crowd and the steady, sure purpose of the soldiers.

cumulative effect. He also saw no reason why metaphoric images also had to be literally relevant. Thus in his first film, *Strike* (1924), he intercut the final massacre of workers and children with shots of cattle being slaughtered in a slaughterhouse. The metaphor is clear, but the slaughterhouse has not figured in the film before. Eisenstein, disagreeing with Pudovkin's theories of editing, theorized that meaning was created not through an accumulation of separate images, but from the clash or attraction between images and the elements contained in them (composition, movement, idea). Thus in *October* (1928) Eisenstein intercuts shots of the provisional leader Kerensky with shots of a mechanical golden *objet d'art* peacock. The viewer therefore sees Kerensky as foolish, trivial, and as vain as a peacock. However, Eisenstein also expanded the range of meanings possible through juxtaposition of images — beyond the simple verbally inspired metaphor. In *Potemkin* (1925) he constructed, entirely through editing, or as he called it, **montage,** an epic of the Russian revolutionary spirit. Screen time is expanded and contracted as actions are broken down and reassembled into separate rhythmic units. In the famed sequence on the Odessa steps, the meaning of the event — a massacre, by Cossack troops, of civilians friendly to the

mutinous crew of the battleship — is powerfully communicated by the interaction of motion in the various shots as well as by the expansion of time (Figure 2). The soldiers' boots march relentlessly down the steps, moving from the upper left-hand corner of the frame to the lower right. Intercut between this repeated image are shots of objects and civilians moving up the steps in the opposite direction to the Cossacks, of groups of civilians huddled together, and of the wild dispersement of multitudes in all directions. Each is visually linked to the others — round shapes are followed by round shapes, movements across the frame are followed by similar or opposed movements — yet at the same time the content is amplified and charged with an intensity of feeling that is the product of the collision of images on the screen: the combination of diverse images in this way has created intellectual and emotional meaning not inherent in any one of the images alone.

Throughout the rest of the 1920s the silent film developed and refined the two kinds of editing upon which Soviet cinema was based: the dynamic and visually exciting use of juxtaposition through collision of images (the Eisensteinian montage), and the less jolting, more organic, accumulation of images, which supplied emotional depth through detail as well as metaphor (Pudovkin's building-block editing). However, the smooth transitions from long shot to medium shot to close-up (Griffith's invisible style) became the staple of the popular and commercial cinema around the world.

SOUND AND EDITING

The arrival of sound in 1927, however, soon created new problems for filmmakers and editors. Sound and pictures now had to be matched. In the first successful sound process, a phonograph disk recorded the sound while the camera photographed the action. Because little or no editing of the **sound track** was possible, the film editor was confined simply to editing the movie so that it would match the recording. Little innovation in the use of sound was possible. By 1930, however, sound-on-film had all but replaced the disk system and given back flexibility to the film editor: the optical sound track and the photographed action of the film were recorded on separate rolls of film, and each could be edited separately and then matched together in the final print. The development of the sound Moviola editing machine in 1931 made this process relatively simple, and soon filmmakers were no longer emphasizing talking heads but were exploring the possibilities of sound editing, of contrasting or paralleling visual imagery with music and dialogue and sound effects.

Nineteen thirty also saw the introduction of the **optical printer,** a machine that could make fancy optical editing such as the **wipe** and **dissolve** with incredible ease compared to similar in camera editing practiced in the early days of film. From 1931 to 1935, wipes (when one scene appears to push the next scene off the screen as if an eraser were being moved across a blackboard) were all the rage. Diamonds, triangles, and flip-flops can be seen in many films of the period. In 1932, **edge numbering** (also called *rubber* numbering) was introduced as a method of making the editing of sound and picture and picture and picture a simpler, more efficient procedure. Now an editor could match up numbers, and the picture and sound would be in perfect synchronization. Because of the increased mechanical ease of editing, many of the films of the mid-1930s contain far more shots than those of the first years of the sound era.

Originally, all editing was done by hand. Each piece of film footage was physically cut and spliced by someone hired for that specific and tedious job. A special print of all footage that might possibly be needed in the final assembly of the film was made, called a **work print.** If it was cut and spliced incorrectly — that is, not to the director's or producer's satisfaction — new lengths of work print could be made and recut without damaging the original negatives. This system also allowed the filmmakers the opportunity to experiment with editing patterns before deciding on the final cut. Today much of the work in editing is done mechanically. New technology makes the job of actually cutting and joining together film footage easier and faster. In 1962, the guillotine splicer was introduced and revolutionized cutting. The splicing tape no longer needed sprocket holes as did the film, for the new machine made its own; splicing thus became more economical and much faster, liberating the film editor to change and experiment more. The latest development in editing technology is a device that transfers the photographed footage to video disks stored in a large computer. These are viewed at will on a small television screen and the editor can electronically mark the footage where he wants to cut; then the edited material can be played back to see how it works. If the editor and the director wish to make further changes, the image is simply electronically erased and then electronically reedited.

Because a variety of sophisticated technology is available today, filmmakers can arrange all the visual and sound footage to their satisfaction. They can superimpose, dissolve, fade in, fade out, **straight-cut,** and rearrange images and sounds in millions of possible combinations. They can go forward or backward in time, slow up an action, speed up an action, or remove unnecessary material in order to best convey the meaning and emotion desired.

3

⊛ FILM TIME

Many art forms produce their meaning in time and through duration: dance is movement in time, music is sound in time, drama and prose fiction are actions in time. The moving image in film is an image in time, and — unlike the experience of looking at painting and sculpture — the experience of viewing a film requires the viewer to be in some way aware of the flow of time. This flow of time, however, is not a simple thing, for there are several different kinds of time in the cinema.

Each film has a **running time,** an exact number of minutes during which it will occupy the space on the screen. Thus, running time is the time it takes for all the frames in the film to move past the lens of the projector at twenty-four frames per second (or sixteen to twenty-two frames if the film is silent). This time can range anywhere from a few seconds for an experimental short to many hours for some less than commercial narrative and documentary films. Recently reconstructed to its original length, Abel Gance's silent film *Napoleon* (1927) runs about four hours; *Shoah* (Abe Stern, 1985), a documentary on the Holocaust, is nine hours long. Rainer Werner Fassbinder's *Berlin Alexanderplatz* (1983) lasts fifteen and a half hours (Figure 3-1).

Running time describes the length of the film, but **screen time** describes the narrative time represented by the actions or events within the film. (This narrative time is sometimes critically referred to as **diegetic time** to distinguish it from the time of the narration, the running time.) The running time of *2001: A Space Odyssey* (1968) is less than $2\frac{1}{4}$ hours, but the screen time spans millions of years of human evolution. On the other hand, although the running time of *An Occurrence at Owl Creek*

3-1 Though most theatrical films have running times of around two hours, a few are so long that they are seldom viewed in a single sitting. Rainer Werner Fassbinder's 15½-hour *Berlin Alexanderplatz* (1983) has been shown in a marathon session with a few breaks in a single day, but it is usually run on television as a miniseries over the course of a week or so.

Bridge (Robert Enrico, 1961) is around a half-hour, most of the screen time of the film represents only a split second.

Finally, much more subjective and less controllable than either the running time or the screen time of a specific film, there is *experienced time*. Experienced time describes the viewer's sense of the pace and rhythm of the film, in other words, how long the film *feels*. A film running only 5 minutes may feel much longer, or a long film might seem as if it were really quite short. We may feel that a film is swift because we are interested in the subject matter, or slow because we are bored; we may also be responding to the film's construction. Experienced time is produced from an individual engagement with the film's patterns of editing.

Although a film's running time is precise and specific (unless, of course, the film has been damaged or there are various versions of a particular movie in release — for example, movies edited for television), both screen time and experienced time can be manipulated in an almost endless variety of ways (Figure 3-2). When separate shots are joined together to represent an action, the time of that action can be compressed or expanded. A shot, for example, showing a character entering an airport in New York can be joined to one showing her leaving an airport in California, thus compressing her trip. Or several shots of the details of a character involved in a car accident may be joined together to

a.

b.

3-2 Japanese filmmaker Kenzo Mizoguchi uses what appears to be a continuous tracking shot to collapse time in *Ugetsu* (1954). Actually, there are invisible cuts as the camera moves to the left, leaving the potter and his ghostly bride in a room, and then picks them up an instant later in a hot spring bathing. The camera pauses. Several lines of dialogue take place. Then the camera moves to the left slowly through some trees and then moves out onto a tilled field, where it again picks up the couple, this time having a picnic. The meaning of this tracking shot is quite clear. This must be a dream or a fantasy because it would be impossible in real life for the two people to run around behind the camera and get to the hot spring before the camera, if it were a single continuous pan, and of course the picnic takes place in the daytime, whereas the pan began at night.

c.

d.

expand the action. Through this joining together of separate pieces of film, the process called *editing,* we can be made aware of simultaneous actions and sequential actions; we can enter a character's mind, we can relive the past, we can be dislocated from any sense of real time and transported to a place where time seems not to exist or where it seems to operate in ways that defy logic. In *Betrayal* (David Jones, 1983), for example, the film begins as a couple have just ended a lengthy love affair. The film moves backward in time — impossibly but inexorably bringing us to the final moments in which these lovers first touch. After all we have seen of their doomed future, that first moment of feeling is temporally revealed as inutterably futile and painful to watch.

The kinds of transitions the filmmaker uses to move us from one shot to another are also the result of choice; the editing may move us abruptly from one time to another or it may bridge time gracefully and slowly. All these manipulations of time, of both screen and experienced time, are the result of editing. Editing, the joining together of separate pieces of film footage by various techniques to form an entire and cohesive film, establishes the narrative or expository structure and rhythm of a movie. This chapter, examining the role of editing, will first deal with the simplest form of structuring shots to form a coherent whole and will then go on to examine the more complex techniques used to constitute different sorts of film time.

Manipulation of Time

> Kino-Eye is the overcoming of time, a visual bond between chronological-ly separated phenomena. Kino-Eye is concentration and decomposition of time. Kino-Eye is the opportunity to see the process of life in any chrono-logical order and at any speed.
> Dziga Vertov [1]

Although we can isolate three time schemes that operate and intersect during the course of viewing a film — running time, screen time, and experienced time — there is yet another kind of time involved in the motion picture process, a time that almost never plays a specific role in the finished film. This is **shooting time.** Shooting time represents not only the time when the camera is actually recording the actions in front of it (including any retakes), but also the total number of days required to collect all the footage deemed necessary so that the director and editor may have some choice of shots when it finally comes to assembling the finished print. Shooting time, therefore, also includes setup time for camera and lighting equipment, for building the sets, for preparing the performers, for travel to locations — in other words, for all those pro-cesses in front of or behind the camera, which go on from the beginning to the end of shooting.

As mentioned in Chapter 1, shooting time is expensive time, and to keep it to a minimum, filmmakers will arrange to shoot consecutively all the scenes taking place in one location or all the scenes using the same performers. All interior scenes that take place in a certain room, for example, will be shot on the same day whenever possible, even though these scenes will appear at different points in the completed film. Thus, the simplest and most basic manipulation of time demanded of the editing process is to rearrange the shot footage, the selected pieces of shooting time, into the desired screen or narrative time. The breadth of choice the filmmaker has in selecting various shots from all the footage available is called the **shooting ratio;** a 1 to 1 ratio indicates that the filmmaker used all the film that was shot; a 1 to 10 shooting ratio indicates that the filmmaker used one foot of film in the finished movie to every ten feet of film that was shot. Once this footage has been selected, the various pieces of film shot at different times and in different locations must be physically joined together in the appropriate order so that shots become coherent **sequences** and **scenes.**

The footage can be joined so that the transition from one shot to another on the screen is gradual, as in the **dissolve** (when one image appears to dissolve into another), or gradual but flamboyant as in the **wipe** (when the edge of the new image appears, like a windshield wiper, to push the old image offscreen). The images can be joined so slowly that there appears to be a large gap of time between the end of one and the beginning of another, that gap represented by the blackness on the screen between shots as the first image fades to black and the second eventually fades into view. Created in the laboratory, these kinds of editing transitions are called **optical effects.** Because these devices have been long used in certain contexts, they tend to have conventional meanings. The dissolve, the wipe, and the **fade out/fade in** normally indicate fairly long gaps in screen time.

Most of the situations in a film where shots must be joined together, however, indicate a much shorter gap in time or no gap at all. Crosscutting between the pursuers and the pursued in a chase may reflect nearly simultaneous time and, of course, when a change in camera position occurs within a scene, moving from a medium shot to a close-up, or from one character speaking to another character listening, it is clear that no gaps in diegetic time are indicated, even if there had to be such gaps in shooting time. In these situations shots are joined together by **direct cuts.** A direct cut is a simple splice — using tape or cement — between two pieces of film.

INVISIBLE EDITING — DECOUPAGE

> If a film is well edited, one is never aware of cutting from one shot to another.
>
> Reginald Mills[2]

It is almost impossible to make a film without editing. Although there have been experiments with fiction films using minimal editing, the exception tends to prove the rule. An interesting example is *Rope* (Alfred

Hitchcock, 1950), an attempt at the illusion of a one-shot film. Apart from the first shot of the film, the locale is a single apartment; the film was shot in 10-minute takes and every time the film had to be replaced, the camera would move in to focus on a dark object like a man's jacketed back so that the change of film would be masked. The viewer's eye detects no break between the takes. All the camera movements were rehearsed for days in advance of shooting and the resultant film is a bravura example of technical expertise.

Invisible editing or decoupage, for the most part, means unobtrusive editing. When cuts go unnoticed by the viewer there is an illusion that the material has not been manipulated. Generally, the principle behind such invisible and discreet editing is for the editor to cut on an action (for example, a person begins to turn toward a door in one shot; the next shot, taken from the doorway, catches him completing the turn); if the viewer's eye is absorbed by the action, the movement of the cut itself will not attract notice. Although this kind of editing was perfected by Hollywood, it is probably accurate to say that today the vast majority of narrative films — no matter where they are made — are edited this way.

Invisible editing is, in fact, not so much unseen as disregarded. We have seen so many films use these devices, always for the same purpose, that we do not notice them any longer. When, for example, we see a close-up of a character's face looking off-screen and there is a cut to a landscape, we instantly know from past movie experience that the particular editing sequence means that the character is looking at the landscape. We read this meaning into the juxtaposition so unconsciously that we are not even aware that the two shots have been edited together.

Other similar conventions that create their own invisibility are the editing patterns based on the establishing shot, the medium shot, and the close-up. In the classical Hollywood style, a **master shot,** a long shot containing the entire dramatic action of the scene is shot first. This is not what the audience will usually see on the screen in the finished film. We may see part of the master shot (called an *establishing shot* in the finished film because it places the characters and the action in a context) — but inserted or edited into this master shot are various medium shots and close-ups. In the finished film, for example, we may see a long shot of a wagon train wending its way, slowly across a desert. Intercut with our view of the whole may be a medium shot of a particular wagon and a close-up of a particular face or a particular wagon wheel. The filmmaker will shoot these insert shots after shooting the master shot. In the editing process, these insert shots and the master must be put together to convey some dramatic emphasis or emotional nuance. Our response to all this editing, however, is likely to be preconscious and the editing process is likely to seem invisible.

Invisible editing, then, creates dramatic or internal realism: what we are watching is happening uninterrupted by *obvious* references to the presence of the camera and the participation of a godlike editor, manipulating pieces of film. Since the obvious juxtaposition or contrast of images is an artistic effort that calls attention to itself, filmmakers who wish to achieve a realistic rather than an obviously artistic effect tend to emphasize the narrative and action either by using the standard editing conventions or by using as little editing as possible. They authenticate the space and time of their cinematic worlds chiefly by using the long shot and the long take and/or invisible editing.

NONCONVENTIONAL EDITING: JUMPCUTS

The idea behind decoupage or the Hollywood style is to make viewers forget they are watching a mediated world. The best praise an editor can ask for is that no one noticed the shifts from shot to shot. Some film-makers, however, desiring to jolt viewers' complacency, to dislocate the audience's conventional sense of spatial and temporal continuity, have blatantly disregarded Hollywood grammar, joining shots together that do not match, making their cuts highly visible. Experimental and avant-garde filmmakers practiced this method of joining shots together for years, but it was not until Jean-Luc Godard released his first feature *Breathless* (1959) that a term was coined to describe this technique: a **jump cut**. The word accurately describes the abrupt editing used in this film. For example, during a conversation between the protagonist and a cab driver, the background outside the cab windows changes several times, indicating that a number of shots have been edited together, but the flow of conversation implies that the scene should be continuous. At first a viewer might feel that such obvious breaks with conventional expectations of how such a scene should be edited indicate sloppy workmanship. In fact, many reviewers who saw the film at the time of its original release made such comments. They thought the film was simply poorly edited. A closer viewing of the film (and interviews with Godard) made it clear that the jump cuts were there on purpose to disturb viewers and remind them the film was playing with the conventions of the Hollywood film.

Today, it is more difficult to define a jump cut. A cut that is disorienting to one viewer may not be disorienting to another. Our exposure to rapid fire, razzle-dazzle television commercials and music video's penchant for violations of traditional filmic continuities may make jump cut an obsolete term since it depends so much on the viewer's experience of the medium.

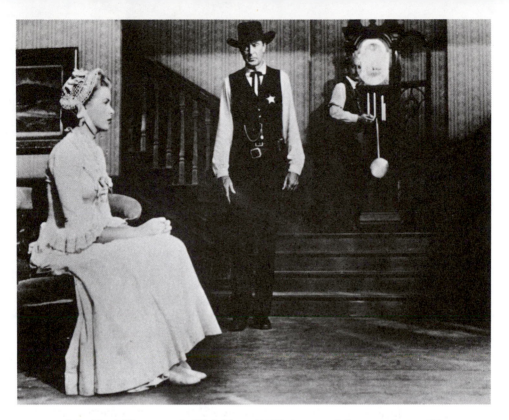

3-3 Fred Zinneman's *High Noon* (1952) is one of the rare fiction films in which screen time (the time of the story or diegetic time) and running time (the film's narrational length) are nearly identical. Screen time is about an hour and a half and the film is only a little shorter. Most films compress weeks, months, and years into a two-hour running time.

COMPRESSION OF TIME

By far the most frequent manipulation of time in the movies is its compression. Indeed, Hollywood commonly uses the word *montage* to connote a sequence that compresses large hunks of time (months, years) into seconds by rapidly linking separate shots with various transitional devices. There are very few narrative films whose screen time is supposed to be the same as their running time — that is, in which the events on the screen are supposed to be ninety or so consecutive minutes in the life of the characters. Two notable exceptions, however, are *High Noon* (Fred Zinnemann, 1952) and *My Dinner With André* (Louis Malle, 1981), both of which come remarkably close to making screen time and running time equivalent. *High Noon's* story begins approximately at 10:30 A.M. screen time and lasts until shortly after noon, covering slightly over 90 minutes; the actual running time of the movie is 85 minutes (Figure 3-3). *My Dinner With André* has some preliminary action in which time is compressed as Wally gets to the restaurant to meet André. But the dinner and conversation takes up just about all of the film's 110 minutes.

Screen time in most narrative films, generally, is far longer than running time, compressing days, weeks, or even years into an hour or two. And the same is true of most documentary and nonfiction films — for although there is a concerted attempt in certain types of nonfiction film such as **cinema verité** or uncontrolled documentary to preserve real time and space by not editing *within* sequences, those sequences themselves are finally edited to other sequences and the time *between* the sequences is not often specified or identifiable. It is, usually, only the **abstract film** (designs, patterns of light) that has no relation to the reality of the external world and common notions of time and space; thus, the abstract film is often easily able to erase distinctions between screen time and running time. What takes place on the screen (which is the only place and space where it is able to take place) occurs exactly in the time it appears to take place.

Compression of time in the movies most obviously takes place *between* scenes, between cuts or dissolves or various transitional editing devices. Thus, in *Citizen Kane* (Orson Welles, 1941), Charles Foster Kane ages from childhood to maturity *between* two shots: the first shows him as a child opening a Christmas gift from his guardian, Mr. Thatcher, whose voice says, "Merry Christmas, Charles," and whom he answers with a dispirited "Merry Christmas. . . ." There is a quick direct cut — linked by Thatcher's voice continuing — to an image of Thatcher caught in midsentence dictating, ". . . and a Happy New Year" in a letter to Kane, who he indicates has now reached adulthood. All those years disappear between two shots linked by a direct cut. The entire life of a character from birth to death, the history of a nation, of a world, all can be encompassed in a single two-hour film by the filmmaker's omission of material between one incident and another. We simply do not see whatever the filmmaker decides is unimportant to the movie.

The compression of time is not limited to the time between sequences or scenes. By means of editing it can occur *within* scenes as well. In real life, it takes, say, eight seconds for a man to climb a given flight of stairs. But in reel life that time can be compressed to increase the pace of the film or to remove irrelevant dramatic material. If climbing the stairs is not dramatically essential to the film's plot, the filmmaker may show us the character starting up the stairs in one shot and then cut directly to him entering a room in which important dramatic action will take place. We automatically recognize — because of the logic of the situation and our past movie experience — that the room is somewhere at the top of the stairs. A character's entire plane trip to Africa can be compressed into seconds. We see her board, we get a shot of the plane in midair, we see it land at the Nairobi airport. We may not even see that much; the character in one shot can indicate through dialogue that she is going to Africa shortly, and in the next shot she will be there.

Another sort of compression of time within a dramatic sequence can occur when the editor repeatedly cuts away from one piece of action to another piece of action. Thus, in a chase sequence in which shots are alternated between a fleeing bandit and a pursuing posse, each time we return to the bandit from the cutaway shots of the posse, we see an indication that time has passed — in one shot we see the bandit galloping down a road, in the next he is crossing a river, in the next his horse has dropped a shoe. Likewise, during each cutaway to the bandit, the posse has been moving in time: the first shot shows the posse stopped at a crossroads, attempting to read the trail, the second shot shows them galloping across a previously unseen terrain, and the last shows them waiting in a grove of trees — until the bandit comes riding into the shot and their custody. In each shot — whether of the bandit or the posse — we see that time has elapsed because space has been covered since the previous shot.

Most filmgoers today are visually literate. They have been trained (partly by television commercials, which have offered viewers a cram course in rapid editing) to understand visual images much more quickly and with fewer explanations than movie audiences of previous decades. Films from the thirties through the fifties used very obvious visual and aural clues to provide the viewer with information about the compression of time. Classic Hollywood films depended heavily upon the transitional devices of the fade and dissolve to show the viewer that a relatively long period of time was passing. In *The Grapes of Wrath* (John Ford, 1940), for example, the Joad family's odyssey to California is conveyed by a sequence of shots, which uses dissolves of various highways but gives the viewer a visual/verbal clue by showing road signs that indicate a movement west; since movement in space indicates a movement in time as well, the viewer has a sense of the long trip even though the sequence compresses the trip's actual time. To distinguish it from the smooth flow and relative invisibility of decoupage editing, this kind of compression is often called a *montage sequence* (although it differs from Eisenstein's use of the term). *Citizen Kane* uses many such montages to compress time. Charles and Emily Kane's years of marriage are compressed into a montage, which, through a series of rapid cuts and pans, shows the changing relationship between Charles and Emily at the breakfast table; visual cues are abundant: the characters' clothes change, the hairstyles change, and the newspaper headlines change

a.

b.

c.

d.

e.

f.

(Figure 3-4). In the same film, Susan Alexander Kane's unsuccessful operatic career is compressed into a montage of dissolves, which link newspaper reviews, backstage and onstage shots, shots of audience reaction, and close-ups of Susan and a dimming stage light. Audiences of the period were also used to what has since become a cliché — the pages of a calendar (either monthly or yearly) blowing off the screen in some sort of temporally induced wind, or the autumn leaves falling off a tree, then dissolving into its spring bloom and summer ripeness. Such

g.

h.

i.

j.

k.

l.

3-4 One of the most brilliant examples of time compression occurs in the breakfast sequence in *Citizen Kane* (Orson Welles, 1941). In two minutes of running time, several years and the disintegration of Kane's first marriage are revealed in quick cuts and short swish pans. The last shot of the sequence finds Kane's wife sitting far away from him and reading the opposition newspaper.

clues to the passage of time, though obvious, can be charming; in *Meet Me in St. Louis* (Vincente Minnelli, 1944), the period atmosphere of the movie is enhanced by the seasonal paintings, which divide the film into four parts and also compress its time. The opening montage of *All That Jazz* (Bob Fosse, 1979) compresses the director's morning wake up routine and the dancers' audition into only minutes of running time.

EXPANSION OF TIME

Screen time can be expanded as well as compressed. An action that takes, say, three minutes of running time may take only one minute of real time. This expansion of time can be accomplished either by intercutting a series of shots (either small portions of the whole action, which are inserted into the main action, or shots of some other simultaneous but related action) or by filming the action from different angles, which can then be edited together with cuts or dissolves so as to extend the length of what might have otherwise seemed a brief action.

The example of the man climbing the stairs can again illustrate the expansion of an action through the use of insert shots that are intercut as details of the main action. Let us say that the act of climbing the stairs is important to the film (it is a horror film and there have been strange noises coming from the attic) so that the director wants to create suspense by expanding the actual time it takes to climb the stairs in real time. All the editor need do to expand time in such an action is to intercut details of the character's journey up the stairs — shots of a hand clutching the banister, wind blowing through bare trees in an exterior shot, a foot on a creaking step, a view of the blackness at the top of the stairs, a flickering candle held in the man's other hand, a cloud passing over the moon. In this way, intercutting can protract and expand the actual time an action may take to perform. A classic example of this kind of expansion, in which separate shots of details are cut together, is the shower murder sequence in *Psycho* (Alfred Hitchcock, 1960). The real time of the murder might be about ten seconds; the actual running time is about forty-five seconds, but in experienced time it seems a great deal longer. Hitchcock used seventy-eight separate shots to convey the murder, revealing its separate parts rather than showing it in one continuous shot.

The cutaway to a completely different action is in some ways similar to the insert shots of details within an action. Cutaway shots serve to compress time, but they can also extend time. Imagine in a film that burglars are attempting to open a safe and we watch them drill and drill. Then there is a cutaway to a policeman patrolling outside the building followed by a direct cut back to the burglars still drilling. Such crosscutting serves to extend time, creating suspense as the viewer anticipates the resolution of the action.

The second method of expanding time in a scene is to film the action from multiple angles and then to cut together (or dissolve) these different views of the same action; we see the action repeated in the finished film, but the repetition is emphatic and dramatic, giving us a sort of God's-eye view of the action — as well as extending either running time or experienced time. Sometimes this method of extending time can be combined with slow motion, as in the climactic shoot-out in *The Wild Bunch* (1969). Or it can be used to create anxiety and suspense when it uses complementary camera composition and involves a perilous activity. In *An Occurrence at Owl Creek Bridge* (Robert Enrico, 1961), for example, the main character has supposedly escaped from hanging because of a faulty rope and has plummeted downward from the bridge into deep water below. We are shown, from a variety of camera angles, which are cut together, his underwater struggle to free his bound hands and to take off his heavy boots and to rise to the surface. The man's progress seems incredibly slow in terms of experienced time, so much so that it feels as if it would be impossible for someone to remain underwater so long and still live; when the man surfaces and lets out a gasp for air, the audience tends to gasp also. What is fascinating is that the running time of this edited sequence is only ninety-seven seconds. What makes experienced time seem so much longer is not only the number of cuts in the sequence and when they are made, but also the composition of the individual shots. In most of the shots, the protagonist is shown in the lower third of the frame or moving laterally rather than vertically. Every time it seems as if the man is about to reach the top of the frame (and the water's surface), there is a direct cut to another shot, which shows him again submerged in the lower portions of the frame. The editing of the various angles of his attempts to surface conveys to the viewer physically and visually a monumental struggle, which then seems to last much longer than it actually does. Indeed, the entire film in which this sequence occurs demonstrates the expansion of time dramatically. About a half-hour in running time, the bulk of *An Occurrence at Owl Creek Bridge's* screen time consists of the split second in which a character is hanged and passes from life to death.

SIMULTANEOUS TIME

Editing can be used not only to expand or compress time, but also to convey to the viewer a sense of simultaneity. The viewer understands that separate actions linked together are occurring not one after the other but simultaneously. How do we know that events or shots are taking place at the same time as each other? The conventional clue is that there is no *progression* of shots. Instead, into the main action to which we always return (bank robbers patiently working on a safe), shots are inserted (a lookout, a police car); or shots are alternated with each other (the fleeing bandits, the pursuing posse) until there is a resolution — a shot that unites elements of the two separate shots or reveals to us in some other way (through dialogue, perhaps) how the two events we have been seeing alternately relate temporally to each other. Much of our sense of cinematic simultaneity has been learned from our past cinematic experience. Although certain content presented through certain editing patterns suggests we are watching simultaneous time, other cues may also be necessary for us to understand this alternation of sequences as occurring simultaneously.

Inserts

Imagine a scene that takes place in a western saloon. The first shot is a long shot, an **establishing shot,** which gives us a sense of context. Let us say it shows a group of players involved in a card game. The long shot cuts directly to a medium shot of one of the players who wipes his face with a bandanna and then moves to put it in his pocket. That shot cuts to a close-up of another man looking at his cards. The next shot cuts to a close-up of another man lighting a cigar. That is cut to a medium shot showing all the players around the table. The close-up shots just mentioned supply us with details already broadly established in the opening long shot. They make us aware of individual pieces of action occurring within the time span of the dramatic scene. They can seem to indicate pieces of simultaneous action (all the players do what they do at the same time), or they can suggest sequential action (the players do what they do progressively as we see them do it). Distinguishing whether the inserts are simultaneous or sequential is often difficult and is in part dependent upon information supplied by the situation of the story as well as the conventions of the editing. Insert shots are just that — they are inserted into a larger context and are details plucked from it. The insert is perhaps the most invisible form of editing because it is so expected, particularly when it gives the viewer close-ups of a character's facial expression.

Parallel Editing or Crosscutting

Parallel editing or crosscutting can be used to compress time or expand it, but it can also be used to keep the viewer conscious of two or more separate actions taking place at approximately the same time. Parallel editing or crosscutting is most often used to create a sense of suspense, because neither action is resolved before we cut away from them. Such editing alternates between events that are happening at the same time in different places; each scene (itself composed of separate edited shots) therefore serves as a cutaway for the other.

In Alfred Hitchcock's *Strangers on a Train* (1951), for instance, parallel editing creates enormous suspense. The police suspect Guy, a professional tennis player, of murdering his wife, and they keep him under surveillance. Guy knows who the real killer is, and he knows that during the tennis tournament he is playing at Forest Hills, the killer is attempting to implicate him further. It is imperative then, that he finish the match quickly and go after Bruno, the murderer. Crosscut with scenes of the tournament, in which the match seems to take forever, we see the killer on his way to an amusement park to plant incriminating evidence — Guy's initialed cigarette lighter — at the murder site. He accidentally drops the evidence down a sewage drain and tries to retrieve it. We see both scenes, each given equal importance, and each serving as a cutaway for the other; the scenes are cut back and forth at an accelerating pace (that is, each is briefer than the one before it) until the suspense is almost painful. Parallel editing creates this suspense not only by showing the viewer a series of unresolved scenes but also by allowing the viewer an omniscience that the characters themselves do not have. Further, alternating those scenes at an accelerating pace creates a forceful and rhythmic momentum. It is, therefore, no accident that such parallel editing is so often used at the climactic moments of action films; it is the stuff of which chases and last-minute rescues are created.

Split Screen (Multiple Images)
Parallel editing, of course, does not actually show the viewer simultaneous events simultaneously on the screen. But filmmakers have tried to show simultaneous activities on the same screen at the *same* time. The screen may be split in half or thirds by two or three separate moving images that occur simultaneously and side by side. **Multiple images** (sometimes repeated shots of the same action, sometimes contrasting images) may appear simultaneously on different parts of a single screen, dividing the screen into two or more segments.

Although the split screen had been used by D. W. Griffith in *The Birth of a Nation* (1915) and Abel Gance in *Napoleon* (1926) — Gance used three screens and three projectors flanking the center screen image with supplementary images — the use of multiple images stayed in its experimental stages until the New York World's Fair in 1964. The wealth of split-screen short films exhibited there influenced subsequent commercial theatrical features, but except for its exploitation by music videos the split screen or multiple image is still somewhat neglected as a major editorial device.

An interesting use of the split screen occurs in Richard Fleischer's *The Boston Strangler* (1968), the semidocumentary story of a schizophrenic murderer. The use of split screen is appropriate not only because it communicates the simultaneity of a big city manhunt, but also because it is a perfect visual metaphor for the split personality of Albert DeSalvo, the Boston strangler. Often the various images simultaneously shown on the screen substitute for the conventional montage sequence in which shots of action (for example, events taking place at the same time in various parts of a city) are dissolved or cut together to convey simultaneous activity. For example, one multiple-image sequence communicates the rounding up of all known sex offenders in Boston, while another shows the simultaneous efforts of women all over the city to take precautions against the murderer. In other episodes, the multiple imagery substitutes for parallel editing or crosscutting, showing us simultaneous events leading progressively toward a dramatic resolution. Moreover, because the split screen offers a visual overload of stimuli, it helps to convey the sense of panic and urgency caused by the strangler. But the split screen is also used to create emotional conflict in the viewer, to create a tension between two opposing feelings, which duplicate — to a degree — the schizophrenia of the film's central character. At one point, early in the film and before we have seen DeSalvo's face on the screen, the audience is visually forced to identify with the killer and his victim simultaneously. We watch multiple images of buzzers and microphone speakers in an apartment building and we hear the voices of an elderly woman and the killer who is posing as a plumber. A hand-held camera shot then takes us up the stairs, duplicating for us the subjective, murderer's-eye view as he climbs toward the victim, and we simultaneously watch, in another and smaller image, an elderly woman getting ready to open the door.

Another example of split screen is the 1975 Academy Award–winning documentary *The Great American Cowboy* (Keith Merrill), which used the technique to communicate the violence and excitement of rodeo life. A cowboy eases onto the back of a bucking horse; the gate is opened and the screen splits into two, four, or more images of the same action photographed from different angles. Multiple images also show different cowboys on different horses, but all of them plunging and rearing wildly. Thus, the split screen not only can show the same action from slightly different perspectives, but can also emphasize the relationship of similar actions actually performed at different times. Moreover, the split screen is well suited to conveying the excitement and frenzy of certain activities. Watching more than one image simultaneously places a demand on the viewer because of the uncommon quantity of visual stimuli, but it also may lead to an intensification of the viewer's attentiveness.

Superimpositions and Dissolves
Superimposition places and holds two or more images on the screen directly over each other. A related device is the dissolve, in which the two images appear directly over each other only momentarily before one of them dissolves away leaving the other alone — and clear — on the screen. Both superimposition and the dissolve can be used to show simultaneous time if the proper diegetic information is supplied. A superimposition of the heroine putting on lipstick before a dressing table mirror, for instance, and the hero knotting his tie before another mirror would convey simultaneity because of their related activities and our knowledge that they were preparing for a date. Similarly, a sequence connected by dissolves in which an image of a woman sleeping is dissolved into a milkman putting bottles near a door, which is dissolved into a paperboy putting a paper in front of an apartment door, which is then dissolved into a man sleeping would tend to convey to the viewer a sense of simultaneous time. Although both dissolves and superimpositions are less clearly able to communicate simultaneous time than parallel editing, insert shots, and multiple imagery, they are occasionally used because they tend to establish a lyric or languorous mood, which may be more suited to the subject matter than the abruptness of direct cutting or the objectification of relationships between events accomplished through use of the split screen.

Stopped Time: The Freeze Frame

One of the most startling manipulations of time in the cinema occurs when it is stopped altogether, when motion is frozen on the screen. Since the essence of film is the illusion of motion — sequential activity in space taking place in time — to stop that motion, to turn the moving film into a still photo, a slide, disrupts identification and participation with the illusion, reminding the viewer that the motion which appears so natural in the film because it seems to duplicate the activity of the everyday world, is in fact an illusion. Dziga Vertov illustrated this proposition in his *Man with a Movie Camera* (1929). We see someone working at an editing table. A pair of hands unrolls a coil of film. The camera moves close enough for us to see several frames on the strip of film. Then a single still frame fills the screen. In an instant the people in the still frame begin to move — we are now seeing the coil of film as it would appear when projected. Other still frames appear and are either started or stopped, brought into and out of motion, given movement and life or a frozen timelessness. We become aware of the film as an illusion, a mediated image, a mechanism controlled by the film's makers.

Subjective Time: Dream, Fantasy, Memory, and Perceptual Distortion

We customarily assume that what is happening before our eyes on the screen is happening in present time. And as each action passes, it leads inexorably to the next and the next and the next, establishing a forceful sense of both continuity and chronological progression. We know that what has come before our eyes is now past, and that what will occur next before us is the future — and that what we are actually watching is the now, the present. Through editing, however, all of the normal chronological time schemes can be rearranged to create a sequence out of chronological order.

How long is a dream? A fantasy? A thought? A memory? A drugged or drunken perception? We do not measure such occurrences of mind and feeling and perception by time — though, obviously, they occupy time in some fashion. Within a film, subjective time arises from a filmmaker's attempts to convey the consciousness of a character (and sometimes the narrational consciousness as well).

In literature, the kind of rambling, digressive, and highly personal associative thought processes in which we constantly engage may be revealed by a literary technique known as *stream of consciousness*. With film, such mental and emotional processes as dreams, fantasies, memories, and distorted perception must be conveyed visually. And the spectator must be able to distinguish these interior processes from the seemingly more objective narrative of other portions of the film.

During the studio years, a dream sequence in a movie was almost always introduced by extremely conventional transitional devices. We usually knew who the dreamer was and when and where she or he was having the dream. The filmmaker provided us with a narrative context, such as a character preparing for bed, or eyelids becoming heavy, and also provided us with certain conventional editing devices that signaled a dream was going to occur: the sleeper would dissolve into the dream as if waves were undulating across the screen, or a whirlpool would be superimposed over the sleeper and we would know we were descending into the vortex of a deep sleep. And, after the dream was completed

3-5 In the opening sequence of Fellini's *8½* (1963), the rope tied to the dreamer's leg, pulled by two men on the beach, brings him to the ground; instead of crashing to his death, he wakes up in his hotel room. Prior to that moment, no fictional "real" present time has been established.

we might see the dreamer, so we would know we were back in present screen time. The dream itself would be visually different from the rest of the film, either in its style or its content. A dream might be seen as through a veil or on tinted stock. More elaborately, in *Spellbound* (Alfred Hitchcock, 1945), the dream sequence, designed by Salvador Dali, mirrored the surreal artist's style and strange perspectives and thus drastically differed from the rather flat style of the rest of the movie.

Today, filmmakers are far less likely to signal a dream clearly as a dream. In fact, the movement into or out of a dream sequence may be disjunctive, and the editing may depend on disorientation cutting. In Federico Fellini's *8½* (1963), for example, the movie begins with a dream, but we do not know this at the start. We see an unknown man caught in a traffic jam in the claustrophobic interior of his car. He crawls from the auto and suddenly floats over the silent line of cars to the end of a tunnel and then out above a beach and ocean. We see a rope attached to his leg, and then, as if he were a kite, he is pulled down to the beach by two men and falls toward the sea (Figure 3-5). Although we may have a hunch that what we are watching must be a dream, we cannot know for certain until a character (in this case, a film director, Guido Anselmi) awakens from it. The imagery is certainly strange, but until Guido awakens no ground rules have been laid for the viewer and it is difficult to know precisely whether we are watching a surreal experimental feature or a dream or a fantasy.

Like dreams, fantasy used to be signaled to the viewer by certain visual and aural clues. A classic example of a visual signal is the change from black-and-white film to color film as Dorothy half dreams, half fantasizes her journey to Oz in *The Wizard of Oz* (Victor Fleming, 1939). In the musical film *On the Town* (Stanley Donen and Gene Kelly, 1949), one of the sailors daydreams about the girl whose picture is on the "Miss Turnstiles" sign in front of him; the sign image dissolves into the image of the girl herself and a dance number begins, taking place in a nonspecific space (the entire background is yellow and all the props are highly stylized). After the number's completion, this space is dissolved back into the yellow background of the "Miss Turnstiles" sign and the image of the girl's face.

Today, fantasies or daydreams are not signaled so obviously, probably because many artists, psychologists, philosophers, and laypersons now believe that fantasy and reality are not so readily separable, or to put it a little differently, that fantasy is a part of reality. Whatever the reason, today's viewers are expected to understand, by means of the content and the context and the dream logic of fantasies, when they are watching a daydream and when they are watching a supposedly objective reality. Sometimes filmmakers go out of their way to confuse reality and fantasy, since we live as much in our consciousness as we do in the external world. Fellini's *Juliet of the Spirits* (1965), for example, scarcely separates fantasy and dream from reality. The protagonist, Juliet, a housewife whose husband has lost interest in her and who seeks some kind of confirmation of identity, has visions peopled with characters who are no more strange than the friends and neighbors and relatives in her ordinary life; it is therefore difficult to distinguish between a fantasy and a party, between a spirit and a spiritualist.

Like dreams and fantasies, memories are generally linked to a specific character in a film. Someone has to remember — and therefore memory is (or can be) highly subjective. What the viewer sees on the screen is not an objective depiction of the character's past, but a depiction of the past as it is remembered and recreated by the character. In Ingmar Bergman's *Wild Strawberries* (1957), the protagonist's memories of his childhood are treated subjectively. The elderly Isak Borg walks through his own past as a ghost. He attempts to explain himself, but no one sees him. Perhaps the quintessential demonstration of the subjective nature of memory is Akira Kurosawa's *Rashomon* (1951), a film in which four different characters recall vastly different versions of an attack by a bandit on a husband and wife traveling through a forest; characters remember what reflects favorably upon themselves, and even the most impartial of the characters (an observer of the action rather than a participant) is suspect because of his biases (Figure 3-6). Spectators who watch *Rashomon* come away from the film less secure in their relationship to truth and objectivity.

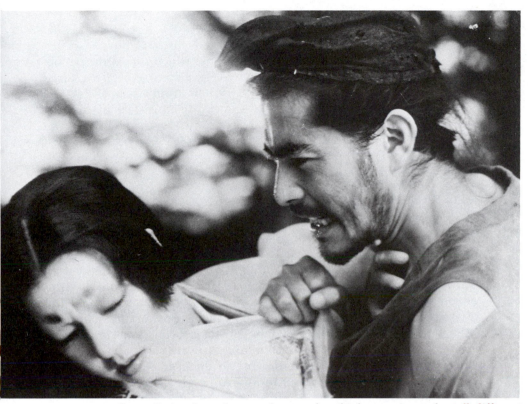

3-6 Prose fiction has often made use of multiple narrators who tell different versions of the same event. Akira Kurosawa, the Japanese director, used the same technique in *Rashomon* (1951). A woodcutter, a bandit, a lord, and his wife each relate what happened one day in the woods. The audience sees each of the told tales as if it were an objective filmed story, but after seeing all four versions, the truth of the events remains ambiguous.

One other kind of subjective time in the cinema is securely attached to a particular character. If a character has been drugged, or is drunk, or is in a state of semiconsciousness, we often witness images in which the content is distorted — the camera has assumed a first-person relationship with the character and thus has taken on that character's distorted perceptions. This active participation by the camera occurs chiefly when a character is in some abnormal physical state; if a character is merely dreaming, fantasizing, or remembering, although the content of what we watch may be strange, illogical, or distorted, the image itself is usually not distorted. A physical abnormality that affects the character's perceptions, however, such as intoxication, is almost always portrayed through the use of a subjective camera distorting what the character sees. Thus, in *Murder My Sweet* (Edward Dmytryk, 1944), when private

eye Philip Marlowe is beaten up and drugged, his return to consciousness is conveyed through camera distortions, which turn ordinary objects in a room into nightmarish and nameless shapes. In *Vertigo* (Alfred
Hitchcock, 1958), an ex-policeman who suffers from a fear of heights,
experiences vertigo or dizziness; the camera demonstrates his distorted perception and fear of falling by tracking in and **zooming** out
simultaneously.

All of the mental processes discussed thus far have been linked to
specific characters. If what we see is a dream, then we shall discover the
sleeper; if what we see is a memory, then we shall see who remembers.
But occasionally, a filmmaker will create a dream without a dreamer —
or with no one identifiable dreamer. In a sense, it is the film that dreams
or remembers. In 1929, for example, surrealists Salvador Dali and Luis
Buñuel made *Un Chien Andalou,* in which there is no real reference point
(Figure 3-7). The film starts out with a title, "Once upon a Time," then
shows a man smoking and sharpening a razor, a cloud passing over the
moon, the man slitting a woman's eyeball with the razor and then a title
that says, "Eight years later," and cuts to a young man riding a bicycle.
All of the actions we see could be in the subconscious mind of a
character, they could be a dream; but then there are none of the comfortable conventions of the movie dream: no dreamer awakens from the
nightmare, restoring the viewer to the real world and to chronological
and decipherable time. In *Un Chien Andalou* nothing is clarified, and the
time we see pass before us on the screen remains ambiguous.

Memory, too, can become detached from a specific character. In *Last
Year at Marienbad* (1961), directed by Alain Resnais, present, past, and
future merge until the distinction between them is meaningless and time
is seen as the merely fluid creation of a subjective consciousness. The
film never clearly establishes a sense of present time or place. Characters
with letters for names move about in a resort hotel; they meet and play
games in which the outcome seems predetermined; they walk about the
halls and grounds, sometimes not even casting shadows in bright sunlight — as if time were no longer measurable by the revolution of the
earth around its axis. Scenes are repeated with variations, conversations, and monologues fragment and repeat. Shot follows shot, but no
secure chronology is established. The entire film could be a dream, a
memory, a fantasy, but it is never clear whose mind or what psychological operation of consciousness or subconsciousness we are witnessing.

In all of the subjective states that the cinema conveys, the nature of
time is ambiguous. While handing in his homework essay on "What I'd
Like for Christmas," the sixth grade protagonist of *A Christmas Story*
(Bob Clark, 1983) fantasizes about how well it will be received. His

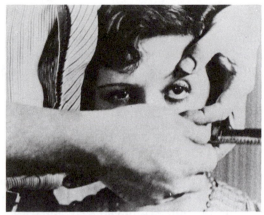

3-7 Some films never present a normal time scheme against which a dream or fantasy can be measured. In *Un Chien Andalou* (1928), surrealists Salvador Dali and Luis Buñuel present what might be a dream, but there is never a dreamer who wakes up — and time itself is mocked by intercut titles.

3-8 In *A Christmas Story* (Bob Clark, 1983), Ralphie, the young protagonist, frequently slips into daydreams, fantasies of heroism, or nightmare as he pictures himself driving off villains or being menaced by wicked witches. These are examples of subjective time in film that is measured against the objective time of the film's narrative.

teacher breaks into song about the masterful prose of the essay, but in chorus with his mother declares that he will never get the Red Ryder Daisy Air Rifle he wants for Christmas because, "You'll shoot your eye out!" The time he is psychologically absent from the school room while witnessing the song and dance number is never specified (nor within the narrative context and the conventions of the psychology of character is it something we wonder about) (Figure 3-8). The running time, of course, is measurable, but the screen time of a subjective sequence is rarely specific. Thus, although transitional editing devices usually locate the narrative in a specific time and place, they also can do exactly the opposite, creating a nontime and a nonplace, the playground of the conscious and unconscious mind.

⊕ Objective Time: The Flashback and the Flash-Forward

The previous pages have discussed some ways in which the cinema can signal and convey to the viewer subjective time, time that is not precisely measurable within the narrative and is generally associated with states of consciousness. But, of course, film can also signal and convey **objective time,** time that we understand is a minute or a day or a week or a year. A case in point is the flashback; a flashback is a memory — or seems to be. Like a memory, it is usually connected with a specific character. And, like a memory, it recalls and recounts the past. Like a memory, finally, how long the remembering of the past takes within the film story is unclear, ambiguous.

Yet flashbacks differ from the subjective presentation of the past. Usually there is an element of impersonality in the flashback, a particular character may be doing the remembering, but the memory that we see on the screen is represented as objective fact — what really happened rather than the way one character remembers it. In *Casablanca*, for example, (Michael Curtiz, 1942) we do not regard the flashback of the love affair between Ilsa and Rick as anything but what actually happened between them. Rick, the owner of a café in Casablanca, is drinking after hours when the first flashback occurs. He has seen Ilsa earlier in the evening and the narrative present has established that they knew each other during the past German occupation of Paris. Rick, trying both to forget and to remember Ilsa, tells Sam, the pianist, to play "As Time Goes By," a song Ilsa had asked for earlier in the evening. As Sam begins to play, a close-up image of Rick is dissolved into a shot of the Arch of Triumph, thus, taking us out of Casablanca and to Paris. There is a cut to Rick and Ilsa riding in a car, obviously in love. After establishing the lovers' relationship to each other and their history as a couple, the flashback ends with a medium shot of Rick standing in front of a train about to leave Paris, being prompted by Sam, the pianist, to board it. The shot dissolves, the figure of Rick being replaced on the screen by a bottle of whiskey sitting atop the bar. We are back in Rick's Café.

Although it is Rick who nominally remembers his and Ilsa's past in Paris, we believe what we see is the narrative truth — uncolored by Rick's nostalgia or bitterness or love. What makes the flashback, even when it is attached to a specific character, seem so objective, so histori-cal? The curious difference between a flashback and a character's sub-jective memory is the establishment of time and narrative logic *within* the sequence. Most often, once the transition is made to a previous time in a flashback, the time sequence of the remembered material is chrono-logical, adheres to the usual laws of cause and effect, and is consis-tent with the rest of the film in which the camera acts invisibly as an omniscient third-person narrator. That is, watching a flashback, the viewer generally watches a continuous and consecutive series of actions that give the illusion of present time. When the sequence is over (the flashback sequence may be composed of a number of smaller units that still progress forward in time), we dissolve or cut back to the real narrative present of the film, established at the beginning of the film's main action. Sometimes entire films are flashbacks, surrounded by bookendlike moments of present time. *Double Indemnity* (Billy Wilder, 1944), *Kind Hearts and Coronets* (Robert Hamer, 1948), and *The Man Who Shot Liberty Valance* (John Ford, 1962) are for most of their duration flashbacks. In the first, a dictaphone confession of murder listened to by an insurance claims agent takes us back into the past; in the second, a man awaiting execution writes his memoirs, which take us into the past in a series of flashbacks; and in the third, an elderly United States senator tells a young newspaperman the true story of a shootout, which leads into the flashback. What is interesting about films which are primarily flashbacks is that because the past occupies so much screen time, it becomes the film's present time; we tend to forget we are watching something that has already happened rather than something which is happening.

The **flash-forward** is a much less common movement in time than is the flashback. The flash-forward, unlike the flashback, usually does not belong to anybody. (The only exceptions are clairvoyant characters, like those in Nicholas Roeg's *Don't Look Now* (1973) or characters who are able to time-trip, like Billy Pilgrim in *Slaughterhouse Five* (George Roy Hill, 1972). The flash-forward is therefore primarily a device connected with the camera/narrator or the film's narrational consciousness — an all-seeing and all-knowing eye whose extraordinary vision the viewer is allowed to share. Although a filmmaker such as Alain Resnais, who views time as an entirely subjective construction, can link the flash-forward to the consciousness of his main character in *La Guerre Est Finie* (1966), films like *They Shoot Horses, Don't They?* (Sydney Pollack, 1969) and *Easy Rider* (Dennis Hopper, 1969) insert flash-forwards for dramatic emphasis, a cinematic forewarning that disorients and jolts the viewer. They also create narrative suspense and a certain sense of dread. In *They*

3-9 A sequence of superimpositions and dissolves can convey a sense of ambiguous time. In *Tom Jones* (Tony Richardson, 1963) Sophie Western and Tom are shown in a courting sequence which implies that young lovers lose track of time.

Shoot Horses, the flash-forwards show Robert on trial for something (we find out at the end it is for shooting Gloria at her own request) and they are filmed through what seem like blue filters so that their eerieness and disjunctiveness is more disturbing; in *Easy Rider* the flash-forwards reveal in tiny and somewhat incomprehensible units the violent death of the hippie cyclist. These flash-forwards are not premonitions that belong to the film's characters; rather, they are insertions by the narrational consciousness, and so once they are understood they are seen as being objective.

Achronological Time

AMBIGUOUS TIME

Within the context of well-defined temporal structures — either clearly subjective or objective — ambiguous temporal sequences may occur. Take for example, a sequence of dissolves and superimpositions used in *Tom Jones* (Tony Richardson, 1963) (Figure 3-9). We see Tom and Sophie Western walking in a country landscape in various combinations of shots superimposed and dissolved with images of trees and flowers. In

3-10 Though the narration in *The Plow that Broke the Plains* (Pare Lorentz, 1936) describes a historical progression — from the settlement of the plains in the nineteenth century to the Dustbowl of the 1930s — the images of tractors moving back and forth across the land, plowing, harrowing, reaping, are temporally unspecific. They exist in achronological, universal time, conveying the notion of many tractors doing this work over and over again, year after year.

what time do these images take place in relation to each other? We know from the context of the narrative that Tom and Sophie are spending — specifically — one afternoon together, but the visual sequence does not let us know whether minutes or hours are passing. Obviously, the aim of the dissolves and superimpositions was not to convey precise information about time, but rather to set up a romantic, lyrical mood and to convey general information about the couple's growing relationship. **Ambiguous time** is most often communicated through dissolves and superimpositions.

UNIVERSAL TIME

There is another construction of achronological time that may be called **universal time.** It is created consciously by the filmmaker who wishes the images in the film to take on a universal quality.

Documentary films, particularly those made in the 1930s, frequently sought to create universal time. In Pare Lorentz's *The Plow That Broke the Plains* (1936), for example, we are shown images of farm machinery working huge midwestern fields (Figure 3-10). Plows and harvesters move back and forth in a series of alternating shots: a group of machines moves across the screen from left to right, in the next image from right to left, and so on. They are never the same machines in the same field. Although the film begins with a map of a specific geographical area — the Great Plains — its purpose seems to be to transcend a specific place and a specific time so that the migrating victims of the drought and wind, which helped create the Dust Bowl, are explained to the public not in geographic or historical terms, with which not everyone might identify, but in terms of humanity's unchanging, universal qualities. Thus, although the film seems to deal with a specific locale and history, the images and narration do not emphasize them. The narration describes, in a most general and simple way, the process of a booming agriculture depleting the land, which then becomes vulnerable to erosion and the ravages of the elements. Because the images as edited lack landmarks and chronology, what we see takes place not so much in, say, Kansas in 1935, as in a universal time and place. By emphasizing the idea rather than the particular chosen example (this is not farmer Smith plowing his Kansas field, but this is the Farmer plowing the Field — the symbol of any farmer in any field), a sense of universal time is created.

Two techniques help the filmmaker to rob time of its specificity: first, the use of a great deal of editing, which links images together in separate shots so there is little sense of context against which time can be measured, and second, the use of a large number of close-ups and/or shots that are not defined by their backgrounds. *The Plow that Broke the Plains*, for instance, rarely shows us a human face that we can inspect and identify as a particular, individual human being; faces are shot in shadow or are not held on the screen for long. The movie also shows us many close-ups of useless or old farm machinery lying on parched ground, objects to which people are no longer attached and which are no longer defined by their activity. Those objects exist in time, but it could be any time. And they also exist in space, but as there are no reference points, it could be any space. Further, the idea of an action becomes important beyond the specific action depicted in the shots. Shots of moving tractors cut to shots of moving tanks, similar shapes and similar directions. The idea conveyed through the montage — that grain and tanks are both weapons of war and are both equally important to the war effort — far outweighs the specific content of the individual shots.

Although perhaps the most obvious examples of the editor's creation of universal time can be found in the heavily edited documentaries of the 1930s from America and Great Britain, where the emphasis is on humanity's universal struggle to endure, examples can also be found today in subtler documentaries. Even the documentary filmmaker Fredrick Wiseman creates universal time. This sounds odd, because one of his primary methods is to present extremely long sequences of activity with no interruption by editing or commentary; real time and real space seem to be captured in the sequence and preserved, minimally controlled by the filmmaker. A Wiseman documentary like *Titicut Follies* (1967), his first film, exploring the world of a mental institution, or *The Store* (1983), recording the various activities in the main Neiman-Marcus store and corporate headquarters in Dallas, seems hardly the place to find universal time. And yet it is there — between the sequences. *Titicut Follies*, for example, begins with a strange variety show in which the participants seem ill at ease, unnaturally stiff. The film ends with the show as well. In between, sequences show us men in an institution for the criminally insane being abused by guards, amusing themselves in the exercise yard, being interviewed by staff personnel, being led through the motions of a birthday party by volunteers, doing in fact all that they do and what the camera has been able to record in the given time it was there. Each sequence preserves its own temporal continuity and spatial contiguity. The screen time and running time within sequences are usually the same. Space is unbroken by editing as the camera moves to change perspective. And yet there is absolutely no establishment of an overall time scheme for the film. Does all this footage come from a typical week? A day? What time relationship exists between the variety show and the events shown after it? By leaving the time between sequences undefined, unspecific, Wiseman takes extremely particularized events and makes them emblematic of such events at mental institutions everywhere and at any time. While preserving the integrity of each specific sequence, because of the film's overall atemporal or timeless editing structure Wiseman is also able to create universality.

Although universal time is suggested chiefly in documentary films, fiction films also occasionally suggest it. A primitive example of an attempt at universality exists in the parallel editing of D. W. Griffith's *Intolerance* (1916), which attempts to link four widely separated periods of history and to emphasize what they had in common. Moreover, *Intolerance* used one recurrent image that was meant to be taken as universal in its spatial and temporal ambiguity: linking the different periods is the image of a woman rocking a cradle, prefaced by the title "Out of the cradle endlessly rocking, ever bringing the same joys and sorrows." In the shot itself the cradle is covered with roses, a strong beam of light shines from above on the woman, and three shadowy figures (the Fates) sit in the background. This image exists in no particular time and in no particular space.

Because the close-up tends to exclude the identifying and specific elements of space and time, fiction films that depend heavily on the close-up are able to suggest universal time. Carl Dreyer in *The Passion of Joan of Arc* (1928) not only gives us a Joan who is alone and in close-up in

3-11 Carl Dreyer in *The Passion of Joan of Arc* (1928) places his central character in a universal time. Frequent close-ups of Joan against bare white backgrounds eliminate temporal clues suggestive of a specific time and place.

the frame, but he also purposely removes background clues suggesting a particular time, using instead white backgrounds for his close-ups (Figure 3-11). The effect creates a sense of timelessness, of nontime, of universal and eternal time. We are not only watching the story of a particular woman engaged in a particular religious and political struggle at a particular time in history, we are also watching the struggle between faith and doubt, which can take place at any time and anywhere. Many of Dreyer's films, as well as those of French filmmaker Robert Bresson, attempt through editing to create images that deal with eternal and timeless states of the spirit.

Visual Rhythm

Running time is absolute in that it can be objectively measured. Screen time is less absolute, and, on occasion, we may have difficulty deciphering it. Usually, however, we can figure out from the dialogue, from visual clues, from knowledge we bring to the film, how long the story or narrative is supposed to be; we can tell if it takes place in a year or ten years, three days or three weeks. Experienced time, which is highly subjective, is created partially by the rhythm of the editing and by the pace of motion within the frame. The rate at which the film is edited, the kinds of editorial transitions, the number of shots in the entire film, and the length of each shot, sequence, and scene imparts a visual rhythm, a pace, to the whole film. This rhythm and pace not only contributes to the mood of various cinematic units but also influences our perception of the entire film.

If images dissolve into each other, the mood produced may be lyric, romantic, graceful, and certainly somewhat leisurely. A dissolve from one image into another takes more running time than does a direct cut from one image to another. A 60-minute film edited primarily in dissolves and fades may seem slower and possibly longer to the viewer than a 60-minute film that is edited primarily in direct cuts. The number and pattern of dissolves, fades, and direct cuts in any given film will partially determine its overall rhythm and pace, and that will in turn influence experienced time.

For example, Richard Lester's *A Hard Day's Night* (1964) was edited so as to achieve a hyperactive rhythm; it greatly depended on disorienting cuts, which were admirably suited to its anarchic and ebullient subjects, the Beatles. When the film was released, it left audiences exhilarated and breathless. Today, however, *A Hard Day's Night* seems much slower than when it was first released; the Beatles retain their charm, but the pace seems almost sluggish. The editing rhythms of the film have not changed, of course, but the audience's sense of them has changed; we have learned to see more quickly, and the techniques that were used so originally in Lester's film have now become commonplace.

Meaning Through Editing — Relationships Between Shots

MONTAGE: CONNECTIONS AND DISLOCATIONS

In front of me lies a crumpled yellowed sheet of paper. On it is a mysterious note:

"Linkage — P" and "Collision — E."

This is a substantial trace of a heated bout on the subject of montage between P (Pudovkin) and E (myself).

This has become a habit. At regular intervals he visits me late at night and behind closed doors we wrangle over matters of principle. A graduate of the Kuleshov school, he loudly defends an understanding of montage as a *linkage* of pieces. Into a chain. Again, "bricks." Bricks, arranged in series to *expound* an idea.

I confronted him with my viewpoint on montage as *collision*. A view that from the collision of two given factors *arises* a concept.

Sergei Eisenstein[2]

Montage — the juxtaposition of separate images — is one way of creating meaning in the cinema. Originally, the word *montage* was used simply; borrowed from the French language by the Russian filmmaker and theorist Sergei Eisenstein, it literally means mounting and was used to signify the physical act of editing, the cutting and splicing of one piece of film to another. However, the word has undergone an interesting and somewhat confusing evolution. Refined and qualified by Eisenstein himself, it has come to be associated with the Russian principles of editing, principles that stress combining images so that they will produce an idea. The word has also been used to describe a certain kind of editing common in the German silent cinema: sequences were constructed primarily with dissolves, and their aim was less to create intellectual meaning than it was to create mood. In Hollywood, the word has been used generally to describe sequences that compress and link time, whether they do so by cutting, dissolving, or superimposing images.

All of these definitions of montage share a common denominator; they all imply that meaning is not inherent in any one shot but is created by the juxtaposition of shots. Simply and dramatically, this basic principle of editing was demonstrated by an experiment conducted by Lev Kuleshov, an early Russian filmmaker. He intercut images of an actor's expressionless face with images of a bowl of soup, a woman in a coffin, and a child with a toy. Audiences who saw the film praised the actor's performance — they saw in his face, emotionless as it was, hunger, grief, and affection. They saw, in other words, what was not really there in the separate images. Meaning and emotion, then, were created not by the content of the individual images, but by the contextual relationship of the images to each other. Alone, his actor's expressionless face is expressionless, his bowl of soup is just a bowl of soup; shown in relationship to each other, however, the shots will communicate a man's hunger to the viewer.

MONTAGE BY COMPOSITION

The composition of shapes and masses in the film frame can be used to link one image to another. A relationship can be established between two shots emphasizing either their similarity or dissimilarity in composition.

An example of a relationship established by shots with a similar composition can be found in Eisenstein's *Strike* (1924). One image shows us a close-up of a man's hand dangling a child whose body, precariously angled on a diagonal plane, fills the major part of the frame. Another is composed similarly, although its subject seems to have no relationship to the image of the child: a cow's head, filling most of the frame, is also angled diagonally and a man's hand has just finished cutting its throat. Because the composition of both shots is similar, the shots are linked together by the viewer who looks, then, for the meaning of the juxtaposition of such seemingly different content. The relationship emerges: the child is being slaughtered in a massacre of strikers by police, much as an animal is slaughtered in a slaughterhouse.

The relationship of shots based on diametrically opposed compositions is best illustrated by those numerous scenes in westerns or war movies in which we get an image of the good guy on screen left followed by an image of the bad guy mirroring the previous shot on screen right, or the army of one group advancing from screen right and the army of its enemy advancing from screen left. This opposition of composition in such an exact manner again makes the linkage of the two shots meaningful. Not only does such a juxtaposition make physical the notion of conflict between opposites, but it also implies — particularly when there is accompanying movement — that the two opposing forces and masses will eventually converge in the frame.

MONTAGE BY MOVEMENT

Since few shots in a film are static, composition alone rarely provides the basis for linking two images. Usually similar movement or opposed movement is combined with composition, providing another element, which can provoke associations between two separate images. This directional flow from image to image can indicate a great deal when it is made noticable as opposed to standard decoupage where cutting on an action or matching similar actions on either side of a cut are meant to be invisible. To be effective montage editing must be perceived.

A montage sequence in *The Graduate* (Mike Nichols, 1967) compresses time, as usual, but it also creates meaning through the similar movement of its central subject in the juxtaposed shots (Figure 3-12). We see Benjamin jumping into his family swimming pool, then Benjamin jumping into bed with Mrs. Robinson in a hotel room, then Benjamin idly floating in his pool on an inflated rubber mattress, then Benjamin in a similarly relaxed position and movement in the hotel bed. The montage communicates not only the recreational aspects of Benjamin's summer but also the feeling that Benjamin's affair with Mrs. Robinson is as idle, emotionally casual, and repetitive as his time in the family pool.

Opposition of movement within a montage sequence, like similarity of movement, can also tell us a great deal. At the beginning of Alfred Hitchcock's *Strangers on a Train* (1951), for example, we are introduced to the two central characters feet first: we literally see their shoes and watch them walk before we ever see their faces. Besides the differences in their personalities indicated immediately by their contrasting taste in footwear (one pair of shoes is sober and plain, the other pair flamboyant

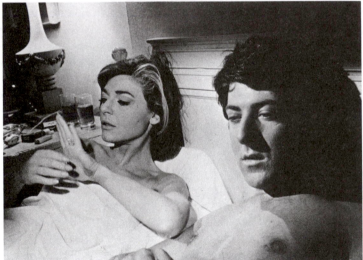

3-12 In *The Graduate* (1970), Mike Nichols punctuates a sequence showing the affair between Benjamin and Mrs. Robinson with an example of cutting together two similar motions. Here he alternates between Benjamin relaxing in his family's pool and lounging in bed with Mrs. Robinson in a hotel room. Later, we see a shot in which Benjamin comes out of the water onto the float in the pool cut to another shot which appears to continue that movement as he slides onto Mrs. Robinson in the hotel bed.

and decorative), we sense a difference between them because the physical direction of their movement is opposed. They each get out of cabs, which have arrived at a train station from contrasting directions and they each walk toward the train, on which they will finally meet, from opposite directions. And, again, because in their respective shots they move toward center screen from opposite directions, we have a clear sense they will converge and eventually come together in the same screen space. Which is, of course, what happens: the two sit down across from each other in a club car, their feet accidentally touch, and the story of two men and a crisscross murder begins. Hitchcock's editing here is formally in tune with the structure and theme of the film.

Editing by this kind of directional flow must be carefully controlled so that the viewer is not accidentally misled. When we see one shot in which a man on horseback is galloping from left to right and that is followed by a shot of another man similarly galloping from left to right, we tend automatically to assume that the second rider is *behind* the first rider and that the action we are watching in the linking of the two shots is a chase of some sort. If the second character is not really following the first, the spatial resemblance is misleading and the editing is probably faulty — unless of course, the filmmaker purposely misled us for some reason.

Contrasting screen movement can also be used to mislead the viewer. In *The Man with a Movie Camera* (1928), for instance, Dziga Vertov crosscuts between a fire engine racing across the screen from right to left and an ambulance racing across the screen from left to right; each shot is accelerated — or shortened — as the two are alternated. There seems to be only one possible conclusion to this montage in which parallel editing also gives us a sense of simultaneous time: the two vehicles are on a collision course. But Vertov simply cuts away from this sequence to other unrelated shots and the two vehicles never crash; their movement toward each other — created by artificial means, Vertov seems to say — is never resolved. In a film that did not pay so much attention to the actual processes of filmmaking (for Vertov shows us the camera, film editing, and so on), we might be inclined to think the editor had made a careless mistake. But Vertov is likely to be poking a little fun at the expectations of the film audience. Throughout the film — which is a virtual textbook of editing technique — motion is used to link shots together. Spinning wheels on machinery are linked to other spinning objects. Some movements are contrasted, others are similar. In one particularly fascinating sequence, Vertov shows us, by juxtaposed shots, spectators watching athletes perform. Although we do not see the spectators in the same shots as the athletes, because of their eye move-

3-13 Dziga Vertov intercut a rotating spindle in *The Man with a Movie Camera* (1928) with other shots of rotating objects to develop a pattern, a visual harmony, based on a particular motion and enforced by repetition.

ment and reactions we link the following shots of the athletes to them and assume that the spectators are actually seeing the action. This in itself is not unusual; most editing makes the viewer assume the existence of an action not really seen on the screen. What is strange, however, is that the spectators blink their eyes, move their heads, in what we consider normal time, in natural lifelike motion — but the athletes move in slow motion. Vertov not only juxtaposes shots to create action, he juxtaposes the dimensions and movements of time as well.

MONTAGE BY REPETITION

So far we have been talking about repetition of composition and/or motion, but not repetition of the image itself. On occasion, however, an editor may choose to repeat a shot exactly as it appeared on the screen before (and may appear again).

Repetition of images requires the juxtaposition of different shots intercut with a repeated image. The effect of this repetition can be soothing or anxiety-provoking; it can function to *unify* disparate images, or, because it destroys normal time, it can function to *shatter* images connected chronologically. In Vertov's *The Man with a Movie Camera*, for instance, the repetition of a rotating machine spindle (Figure 3-13) between shots of different objects, which are rotating, creates a pattern, a rhythm, a visual harmony because the image of the spindle draws all the other shots together and cements them into a unified sequence. In *An Occurrence at Owl Creek Bridge* (1961), on the other hand, we are disturbed by the repetition of several shots within a montage sequence. Telephoto shots of a man running toward the camera are juxtaposed with shots of a woman moving down plantation steps and then laterally across the screen. Because the man, who is running toward the camera (and the woman), is shown repeating the action from the same point in space, the viewer becomes aware of the realistic narrative's transformation into an explicit fantasy or dream.

MONTAGE BY RHYTHM

Let us imagine a series of shots consisting of three 2-second shots, one 3-second shot, and then two 1-second shots. This series creates a rhythm or pattern. This pattern might be altered and/or repeated. In some abstract films such rhythmic alterations of shots are synchronized to music, as in the animated design sequence to Bach's Toccata and Fugue in D minor in Walt Disney's *Fantasia* (1940).

The intrusion of such rhythmic editing into an unrhythmic context occurs at the climax of *An Occurrence at Owl Creek Bridge*. Some shots are repeated, and a very formal rhythm between shots is used in conjunction with rhythmic music on the sound track. The result is very disturbing; it immediately tells the viewer something is unnatural or wrong, and it finally severs the viewer's identification with the escaping protagonist. We get crosscutting between a head-on telephoto shot of the protagonist running — but seeming to make no progress — toward his wife (and the camera), and a normal-lens shot of his wife moving in slow motion laterally to greet him (Figure 3-14). Each of the images of the protagonist lasts for five bars of music, and each of the images of the wife — except the last one — lasts for seven bars. Further, the cut from the wife to husband occurs on the first beat of the musical bar, but the cut from the husband to wife occurs on the last beat of the fifth bar. The formal rigidity of the rhythm makes viewers aware of artifice and withdraws them from too intimate a connection with the characters, so that the protagonist's death will come as a proper narrative conclusion to the film rather than as a cruel joke on them.

MONTAGE BY CONTENT: DETAIL AND METAPHOR

All the juxtapositions between shots thus far discussed have had one thing in common: visual resemblance of the images (whether though composition, movement, or repetition) connected them into a unit or sequence. But there is another basis for the juxtaposition of images: their content, what their subject is, what they are about.

Juxtaposing images with related content (for example, shots of factory workers and shots of smoke stacks) creates meaning as the shots accumulate. This accumulation of juxtaposed shots — for instance, a close-up of an ashtray full of cigarette butts, following a long shot of a man smoking at his desk — also helps create a sense of duration, a sense of a sequence being built up from separate images bit by bit, rather

3-14 Rhythmic montage can be used to create narrative tension. In a sequence from *An Occurrence at Owl Creek Bridge* (Robert Enrico, 1961), the crosscutting between the husband and the wife is set to music with the image of each having a distinct number of beats. The repetition of the pattern signals the viewer that something is wrong, that the scene is too artificial to be real.

as if the images were building blocks. This sense of the montage sequence being constructed as detail is linked to detail was first articulated by the Russian filmmaker V. I. Pudovkin, who not only made films but who also wrote about film and explored film theory. Pudovkin was not in modern terms a realistic filmmaker (he did not think that editing should be either invisible or linked solely to notions of natural time and space), but the traditional Hollywood film nevertheless has relied heavily on his method of creating meaning through the invisible accumulation of separate images.

Suppose, for example, a filmmaker wishes to show us commuters catching a train in the morning and wants the images to suggest that the people hurrying to work are all alike, that their lives are uniform, and that the mass rush for the train is an indication of the lack of individuality in modern life. These are *ideas* we are supposed to draw from the imagery, but ideas cannot *literally* be photographed. Of course the filmmaker could *tell* us this on the sound track, or could add titles to the picture. But if we are not meant to be aware of a narrational presence outside the movie, the filmmaker will suggest these ideas to the viewer by editing together appropriate details from the scene. After establishing the context in a long shot (people appearing on the station platform), the filmmaker probably will create a montage sequence out of close-ups of objects in the scene itself, and through them will attempt to establish uniformity. For example, many images of briefcases, newspapers (perhaps all of them the *Wall Street Journal*), similar gray flannel suits, and close-ups of faces with the same expression may be juxtaposed. These images in quantity and in juxtaposition will indicate to the audience the sameness of the commuters, yet all of these images arise naturally out of the entire scene and the context of the characters' daily life.

Instead of accumulating details over a period of screen time, however, the filmmaker could create a quick and economical visual metaphor — which, although it would not conform to the conventions of realism and would probably call attention to the manipulation of images, would communicate the idea visually. This kind of juxtaposition of images relies on linking shots in which the content is usually unrelated in the context of the film except by an idea. An example of this

 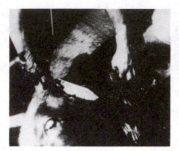 

3-15   These three shots from Eisenstein's *Strike* (1924) demonstrate intellectual montage. The shot of the animal being slaughtered is inserted into the sequence of the workers being massacred by the Czar's troops. The viewer is presented with an idea: the workers are being slaughtered as if they were cattle.

editing approach — and one which brings us back to our commuters — exists in Charles Chaplin's *Modern Times* (1936). In the film we see a shot of commuters descending into a station. The next shot shows us a flock of sheep pushing each other into the depth of the frame, in the same movement seen in the previous shot. Although these juxtaposed images are completely different in photographic content and context, we understand the metaphor: the commuters are like those sheep, mindlessly following each other. The meaning of the juxtaposition arises from nowhere in the world of the film but from literary and cultural convention, and from a connecting movement.

This kind of montage was first practiced by Sergei Eisenstein, a contemporary of Pudovkin and like him both a filmmaker and a theorist. The two men were friends but disagreed strongly on editing practice. While Pudovkin believed images of the details of the narrative were building blocks whose accumulation led to meaning, Eisenstein saw images as more like Chinese or Japanese ideograms, which, by juxtaposing unrelated word pictures (such as *eye* and *water*), create a new idea and a new word (such as *crying*). Eisenstein applied this principle to cinematic images. Two images — quite unlike in content — could be juxtaposed to create a new image, an idea in the mind of the viewer. He called this collision of unrelated images **intellectual montage** (Figure 3-15). A classic example of intellectual montage is the juxtaposition of shots in Eisenstein's *Potemkin* (1925) after the sailors on the battleship open fire on the town of Odessa to retaliate for the city's massacre of those citizens who were sympathetic to the sailor's plight. A shot of the battleship's cannons firing is followed by a shot of the target, cupids on a theater; in turn, that shot is cut next to a shot of a shell bursting against

3-16 Chaplin, like other silent film directors, resorted to literal visual imitations of verbal metaphors. When his starving partner in *The Gold Rush* (1925) looks at Charlie strutting around the cabin and hallucinates that he is a chicken, a dissolve shows us a strutting Charlie in a chicken costume.

the gates of the theater, filling the screen with smoke. This shot is followed by a series of three separate cuts of sculptured stone lions: the first is shown at rest, the second has its head raised, and the third is upright with a snarling expression on its face. The film then cuts to another shot of the theater gates and smoke, which thins enough to show that the theater has been destroyed. What is notable here is that the stone lions have no context in the particular sequence; they are placed within it because they create an idea by comparing or metaphorically equating the sailors' angry fire and rebellion with the awakening of a previously passive animal and its arousal to rage. The metaphor is enriched by Eisenstein's decision to show us *stone* lions awakening. He suggests not only the ultimate kind of arousal from a state of dormancy (shots of a real lion would do that although not so emphatically) but also that the very stones of the city are incited to sympathetic anger with the mutineers.

A visual comparison or metaphor to convey an idea to the viewer may, of course, be too obvious, or, on the other hand, it may be obscure and confusing. It can also be used for comic effect. In Chaplin's *The Gold Rush* (1925), the little tramp visually changes on screen from a man into a human-size chicken through a dissolve (Figure 3-16). The tramp, shuffling his feet to keep warm, seems to his starving companion to be a chicken scratching the ground; therefore, the little tramp *is* a chicken in the image. A visual metaphor is created.

3-17 A superimposition occurs when two different shots are printed one atop the other. In *The Man with a Movie Camera* (1928) Dziga Vertov superimposed an eye on the camera lens to create a visual metaphor: the camera lens is an eye.

Less comically but just as simply, Dziga Vertov in *The Man with a Movie Camera* creates an instant metaphor and communicates a complex idea by juxtaposing an image of an eye opening and an image of the aperture of a camera lens widening (Figure 3-17). This is the central metaphor on which he bases the entire film (and also his writings about the Kino-Eye), but he also juxtaposes other images with these, for example, the lifting of a retractable shop-front covering as the owner starts the business day, the opening of window shutters, and the opening of the slats of venetian blinds to let in the morning sunlight. Thus, not only does he show us metaphorically that the camera is an eye, but he also extends the metaphor so that a city, its inhabitants, and a camera all awaken to movement and the happenings of a day together.

Although this kind of intellectual montage reached its peak during the days of silent cinema and has been used to a lesser degree since, modern cinema does regularly use the juxtaposition of images to create in the viewer's mind what is not really there — photographed — on the screen. The lessons of Lev Kuleshov's editing experiments showing an expressionless face are still in use: the meaning of a shot is not necessarily inherent in the shot but in the juxtaposition of shots.

One can see this principle in action whether one looks at a film like Eisenstein's *Potemkin* or Alfred Hitchcock's *Psycho* (1960). In the Odessa steps sequence in *Potemkin*, for example, Eisenstein juxtaposes images of boots, guns, horrified faces, and various objects, and the result is a massacre that remains violently imprinted on our minds, but which we do not really see in its entirety on the screen. In *Psycho,* Alfred Hitchcock constructed the shower murder sequence out of a montage of seventy-eight separate short shots. A close examination of the sequence reveals that the murder weapon, a knife, never touches the body — and that the body is not necessarily the body of the actress who plays the victim. Yet when we watch the movie, we are convinced that we have seen a violent and bloody murder.

Although this kind of editing seems especially suited to the world of movie melodrama, it is also employed in ostensibly realistic films, which will occasionally juxtapose two images that reveal an idea not inherent in either of the two shots shown separately. For example, the documentary, *Hearts and Minds* (Peter Davis, 1975), has a sequence in which a shot of General William Westmoreland glibly discussing how cheap life is to the Oriental is juxtaposed with a shot of a small Vietnamese boy crying uncontrollably at a relative's graveside. Earlier propaganda films also used this kind of montage — whether they were the product of Axis or Allied filmmakers. In the German *Triumph of the Will* (Leni Riefenstahl, 1934), shots of Hitler's airplane descending are juxtaposed with shots of majestic clouds and church spires; in the American *Why We Fight* series (Frank Capra, 1942–1945), shots of children playing in some American suburb are juxtaposed with staged shots of Japanese and German children playing with war toys.

Filmmakers eager to convey a message, whether in a fictional or documentary film, usually employ montage more frequently than do other filmmakers. In this way, not only can they manipulate time and space through editing, they can manipulate the very content of their images and control the meanings of their films with a minimum of ambiguity.

Meaning with Minimal Editing — Relationships Within Shots

MISE-EN-SCÈNE

> The search after composition in depth is, in effect, a partial replacement of montage by frequent panning shots and entrances. It is based on a respect for the continuity of dramatic space and, of course, of its duration.
> André Bazin [3]

Mise-en-scène, a French phrase, was originally a theatrical term meaning "to put in place." (A stage director in France is called the *metteur en scène*.) While montage achieves meaning through the relationship *between* shots, the juxtaposition of separate images, mise-en-scène achieves meaning through the relationship of things visible *within* a single shot. The filmmaker who uses montage wants the viewer to see the art, the manipulation of the raw materials — the photographed images; there is no attempt to imitate or present an illusion of the everyday world, to respect the continuity of space and time, that unity perceived by viewers outside the filmed world. The filmmaker who uses mise-en-scène tries to hide the art, the manipulation of the photographed images in order to present an illusion of reality. In other words, mise-en-scène is a style of **realism.** The frame in montage style is like a painter's canvas, a place where pictures are composed; the frame in mise-en-scène style is like a window on a world that seems to be taking place spontaneously with the camera simply an objective observer. But, of course, the camera can never simply be an objective observer. Everything that takes place within the mise-en-scène frame is as artfully composed as anything in the montage frame. Jean Renoir's films, noted as paradigms of mise-en-scène filming, are as artfully structured as any of Eisenstein's. Indeed, except for some experimental films, no one film can be considered totally montage or mise-en-scène. Renoir used decoupage where necessary to achieve the desired effect; when he needed to, Eisenstein used long takes. Most filmmakers edit and move the camera, create and record, impose meaning, and find meaning. Yet when a film employs one or the other style extensively, a different effect will be achieved. The mise-en-scène filmmaker minimizes editing or fragmenting a scene into separate units to present the illusion of reality. Thus, cinematic devices (such as Eisenstein's stone lions that seem to rear up), which call attention to themselves and to the film as film, tend to be avoided. The meaning and texture of a mise-en-scène film is primarily created by context; the film appears realistic and the filmmaker invisible. The meaning and texture of a montage film is primarily created by frequent editing; the film appears more expressionistic and the filmmaker's presence is more obvious.

The mise-en-scène filmmaker prefers to communicate meaning *in* the shot rather than to create it from separate shots. But how is that meaning achieved and where is it found in any single shot? The spatial relationships between people and other people, between people and objects, between objects and other objects convey meaning. Thus, the composition within the mise-en-scène shot is extremely important, whether the shot is static or the subjects move or the camera moves or both subject and camera move. Since it is necessary for the viewer to see these elements, people and objects in the foreground as well as people and objects in the background, mise-en-scène shots will nearly always employ deep focus. All of these variables can change the meaning of a single shot without the intervention of a single cut.

Consider, in Jacques Tati's *Mr. Hulot's Holiday* (1954), a comic shot in which the camera is static and the subject moves. Mr. Hulot, sitting in a canoe in the ocean, is barely discernible in long shot; we watch the canoe slowly fold up on him as the prow and stern rise from the water and close on the gentleman, quietly gulping him down. What makes the scene (of one shot) so funny is that we can see the man in relationship to his environment: he is being defeated by both the human-made contraption and the sea. Watching the action in a single take also emphasizes the inexorability of the forces marshaled against him.

Movement becomes the important element of the impressive mise-en-scène of the beginning of Orson Welles's *Touch of Evil* (1958), in which both the subject and the camera move. A 2½-minute shot, in which relationships between people and objects and place are constantly shifting, starts with a close-up of a time bomb planted in an automobile. The camera then introduces us to the hero and heroine, and moves above the mazelike confusion of an unknown place and the distortions of night and neon to come finally to a stop (followed by the film's first cut) as the bomb explodes and the car is consumed in flames. Besides conveying a wealth of information central to the narrative, the restless and inquisitive camera (which is constantly seeing things from new perspectives) mirrors the film's thematic emphasis on the search for concrete answers to a complex and puzzling mystery, a complex and puzzling person, the complex and puzzling issues of morality, public and private.

In order to reveal spatial relationships within the frame during the length of a shot, there must be room as well as time. In a mise-en-scène film, the ideal distance of the camera from the subject will emphasize space. Therefore, the basic spatial unit of a mise-en-scène film is the long shot showing a figure or object and its surroundings. The close-up and even the medium shot usually exclude too much of what makes up a spatial context. In addition, in order to allow enough time for the viewer to perceive and understand the spatial relationships within the frame, the basic temporal unit of the mise-en-scène film is the **long take,** a shot lasting, say, at least several seconds. If a shot disappears too quickly from the viewer's field of vision, the shifting and changing relationships in the frame will be harder to grasp. What constitutes a long shot or a long take, however, is relative to the subject matter of the shot — its importance and relationship in the context of the whole.

THE ILLUSION OF ACTUAL SPACE: THE LONG SHOT

The long shot, in which both subject and background context are clearly visible, accentuates the notion that the space within the frame is the same kind of space that the film viewer inhabits. The space within the

frame is contiguous, as it is in our daily lives, and this spatial connected-
ness is heightened and authenticated the longer the shot is on the screen
and the more the camera follows the subjects around in it. The moving
camera within the context also helps to define the space and to create
depth, again qualities associated with space as we know it outside the
theater. Together, the long shot and the moving camera strengthen our
belief in the reality of the actions going on within the frame. (Jean-Luc
Godard in *Breathless* proves the exception to the rule. Some of his long
takes with a moving camera go on so long, the viewer is reminded that
this, too, is a convention of *realism* and not an image of a real world.)

Contrast the use of the long shot and moving camera with the shorter
and more static shots in Walt Disney's animal adventure films. The
frequent cuts fragment real space. Instead of a long shot showing us,
within the frame, a bear chasing a raccoon, we may see in one shot the
image of a bear about to attack. Then there is a direct cut to a raccoon
looking startled. Then a direct cut back to the bear starting to run and
a direct cut to the raccoon running. The edited sequence continues
alternating between separate shots of the two animals. Although we are
offered the illusion of a chase between the bear and raccoon, we know
that this particular chase might never have really taken place. The
running sequences could have been filmed at different times and in
different places; the bear and the raccoon might have been introduced
only in the cutting room.

On the other hand, if we watch *Nanook of the North* (Robert Flaherty,
1922) we see Nanook wait before a hole in the ice in which he's speared
some unseen animal and we watch him move backward, pulling in his
line, only to be dragged sprawling to the hole again and again until he
and some Eskimos who have joined him in the shot, after what seems
like an interminable struggle, finally pull in a huge seal. We know from
the shot not only that we are watching a documentary, but that we are
watching Nanook actually catch the seal before our eyes. Everything
happens in the one frame, in the one shot, and it is evident that the
editor has not manufactured the situation. (Or, rather, it *seems* evident
that there was no trickery; in fact the seal hunt was staged, but the long
shot makes it look thoroughly convincing.)

Even in films that make no attempt to be faithful to the usual behavior
of the external world, the use of the long shot and the moving camera
may make the space within that otherwise fabricated world seem real. A
prime example of the creation of real space in an otherwise unbelievable
world would be one of Busby Berkeley's dance numbers. Rationally, we
know that no space exists outside the film set equivalent to the space of a
production number like "Dames" in the movie *Dames* (Ray Enright,

1934). During part of the number, girls wearing white organdy gowns and Ruby Keeler hairdos and masks swish their skirts and pose on a piece of 1930s architecture, which looks like a combination of stairs and treadmill. What is so surreal about the number is not only its depiction of duplicate women by the multitude, but also the incongruity that such an unreal subject is being photographed by a camera which moves and inhabits and *authenticates* what should — by all rights — be an *unreal* space. We know by the camera's creation of depth and its movement that such space existed — if only on a movie set.

THE ILLUSION OF ACTUAL TIME: THE LONG TAKE

If there are no cuts in a scene, if the scene is recorded in one continuous take and is in fact one shot of at least several seconds, then the viewer must accept the idea that screen time and running time are the same. Combined with the long shot, the long take creates an overpowering sense of real time, of the viewer's witnessing a real event, the sense that there's been no trickery. Time has not been manipulated in the editing room. It is, like the space in a long shot through which the camera moves, continuous, unbroken.

What also makes the long take authentic is that it is not inherently dramatic; there is (as in real life) time wasted with little happening, and when actions happen, they seem to happen spontaneously. Editing can impose drama on actions, removing what seems dull or simply unessential. But the preservation of continuous time in the long take makes the shot resemble time as we experience it in our daily lives. Continuous time in film, like contiguous space, authenticates the action in the frame.

Because of this quality, the long take is chiefly associated with the documentary film. We could look again at Nanook catching the seal in *Nanook of the North* and appreciate the scene for its duration as we did for its distance and creation of context. A more recent example is Fredrick Wiseman's *Welfare* (1975), an almost three-hour documentary based on the pain inflicted upon both the film's subjects and the film's viewers by interminable bureaucratic time. One funny, moving, sad, and horrible confrontation between an elderly welfare client and the building security guard goes on for fifteen minutes or more. The two men insult each other, trade witticisms and sarcasms, affirm their isolation and yet meet on some emotional ground without even knowing it — and all in real time.

The long take, however, like the long shot, can also be used in an unreal context. The space can be faked, but the action within it can still be authenticated by duration. This authentication of an action in an unreal space is particularly important to films in which the talents of a

3-18 The long take, giving the sense of real time, adds a sense of reality to dance sequences. Most Ginger Rogers and Fred Astaire dances, like this one from *Swing Time* (1936), were primarily filmed and presented as one continuous take, allowing the viewer to marvel at the stamina and perfection of the dancers' artistry. We would be less admiring if we thought that a two minute dance was made up of the best snippets of dozens of hours of filming.

performer are showcased. The dance sequences in a Fred Astaire and Ginger Rogers musical, for instance, must exist as much as possible in real time or the viewer has nothing to marvel at (Figure 3-18). The reality of the space that Rogers and Astaire inhabit in *Top Hat* (Mark Sandrich, 1935), for instance, is patently unreal; the cardboard and plywood bridges of its Venice bear no relationship whatsoever to the Italy where Benito Mussolini was in power. But time in the dance sequences must be real or we cannot see the talent we have come to admire. Astaire and Rogers dance together flawlessly in time; they defy gravity and match each other's steps in time. We would admire the dancers far less if we thought that a 2-minute dance was in fact made up of the best fragments of dozens of hours of filming, a practice common in more recent films like *All That Jazz* (Bob Fosse, 1980) (Figure 3-19).

The long take may do more than authenticate reality (as in the documentary) or create a temporal reality within an unreal space (as in the performance musical). Vincente Minnelli in *Meet Me in St. Louis* (1944) projects a romantic, fluid movement and mood in the scene when

3-19 Dance numbers in contemporary films are usually constructed with montage. A multitude of short shots, including close-ups of faces, hands, and feet from many different camera positions, are edited together to form a dynamic whole. *All That Jazz* (Bob Fosse, 1979) uses this method throughout the film.

Judy Garland and Tom Drake turn out the lights in the house after the party. One continuous take, the whole scene has a gentle, suspenseful quality; we wonder whether the journey through the house and the increasing darkness will end in the couple's first kiss. If this long take had been pieced out of many separate shots, the rhythm and smoothness of this almost dancelike courtship would have been greatly de-emphasized.

Editing — how the bits and pieces of a film are put together — always conveys some kind of information about the film and its intent. If it is natural and unobtrusive, it tells us to watch the other filmic elements, to watch the plot unfold, to find significance in the dialogue, to notice the lighting and the composition; these are the main carriers of meaning. If, on the other hand, the editing calls attention to itself, it has something particular to announce: these images juxtaposed in this particular way have a special relationship to each other, are saying something important.

We have been discussing editing in a fairly narrow way, specifically defining it here as the ways in which pieces of film — images — can be joined together and to what effect. These images can be joined in the laboratory (with dissolves and fades), found and joined by the camera within one shot (mise-en-scène), or spliced together on an editing table (montage). Speaking broadly now, we can say that editing is the creator of *all* the relationships in a film; it is the relationship of what we see to what we see, of what we hear to what we hear, and, finally, of what we hear to what we see. Editing shapes the whole film, generating meaning from the relationship of all of the parts.

NOTES

[1] "The Vertov Papers," translated by Marco Carynnyk, *Film Comment* 8, no. 1 (Spring 1972): 48.

[2] *Film Form* (New York: Meridian Books, 1957), p. 37.

[3] *What Is Cinema?* (Berkeley, University of California Press, 1967), p. 34.

[4] "Film Editors Forum," *Film Comment* 13, no. 2 (March–April, 1977): 24.

Historical Overview:
The Development of Sound

SOUND AND THE SILENT FILM

The first motion picture audiences were fascinated less by little stories or fantasies than they were by images of life, captured and moving before them on the screen. Therefore, it is in some ways natural that from its very beginnings, the moving photographic image has been in search of accompanying sound. The two major problems that had to be solved before sound film could be produced were those connected with **synchronization** and amplification; yet even at the birth of the motion picture, sound was in attendance.

When William Dickson first demonstrated his moving-picture machine to Thomas Edison in 1889, he also played a phonograph cylinder of his own voice, which roughly matched the film's flickering images. By 1894, Edison had issued a number of short films with accompanying phonograph cylinders for the home market, but these cylinders were more a curiosity than a commercial success. Thus, Edison's Kinetoscope went into peep-show parlors as a silent entertainment. However, after projection of the filmed image became standard practice, several French companies matched their films with voice recordings on cylinders and disks. Although these worked fairly well in a very small hall, the fidelity was poor and the volume extremely low. As the popularity of the cinema grew, and theaters became larger and larger, disks and cylinders were abandoned because there was no way of amplifying the recorded sound.

By 1900, live musical accompaniment had become the aural mainstay of the silent cinema. As anyone who has sat through an otherwise totally silent movie screening can attest, something is needed to camouflage the sounds of the projector (which, in the early days of cinema, was frequently in the same room as the audience rather than in a separate projection booth) and to muffle the noises of the audience itself. The very first public screenings of the Lumière brothers' films in 1895 used piano accompaniment, and it was soon discovered that music could actually enhance the viewing experience. Music — loud or soft, lively or mournful — added emotional undertones to the scenes on the screen, cued the audience and moved them transitionally from one scene to another, and it provided sound effects.

Thus, nearly every picture house or palace had live music of one sort or another ranging from a rickety upright piano to a full-size symphony orchestra. As early as 1909, the Edison Company distributed a guide for instrumental accompanists called "Suggestions for Music." This practice gave rise to the creation and development of **cue sheets** indicating where in a given film certain kinds of music creating certain kinds of rhythms and moods might be played, and recommending certain pieces the accompanist might choose to follow. With the longer and more prestigious films, the musical accompaniment became more elaborate. Following European example, in 1915 D. W. Griffith commissioned and co-wrote with Joseph Briel a compilation of symphonic themes for his epic *The Birth of a Nation;* the music was arranged for a seventy-piece orchestra, and when the film opened in the larger cities such was the accompaniment. Throughout the silent period, film studios supplied musical scores and cue sheets for their movies, which local musicians could follow.

Sometimes the orchestra supplied sound effects as well as music, with most of the responsibility falling on the shoulders of the percussionist, whose array of noisemaking instruments became larger and larger. Even smaller theaters could provide a clanging, buzzing, trilling aural experience for their patrons with the Mighty Wurlitzer theatrical organ, which could duplicate a host of nonmusical sounds through its intricate series of pipes and air-operated percussion devices.

The human voice was not forgotten either. Many nickelodeons in large cities employed a person *(der Spieler)* who would read the titles out loud for the immigrants in the audience who were unable to read English. Sometimes the reader would provide a continuous narration to help make the story more comprehensible. But these attempts to add the human voice to the moving picture image were too unwieldy and impractical to become successful, and by the time of World War I audiences and filmmakers had arrived at a mutually understood set of visual conventions to make up for the absence of spoken dialogue. What sometimes appears to us as bizarrely exaggerated dramatic performances in silent films is, in fact, a kind of visual code that audiences of the time understood and responded to.

EARLY INVENTION

Progress toward the modern sound cinema began with the invention of a device that solved the problem of amplifying recorded sound. Dr. Lee De Forest's selenium audion tube was as crucial to the development of sound cinema as it was to the development of the radio. De Forest's invention was patented in 1907, but the possibilities of the application of the audion tube to sound film went unappreciated for twenty years. Although various crude methods of synchronizing **sound-on-disk** with images on film had been demonstrated and exhibited sporadically since 1889, the emergent film industry did little to link De Forest's solution to the problems of amplification with a sound-on-disk process.

By the end of World War I, in Germany Josef Engle, Joseph Massole, and Hans Vogt discovered a method of recording sound directly onto film. Their "Tri-Ergon" **sound-on-film** process was based on the principle of the oscilloscope, which turns sound into light impulses. These light impulses could then be recorded on the film **emulsion,** after which the light was converted back into sound by a device that read the light images as they passed through the projector. After the war, De Forest also invented a process based on the same principles. He developed a photoelectric cell that could translate sound into light. The light was then photographed as a series of bars of varying shades of gray and black on the celluloid. By placing this pattern of bars on a thin strip next to the film's sprocket holes, image and sound could be locked into one synchronized unit.

By 1923 De Forest was exhibiting short subjects in his Phonofilm process at various theaters around the country. But these song and dance numbers by vaudeville stars (including Eddie Cantor) were treated simply as a novelty. Finally, in 1925, Bell Laboratories (Western Electric) perfected a special turntable for 17-inch disks, disks large enough to hold sound for an entire reel of projected film. They called the system *Vitaphone* and attempted with little success to interest various large, successful film studios in buying it. But Warner Brothers — new, little, and aggressive — gambled on Vitaphone; unlike their more successful and complacent competition, Warner's had nothing to lose. They purchased the rights to the system and kept the name Vitaphone.

In August of 1926, Warner's released a program of various sound shorts, which used the new sound-on-disk process. Also included was the first sound-on-disk feature, *Don Juan* starring John Barrymore, with a synchronized musical score. Audience response, though favorable, was neither ecstatic nor indicative of the effect the Vitaphone process would have on the entire film industry the following year when Warner's released *The Jazz Singer* (Alan Crosland), starring Al Jolson (Figure 1). Perhaps Jolson's personality captured the imagination of the public, or perhaps it was the *songs,* a change from mere accompaniment; there were, in addition, a few words spoken by a performer on the screen. Whatever the reasons, when *The Jazz Singer* opened on Broadway, October 6, 1927, it immediately captured the fancy of the moviegoing public. This first sound feature was not in sound except for four singing or talking sequences; the rest of the film depended on titles. But because of the enormous impact this film had on the history and production of film, *The Jazz Singer* might as well have been

1   Al Jolson in *The Jazz Singer* (Alan Crosland, 1927). This film opened on Broadway in October 1927. Though sound had been technically possible from the beginning of the decade, the box-office success of the film made Hollywood invest in "talking pictures."

the first sound feature (*Don Juan* was) or the first all-sound feature, which in fact was the unmemorable *The Lights of New York,* released in 1928 by Warner's as a follow-up to *The Jazz Singer.*

THE MOVIES TALK

The Jazz Singer moved Warner Brothers ahead of its competitors, who quickly followed the leader by rushing into sound production. Unreleased films, which were essentially silents, either completed or currently in production, were hastily altered by adding sound segments. Within a year nearly every film talked to audiences in those theaters that were equipped to hear them, while silent versions of the same films were distributed to theaters not yet converted to sound.

Early in 1927, William Fox of the Fox Film Corporation (eventually to become 20th Century Fox) purchased the rights to the German sound-on-film Tri-Ergon system and then added to the system the process developed or borrowed by Theodore Case, a former associate of De Forest's. Fox released the first largely distributed sound-on-film newsreel, the popular Fox Movietone News series, which played to packed houses with its synchronized pictures and sounds of Charles Lindbergh's triumphal return to America after his transatlantic solo flight in May of that year. The sound newsreel became a fixture in movie

2   At first, sound recording techniques required that the camera be placed in a soundproof booth (the large box in the right middle background), thus making camera movement virtually impossible. (Notice the large microphones hanging from the ceiling in the background.)

houses for many years — until television in the 1950s made theatrical filmed news out of date before it could reach the theaters for exhibition. The following year, 1928, brought the public the first sound cartoon, Walt Disney's *Steamboat Willie*, in which an imaginative mouse makes musical instruments out of various farm animals. During the next several years, sound-on-film systems appeared all over the world and competed with the sound-on-disk system, and by 1930 the practicality of the sound-on-film system had won out and the Vitaphone disk system was retired.

   The new technological miracle of sound film, though appreciated by filmgoers, caused a great many headaches for the filmmakers. To record the sound and the image at the same time, even though they were recorded on separate machinery, the camera had to be placed in a soundproof booth so that its noise could not be picked up by the unselective microphones. And, since the studios wanted all-talking films (since they presumed that was what the public wanted), the camera had to be immobilized. The camera remained stationary because it was too bulky to move in its housing, and static medium shots became the standard. Composition of shots was also greatly affected. Actors could not move about the set because of the position of the microphone; like the camera, they were immobilized, generally forming close groupings so all could be heard (Figure 2).

But as early as 1929, the more creative filmmakers began to experiment with ways of overcoming the limitations sound had placed upon them. In Hollywood, a number of fine filmmakers developed techniques to realize their films visually as well as aurally. Rouben Mamoulian, for instance, used two microphones for a single scene so that his performers could stay at the dramatically proper distance from each other rather than having them huddle together inappropriately around the traditional single mike. Thus, his *Applause* (1929) instituted the use of **multiple-channel** sound recording and of **soundmixing,** the latter a process whereby multiple recorded tracks are balanced with each other to form finally a single and selective sound track. Mamoulian also shot a great deal of the film silently so that the camera could again move; the sound was added afterward through the process called dubbing or **postsynchronization.** Ernst Lubitsch, a director who had made a reputation in the silent cinema for his sophisticated comedies, also added sound to many scenes in his *The Love Parade* (1929) *after* they had been shot. Lubitsch was particularly creative in his imaginative use of silence and in his ability to create an integrated and rhythmic balance of sound and image in his films. Again recording the sound after the image was shot, King Vidor created wonderful atmospheric effects with selective sound effects in his *Hallelujah!* (1929); to a chase sequence in which a character runs through a menacing swamp, Vidor added postsynchronous bird cries, panting, the sound of twigs underfoot not only to create realism but also to heighten the suspense. Abroad, other filmmakers were also learning how sound could be manipulated artistically. In Great Britain, Alfred Hitchcock used a subjective sound track in *Blackmail* (1929), which was added to what had been shot as a silent movie; words that have special significance to the heroine are amplified and reverberate according to their emotional importance. And in France, director René Clair, at first an outspoken opponent of sound films, used the new element unrealistically to create humor and irony in *Sous les Toits de Paris* (1929). The experimentation and success of these innovative filmmakers set the standard for what could be achieved by adding sound not at the time of shooting, but afterward through dubbing and postsynchronization. Song and dance numbers worked the other way around. The music was recorded first and then played back over loudspeakers while the camera recorded the singers and dancers matching the music.

Although by 1931 techniques that could suppress track **noise** were developed, making feasible the dubbing of dialogue, postsynchronizing dialogue was a great deal more difficult than postsynchronizing music and sound effects. The sound Moviola editing machine perfected in that same year, however, facilitated the matching of sound and picture. And by 1933, the mechanics of mixing multiple postrecorded sound tracks without any loss of quality had been refined enough to allow filmmakers to use an amalgam of simultaneous sounds in their films. Thus, after 1933 continuous background music became common because the quality of the several combined tracks — music, dialogue, sound effects — could be selectively controlled.

Sound has become the norm in cinema. Silent films are generally thought of as primitive or experimental. Most all of the basic sound hardware used today has been available since the mid-1930s, which already seems like a very long time ago. The only fairly recent technical additions to the sound process are **stereophonic sound,** developed in 1952 to accompany Cinerama's wide screen, lightweight and portable **magnetic tape** recorders, more sensitive and selective microphones and mixing equipment, and — most recently — **flatbed editors,** TV tape transfer editing systems, and the **Dolby sound system,** which allows for clear multichannel recording and playback by electronically suppressing tape noise. *Brainstorm* (Douglas Trumball, 1983) used the Dolby sound's depth and dynamic balance to enhance the visual special effects.

4

 *FILM SOUND*

Movies have always been heard as well as seen. After their initial demonstration, even those films we refer to as silent were commercially projected along with some sort of sound, usually live musical accompaniment. Nevertheless, something was still missing. Those images, which appeared so lifelike on the screen were mute. People moved their lips and "spoke," dogs "barked," doors "slammed," telephones "rang," but these screen images of people, animals, and objects were themselves silent. Music and sound effects might well up from a Wurlitzer organ, a pit orchestra, or a lone piano, in an attempt to cover the silence, but such sound — no matter how effective — was separate from the film and from the artistic control of the filmmaker. And though the film's title cards were under the control of the filmmaker and actually *in* the movie, titles tended to break up the flow of images. The sound film changed all this.

The process of creating a rich, complex, and meaningful sound track is as complicated as creating rich, complex, and effective images. Each filmmaker must decide whether to use performers whose voices are as suitable to their characters as are their physical characteristics, or whether to **dub** in voices of other actors with more suitable voices. The filmmaker must decide what sort of background sounds and special effects are desirable. The kind of music suitable to the film, how much of it to use, and where to use it must also be decided. Finally, the possibility of using silence expressively must be considered. All these sounds must then be recorded successfully, and the various sound tracks must be mixed and balanced with the necessary emphasis in order to produce the desired effect. In short, sound in the cinema is never something that is simply there as it is in everyday life. Rather, it is yet another element that contributes to the structure and meaning of any cinematic work.

The human voice, sound effects, and music are the sounds of cinema. Chapter 4 will investigate and examine both the physical process and the artistic potential of sound in the cinema.

The Process

> We used an eight-track system and it's really unmixing rather than mixing sound. We'd just put microphones on all the principals and hang them out the window and stick them in the clock and under the doorbell and wherever we want a live sound. And they all go down on different tracks, pretty much the way music is done today. And in our musical sequences we had an additional sixteen tracks. We didn't have to come back later and put in dead sound effects.
> Robert Altman [1]

The early attempt to synchronize moving images with sounds recorded on large phonograph disks presented problems: if there was a break in the film and a few frames were lost, there was no way to make a corresponding correction on the disk; one could only add a few black frames to the film. The ideal solution to the problems of synchronization was to put the sounds on the film itself — so that if a splice became necessary, only a small portion of the sound track would be lost and the remainder of the reel would still be in perfect synchronization. After a few years in which both systems competed, the sound-on-film or **optical sound** system became standard. Today, sound is recorded on tape **(magnetic sound)** during shooting, then mixed with any number of sound effects or music tracks to form a final composite sound track. In most theatrical release prints this final composite sound track is optical. In the optical system, the desired sound — dialogue, background noise, or music — is captured by a microphone and converted into electrical impulses, which in turn are changed into light impulses. These impulses of light are then photographed on film similar to that used to photograph the image. Eventually, in the final print of the film, these impulses appear in the narrow space between the frames, which hold the images, and the **sprocket holes,** which control the film's progress through the projector. During the projection process, this optical sound track runs past a light bulb (the sound reader) and the process is reversed: the light impulses are converted back into electrical impulses, which are then converted into the sounds we hear coming from the speaker. Thus, each sound projector has two light bulbs — one to project the visual image onto the screen and one to read the sound track. The most recent technological development replaces this optical sound track with a magnetic strip upon which the sounds have been recorded.

Though simple in concept, the recording of the sounds we finally hear in a released movie is a complex process. **Synchronous sound** is the sound in a film that is synchronized or matched to an onscreen source — an actor's lips, an axe chopping wood, a musician playing an instrument. (It may have been recorded after the image, but it nevertheless is called synchronous sound if the viewer perceives it as matched to the image.) **Asynchronous sound** is the sound in a film that is not synchronized or matched to any source visible onscreen at the moment — the sound of wind and waves when the image is of the interior of a ship's cabin, background music when no instruments are visible, any voice speaking when the lips are not clearly visible in the image, the sound of footsteps when the image shows only the upper body of the actor.

Although sound that is synchronous in the finished film can be recorded at the same time the image is being photographed (the sound recorder and the camera are electronically in sync, running at the same speed), it can also be recorded **wild** (with a sound recorder alone) and then synchronized with the appropriate image. Sounds recorded wild and then dubbed in can vary from orchestral background music to lines of dialogue actors have fluffed at the original shooting, from the sound of waves to the computer talk of a robot. And any of these sounds, whether recorded in sync or not, may be used as either asynchronous or synchronous sound in the final print. For instance, dialogue that appears in sync in one scene in a film may be repeated on the sound track in a later scene in which the character may be remembering what was said earlier: the second use of the dialogue would be asynchronous.

The **sound mixer** works with a multitude of sound tracks — tracks of dialogue, tracks of natural and synthetically created sound effects, tracks of the music selected for the finished film, and tracks of the **narration,** if any. It is the sound mixer's job to blend those tracks together at the right volume and with the right emphasis, thereby creating a unified sound track (composed of many different sounds) that is appropriate to what the film is trying to communicate.

The Human Voice

Relatively few movie patrons become analytical enough to be aware of the voice as an independent medium of artistic illusion on the screen.
Parker Tyler [2]

The storytelling arts have traditionally depended on words. Painting, music, and dance can tell stories also, but their storytelling ability is limited to simple narrative, high in emotional intensity but low in communicating cause and effect. Words are the most explicit, specific, and commonly understood means of telling a story.

Even in its silent infancy, the motion picture needed words to exploit its narrative capacities fully, to satisfy completely the demands of the stories it wished to relate. Title cards supplied those words. But title cards were no substitute for human speech and **dialogue.** They interrupted the rhythms of a film, stopping the action. If few cards were used in an effort to maintain the film's visual rhythms and momentum, the film might sacrifice complexity. If many cards were used, the film often became dull and inert when rhythm and momentum were sacrificed to a complexity never animated by the visual images. It is true, however, that certain films by gifted directors avoided excessive dialogue titles without sacrificing meaning and complexity. F. W. Murnau's *The Last Laugh* (1924) had only one title, but it was able to tell the story of its central character visually and to tell it well with the use of a few verbal devices like writing on a wedding cake and a newspaper.

Generally speaking, however, a cinema primarily concentrating on narrative needed some way of delivering the voices of the actors to the audience some way of providing the audience with a direct sense of reality, so that the story could be experienced without the interruption of title cards. When synchronized sound communicating the voice of the actor on the screen finally became a commercial reality in 1927, the movies were no longer silent and title cards were replaced by spoken dialogue.

DIALOGUE

Dialogue can appear and function in all sorts of films: story films, documentaries, some experimental films, animated films. In most cases, dialogue physically authenticates the speaker as an individual (whether human or cartoon animal) and continues to do so whenever we see that individual in the frame move his lips. Dialogue tends to confirm the audience's assumption that the image projected on the screen is that of a real person and not simply a character, an imaginary creation of the storyteller. Curiously enough, this confirmation of a character's reality works in animated films as well as live-action ones. For example, the voice of Bugs Bunny sounds the same each time we hear it, and each time we see the animated rabbit supposedly speaking, we hear the same accent, the same nuances of phrasing; indeed, we would easily be able to identify the voice as that of Bugs Bunny without its accompanying image. We may know from a cartoon's credits that Jim Backus is the actor responsible for the voice of Mr. Magoo, but when someone does an imitation of Backus's voice, everyone identifies the voice as belonging

4-1 The characterization represented by the dialogue in a film and the voice and physical presence of the actor playing the part seem to merge, to become one. We may know somewhere in our minds that Barbra Streisand and Mandy Patinkin were speaking dialogue written for them by a screenwriter in *Yentl* (Barbra Streisand, 1983), but it is difficult to separate the actor from the character during the performance.

not to Jim Backus but to the cartoon figure of an impossibly near-sighted gentleman.

Although there are similarities, dialogue in the cinema is not the same as dialogue in drama. Dialogue in drama is the words that actors will say when they perform the play (this definition of dialogue also applies to a film **script**), but it is also the words a reader may read unperformed, without an actor present. Dialogue in the cinema, however, is the words spoken by a particular human voice; it is both the words and the voice speaking the words. Dialogue in drama can be interpreted and reinterpreted with each performance of the play. Dialogue in cinema is what it is when we hear it; a subsequent viewing of the film will reveal the same reading and interpretation of the words — even if our experience of them is different. Because the words and the performer who speaks them are less obviously separable in films than they are in theater (Citizen Kane is only Orson Welles, but Hamlet is innumerable actors from Shakespeare's day to our own), often the characterization represented by the dialogue in a film and the human voice and physical person of the screen actor playing that character seem to merge, to become one. As far as the audience is concerned, there is often little or no difference between the performance and the performer, between the character and the actor (Figure 4-1). Sam Spade sounds like and speaks like Humphrey Bogart; Humphrey Bogart sounds like and speaks like Sam Spade.

In addition to establishing the speaker as unique, the dialogue in a film will do what it has done in drama for centuries. It will tell what must be told and provide the characters with a way of expressing their motivations, past experiences, feelings, attitudes, philosophical questionings. For this reason, even if for no other, dialogue must be clearly recorded so that the audience will be able to follow what is going on in the character and in the film.

Dialogue that will appear in sync with an image of the actor's lips is usually recorded at the same time that the image of the actor is being recorded by the camera. This is the easiest way of assuring that the words and lips are synchronized. But lines of dialogue that do not have to be in sync (the actor is out of the frame, or is in long shot so that we can hardly see his lips, or she is not facing the camera or not moving her lips because the lines of dialogue represent internal thoughts) can be recorded after the images are recorded. With sophisticated equipment, dubbing of actors' voices can be perfectly synchronized. Such dubbing may be necessary because of a bad sound recording made while the film was being shot or because the director wishes the actor to change the reading of a particular line of dialogue or wants to add something that wasn't there in the first place. Nonsinging performers, for example, have often had a singer's voice dubbed in when the film demands a song. For example, Patsy Cline's own recordings were used when Jessica Lange played the singer in the biographical *Sweet Dreams* (Karel Reisz, 1985). And network television's moral code, which is a great deal stricter than the cinema's, has frequently required the doctoring of a movie's sound track to eliminate objectionable language. Modern methods of dubbing can easily alter Jackie Gleason's four-letter words in the *Smokey and the Bandit* series to more acceptable euphemisms like *damn, crud*, or *hell*, and the resulting sound track will still give the impression that he is indeed saying the less objectionable words. (The original sound track is used, of course, on a pay television service or on video cassette.)

Most of the time, viewers hardly think about such postsynchronous sound — except, perhaps, in the case of television bowdlerization of a movie they have previously seen. But one kind of dubbing presents more obvious and difficult problems for both the editor and the audience: the dubbing in of one language for another. Shortly after World War II, in an effort to keep down production costs, the Italian film industry pioneered in dubbing entire films; today, they and other European countries are equipped to dub a film into any one of a dozen languages so that the completed film will have a broad market. This kind of dubbing also allows a film's director to cast performers who may not even be able to communicate with each other in the same language. The results of such dubbing are not always of the highest order; it is almost impossible to achieve absolutely perfect lip-sync from one language to another, and often the performer doing the dubbing for the actor on the screen is not able to give a performance equal in artistry to the original. These problems and the distractions they cause arise when any foreign film is dubbed into English. On the other hand, the only alternative — English-language subtitles — also causes problems and distractions. Subtitling clutters up the image, causes the viewer to do more reading than viewing, and often fails to translate adequately and communicate the complexity of the original dialogue; we obviously hear a lot more in a second than we could possibly read. Viewers who are irritated by out-of-sync lip movement and dialogue will usually prefer subtitled versions of foreign films; those who feel the subtitles interfere with the visual experience of a film will usually prefer dubbed versions. Many films are available both ways — for example, Federico Fellini's *Amarcord* (1974) or Werner Herzog's *Fitzcarraldo* (1982) — and sometimes both versions will play in the same city, particularly in larger metropolitan areas (Figure 4-2).

The decision to see a dubbed or subtitled foreign film becomes even more complex if one realizes that the original language in which a film was made is an element of its meaning, constituting the atmosphere of the region in which the film takes place and the rhythms of a particular culture. Italian and German do not sound alike; their cadences are strikingly different. Actually *hearing* the differences in language helps the viewer to locate the film physically and to place it culturally and emotionally.

The notion that the sound of a voice can do more than merely relate the meanings of words spoken by characters visible on the screen can be extended to English-language pictures also. Certainly, the meanings of words are crucial to any film, for certain abstractions and ideas (like love, honor, and duty) are impossible to photograph. Very often characters in films will tell us the meaning of events in their lives. But, again, it is important to remember that dialogue is not the words alone; it is also the *sound* of those words being spoken as human speech. The very texture of a performer's voice also supplies a certain element of character, as much a part of the performance as is the actor's physiognomy, stance, and gesture. All of the great film stars of the past (and to a

4-2 Made by a German director and acted by an international cast of Spanish, Italian, and German performers, *Fitzcarraldo* (Werner Herzog, 1982) appeared in American theaters dubbed in English. Though this makes all the nuances of the dialogue available, many viewers prefer subtitles for foreign language films because the sound track more accurately indicates the milieu.

lesser degree, of the present) had such distinctive voices that they could be and still are easily caricatured. The sincere and somewhat garbled drawl of Jimmy Stewart, the smooth, brusque and well-oiled voice of Clark Gable, the sinister and reverberant quasi lisp of Boris Karloff, the clipped, impatient, and slightly grating voice of Bette Davis — all were as much a part of these performers' screen personae as the lines they had to say.

Finally, the viewer has to evaluate a film's dialogue not only in relation to the meaning of the words, but also in relation to how much dialogue there is in the film and how it is used. There is a great deal of dialogue in Howard Hawks's *Bringing Up Baby* (1938), for example, but because it is delivered at breakneck speed one does not feel the film is talky. The breathless and seemingly incessant chattering of Katherine Hepburn's portrayal of a daffy yet shrewd socialite comically wears down the audience as much as it wears down Cary Grant's eventually exhausted paleontologist. Stanley Kubrick's *2001: A Space Odyssey* (1968) runs for 138 minutes, yet there are only 43 minutes of dialogue in it and that dialogue is incredibly banal. The banality of the dialogue, however, always seems to come as a bit of a shock, for the long periods of verbal silence in the movie lead the viewer to expect that if someone opens his mouth to speak, what will be said will be important. Instead, the dialogue is intentionally insignificant. It is Kubrick's way of pointing out the inadequacy of human responses to the exquisitely specific and complex technology human beings have developed and to the visual beauties of the universe around them. This way in which dialogue *functions* in a film is as important as the overt content of what it says.

NARRATION

Narration in film is the words spoken by a human voice, addressed to the audience, but not heard by the subjects of the film. Although within the film, that is, it places itself outside the story, the diegesis. Most often, narration is asynchronous, that is, the speaker is not seen on the screen addressing the audience. Narration, thus, is also referred to as **voice-over**, particularly when it is used in documentary, news, and commercials. Although most viewers tend to associate narration with the documentary or nonstory film, narration is used widely in all kinds of film and for all kinds of purposes.

In *Tom Jones* (Tony Richardson, 1963), for example, an omniscient narrator — who is never seen and who takes no part in the action — speaks to the audience and comments on the action and characters with an amused, slightly condescending vocabulary and tone of voice; indeed, he functions like the authorial voice in the Henry Fielding novel from which the film was adapted, a voice that creates a conspiracy of intelligence and superiority between the narrator and the audience (Figure 4-3). Like the storyteller who begins "Once upon a time . . ." the narrator leads us through the story as an ally and friend, and also as a presence who exists in our present temporal frame of reference. Narration in *Barry Lyndon* (Stanley Kubrick, 1975) functions a bit differently. It transforms the present into the past by telling us what is going to happen and, thus, creates the fictional world as suspenseless and predetermined. A film that is narrated is a film in which *past* events are being recalled or structured; the narrator already knows how the story turned out, how the documentary will make its point. It is no accident that a film's narrator almost never speaks in present tense.

In fact, because a narrator *now* is telling us what happened *then*, many films structured around flashbacks use narration. In these instances, the narrator *is* a character in the film but a character who has already experienced what we are about to see; the entire film is therefore the means of bringing the viewer through time past into the character's present. In *Great Expectations* (David Lean, 1947), the central character Pip speaks to us about his childhood from his present vantage point as an adult. In *Murder, My Sweet* (Edward Dmytryk, 1944), we are at least aware that the detective Philip Marlowe has survived the events we are

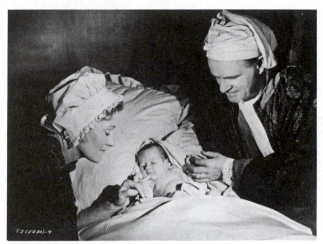

4-3 During this shot from *Tom Jones* (Tony Richardson, 1963), we do not hear the voices of the performers we see. Rather, we hear an omniscient narrator who is never seen. The narrator comments on the action and the characters with an amused, slightly condescending tone of voice, which creates a conspiracy between audience and narrator. This allows the audience to distance itself from the follies and foibles of the orphan, first found in Squire Allworthy's bed.

about to see. But in an ironic and impossible reversal of that surety, the narrator of *Sunset Boulevard* (Billy Wilder, 1950) is dead from the film's beginning — since we see him shot *before* he brings us up to the present and the flashback ends (Figure 4-4).

Besides providing a tidy flashback structure for the story film, narration by one of its characters also reveals that character to the viewer. In *Badlands* (Terrence Malick, 1974), Holly — the narrator — tells us as much about herself as she does about the events we witness in this film of two teenagers in the 1950s who go on a killing spree for no particular reason. Her language is so artificial and unoriginal that the sadness and smallness of her aspirations are revealed when she says to us: "Little did I realize that. . . ." When she tells us how her boyfriend murdered her father, her tone is as unemotional as it is when she talks about her life in high school or the lovers' drive through the Dakota Badlands. And she also reveals a chilling and quiet aberration by what she chooses to emphasize as important and what she chooses not to mention at all as we hear her voice comment on events we are watching.

When the narrator is also the film's central character, then, there may be a counterpoint between the narrator's perceptions and the perceptions of the audience watching the event. But this is not the only

4-4 Narrators are often found in films which are told in flashbacks. One of the strangest examples is *Sunset Boulevard* (Billy Wilder, 1950) in which the narrator of the story is found dead at the beginning (we see his body floating in a pool). Nevertheless, he narrates the story as the rest of the film brings the action up to the moment where his body is fished out of the pool by the police.

function of a character's voice-over narration. Like counterpoint, the agreement of the narration with the visual event can also function meaningfully. In Robert Bresson's *The Diary of a Country Priest* (1951), the tortured young priest of the title delivers his innermost thoughts to the viewer through his narration as he composes his diary. As we see his pen write the words, we hear him think the same words in an emotionless voice. In one sense, this is the cinematic version of the theater's soliloquy: the character is not addressing another character but rather is thinking to himself in a moment we are privileged to be able to hear. This kind of private narration is one way film represents interior dialogue, the mind thinking, talking to itself. But in Bresson's film, such narration serves an additional dramatic purpose. *The Diary of a Country Priest* attempts to deal with matters of the spirit through the physical images of film; it attempts to convey to the viewer the mystery and wonder of divine grace, the irreconcilable separation of the earthly from the spiritual. When the priest writes in his diary and we see and read the words on the page we also hear his voice saying those words; the written words are confirmed by their spoken repetition, and yet as we see and hear them they tell us nothing about the priest's tortured soul. The movie's insistence that we have been told and shown *all* there is to know makes us doubly aware that we have been told nothing at all.

We are, of course, much more consciously aware of narration in the nonfiction film than we are in the narrative film, perhaps because most viewers have been exposed to teaching films in school in which information was conveyed by a narrator and illustrated by the film's images. Voice-over narration strongly influenced the viewer's attitude toward the images. The voice of Westbrook Von Voorhis, narrator of *The March of Time*, the news series that originated in the 1930s was aptly called "the voice of God." The voice of a documentary narrator can be male or female, loud or soft, emotional or unemotional — and because it is a human voice, it will speak through its tone, timbre, and inflection as well as through the words it utters. Two versions of the documentary film *Nanook of the North* (Robert Flaherty, 1922) provide an interesting example of how a narrator's voice can affect the meaning of the visual images it accompanies. *Nanook* was made as a silent film about an Eskimo and his family, but some versions in circulation have substituted a narrator and sound track for most of the film's original titles. The sound version of *Nanook* is condescending in both the commentary and the tone of the narrator's voice. Nanook is made quaint and primitive, his skills are regarded as curious, and his accomplishments are minimized by overstatement. The silent version, however, allows us to view Nanook relatively uninterpreted. The titles give us information, and occasionally they editorialize, but when we *see* Nanook, what we see speaks for itself and is not qualified by the attitudes and tone of someone else's voiced perceptions.

Narration can also serve yet another purpose, an aesthetic one. A continuous sound track in which a narrator speaks to the audience throughout the film can unify what would be otherwise fragmented and disconnected visual images. This is a particularly effective function of narration in compilation films, which are composed of materials from diverse sources: historical footage from archives, paintings from museums, clippings from newspapers, sections of newsreels, footage taken in the present by the filmmaker to augment the collected materials. Edited together, all this film might seem disjointed and arbitrarily chosen. Space and time are constantly shifting within a compilation film. The narration binds the film and creates a cohesive whole, for the narration takes place in continuous time. This unifying function of voice-over narration can be used to great emotional effect, as in Alain Resnais's *Night and Fog* (1955). This short film about the Nazi extermination camps alternates relatively static footage of black-and-white archival materials with moving-camera footage in color showing the empty camps as they were when the film was made. The method of the film is contrast: black-and-white images are contrasted with color ones, static images are contrasted with images from a nervous, moving camera, death is contrasted with life, the present is contrasted with the past. The one element in the film that unifies and finally synthesizes these opposites at a higher level is the narration. The narration brings the past into the present, animates the dead into a connection with the living, and enables viewers to connect and reconcile their own often conflicting emotional responses to the film's images of the holocaust.

Sound Effects

SYNCHRONOUS SOUND

When an object in the frame (say, a door) reveals itself by its sound (a slam or a creak) as well as by its visual presence, we are convinced that the object is real and not constructed of cardboard. Of course, in actual fact, the door frame visible on the screen may be constructed of extremely lightweight material, and closing that particular door would result in a sound that bore little resemblance to the sound of a real door closing. The sound technician, however, can dub in the sound of a real door closing, and because it is synchronous with the image, the audience is convinced of the substantiality of the door it sees, and by extension, of the film's physical world (Figure 4-5). Though we take this ordinary function of synchronous sound for granted, its contribution to the illusion of reality is crucial to films that are fantasies such as *E.T.: The Extra-Terrestrial* (Steven Spielberg, 1982) or *Gremlins* (Joe Dante, 1984); in a visual setting that bears little resemblance to the world we know, synchronous sound effects authenticate fantastic objects and fantastic places (Figure 4-6).

Like dialogue, synchronous sound that seems to emanate from objects onscreen may be recorded at the time of shooting the film or it may be dubbed in later. Either way will create the illusion that what is heard is the natural sound made by the machine gun, the waterfall, the car engine, the door.

Synchronous sound not only contributes to realism; it can be manipulated to create atmosphere, meaning, and emotional nuance. The sound mixer can emphasize an onscreen sound, such as a telephone

4-5 Sound can be used to substantiate the solidity of the image. Though the set used to represent the Thatcher Memorial Library in *Citizen Kane* (Orson Welles, 1941) was made of plaster and painted canvas, the hollow-sounding voices and the reverberating slam of the vault door made it seem to be made of stone and steel.

4-6 Sound is an important device for creating the illusion of reality in such fantastic films as *Star Wars* (George Lucas, 1977). The sounds created for various pieces of machinery and the robots convince the viewer by their appropriateness. For instance, C3PO's voice began as an actor's voice, but then it was altered electronically to make it seem more metallic.

ringing, so that it becomes an extremely urgent call or, on the other hand, a call that is simply part of everyday existence and background noise. Even in the most ordinary circumstances, the sound track of a film must be blended for dramatic effect or merely for clarity; this blending and emphasis and clarity are achieved not by the microphone, which recorded the sounds, but by the sound mixer. Although modern microphones are extremely sensitive and are able to pick up sounds from a selected and specific location, so that on-location recording has become more common than it once was, the microphone is still not able to distinguish between what is dramatically important and what is simply part of the background sound. Turned in a specific direction, it will listen impartially to everything it hears. Like a microphone, the human ear picks up everything in its range, but the brain focuses selectively, picking out important sounds and ignoring others even when they are heard at the same volume. The sound mixer functions as the brain behind the microphone, selecting and focusing on only those recorded sounds that are dramatically relevant to the scenes with which they will be synchronized. Therefore, just as filmmakers use illumination or framing to call attention to important visual elements of their composition, the sound mixer arranges the sound track to call attention to a specific object within the frame with which the sound is synchronized. If, for example, a family appears in a shot watching television when the phone rings, the sound mixer can heighten the sound of the phone and reduce the sound of the television set.

ASYNCHRONOUS SOUND

Much of what has been said about synchronous sound effects can be applied to asynchronous sound effects, those whose source is not visible on the screen. If, for example, we see a face in close-up but hear thunder, we have asynchronous sound. Asynchronous sound extends the filmmaker's freedom in ways that synchronous sound does not. Synchronous sound, after all, chiefly gives us more of what we see. If, for instance, a train appears on-screen, it gives us some sort of train sound no matter how subdued. But by using asynchronous sound, let us say the sound not of a train but of someone screaming, a director may shock the viewer or create a surreal world. René Clair in *Le Million* (1931) shows his actors fighting over a coat containing a lottery ticket, while we hear the sounds of a rugby match (Figure 4-7).

Because asynchronous sound need not be in sync with anything on-screen, filmmakers may introduce a sound that has just the right emotional nuance for the drama, even though this sound is not really related to the images. In a scene, for instance, showing a couple having a heated argument and then suddenly silently and angrily confronting each other, a filmmaker might choose to introduce the sound of an ambulance, increasing in volume as it nears and decreasing in volume as it races off (unseen in offscreen space). Because of the viewer's associations with ambulances — their urgency, their connection with someone's misfortune, their piercing and whining sound, which is both commanding and plaintive — such a sound asynchronous with the

4-7 Asynchronous sound — sound that does not come from any visual source in the image — provides a way of counterpointing the primary meaning of the image. In *Le Million* (René Clair, 1931) the actors are seen fighting over a coat that contains the winning lottery ticket, while the sound track contains crowd noises and officials' whistles from a rugby match.

image will enhance the dramatic tension on the screen and comment implicitly on the couple's painful and precarious relationship.

Asynchronous, wild sound effects (and human voices, to a lesser degree) also complement the image in another way: they extend the world beyond the confines of the frame. They help to make the film frame seem less like a container for the action than like a window, which reveals to the viewer only a portion of the world that continues beyond the window's limits. We may, for instance, hear traffic noises although the camera is focused on an interior setting; the previous example of the off-screen ambulance siren heard while we are watching an action set in a confined interior is pertinent here. What is created is not only an off-screen sound accompaniment, which is emotionally suitable to the action of the couple arguing, but also the illusion of a world extended beyond the limits of the rectangular screen, a life going on outside the field of the camera's vision. Though we may be watching the safari guide and the client's wife making love in his tent in the corniest of adventure films, our notion that they are really in the middle of the African plains and not on a sound stage is created by the careful addition to the sound track of insects chirping and buzzing, monkeys chattering, and an occasional lion roaring. The constant clickety-clack of wheels on rails encourages us in our belief that Cary Grant and Eva Marie Saint are actually on a real train in *North by Northwest* (Alfred Hitchcock, 1959) and not on a cutaway mock-up produced by the prop department. Even when we do not really believe in a film's contrived story, we often do believe in the authenticity of the same film's place. Because sounds from a multitude of unseen sources fill up our lives, asynchronous sound must be audible in a film character's life as well, if the filmmaker wishes us to feel that what we are seeing and hearing is credible.

⊛   **Music**

> To comprehend fully what music does for movies, one should see a pic-
> ture before the music is added, and again after it has been scored. Not
> only are all the dramatic effects heightened, but in many instances the
> faces, voices, and even the personalities of the players are altered by the
> music.
>
> Dmitri Tiomkin[3]

BACKGROUND MUSIC — THE FILM'S SCORE

Background music — at first the piano or organ played for silent
films — has long been used by filmmakers to add emotion and rhythm
to their pictures. From travelogues to westerns to serious dramas, music
has complemented the mood of countless scenes, to such an extent that
certain kinds of musical passages are instantly recognized by the audience as fitting certain kinds of films or certain parts of films. We are all
familiar with chase music, circus music, western music, and Oriental
music, and with the strains of ukuleles playing as the sun sets on
another visit to some island paradise. No horror film would be complete
without ominous bass notes or sudden piercing shrieks of strident
violins. Science fiction films are often accompanied by synthetic and
atonal music or by music that grandly evokes the vastness of a universe.
Lyrical passages underscore romantic love scenes and sad melodies in a
minor key evoke the nostalgia of love lost.

Background music may be more distinctive and noticeable than its
name suggests, so much so that an audience may, after seeing a film,
always associate the selected music with the visual images that accompany it. If you have seen Stanley Kubrick's *2001: A Space Odyssey* (1968),
when you hear Richard Strauss's "Also Sprach Zarathustra" you recall
Kubrick's images. Sometimes, too, a particular composer of film scores
has such a distinctive style that viewers who have seen a number of
films accompanied by that composer's music will feel (if not actually
identify) something familiar about what they hear (Figure 4-8). The late
Bernard Herrmann and Nino Rota were just such composers. Herrmann
created music totally in keeping with the various films he worked on,
giving all of them an added suspense and psychological depth; yet
despite the appropriateness of his music to each film, an identifiable
and evident similarity exists between the music of *Citizen Kane* (Orson
Welles, 1941), *The Day the Earth Stood Still* (Robert Wise, 1951), *Psycho*
(Alfred Hitchcock, 1960), and *Taxi Driver* (1976), to name but a few of the
films he scored. Nino Rota did the same for nearly all of Federico
Fellini's films. Certain background music also can be accentuated at the
beginning or end of a film by including a voice-over song that picks up

4-8 John Williams is one of the best-known composers and conductors of film music today. His credits include *Jaws* (1975), *Star Wars* (1977), *Close Encounters of the Third Kind* (1977), *Superman* (1978), *Raiders of the Lost Ark* (1983), and others. Even though he writes music specifically for each film, the symphonic style of his work has made it possible for the music to achieve popularity independent of the film.

4-9 Background music at the beginning or the end of a film often includes a voice-over song that picks up the major themes of the movie. The song from *Flashdance* (Adrian Lyne, 1983) became so popular in itself that it can hardly be considered background music any longer.

the major themes in a movie. Such music — for example, the title songs for *Flashdance* (Adrian Lyne, 1983) and *Ghostbusters* (Ivan Reitman, 1984) — may become so popular that one can hardly consider it background any longer (Figure 4-9).

Generally, however, background music, whether composed for the film or taken from already composed sources, is not meant to be noticeable. Rather, background music is conceived of as a relatively inconspicuous support for a film's images, evoking time and place and mood. It serves, in a way, as the film's narrational consciousness — providing tone and an emotional attitude toward the story and the characters. The sprightly harpsichord music, for example, played as background in *Tom Jones* (Tony Richardson, 1963), helps locate the viewer in the eighteenth century, carrying with it associations of the polite and structured society of that era. Because the music is often played at breakneck speed, it also creates a light, tongue-in-cheek, comic climate, which supports the **tone** of the film. Background music may contradict a film's images, for example, the ironically gay zither melodies that accompany Carol Reed's *The Third Man* (1950) or the ballad that accompanies the world blowing up in Stanley Kubrick's *Dr. Strangelove* (1963). Background music, however, chiefly complements the image rhythmically, tonally, atmospherically. Thus, a chase sequence will be accompanied by lively, suspenseful, action music; a love scene, by violins that swell in harmony with the rising and falling dramatic action.

Background music may also have more specific narrative functions. Through repetition it can link shots, scenes, and sequences. A certain musical theme, for instance, may be played early in a film when a particular character appears on the screen, as in *Once Upon a Time in the West* (Sergio Leone, 1968) or it may be associated with a particular situation — a lover's tryst, for instance. The character or the situation can then be evoked later in the film by repeating the musical phrases. Background music can also foreshadow a change in mood, signal to the viewer that there will be a dramatic shift in the plot. The music played, for instance, during a happy family reunion scene may change into a minor key — usually associated with gloom and foreboding — just before there is a knock at the door. Viewers sense that the visitor will bring bad news, even though they may not realize that it is the background music which has affected their feelings.

The invisibility of background music is one of its most important characteristics. For background music is, of course, extradiegetic. Music will begin with the credits (or before), underlining and amplifying the content of the film. But it will always be music that does not originate from any onscreen source; it is asynchronous sound. In this sense, the use of background music in, say, a western, is incredible, illogical, patently not present. The wagon trains actually crossing the prairies were never accompanied by 101 strings playing a stirring epic melody.

FOREGROUND MUSIC

There are other ways to bring music into films, however, which are credible and dramatically plausible. For example, characters may be in a room with a radio, a television set, or a stereo set. Although some of this music may arise from offscreen sources and thus be asynchronous sound, it may just as often be synchronous, arising from some image on the screen. Instead of using a score written for the film and played by an offscreen and unrealistically placed studio orchestra, a filmmaker who wishes to create a relatively representational film, a conventionally realistic movie, may instead place characters in bars, in automobiles, in rooms in which there are radios, televisions or stereos to provide atmosphere without betraying the film's realistic premises. *American Graffiti* (George Lucas, 1973), for example, set in the 1960s, uses dramatically appropriate songs, which happen to come from the radio, atmospherically supporting the actions of the characters and also commenting ironically upon them.

Most foreground music, however, is that performed by on-camera musicians and singers. Film musicals, of course, contain the greatest number of such performances. Whether an on-screen but subordinate orchestra is playing the absolutely necessary music so that Ginger Rogers and Fred Astaire can dance for us or whether Barbra Streisand or Neil Diamond are singing, music performed onscreen is the main attraction in the musical film.

There are two primary conventions for such performances: either the personality is a performer in a story about show business and thus will appear onstage or in rehearsal, as in *All That Jazz* (Bob Fosse, 1980), or else the performer will simply be an ordinary person who must sing in the middle of a narrative to reveal his or her emotional state, as in *West Side Story* (Robert Wise and Jerome Robbins, 1961). Sometimes a character in a musical film will do both. In *Top Hat* (Mark Sandrich, 1935), for example, Fred Astaire plays a character who is a professional dancer performing in a show. The number "Top Hat" is presented on a stage as part of the show, but most of the other songs and dances, such as "Isn't It a Lovely Day?" and "Dancing Cheek to Cheek," are done in the middle of the narrative simply because the characters feel like bursting out into song and dance. In a later musical, *Funny Face* (Stanley Donen, 1957), however, Astaire plays a fashion photographer, not a professional dancer; thus, all of his song and dance numbers occur as part of the story, not as the performances of a dancer. Though Mozart's career and music were featured in *Amadeus* (Milos Forman, 1984), modern musicals are more likely to focus on the career and performance of rock stars — Prince appears more or less as himself in *Purple Rain* (Albert Magnoli, 1984).

In the popular revue films of the 1940s, a contrivance of the plot required the main characters to attend an opera or a ballet performance or go to a nightclub where those in the audience would be treated to a musical performance by some famous opera star, singer, or swing band.

The ways to get on-camera music into a film are many, some obvious and some devious. Although it is unlikely that viewers would describe Robert Altman's *Nashville* (1975) as a musical, the director used the country and western music capital of the world — the city of Nashville, Tennessee — as a means of exploring life in contemporary America. All the music was performed on camera by actors representing country and western stars or would-be stars, and this music served to authenticate the film's physical world, to lend atmospheric support to the film's plot and its visual imagery, and to comment ironically on the characters and their actions.

Offscreen or asynchronous music can also be used in a way that calls attention to itself, which makes it part of the foreground in the audience's consciousness. Functioning almost like narration, it can lend rhythm and atmospheric support to major transitions, it can structure and cement images that may lack inherent continuity, and it can guide the audience in shaping its attitudes toward the characters or actions. Most asynchronous foreground music is vocal as well as instrumental, featuring songs sung by prominent singers who can hold the audience's attention. Such music occurs in *McCabe and Mrs. Miller* (Robert Altman, 1971), which uses the songs of Leonard Cohen. Because Cohen's lyrics are fairly complex, the music does not so much give voice to a character's feelings (like, say, Simon and Garfunkel's music in *The Graduate*); rather, it is a means of making the audience consider the characters and events from a distanced perspective. Thus, Cohen's "The Sisters of Mercy" functions paradoxically when sung over images of the prostitutes who have been brought to the mining town of Presbyterian Church; the song simultaneously supports the imagery and ironically contradicts it.

The Artistry of Sound

> In the early period of talking pictures, while writing the film script for *Le Million*, I amused myself by making the conscience of one of the characters talk, or more exactly, sing. This innovation had a certain success and it was confirmed in the most flattering way: by the numerous imitations that were made of it. Some time later, I conceived the project of a film in which the entire action would be commented on in the manner of the "voice of the conscience" — that is to say, in which the thoughts of the characters would be expressed by sound, either according to or contrasting with the actions of the images shown on the screen.
> René Clair [4]

Like the images in a film, sound is edited or molded to suit the needs of the individual film. Sound can be used to emphasize or alter our visual perspective of a character or place, to bridge transitionally a cut, or to contradict the image or a previously established mood, and it can be used to establish the identity of a particular kind of film, such as a western or a gangster film.

SOUND PERSPECTIVE

The perspective (or distance) from which we hear sounds in a movie can affect our understanding of what appears in the frame and can affect our emotional responses to what we see. Voices or gunshots or music can be near or they can be far away; they can come from one speaker or, as with the new Dolby stereo system, from several so that they may appear to travel across the screen as their source in the image travels. Usually, sound perspective is created through the use of **selective sound** (some sounds are removed from the track, others are retained), or by a change in the quality of the sound (amplification is changed and/or the sound is distorted).

Selective sound obviously emphasizes some sounds (for example, a watch or a bomb ticking) and omits others. Usually it tends to function subjectively, indicating how a *character* hears rather than presenting a natural **sound mix**. The selective sound track puts us physically inside the character we see on the screen, allowing us to feel as if we are participating in the action. In *Downhill Racer* (Michael Ritchie, 1969), a movie about ski racing, the sound becomes highly selective in the racing sequences. The sound track lets us hear only heightened sounds of breathing, skis scraping against icy snow, and a watch ticking away the seconds. These isolated sounds link the viewer to the central character, helping the viewer to experience the racer's intense concentration. Another instance in which selective and amplified sound creates subjective engagement with the film occurs in *An Occurrence at Owl Creek Bridge* (Robert Enrico, 1961). At first it appears we are watching an objective presentation of Union soldiers preparing to hang a Southern civilian, but boots striking the wooden ties of the bridge, the rope rubbing against a crossbeam, the sound of fabric as it is tied around the condemned man's legs to hold him secure, all sound louder than normal. The viewer feels uneasy, although perhaps not even aware that this unease is caused by the discrepancy in perspective between the selectively subjective sounds and the initially omniscient and objective images. This amplification of sound adds to the tension generated up to the moment when the prisoner drops from the bridge and makes us identify ourselves with the condemned man even before we visually enter his consciousness.

The selective sound track can combine amplification with distortion to achieve an even more intense psychological subjectivity. The audience is not only linked with the protagonist but is also involved in the

4-10   Distorted sound can often be used for aesthetic purposes. When the protagonist of *An Occurrence at Owl Creek Bridge* (Robert Enrico, 1961) seemingly escapes his bonds underwater and rises to the surface, he appears to see and hear the soldiers' reactions to his escape in slow motion. The slowed-down sound and images indicate the subjectivity of time.

process by which other characters are dehumanized or objects are made unfamiliar. An obvious example occurs in *An Occurrence at Owl Creek Bridge* when the protagonist, who has just survived his own aborted hanging, surfaces from a prolonged underwater escape to hear pursuing soldiers on a bridge yell at him in what seems to be slow-motion sound (Figure 4-10). In keeping with the notion that under stress one's mind operates hyperactively, the technique connects us aurally with the protagonist, and also dehumanizes the soldiers, who sound like grotesques. One problem with distorting sound, however, is that the audience, rather than realizing that the sound has been purposely distorted, may think something has happened to the theater's sound system or the projector. Enrico guards against this misconception by recording the sound of birds at normal speed, and those sounds, unobtrusive as they are, provide the audience with a frame of reference. Another example of amplification and distortion occurs in *The Graduate* (Mike Nichols, 1967). The alienated Benjamin puts on his birthday present, a complete scuba diving outfit. As he walks down into the family swimming pool, having been coerced by his incessantly chattering parents to try it out, the water covers his face mask (the subjective camera places us in his position, looking out through the glass), and the sound track alters. The voices of the adults gathered around the pool thicken, distort, and finally disappear. All we hear is the amplified gurgle of the breathing apparatus, which, in comparison with the previous meaningless and unpleasantly grating chatter, sounds peaceful and contented.

Amplification of a sound track need not be used solely to produce identification with a character. It can be used more neutrally, less as a subjective device than as a dramatic one. In some films, an extreme long shot may show a couple walking along the beach or sitting high on a hillside; in contrast, we hear their voices close up so that their conversation seems exceedingly intimate, more so perhaps than it would if we were watching a close-up image where we would tend to take the match in perspective between image and voice for granted. Besides heightening intimacy, amplification can heighten excitement and drama. In a contemporary chase sequence, such as the opening one in *Beverley Hills Cop* (Martin Brest, 1984), sounds of screeching tires, shifting gears, metal cracking against metal, are often amplified to increase the dramatic intensity of the visuals.

The entire range of sound selection, amplification, and distortion is itself demonstrated in a film that shows the recording and manipulation of a couple's conversation obtained as they talk in the middle of a busy plaza. *The Conversation* (Francis Ford Coppola, 1974) not only shows us how sound can be manipulated technologically, but also how it is always finally interpreted — or misinterpreted — by a human consciousness (Figure 4-11).

THE SOUND BRIDGE

Sound can be used not only to complement or contradict the content of the visual image, but also to bridge the gap often caused by the abrupt juxtaposition of disparate images. The **sound bridge** is an effective transitional and artistic device that can connect two or more differing images, helping the audience to realize that some connection between them is intended. We have already seen how, for example, continuous narration can create continuity between images, say, of airplanes bombing a ship and of infantrymen advancing on land, collected from various archival sources, to make a compilation film. And we have mentioned that music, too, can bridge images unconnected in time.

The first device, narration as a transition, is commonly used by the documentary film. Its most flamboyant transitional functions are best illustrated by examples from films made during the 1930s and 1940s, but the technique in more circumspect forms is still used today. Pare Lorentz's *The Plow That Broke the Plains* (1936) and *The River* (1937) both use continuous narration to link images filmed at different times and in different places. Both films show us images that are essentially abstract, contextless: close-ups of rusted farm implements lying on parched

4-11 The entire range of sound selection, amplification, and distortion is demonstrated in *The Conversation* (Francis Ford Coppola, 1974). The film shows how a surveillance company cleverly records a couple's private conversation as they talk in the middle of a busy plaza: as we hear snatches of conversation that only the man in the left foreground could be hearing, we come to realize that the man has a microphone in his hearing aid and a tape recorder in his shopping bag. The film shows not only how sound can be manipulated technologically, but also how it can be interpreted — or misinterpreted — by the human consciousness.

ground, drops of water dripping slowly from a twig. But the narration, with its temporal continuity, its single voice, and its rhythmic cadences, links these images.

The second device, the use of music to effect the transition between images that are not inherently connected, is extremely common. The music accompanying a scene begins to change to a major or minor key, or we hear a musical **motif** connected with a character we will see in the next scene. A song can link or unify images that, though edited together, have little spatial or temporal relationship. In *The Graduate*, for example, there are several juxtaposed shots, alternating Benjamin on a rubber raft in his swimming pool and Benjamin in bed with Mrs. Robinson. Some of these are linked by motion (Benjamin dives into his swimming pool and lands in bed with Mrs. Robinson), but even these visually strong connections would seem extraordinarily contrived were it not for the smoothness and unification of the sequence provided by Simon and Garfunkel singing "The Sounds of Silence" on the sound track. The song bridges the spatial and temporal gap between the intercut shots and communicates a relationship. The total effect of the unified sequence (or montage) is that Benjamin drifting into an affair with Mrs. Robinson and Benjamin drifting in his swimming pool are equal activities — both for Benjamin and for us.

Dialogue and sound effects can also function effectively as sound bridges. A change of image, moving abruptly in time and space, can be bridged without confusing the viewer if the shift is softened by the use of continuous sound. In *Citizen Kane* (1941), the director used his previous radio experience with sound bridges to compress great periods of time, as when we see the young Kane glaring up at the torso of his guardian, who is saying, "Merry Christmas, Charles," and who finishes the phrase years later to the mature Charles in the next directly cut image: "and a Happy New Year." The direct cut from one image to an image of years later might have disoriented the audience, but because there is no pause on the sound track, the years are intelligibly connected. In the same film, a sound bridge unifies and compresses the unhappy and short-lived operatic career of Susan Alexander, Kane's second wife: her creaky rendition of an aria bridges the images of newspaper accounts of her tour, theater lights, audiences, and people running about onstage.

A sound bridge can also act as a foreshadowing device, preparing us for a change in mood, a flashback, a scene to come. In *An Occurrence at Owl Creek Bridge*, the escaping protagonist flees from pursuing soldiers, gunfire, and cannon shot. He finally comes to rest in an idyllic spot, which visually conveys a sense of release, of life's beauty and value. The man moves forward in one shot to smell a flower. During the latter part of this shot, we hear a barely perceptible whistling noise, which becomes louder and finally is recognizable in the next shot (effected by a direct cut) when a cannonball explodes. Thus, the ominous, almost unidentifiable sound we hear in one shot not only begins to make us uncomfortable, even though we are looking at an idyllic scene, but also prepares us for the next scene. We also are able to recognize the source of the sound a moment before the film's protagonist; as the sound becomes clearly audible and we realize what it is, we want to warn the protagonist to run from the danger before he is even aware of it.

SOUND COUNTERPOINT

When various elements of film are used simultaneously to contradict each other so that new meaning is created, we speak of counterpoint.

Obviously, not every kind of contradiction between filmic elements deserves consideration as counterpoint. Sloppy filmmaking can also result in contradictions, but these contradictions do not produce a purposeful meaning or effect.

Because, in a nonoral culture, we do not discriminate so easily with our ears alone, most counterpoint involving sound is not between sound and sound but between sound and image. But one fascinating experimental short, *Frank Film* (Carolyn and Frank Mouris, 1973), combines two voice tracks to accompany its animated collage of images. One voice track, presumably using the voice of the actual filmmaker, narrates an autobiography: Frank is being "frank," candidly telling us just how he came to be a filmmaker and how he came to make this particular movie. The autobiographical track moves along chronologically and coherently. Simultaneously, a second voice track (again using Frank's voice) rattles off a barrage of numbers and of nouns, which constitute a free association, and more or less match the bombardment of quickly changing images of objects. The combination of both tracks with the visual imagery results in such an overabundance of stimuli that many people have trouble watching the film without discomfort, yet this method is perfectly suited to this particular film's subject matter, which combines several levels of consciousness and explores the ways in which an individual is bombarded and influenced by the visual and aural stimuli of his culture.

This kind of sound counterpoint — dialogue with dialogue — is unusual. The problem it presents is demonstrated by *Frank Film*, for it is extremely difficult to absorb both sound tracks and equally difficult to concentrate on only one sound track at a time when both tracks consist of a voice speaking language that is supposed to mean something. The most common counterpoint created by spoken language in a film is a great deal more simple and seems, as well, more realistic: in a given crowd scene — such as in a restaurant or at a party — various conversations will overlap, but the viewer tends to find that one conversation is dominant and more continuously audible although key words which counterpoint that dominant conversation are heard clearly arising from the more subdued babble of the other conversations. Thus, the viewer need not pay equal attention to separate dialogues, but the illusion of spontaneous counterpoint will be effectively created.

Sound and sound, however, can be easily and creatively juxtaposed when one of the sounds we hear is music and the other is dialogue (Figure 4-12). Such juxtaposition is used frequently throughout *American Graffiti* (George Lucas, 1973). Nearly everyone in the film listens to the radio and so the sound of the sixties, the actual instrumental and vocal

4-12 Music can be creatively juxtaposed with dialogue. Throughout *American Graffiti* (George Lucas, 1973), the actual instrumental and vocal recordings of the 1960s add an extra dimension of irony. The banal, sentimental lyrics of pop music heard from car radios and at the sock hop suggest drama and romance, life as imagined, whereas the actions, predicaments, and frustrations of the characters reveal the ordinary contingencies and ambiguities of everyday life.

recordings of the times, provides an extra dimension of cinematic irony to the sound track.

Most often, we have said, the counterpoint is of sound and image, creating meanings not inherent in either by itself. What is created by such counterpoint is similar in many ways to the counterpoint created by editing two disparate images together so as to form a new image — an idea in the mind of the audience. Much as Sergei Eisenstein, the great Russian filmmaker, demonstrated that shot A + shot B = shot C, one could demonstrate that shot A accompanied by sound B = shot C. The difference, of course, between editing together two disparate images and editing together a disparate sound and image is that one image comes after the other but the sound and the image occur simultaneously. The economy, clarity, and comparative subtlety of such counterpoint of image and sound makes it a favorite device of contemporary directors who find the traditional counterpoint of image and image too unwieldly and heavy-handed.

Federico Fellini, for example, creates ironic counterpoint in *8½* (1963). Against images of elderly men and women shuffling slowly in long winding lines toward the fountains of a spa where mineral water is being dispensed, Fellini juxtaposes the sounds of a brisk orchestral arrangement of Wagner's "Ride of the Valkyries" on the track. As the camera pans we discover that the music is being played by a band meant to entertain the elderly spa guests. The contrast between the heroic, dynamic music and the slow-moving image — the feeble, the elderly, the ill — produces a sharp sense of discrepancy between human aspirations and realities.

Stanley Kubrick is another filmmaker who frequently creates an ironic counterpoint between image and sound track. In *Dr. Strangelove* (1963), Kubrick begins the film (and its credits) with a shot of two Strategic Air Command B–52 bombers in midair, one refueling the other. On the sound track, however, one hears not the complementary sounds of droning engines but a saccharine instrumental ballad, "Try a Little Tenderness." The counterpoint between the utterly different content of these two cinematic elements creates an entirely new meaning, one inherent neither in the image nor in the sound by itself: the B–52's are not refueling, they are copulating. The sound track forces us to regard what we watch in an entirely new way. Kubrick again uses music as an integral and highly important element of *A Clockwork Orange* (1971). The film follows the adventures of Alex, a violent hoodlum in a futuristic society. Although music is used in ironic counterpoint to the images it accompanies in many scenes, perhaps none is so shocking as the one in which Alex brutally beats up a writer and sexually assaults his wife — while he sings "Singin' in the Rain" and tap-dances in his stormtrooper-like boots, punctuating his performance with the painful thud of kicks.

One other way in which sound and image can be used in counterpoint in a film is by the juxtaposition of an image and silence (Figure 4-13). Just as the freeze frame in a moving picture frustrates the expectations of continuous, lifelike movement, so does the sudden absence of sound in a sound film frustrate our sense of the reality of a given situation. Continued for a long period, cinematic silence becomes almost tangible and extremely discomforting. Thus, an absence of sound over images of activity tends to distance the viewer, pushes us away from our absorption with the illusion of reality and makes us aware of the artificial nature of sound in the cinema.

SOUND CONVENTIONS

A convention is commonly defined as a general but abitrary agreement on usage and social practice. Policemen, for example, wear a standard uniform, and we cover our mouths when we yawn in public. In the arts, too, there are agreements: when we see *Julius Caesar*, we agree that these

4-13 The creative use of sound can also mean the use of silence. As the young boy in Ingmar Bergman's *The Silence* (1963) walks up and down the deserted corridors of a hotel in some foreign city, his loneliness is underscored by the total absence of sound.

Romans will (for our benefit) speak in English. Thus, a convention in film might be the established use of a particular camera movement joined with a particular content. For example, in 1930s and 1940s films, the camera moves upward and away from embracing lovers, which indicates that they are about to do something together that we have agreed not to watch. The dialogue pattern in a particular sort of movie and the musical or sound accompaniment to a specific kind of dramatic activity, such as the playing of the "March from Lohengrin" to announce the entry of the bride at a wedding, are examples of sound conventions.

We have become so accustomed to hearing some sound conventions that pointing them out may seem unnecessary, and yet it is *because* we take conventions for granted, because they are invisible, they need to be examined. Dialogue patterns can be conventional. Think, for example, of how we expect the snappy cadences and hyped-up, super-fast delivery of newspaper reporters, how, in fact, a slow-speaking reporter would surprise if not disturb us by his unconventionality. In contrast, in a western we expect characters to talk slowly, ungrammatically, and even painfully so that self-expression tends to resolve itself in action rather than words. Slang, though now widely used in many sorts of films, was first associated with the early sound gangster films, and it is still a convention of movies with urban settings rather than rural ones (Figure 4-14).

Music and sound effects have also been used conventionally. Again, the most obvious use is the most taken for granted. It is conventional

4-14 Certain sounds identify certain films. Slang, though first associated with early sound gangster films, is now used in many sorts of films. But the screech of tires on a getaway car, the rattle of tommy guns, the wail of a pursuing siren will always signal a crime film. Edward G. Robinson's distinctive snarl will always be associated with the ambitious hoodlum he played in *Little Caesar* (Mervyn Le Roy, 1930).

that music accelerates for a chase sequence, that it becomes louder to underscore a dramatically important action, that its tempo or pitch indicates whether or not a particular action demands special attention from the viewer. Less obvious are the ways that music and sound effects function to take us back in narrative time by repeating an already established motif or by using echo and distortion to indicate that something unusual — perhaps a flashback — is going to occur. Music in musicals appears out of nowhere, coming up slowly under a dramatic scene so as to lead us gently into a song or dance number, which finishes in a crescendo as the image fades or the characters freeze for a fraction of a second to indicate the end of a scene.

Even the tonal quality of a film's entire sound track may be a convention. Just as the more obvious sounds added to exotic and historical fictional subject matter create an illusion of authenticity of place (jungle sounds in a safari picture, the clank of spurs and snuffling horses in a western), so in a contemporary film an intentionally sloppy sound track can add to the illusion of authenticity and on-the-spot immediacy. Originally, because on-location documentary and news reel sound recording was less selective than it is today, an unselective and unpolished sound track was normal for films recorded on location. If a film was being shot in an actual office, the sound recorder would not only pick up the voices of the principals, but also the peculiar complex of sounds in an office, such as the noise of typing down the hall, people scurrying about off-camera, and also the buzz or feedback that a microphone will pick up in a place that sound technicians call *live*. (In a live space, any sound made simply keeps bouncing around in the space, setting up a nearly omnipresent reverberation, rather than being absorbed. A correctly constructed and draped sound recording room, which absorbs sounds, is called *dead*.) All these sounds authenticate the reality of place and time in a documentary film. Whether filming and recording in a factory, on a ranch, at a press conference, or out on the street, the filmmaker was not technically able to refine on-location recording until the 1960s. The very limitations of documentary recording set up a tradition, a convention: sloppy sound equals immediacy, honesty, a certain measure of objectivity. Feature fiction films adopted the use of sloppy sound tracks to authenticate their contemporary settings and content. Ironically, even current documentary films made on location, though technically able to achieve a clear and clean sound track, often purposely do not clean up their sound tracks because the less professional they sound the more they are accepted as realistic.

There is another way in which sound (dialogue, sound effects, and music) can communicate in a film. A particular sound or combination of sounds can evoke a whole cluster of associated thoughts and feelings from other films or from ordinary life. Lines such as "I wouldn't marry you if you were the last man on earth!" or "Make my day!" after repeated use in many films, may become invested with greater significance than the mere words themselves convey.

Music may function similarly. The most obvious examples are national anthems, which represent the qualities of their respective nations to anyone who hears the familiar tunes. The "Marseillaise" connotes France (the liberty, equality, and fraternity of the French Revolution) much as the "Volga Boatman" connotes Russia (brooding serfs, neurotic aristocrats). Musical instruments, similarly, may convey place: the sitar,

India; castanets, Spain; drums, frontier America or jungle Africa. Sound effects, aurally accompanying the specific film we are watching at a given moment, may also evoke all the other films with similar sounds we have seen. The gangster film has its screeching of tires, its machine-gunning. The horror film has its creaking doors and stair risers, its ominously sudden and expressive moaning winds and claps of thunder. The science fiction film dotes on the sound of machinery, the clicking of circuits, the humming of computers.

Film, then, is an aural as well as a visual medium. The idea that *cinematic* is a term which should be confined to the visual elements of the cinema has surely been put to rest by the outstanding achievements of the sound film. Spoken dialogue and narration, by assisting the un-interrupted flow of images, give us the illusion that we are observing reality — even a clearly alternate reality (for example, *E.T.*). They also contribute effective ambiguity, irony, and ideas to the film medium. Music, too, makes a contribution, extending or counterpointing what is expressed in the images we see. And sound effects not only add tone, mood, and tensions to film, but they can also authenticate a two-dimensional world confined by a rectangle of light beams so that it becomes extended far beyond the boundaries of the theater in which we sit.

NOTES

[1] Quoted in Connie Byrne and William O. Lopez, "Nashville," *Film Quarterly* 29, no. 2 (Winter 1975–1976): 15–16.

[2] *Magic and Myth of the Movies* (New York: Simon and Schuster, 1970), p. 1.

[3] "Composing for Films," in T. J. Ross, ed., *Film and the Liberal Arts* (New York: Holt, Rinehart & Winston, 1970), p. 234.

[4] *Four Screenplays* (New York: The Orion Press, 1970), p. 109.

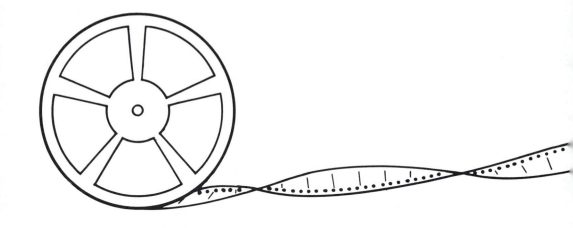

PART III
NARRATIVE
FILM

Knowing and Understanding Narrative Film

Cinema, film, motion pictures, movies — whatever the words, for most people they are synonymous with films that tell a story, a fiction about created characters interacting in situations that are plausible once the premise of the tale is established. The story (the diegesis), then, is the content of a fiction film. Yet it is important to recognize that we cannot actually see some of the attributes of the story, which we nevertheless apprehend. We may *see* actors performing actions, but we *understand* characters and *know* they are in a plot. We may *see* a person working in a factory, but we *understand* the conditions of such labor and *know* that the film is taking an attitude toward those conditions, showing us, for example, the dignity of labor, or the tedium of factory work. In other words what is physically perceivable, what is actually heard and seen in a film, is only part of the content of the film. There is a large component that is only intellectually apprehendable. We might say the audible and visible in the film act like signs to communicate these other meanings.

Even if we cannot see and hear these other meanings directly, we can discuss, study, and define them. What is the difference, for example, between a story and a plot? Some have said a story is what happened; for example, the king wanted some new territories to rule so he raised an army and attacked the neighboring kingdom. Here we have simply a recitation of the chronological events. A plot, however, is the specific sequence of events in a particular narrative. It is an ordering made by someone for a purpose. We could write a script for a film of our story king and in so doing we would have to plot the action. The plot could be chronological, starting with the king's first musings about the need for new subjects, his fight to get Parliment to agree to the plan, the difficulties of forging a large army from scratch, the revelation from spies that the opposing king was also raising an army, and so on until the final attack begins. Or the order could be changed so that a bard was telling the tale to a present audience about a past king. Or we could add a subplot about the king's cowardly son who did not want to go to war and started a revolutionary movement against his father. In effect we would be taking raw material — the story — and by using narrative structures turn it into a plot.

What then are narrative structures? They are certain standard configurations like telling the story from a certain perspective. The same story about the king would be different if it were told from the viewpoint of a loyal subject, a disinterested visitor, or the king him-

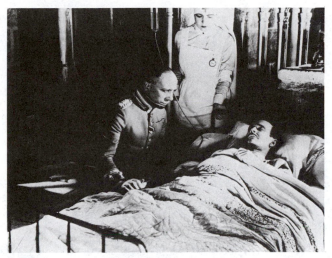

Grand Illusion (Jean Renoir, 1938), a realistic film, probes man's relationship with war and the illusions of heroism, class consciousness, and national pride. In *Grand Illusion,* the passing of the pre-World War I world is symbolized by the death of Boeldieu (Pierre Fresnay) as von Rauffenstein (Erich von Stroheim) looks on.

self. Certain ways of doing beginnings and endings are narrative structures. Having a beginning in which certain information is revealed to the audience (through a narrator, perhaps) that is not known to the characters is a different way of structuring the same story material than having everything presented to the audience and the characters at the same time (if we find out before the king does that the opposing country is preparing a campaign, for example). Narrative structures would dictate the alternatives for endings as well. Is the conflict raised in the narrative resolved? Does the king conquer the territories or do we just see his army ride off to battle? Do we see the battle or simply the results? Do we get any scenes of the enemy camp? Do we ever know anything about them, or are they just the faceless foe? Narrative structures are like empty molds into which the story material is pressed and then it comes out a plot, which can be made into a film (or a novel, a play, even a poem — the journey of a hero is the narrative structure organizing *The Odyssey,* for example). Even the time honored opening of "Once upon a time . . ." is a narrative structure that sets up certain expectations. Thus, narrative structures are organizing principles that interrelate the expectations of the storyteller and the story audience

In *The Seventh Seal* (1956) Ingmar Bergman investigates the age-old search for proof of God's existence through a combination of realistic and nonrealistic means. Death is personified and moves through the film as a character, seen here playing chess with the Knight (Max von Sydow).

and exist, in a sense, as part of the cultural matrix of any group of communicators, that is, the narrative structures are familiar and known.

Though there are reports that some primitive tribes when first shown motion pictures could not *understand* what the images meant because such narrative structures were unknown to them, no one in the modern world has any difficulty in reading these signs. Whether the human figures are six inches tall on a home television screen or 20 feet tall in a large theater, we know they represent average sized human beings. In the same way we understand the who, what, where, and why of the diegesis because the narrative structures, in our particular case, the *filmic* narrative structures are well known to us. They are part of our cultural heritage.

But there is another kind of understanding and knowing that takes place after we watch a film; we may have to think about what we have seen to understand it. The film's theme may not be clearly stated, the filmmaker's ideas may be begging for interpretation. Or reflection about a film may bring an understanding of the film's place in history, its relationship to other films by the same director, or to other films of a similar type.

Some fiction films contain extremely fresh situations and characters, while others, relying on formula plots and stereotyped characters, seem to belong to a group of films, or a **genre. Nongenre** films, such as *Citizen Kane* (Orson Welles, 1941) usually attempt to individualize their characters and situations, thereby making them fresh experiences for the viewer. Formula or genre films, on the other hand, portray representative figures (such as the tough but decent detective) acting in conventional situations. The fiction film, whether a genre or nongenre film, can use the conventions of realism in its setting, time scheme, and character motivations or it can use the conventions of expressionism. Nongenre films, however, tend to have complex, ambiguous themes that challenge commonplace ideas, whereas genre films tend to deal in clearly delineated conflicts, usually between obvious good and evil. The pleasures of the nongenre film derive from its originality and its ability to surprise us. The pleasures of the genre film derive from its familiarity and its ability to meet our expectations in satisfying ways.

Aspects of the fiction film are presented in two chapters. Chapter 5 will deal with genre films, and Chapter 6 with the nongenre narrative film.

Historical Overview:
The Development of the
Narrative Film

EARLY STORYTELLERS: HOLLYWOOD AND THE SILENT FILM

The invention of cinematography in the late nineteenth century provided a new medium through which to tell stories, a medium that literally could combine the tools and techniques of painting, music and dance, pantomime, drama, and literature, and could reach and affect a mass audience. But the idea of using the motion picture camera and projector for narrative purposes was not developed as immediately as one might think. The inventors of motion picture technology were not artists, were not concerned with the fanciful or unreal aspects of the medium. Instead, they were men of science and industry, inventors and tinkers who were chiefly concerned with capturing on film the physical world in which they lived.

It was Georges Méliès, a magician and theater operator involved less with the scientific than with the magical and fantastic, who first consciously realized the narrative capacity of the new medium. Having discovered that the camera could be stopped in the middle of an action and then restarted after the action was altered, so that during projection a scene would appear to be filled with magical transformations, Méliès was able to create realistic illusions in which actors' heads were severed from their bodies and then magically returned and people were transformed into puffs of smoke. Through the magic of animated sequences and fabulous cardboard scenery, Méliès's characters could fly off to the moon or plunge deep into a fairyland world under the sea. It is not surprising that — unlike his more scientifically oriented predecessors, the Lumière brothers and Thomas Edison — Méliès was drawn to filming stories, short versions of childhood favorites like *Cinderella* (1899) and *Little Red Riding Hood* (1901) as well as literary adaptations like *A Trip to the Moon* (1902), *Gulliver's*

1 Edwin S. Porter is credited with creating the first story film that took advantage of the camera's unique abilities. The close-up, parallel editing, camera movement, and subject movement toward the camera are some of the formal devices found in *The Great Train Robbery* (1903).

Travels (1901), and *The Legend of Rip Van Winkle* (1905). But for all his delight in storytelling and for all of his discoveries about how to edit in the camera (he developed the fade-out, dissolves, double exposure, slow and fast motion, and **animation**), Méliès never transcended his own theatrical background or the narrative limitations of the stage and proscenium arch. All the action in Méliès's films was contained in the center of a static frame, and stories were related in a strict chronological order, one complete scene following another.

Edwin S. Porter, head of Thomas Edison's Kinetoscope operations, found the key that eventually allowed the new medium to find its own means of story telling. Porter demonstrated that editing could manipulate time and space to create drama, suspense, and excitement in a way that would be impossible for the theater to duplicate. In 1903, he took pieces of film footage of various fire companies in action from the Edison files, shot several scenes to match this **stock footage,** and then edited the action together to make *The Life of an American Fireman*. Later that same year, Porter made *The Great Train Robbery,* which went further toward refining the storytelling techniques that have become essential to the medium. Porter employed the parallel editing of two simultaneous actions taking place in different locations, the chase sequence, scenes shot from different camera angles, and the dramatic close-up.

Interestingly enough, Porter's techniques were more the result of happenstance and the particular filming conditions imposed upon him by the subject matter of *The Great Train Robbery* than they were the result of conscious discovery. The film tells the story of a gang of bandits who rob a train, are pursued by a posse, and are finally dispatched (Figure 1). Much of the action takes place outdoors in the "wild, wild west" of New Jersey, and this on-location shooting in rough terrain required that the camera be set up in positions other than squarely in front of the action. The camera also moves slightly at one point in the film to produce a brief and tentative pan shot, which keeps the moving bandits in the frame. Further, characters are occasionally forced by the terrain to enter or leave the scene from behind the camera rather than from screen left or screen right, the cinematic equivalent of theatrical wings. Porter's most important achievement, however, was in allowing the action of the story to dictate the narrative structure of the film. Cutting back and forth between the robbers and the posse satisfied the audience's equal interest in both groups as well as creating dramatic suspense. Porter's popular little film clearly established the medium's potential for a distinctly cinematic narrative, articulating conventions further reinforced by D. W. Griffith.

Griffith, a Southerner, came to New York to make his fortune as a great dramatist, but ended up as the most remarkable film storyteller of his time. As a failed playwright, but fairly competent actor, he became a player for the Biograph film company. In 1908, with Biograph's promise that should he fail he would not lose his acting job, Griffith tried his hand at directing a movie and thereafter made two or three or more short story films each week, constantly experimenting with the camera's narrative capacity. It is intensely ironic that this man who had trained himself for the serious theater, and who was never an avid fan of cinema, should so brilliantly have modified the theatrical conventions practiced by other filmmakers of the period. Whereas other filmmakers tended to use the single static camera position for an entire film, exaggerated stage acting played to the balcony rather than to the more intimately located camera, and bright, flat, unimaginative lighting, Griffith moved the camera between shots, occasionally within shots, restrained the performers' gestures and posturings, and used dramatic lighting parallel to stage mood lighting. He also realized the selective nature of the medium, understanding that it was capable of isolating elements of the drama through the use of **irises** and **masks** and close-ups in a way unavailable to the stage even though the stage could do something like this with spotlighting. Although Griffith retained a great deal of the content of the theater — most of his films were nineteenth-century melodramas — he was able to tell his stories with an astonishing narrative forcefulness and involve the audience more intensely. Griffith's filmed stories had an energy, fluidity, and vitality that took advantage of the motion picture's ability to move.

This illusion of motion, of movingness, is essential in cinematic form and in cinematic storytelling. It is not only that images on the screen move, but also that the audience seems to change location and perspective. Griffith could place an audience high on a hill overlooking the battle lines of the Northern and Southern armies and fill it with the sense of epic spectacle as he does in *The Birth of a Nation* (1915) and in the next shot bring the audience close to an individual act of heroism on the battlefield, isolating the details of human action necessary to build the audience's empathy with specific characters. The stage, of course, can change the scene too, but not with the rapidity of cinema. Cinema, moreover, has an immediacy and specificity of time and place that drama does not possess. In *Henry V* an actor, speaking on behalf of Shakespeare, must apologize for the limits of the stage, saying, "Think, when we talk of horses, that you see them," and he goes on to say that the audience's imagination must go "here and there," but a film can show us horses and in a second can take us from France to England. The mobility Griffith found through editing meant that film stories did not need to be told like theatrical stories.

Griffith perfected parallel editing to increase suspense. He built up scenes out of shots photographed at varying distances and angles, thereby increasing the audience's involvement with the plot and the characters. He used objects such as the cameo of Elsie Stoneman that Ben Cameron holds tenderly in *The Birth of a Nation,* and small yet significant details (for example, having Mr. Jenkins, the factory owner, stoop to pick up a dime before looking in on the workers' dance in *Intolerance,* 1916) to reveal the emotional states of his characters, and he recognized that a slight change in a facial expression could give far more information than an exaggerated grimace. Aware that the cinema could span time with a cut and could authenticate an imaginary event with its images, he set his characters in significant social and historical contexts in order to establish the reality and the serious intent of his stories. *Intolerance,* a plea for an end to bigotry, combines four stories from four different time periods and places — an urban drama set in modern times, Judea in the time of Christ, the St. Bartholomew's Day Massacre in the Paris of 1572, and Babylon in 539 B.C. — and thus both captures the sweep of history and the meaning that history has for the individuals caught up in it. Griffith was not the first filmmaker to use the **epic** form nor the spectacular mise-en-scène (the Italian cinema developed the spectacular epic first), but he was the first to combine the epic and the personal. One example of many suffices to demonstrate Griffith's fluid movement from the grand to the lowly. During the Babylonian story, a feast for the ruling Prince Belshazzar is held amid the splendor of one of the largest sets ever constructed in Hollywood. Extreme long shots take in the cast of thousands of dancing girls and retainers, the whole whirling mass of people and bodies, garlanded and draped columns, huge statues of ancient temple gods, and all of this is viewed with a godlike omniscience by the audience. But Griffith particularizes the monumental scene by focusing in — via inserted close-ups and masking devices — on the simple and hard-fighting Mountain Girl and recording her reactions to the feasting surrounding her. Though commercially unsuccessful in its own day, *Intolerance* is a monument to the imagination and skill of the motion picture's first great storyteller.

While Griffith refined the narrative structure of epics and melodramas, others developed the art of pantomime and burlesque, taking specific advantage of

2   Much of silent comedy depends upon exaggeration of emotion and broad gestures. Chaplin, however, often extracted laughs using exactly the opposite method. In *The Gold Rush* (1925), while starving in the middle of a blizzard, he calmly polishes off a boiled shoe as if it were a rare gourmet treat served in a fancy restaurant, even going so far as to suck the last traces of food off the shoe nails as if they were chicken bones. The sequence derives its humor from the Little Tramp's straight-faced delicacy.

film's malleable time and space. Thomas H. Ince, a **producer** who supervised every facet of the films in his charge, ran a tight studio, and his films were marked by taut construction, a direct narrative line, believable characters, and lots of action. Mack Sennett, another producer/director, covered the comic elements of storytelling with as much verve as Griffith covered the melodrama and Ince the adventure film. Sennett created the Keystone Cops, and he discovered visual **slapstick** and custard pies, bathing beauties and fast motion. He also found the actors that he needed for his kind of stories: Ben Turpin, Fatty Arbuckle, and, of course, Charlie Chaplin (Figure 2). The narrative structure of slapstick comedy depended less on coherence than on motion, less on nuance than on the ridiculously broad, and less on the development of character and intricacies of plot than on the use of physical space and cinematic time.

Essentially, then, by the start of World War I, the movies had standardized its conventions, types, and forms, its production, distribution, and exhibition system. Hollywood was the place that produced epics, tearjerkers, westerns, and slapstick comedies starring famous screen personalities, films that were then shipped throughout the country to adoring fans who paid to see their favorite performers in action on the silent screen. Stories tended to be made to type and performers were usually cast to type. During and after the war, audiences went to films whose subject matter tended to reflect whatever was popular in pulp novels, theater, and vaudeville. Movies had become big business and producers

had become the dominant force in Hollywood filmmaking, listening more atten-
tively to the ring of the cash register than to the creative artist. The practice of
giving the producer the right to final cut became an industry standard. Thus, if a
director turned in a finished film that the producer did not like, the producer
simply recut it, shot extra footage if necessary, and changed the whole to suit
what he thought was the public's taste.

EARLY STORYTELLERS: EUROPE AND THE SILENT FILM

Early in the 1920s other national cinemas arose to challenge the supremacy of
Hollywood. Though each nation had its own distinctive cinematic character, all
of the famous European filmmakers of the period shared the assumption that the
cinema was an art equal to literature and was thus capable of treating the most
serious, complex, and profound material with sensitivity, subtlety, and expressive technical daring. Film in Europe had never been regarded, as it was in the
United States, simply as lower-class entertainment.

From Germany, perhaps the most innovative national cinema of those years
between 1919 and 1925, films such as Robert Wiene's *The Cabinet of Dr.
Caligari* (1919), Ernst Lubitsch's *Anna Boleyn* (1920), F. W. Murnau's *The Last
Laugh* (1924), E. A. Dupont's *Variety* (1925), G. W. Pabst's *Joyless Street*
(1925), and Fritz Lang's *Metropolis* (1927) stunned the world with their in-
ventive camera work and serious subject matter. Often this inventiveness and
seriousness took the form of **expressionism,** in films that explored dream, nightmare, and psyche and that found their narrative shape determined less by action
than by emotion (Figure 3). Sweden contributed two masterful and creative directors, Mauritz Stiller and Victor Seastrom, who, like so many of the German
directors, were lured to Hollywood by large salaries and promises (not always
fulfilled) of artistic freedom. In Denmark, Carl Dreyer developed a cinematic
style that also subverted traditional notions of what constituted the story film.
Dreyer was fascinated with what a pared-down cinema, concentrating on close-
ups and minimal but intense details, could communicate about the human soul;
working in France he made *The Passion of Joan of Arc* (1928), a masterpiece
that reveals the spiritual agony Joan underwent during her trial for heresy.

René Clair and Abel Gance, two French directors, also notably expanded the
narrative limits of film storytelling. Clair's filmmaking ranged from the avant-
garde (*Entr'acte,* 1924) to the farcical (*The Italian Straw Hat,* 1927), but he was
consistently interested in telling a story visually through rhythmic editing. Gance
also experimented with various camera techniques and made an epic, *Napoleon*
(1926), using a triptych screen, which not only created the wide-screen effects
we tend to associate only with Cinerama but also made use of multiple images.

The Russians, too, contributed to the development of film narrative following
the Russian Revolution of 1917. Influenced by their careful study of D. W. Griffith's films (especially *Intolerance*), new Soviet filmmakers like Sergei Eisenstein,

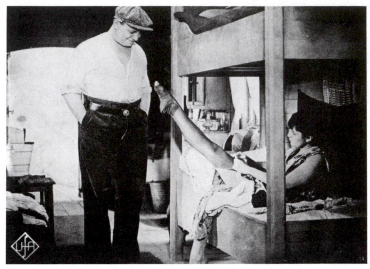

3 Some German expressionist films employed realistic settings to tell stories that were closer to everyday life. Yet they were still able to use subjective camera and harsh shadow effects to add an eerie quality to the depiction of elemental conflicts. In *Variety* (1925), E. A. Dupont blended the real and the expressionistic in his story of jealousy and murder under the "Big Top."

V. I. Pudovkin, Alexander Dovzhenko, and Dziga Vertov became masters of editing, expanding the possibilities of manipulating narrative time and meaning.

By the time sound was introduced in 1927, the movies had reached technical and artistic heights almost unimaginable. The camera and the written title had combined with the pantomime of actors to create every conceivable kind of story, from the silliest and simplest of slapstick comedies to sophisticated farce, from the most familiar shoot-'em-ups to the most profound evocations of historical epochs, from trite melodramas to emotionally draining dramas of heroes and heroines caught in the grip of fate, and from cheap thrillers to exotic and expressionistic nightmare worlds. Based upon the structural principles and conventions evolved by Méliès, Porter, and Griffith, filmmaking in the 1920s, both in Europe and in America, achieved a consummate artistry.

SOUND AND THE NARRATIVE FILM

The conventions and structures of cinematic storytelling changed, however, with the advent of sound. Once actors could talk and be heard and music could be synchronized with the action, audiences demanded verbal as well as visual drama. People wanted to hear voices in conflict, in love, or describing what had happened or what was about to happen or what things meant. Audiences demanded a glib sort of realism. The first years of talkies produced a spate of filmed plays and musical revues, and so total was the concern with sound that the camera again became a static observer seated front-row center. In effect, the camera was immobilized by the microphone.

4 Sound ushered in the era of musicals: "All Talking, All Singing, All Dancing." Dick Powell and Ruby Keeler became stars, playing the lovestruck couple in several Busby Berkeley musicals of the 1930s. The production still above is from *Gold Diggers of 1933.*

Within a year or so of the success of *The Jazz Singer* (1927), however, creative filmmakers began to discover and develop more effective means of using sound to enhance their stories. The use of **multiple sound tracks** and asynchronous sound originating offscreen made contemporary dramas seem authentic and real and immediate. Sound also allowed the filmmaker another element through which to create humor or pathos. And sound was extraordinarily economical; information could be conveyed quickly without unnecessary visual emphasis.

Sound had an influence on what kind of stories got told, too. Musicals (Figure 4) and gangster films, for example, would not have been made in such great quantity without a sound-on-film process, which could provide delightful songs and terrifying machine-gun blasts. And comedy changed drastically in its orientation and structure. Silent comedy depended on visual momentum, on broad and simple actions that snowballed in accelerating images until they left the audience laughing breathlessly. Although title cards occasionally made puns, the viewer's apprehension of the comedy primarily depended on the physical and the visual. Sound changed that. The images in comedy might seem ordinary — or at least normal — while the dialogue might snowball and accelerate. Funny lines were often more intellectual, dependent upon a play on words, or on class distinctions.

THE HOLLYWOOD FICTION FILM

Other technological advances since the 1930s (color and wide-screen processes, for example) have had relatively little impact upon the kinds of narrative films made and the way in which narratives are put together. The Hollywood staples — proven successful by box office receipts — were genre films: gangster films, westerns, musicals, adventure films, science fiction and horror films, family melodramas (weepies), Biblical epics, and costume dramas (Figure 4). Although enhanced by the addition of sound and color and wide screens, most of these genres were established in the days of the silent cinema and their storytelling patterns were not significantly altered by the introduction of new technology alone. One either has to look at certain nongenre films, which used the new technology in an idiosyncratically creative way, or at certain film movements (usually associated with a national cinema), which absorbed the technology as another tool through which new narrative patterns could be realized.

One such nongenre film that has had a tremendous impact on the art of contemporary cinematic narrative as well as on other aspects of cinematic art was Orson Welles's *Citizen Kane* (1941). The use of multiple flashbacks, overlapping narrative segments, and a film within a film created enormous complexity in what might have been a simply conceived, chronologically executed fictional biography of a powerful man. *Citizen Kane* was as innovative in its day as *The Birth of a Nation* and *Intolerance* had been in theirs.

During World War II, Hollywood film stories were for the most part conservative and patriotic — and European cinemas, except for Germany's propaganda machine, scarcely existed. After the war ended, however, several interesting cultural and technological realities influenced the shape of film narrative, its substance and its form. In America, for instance, awareness of the effect of the war — for example, of returning veterans who would face psychological and employment problems, and of women who had been financially independent and gainfully employed — affected even what seemed the most escapist film fare. A genre (or, some maintain, a film style) appeared that has since been given the name, **film noir** (literally, black film) (Figure 5). Stylistically the ancestry of these films could be traced to the horror films of the 1930s and early 1940s, films whose use of light and shade *(chiaroscuro)* had been imported with German directors and cameramen during the late 1920s and the 1930s. Thematically, their ancestry owed something to the gangster film. Film noir, however, was post-World War II, focusing on the seamy underbelly of the

5 Barbara Stanwyck, Fred MacMurray, and Edward G. Robinson appeared in *Double Indemnity* (Billy Wilder, 1944), an early *film noir* — literally "black film." In opposition to the traditional optimism of Hollywood films, the *film noir* explored the seamy side of urban life in post-World War II America, focusing on a corrupt and deceitful world.

urban world, the big city full of corruption and deceit, a disillusioned world with few heroes and few if any redeeming social values. True, most Hollywood films still echoed the optimism about the future that has always seemed a part of American culture, but films like *Double Indemnity* (1944), *The Big Sleep* (1946), *The Strange Love of Martha Ivers* (Lewis Milestone, 1946), *Out of the Past* (Jacques Tourneur, 1947), *The Asphalt Jungle* (John Huston, 1950), and *The Big Heat* (Fritz Lang, 1953) indicated a deep-seated pessimism, which was far more brooding and disturbing than those films that, like the intelligent and narratively satisfying *The Best Years of Our Lives* (William Wyler, 1946), dealt more overtly with postwar themes (Figure 6). After World War II films in America began to mature in their thematic content; the emergence of film noir signalled a trend toward psychological realism.

FILM MOVEMENTS

This move toward realism, dramatically evident in filmmaking in postwar Europe, was especially evident in Italy. Because Italian studios had been bombed

6 Nongenre films in the realistic mode will often be about something most people consider relevant to contemporary life. *The Best Years of Our Lives* (William Wyler, 1946), for instance, recounted the problems faced by three returning veterans of World War II, exploring their difficult readjustment to civilian life.

and film stock was hard to come by, Italian filmmakers literally took to the streets to find their stories and to film them. Using natural locations, natural lighting, and nonprofessional actors as well as professionals, directors like Roberto Rossellini and Vittorio de Sica told stark, episodic narratives of ordinary people living ordinary lives in a war-torn country governed by a usually unfeeling and inadequate bureaucracy. This movement, called **Italian neorealism,** changed the shape of film narrative. Storytelling no longer needed to be neatly fashioned, tidily resolved, artificially constructed; narrative — in imitation of life — became more open-ended and less dramatically symmetrical. And because these films were financial as well as critical successes in the United States, Italian neorealism influenced the narrative traditions of American film.

Factors other than the war influenced a further change in narrative cinema in France during the 1950s. There, the champions of a new cinema were a number of young film critics who had studied and written about film history and particularly enjoyed the taut and dynamic Hollywood films made in the 1940s.

7   Alain Resnais, a French new-wave director, uses the fiction film to explore the relationship between memory and history, between what really happened and what we remember. In *Hiroshima, Mon Amour* (1959), he contrasts the painful memories of two participants of World War II, a Japanese man whose parents died at Hiroshima and a Frenchwoman who had a love affair with a German soldier during the Occupation. Resnais uses film's ability to manipulate time to indicate the complexity of the problem.

François Truffaut and Jean-Luc Godard were the leaders of this group of new filmmakers, most of whom had grown up in the Paris Cinémathèque, a film archive that showed films from around the world around the clock. Although each filmmaker who emerged from this group was an original and individual talent, all of the filmmakers were united by their desire to abandon — as well as often subvert — formal and conventional and boringly respectable stories usually adapted from novels or plays, and by their desire to make films which went to the center of contemporary concerns and dealt with them through contemporary forms. By the end of the 1950s, the films of what has since come to be called the **French new wave** (nouvelle vague) began to attract international notice. The new wave introduced many important directors, but perhaps Jean-Luc Godard and Alain Resnais exerted the greatest influence on film narrative: Godard because of his attempts to educate the viewer to the ideology behind the processes of the cinema, and Resnais because of his innovative explorations of time and memory (Figure 7).

A renaissance of British filmmaking occurred at about the same time as the French new wave films began to appear. The **British free cinema** movement began in the mid-1950s, reflecting the English artists' increasing concern with everyday life as lived among the middle and lower classes. Earlier, the narrative cinema (like the drama) had emphasized the upper classes and had tended to ignore social problems or to put them in comic form. But in the fifties British

8 Even though Stanley Kubrick began directing films under studio conditions, he is now in a position to control every aspect of his films. For instance, he adapted a Steven King novel into a screenplay, which he then produced and directed: *The Shining* (1980) is totally a Kubrick film from the casting, through the photography, the editing, to the choice of music.

filmmakers began to fashion an original and gritty cinema, at first adapting other media for the cinema — a novel for *Room at the Top* (Jack Clayton, 1958), and a play for *Look Back in Anger* (Tony Richardson, 1959). Until the mid-1960s, when the movement seemed to lose its impetus, England exported films that combined social drama with innovative forms and touches of wry comedy.

Two other film movements, which have further changed the shape of the fiction film, have been the Latin cinema and the **new German cinema.** Although Latin filmmakers had long used film for political ends, especially to criticize governmental policies which favored the rich and ignored or exploited the poor, it was not until the 1960s that their films gained international recognition as bizarre and innovative combinations of realism, folk myth, music, fantasy, and social documentary, which promoted, in allegorical fashion, revolutionary ideas. First recognized in the mid-1970s, the new German cinema is one of the most recent film movements. Although each filmmaker's vision is unique, the works of Rainer Fassbinder, Werner Herzog, Margarethe von Trotta and Wim Wenders all share a modernist aesthetic, an antagonism toward traditional cinematic narrative, and a critical attitude toward contemporary German values.

NEW DIRECTIONS

American film has chiefly continued to excel in traditional narrative forms. Although the work of filmmakers such as Stanley Kubrick, Robert Altman, Woody Allen, and Terence Malick indicate new directions in American narrative cinema (Figure 8), the basic shape of the Hollywood fiction film has remained relatively constant. Europe, except for the new German cinema, has not seen particularly drastic or significant changes in film narrative either. France, for example, now seems to export humane, domestic, bourgeois dramas and comedies, like *La Cage Aux Folles* (1978) rather than the groundbreaking experimental and existential ones of the 1950s and 1960s. National cinemas, however, throughout the world still continue to pour energy and talent into the fiction film. Peter Weir, Fred Schepesi, and Gillian Armstrong have propelled the Australian film into the limelight with films like *Picnic At Hanging Rock* (1975), *The Chant of Jimmie Blacksmith* (1978), and *Starstruck* (1982).

5

⚙ *GENRE FILMS*

The emphasis . . . is on a description of popular movies, viewed in sets and cycles rather than as single entities. It is an approach that accepts obsolescence and in which judgements derive from the sympathetic consumption of a great many films. In terms of continuing themes and motifs, the obsolescence of single films is compensated for by the prolongation of ideas in film after film.
Lawrence Alloway [1]

Long the staple product of Hollywood, the genre film such as the western or the gangster film is different from other fiction films in that it follows established narrative structures, uses stereotypical characters, and communicates through certain familiar images **(icons).** These structures and images are a sort of shorthand, compressing information about the story, characters, and theme into conventional actions and objects such as décor, costume, and topography. In a western, for example, the derringer (a small, easily concealed pistol) indicates its owner's basically underhanded character. Or consider clothing: both cowboys and outlaws wear loose-fitting and practical clothing, indicating a free and open life-style, but people from the town usually wear suits, vests, and ties to indicate their more restricted way of life. The genre film also builds upon preexistent audience expectations: we go to see a thriller, a gangster film. The experience of the genre film is a familiar rather than a new experience and its satisfactions are based on our previous knowledge of the **formulas, conventions,** and iconography used in the films. Genre films are popular and comprehensible — and although certain critics look down on genre films as escapist, mass, and mediocre entertainment, audiences turn out in droves to see the likes of such genre films as *Poltergeist* (Tobe Hooper, 1982), a horror film; *Star Trek II: The Wrath of Kahn* (Nicholas Meyer, 1982), a science-fiction film; and *Rocky IV* (Sylvester Stallone, 1985), a sports film. More sophisticated critics, recognizing that the popularity and comprehensibility of the genre film do not necessarily mean simplicity, know that genre films are worthy of critical scrutiny for any number of interesting aesthetic and social reasons. Contemporary filmmakers, too, recognize and exploit the audience's familiarity with genre films. Through parodies or reversals of familiar genres — such as *Lust in the Dust* (Paul Bartel, 1985) and *Barbarosa* (Fred Schepesi, 1982) — they have turned the genre film into a modernist, self-conscious, self-reflexive exploration of its own form and content.

The Definition of Genre

What, precisely, is a genre film? It is a film which belongs to a particular group of films that are extremely similar in their subject matter, thematic concerns, characterizations, plot formulas, and visual settings. Such a film somehow depends on these similarities for its very existence and for the satisfactions it brings the viewer. Some genres, such as the western, are easily recognizable; many points of similarity exist between films, linking them firmly into a group. On the most simple level, we know a western is a western because nearly all westerns are set on the American frontier from 1865 to 1900. Certain historical elements recur again and again in western films: we have seen, on many screens, images of the building of the transcontinental railroad, the United States cavalry defending a fort, the wagon train crossing the country. We have seen repeated images of the bounty hunter, the lawman, Monument Valley or the Great Plains, the roundup, the bunkhouse, the campfire, the Indians, the western town with its board sidewalks and saloons and bank and general store. These visual elements help us to identify a western as a western, although all of them, of course, need not appear in any one film. In fact, unless the film is an epic (Ford, Hathaway, and Marshall's *How the West Was Won*, 1962, or Italian director Sergio Leone's operatic *Once Upon a Time in the West*, 1969), the inclusion of too many conventional elements in a single film may result in an effect that is unintentionally comic (Figure 5-1).

King Vidor's *Duel in the Sun* (1947), for example, though it was expensively produced and was much publicized at the time it was released, by today's standards of what constitutes the limits of the conventions of realism and historicism, seems like a parody. *Duel in the Sun* seems to go out of its way to include as many of the conventional

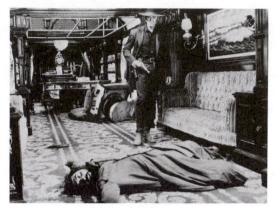

5-1   Genre films are crafted out of formula plots, conventions, stereotyped characters, and icons. Each film contains a selection from the pool of available elements. *Once Upon a Time in the West* (Serge Leone, 1969), however, contains so many elements of the western, heaped one upon the other — the mail-order bride, the fight over water rights, the coming of the railroad, sinister bankers and corporate officials, and obsessive revenge — that the effect is close to opera. Playing against his usual stereotype of the earnest lawman, in this film Henry Fonda portrayed the wickedest, most ruthless hired killer ever imagined.

aspects of the genre as possible. The heroine, Pearl, is a half-breed. The protagonist and antagonist are brothers; one has become a dandified, civilized, easternized lawyer who is genteel with ladies, and the other is still a wild, crude, irresponsible, stallion of a cowboy. Their father (a retired senator) owns a huge cattle empire and favors the toughness of his wild son over the refined manners of his other son. Their mother (a tired but strong-willed Southern belle) prefers the civilized qualities of her favorite over the animal crudity of the son she is sure will come to no good. Both sons confront each other over Pearl; one son wants to improve Pearl's mind, the other is more interested in her body. The railroad enters the picture, its construction threatening the ranchers' rangeland. There is a confrontation between the ranchers and the railroad crew, and the cavalry arrives from nowhere in the nick of time to prevent a full-scale battle. Pearl (whose half-breed bad blood has not been able to resist the advances of the bad son, although she does want her mind improved) and the bad son end up killing each other, leaving the good and civilized son free to marry an eastern lady, who is not too sexy or too dark-skinned and who has turned up on the train, appropriately arriving from the east. The effect of this excess of conventional

5-2 A western need not take place in the legendary past. As long as generic elements are present, the story can be set in the contemporary West. In *Lonely Are the Brave* (David Miller, 1962), set in the present, the traditional underlying conflicts between the individual who seeks the freedom of the frontier and the encroaching society that seeks to tame him are as clearly visible as they are in the more traditional western. In typical "formula" westerns, such as the many films cranked out in the Hopalong Cassidy series, good guys and bad guys are clearly drawn. The only unconventional element in this series was that Hopalong (William Boyd), the hero, always wore a black hat, and the villain (here, Robert Mitchum) frequently wore a white one.

elements is humor. *Duel in the Sun* is difficult to take seriously, because audience expectations have changed.

Other western movies such as *The Wild Bunch* (Sam Peckinpah, 1969), *Little Big Man* (Arthur Penn, 1971), and *McCabe and Mrs. Miller* (Robert Altman, 1971) seem to break with tried-and-true formulas, and yet they are still recognizable as part of the western genre because they retain enough generic elements to bear a strong resemblance to other films in the genre. An interesting example of this sort of departure from classic generic elements in a film that still remains a western is *Lonely Are the Brave* (David Miller, 1962). The film breaks with traditional convention in that it takes place in contemporary times, in a world full of freeways, appliances, cola drinks, and helicopters (Figure 5-2). After purposely getting himself into prison to help a close friend escape (a fairly conventional plot contrivance in the traditional western), the film's protagonist, Jack, himself escapes (his friend refuses) and is hunted down by a reluctantly admiring sheriff, his colorless assistant, a prison guard, and finally by an impersonal helicopter and its crew from a nearby military base. Jack is defeated not by gunshot in a final shoot-out on the dusty streets of a western town, but by the wheels of a huge truck carrying bathroom fixtures cross-country on the blacktop surface of a modern highway.

Why is this film, so dependent upon its contemporary context, still a western? There are enough traditional elements in the movie to remind us constantly of other western movies that we have seen, and the **theme** of the film — the end of frontiers and the toll that progress takes on the lone individual — is basic to almost all classic movie westerns. Jack is a typical western hero: he hates fences and boundaries; he has rejected the stability of marriage and home because it would rob him of freedom and would force him to conform; his true home is the rapidly diminishing wilderness; his only property is his horse and gear; he cannot understand or abide by the bureaucratic and seemingly arbitrary rules of civilization. Then, too, the film's characters are engaged in relationships common to other westerns: Jack and his married friend have grown up together and are almost like brothers, but they have gone their separate ways and chosen dramatically opposed life-styles and relationships to society, each of which is ultimately incomprehensible to the other man (similar to Howard Hawks's more traditional *Red River*, 1948). The prison guard is the typical bully and coward who wants to break the spirit of the hero and who regards Jack's confidence and strength as a personal accusation and threat (similar to a situation in Anthony Mann's more traditional *The Tin Star*, 1957); the sheriff and his deputy provide an almost vaudevillian representation of cool, leisurely efficiency and bumbling ineptitude (reminiscent of many Ford's and Hawks's westerns, which use sidekicks, dramatic foils and comic companions to the more virile hero); the sheriff's admiration for Jack's persistence and ingenuity creates a relationship between the two, and even though they have never met they become adversaries of equal strength (similar to situations in Sam Peckinpah's *The Wild Bunch* and Abraham Polonsky's *Tell Them Willie Boy Is Here*, 1970). Finally, the casting of Kirk Douglas as Jack evokes the traditional western, for Douglas has played many western heroes and even in the contemporary settings of *Lonely Are the Brave* he reminds us of the hero of the traditional western (Figure 5-3).

For a movie to be considered part of a genre, or of a generic tradition, then, it need not include *all* the conventions of that genre, but it should include *enough* generic elements to cause the viewer to associate it clearly and consciously with other films containing similar elements. These similarities of theme, **plot**, and characterization should also be quite

5-3 Setting plays an important part in the western. In addition to its function as a concrete image of the Frontier — the place where, both historically and imaginatively, civilization and the wilderness exist side by side — the wide-open spaces provide the cinematic space for unlimited, exciting action. Here Indians and outriders fight it out during an attack on the wagon train in *How the West Was Won* (John Ford, George Marshall, Henry Hathaway, 1962).

specific. There are countless films built on the relationships between men and women, yet all these films do not constitute a genre because the details, characterizations, and themes of the films may have no other points of resemblance whatsoever.

Primarily then, the genre film is part of a system of well-known narratives, sets of stories, prepackaged and familiar, like breakfast cereals, which have proved popular in the past. Film producers and film audiences (in sum — the culture) together have defined (and continue to redefine) the shape and form of these narratives and the meanings they convey in response to the culture's changing and unchanging desires and needs.

FORMULA

Genre films are constructed from formula plots. The basic conflict of the story is familiar, and we know from past viewing experiences more or less how the story will be resolved. Thus, what happens in a particular genre film is predictable; we do not get *surprise* so much as *suspense* generated by small variations. We can relax and only pretend anxiety about whether the protagonist will live or die at the end of the movie.

5-4 Genre films use formula plots. The adventure film frequently brings together a group of people from different stations in life and places them in a situation of stress. In *The Poseidon Adventure* (Ronald Neame, 1972), passengers on a swamped ocean liner are tested to see who wins and who loses, who is a coward or a shirker, and who has the courage and skill to survive.

Different genres, however, tend to concentrate on different basic conflicts. From one genre to another, then, we get different episodes in the plot and different characters.

Consider, for example, the adventure film. One of the basic conflicts presented in certain kinds of adventure films — whether it is a film about a wild animal hunt like Howard Hawks's *Hatari!* (1962), a war movie like *Battleground* (William Wellman, 1949), or a survival movie like *The Poseidon Adventure* (Ronald Neame, 1972) — is the formation, from a random group of people, of a functioning minisociety, which can accomplish a given task successfully. Because this is the central issue, all these films tend to concentrate on delineating different stereotypical characters (the coward, the braggart, the lover) and on the process whereby these individuals are tested and found to be useful or useless to the group and its single goal (Figure 5-4). Thus, the formula situations (a shipwreck, a jet plane in trouble, a platoon cut off behind enemy lines, a search for hidden treasure) provide a way to isolate and estrange the characters from civilized society so that their true natures may come to the surface. The characters represent a cross section of society, sometimes ethnically and geographically (the Italian-American from New York, the black, the Texan), sometimes occupationally (the banker, the laborer, the farmer), and always morally (the sniveler, the stoic, the sentimentalist) to indicate the democratic nature of group action.

Since this type of adventure film presents a model for a truly democratic minisociety, the hero is not such a loner as the hero in, let us say, the western. He (as in the vast majority of genre films, the protagonist in the adventure film is almost always a male) begins as one of the victims of the initial and major crisis (e.g., the shipwreck), which starts the adventure early in the film. By virtue of his common sense, his knowledge of the goal to be achieved, his ability to organize — in short, by his ability to act decisively and in the group interest — he rises above his peers. Once the goal is achieved, the hero returns to his stance of ordinary man, a functional and average member of the larger society he has rejoined. He does not ride off into the sunset seeking new adventures and tests, but instead seeks refuge in the very society he has gone about recreating on a smaller scale.

In such adventure films, certain formula scenes seem almost obligatory. When we see war movies or disaster movies, we recognize fairly early on which characters will do what, which will die early in the film, which will selfishly betray or desert the group, which will survive. We know that there will be scenes that will individually test the characters. We know that the film will be structured so that it will begin in a normal context in which people take themselves and their social roles for granted. We know that the characters will be in a situation in which a microcosm can be collected on some realistic pretext: on an airplane, in the random unit of an army, on a pleasure ship or railroad train, on a floor of an office building. We also know that after the characters have been shown to us in their civilized guise, a catastrophe will occur that will shut them off from contact with the larger society to which they belong. From that point on in the film, we expect small tests of courage and ingenuity and endurance, and we may even have a fairly good idea of who will fail and who will succeed, and of when and how they will do so — simply by the casting of various familiar actors and actresses in several kinds of roles. [*Airplane!* (Jim Abrahams, 1980) successfully parodies the adventure genre in part by casting Lloyd Bridges and Robert Stack in the same type of roles they played in more serious versions of the airplane disaster film.] We know, because we are familiar with the formula, that in the end there will be survivors of the adventure and that they will rejoin the larger society at the close of the film.

The word formula, of course, denotes a repeated series of activities that result in a predictable end result. Certain formulas underlie specific genres — the natural catastrophe, which tests a minigroup of individuals is the stuff of the adventure film, and the variations on the theme of opposing groups in the American west (settlers vs. Indians, ranchers vs. sheepmen, cavalry vs. Indians, and so forth) is the stuff of the western. But it is also true that certain formulas tend to be the communal property of all narrative film — in fact, of all narrative. For example, boy-meets-girl, boy-loses-girl, boy-gets-girl is one such formula, and another is that of the falsely accused person who must clear his or her name. Part of the enjoyment of watching traditional narrative films is our familiarity with such basic formulas, our recognition of the basic outline which holds together the innumerable small, fresh details that make the film different from the previous one with the same basic outline. Thus, when we watch a genre film, a pleasurable tension is created between the expected and predictable and familiar elements of formula and the unexpected variations of the specific film story we are watching.

CONVENTION

Whereas a formula is an entire structure or series of actions that results in a predictable and familiar end, a convention is a small, relatively separate unit of action in genre films. Conventions are the specific ways in which the formula plot (who did what, when and where, to whom) is translated into visualized action in a particular genre. The showdown gunfight between the protagonist and antagonist in the western, or the love duet between the boy and girl in the musical, are examples of such conventions. These conventional actions recur from film to film, sometimes even in remarkably similar detail.

Most westerns, for example, have a showdown gunfight between the protagonist and antagonist, and these fights are pretty much alike from film to film. The reluctant hero appears in the street, finally provoked to a showdown by the villain. The townspeople scatter and hide. There will be some interchange of terse dialogue, a challenge and acceptance of sorts. The villain must make the first move for his holstered revolver, but — like lightning — the hero draws faster and shoots down the villain.

Besides the gist of content of the convention — the chief thing that happens — there is also the way in which the content is treated, that is, the way in which the camera photographs it and the editor edits it. These, too, become familiar and predictable. Conventionally, in that shoot-out, there will be clear, sunny weather so that long shadows can dramatically enhance the action. There will seldom be any wind. A long shot of the street, usually from a high angle looking down, will give the viewer a clear idea of the spatial relationship between the two characters. This long shot will usually be followed by a series of cuts alternating between each of the men in medium shot and close-up, and these may be followed with a long shot of the townspeople scattering, and a few close-ups of eyes peering from behind windows. Then the cutting of close-ups between the two men will accelerate until the final close-ups show the faces of each, the hands reaching for the hips, the guns being drawn. Then there will usually be a long shot of the villain being struck by the fatal bullet and his fall to the ground. This is customarily followed by a high-angle long shot again revealing the town and letting the viewer see the townspeople and possibly the heroine rejoin the lone hero on the street. Variations, of course, are probable; the street may be larger or smaller, there may be fewer or more witnesses to the showdown, there may or may not be a heroine, there may be shots inserted of the villain's henchman on a hotel roof waiting to gun down the hero before he can fire at the villain. Still, the basic convention in both content and form is clearly recognizable and satisfyingly familiar. This convention is almost never violated except purposely, for example, when a filmmaker parodies the genre or makes a consciously antigenre film, which attempts to subvert our expectations. Otherwise, certain aspects of the gunfight are always maintained: the hero never draws first, he never shoots his opponent from ambush, and he always triumphs in the end.

Although we are perhaps most familiar with the conventions of westerns, we recognize conventions in other genres, too (Figure 5-5). In the gangster film, the death of the protagonist usually shows him cornered, caught in some kind of trap and, unlike the ending of a western, there is no gun duel, no stylized interplay between protagonist and antagonist. Instead, the gangster is surrounded and gunned down. We are also familiar with the convention in a war movie in which the soldier gives his watch or some personal object to his girlfriend, wife, or buddy to hold for him. We know as clearly as if it were spelled out in block letters that that soldier is never going to come back. All of these are conventions of content. But, as in the western, there are stylistic or formal conventions in other genres too. In science fiction films which feature giant mutations threatening giant cities, we expect alternating close-ups of people and creatures and then long shots in which the creature and an identifiable urban landscape are together. And in the musical, we have come to accept lovers singing to each other, cheek pressed against cheek and faces directed out toward the film audience. We tend to be more aware of plot conventions than of formal conven-

5-5 A convention often found in the musical genre is that the lead couple falls in love. Here Polly (Ruby Keeler) has fallen in love with Brad (Dick Powell), a songwriter who lives across the court, in *Gold Diggers of 1933* (Mervyn Le Roy, 1933).

tions, but both are crucial to the genre film and to the pleasure we derive from watching variations on their familiarity.

ICONOGRAPHY

> In *Little Caesar* (1930) a police lieutenant and two of his men visit a night-club run by gangsters. All three wear large hats and heavy coats, are grim and sardonic and stand in triangular formation, the lieutenant at the front, his two men flanking him in the rear. The audience knows immediately what to expect of them by their physical attributes, their dress and deportment. It knows, too, by the disposition of the figures, which is dominant, which subordinate. . . . These examples indicate the continuity over several decades of patterns of visual imagery, or recurrent objects and figures in dynamic relationship. These repeated patterns might be called the iconography of the genre, for they set it off visually from other types of film and are the means whereby primary definitions are made.
> Colin McArthur[2]

An even smaller unit of the genre film is the icon, from a Greek word meaning "image," "likeness." Whereas formula refers to an entire structure or series of actions upon which an entire film is based (the essential plot and characters), and convention refers to a unit of action or episode within a formula that recurs from film to film, the film icon is a yet smaller element of the genre film. Certain costumes (cowboy clothes,

space suits), certain objects (cigarette holders, pistols), certain landscapes (foggy moors, wide-open prairies), and certain performers (John
Wayne, Sylvester Stallone) instantly signify — simply by their presence — elements of plot that have not yet occurred, complete psyches
and motivations in characters, and complex thematic associations regarding the content of the genre and with the past cinematic experience of the viewer.

An icon gets its meaning from its repeated use in many films. The
round glass paperweight in *Citizen Kane* (1941), for example, though
important in that film, is not an icon, because paperweights have not
accumulated, in film after film, any special meaning. Similarly, the tune
whistled by the child murderer in *M* (Fritz Lang, 1931) has no meaning
outside of its appearance in that specific film. (These items are often
called *motifs*.) The sound of a creaking door, on the other hand, tends to
be iconic, conveying menace, dread, potential horror; it evokes all those
moments of terror and all those dreaded figures from past horror films
the viewer has seen. The same is true of a horse neighing or a dog
howling in a horror film; within the context of the genre those sounds
have come to signal impending danger, the presence of some other-
worldly menace sensed by animals but not by humans. (In *Young Frankenstein*, 1974 — one of the funnier genre allusions uses neighing horses
whenever a particularly evil housekeeper's name is mentioned, even
though the animals are not near enough to such conversations to over-
hear them.) The sound of a machine gun with its rapid-fire rat-a-tat and
its specific physical appearance in a gangster film signifies not only itself
in the one particular film, but also signifies the crudeness of gangsters.

Icons in the western genre, the gangster film, the traditional horror
film derive many of their meanings from extrafilmic sources such as
history and literature, as well as from film tradition itself. But as visual
imagery, the icons take on added significance, emotional weight, and
power, and come to communicate enormous amounts of narrative information to the audience. Consider, for example, the meaning generated by the handgun in the western. The Colt Peacemaker is the most
popular handgun used in the western film — and part of its cinematic
appeal may have to do with the fact that the shape of the Peacemaker is
more graceful than those of some of the other handguns of the period.
Since the western hero is often a graceful figure concerned with self-
defining style (the proper patterns of ritual behavior), it is appropriate
that his weapon be graceful and stylish too. The handgun, thus, functions in the western not only as a firearm, but also as a visual means
whereby the filmmaker communicates information about character to
the viewer. Similarly, derringers and other small concealable weapons

have accumulated cinematic associations that make them icons signifying deception, rascality, cowardice, and effeteness.

While the iconic significance of objects in genre films is often easily discernible because we notice *things* in movies, the more pervasive yet less noticed background can also function iconically. We expect a certain physical topography in the western (even if it is actually filmed in Spain or Italy), and that landscape conveys more than its physical self; it communicates a way of life with particular hardships, particular demands, it communicates certain unplayed dramas that have taken place in its arena in other movies or will take place in the movie being viewed and in future movies (the ambush in the box canyon, the Indians appearing on the crest of a bluff, the stumbling descent of a horse through badlands). The city is more than a merely physical characteristic of the gangster film; it communicates from film to film a nightmare landscape, a cold, unnatural world, a world full of hiding places where devious transactions can take place in the shadows.

Finally, certain performers are iconic. They communicate not only themselves as recognizable stars, or as the characters they play in the specific film, but they also communicate a kind of character, a whole set of moral values, from film to film simply by their physical appearance in these films. John Wayne, for example, is an actor who is an icon. He need not have very many lines of dialogue in any given western movie for the viewer to understand, to know almost intimately, who and what the character is, what he believes in and how he will act in a given situation. Because Wayne played in so many westerns, becoming a star in John Ford's *Stagecoach* (1939) as a relatively young man and showing his age most poignantly as the cowboy hero dying of cancer in Don Siegel's *The Shootist* (1976), he accumulated so many lines of dialogue and so many repeated actions performed in similar situations that when he appears on the screen in a western he signifies a whole set of ethics, a predictable range of behavior, a wonderfully familiar sense of a known character (Figure 5-6). Harrison Ford is a contemporary equivalent playing the worldly cynic with a heart of gold in all of his films from *Star Wars* to *Raiders of the Lost Ark*.

Types of Genre Narrative

One gangster film follows another as one musical or one western follows another. But this rigidity is not necessarily opposed to the requirements of art. There have been very successful types of art in the past which developed such specific and detailed conventions as almost to make individual examples of the type interchangeable. . . . One goes to any individual example of the type with very definite expectations, and original-

5-6 Many performers have become icons, their mere presence in a film signifying more than just an actor playing a character. John Wayne played the same Westerner from John Ford's *Stagecoach* (1939) to Don Siegel's *The Shootist* (1976), to the extent that the audience knows from the moment he walks onto the screen what he represents morally and dramatically. This image from Howard Hawks's *Red River* (1948) includes Walter Brennan, who turned up time and again as a foil to the Wayne figure.

ity is to be welcomed only in the degree that it intensifies the expected experience without fundamentally altering it.
Robert Warshow[3]

There are two major types of genre films, **comedy** and **melodrama. Tragedy,** in contemporary films, tends to appear in nonformula films rather than in genre films — although one might possibly argue that certain gangster films and some of the family melodramas in which the protagonist ends badly are both tragic *and* genre films. Undoubtedly, elements of the tragic are present in such films, but when the genre film draws to its conclusion, the audience has usually transferred its allegiance to society's notions of order, which dictate the elimination or punishment of those individuals who violate the norm, such as gangsters and women who seek independence and fulfillment outside the domestic sphere. Tragedy is alien to the ends of genre films, for tragedy demands that the easy resolution of genre films be abandoned. The genre film, by resolving its conflicts easily, does not challenge the audience's values, as does tragedy. It is this easy resolution in genre films that pleases and soothes the viewer.

5-7 Slapstick comedies contain certain conventions — the car chase, the pie fight, the dignified being undone. Mack Sennett's Keystone Kops films used such recognizable material. Physical reaction and pursuit will follow this phone call.

GENRE COMEDIES

There are, of course, many kinds of comedy in film. There is physical comedy and there is verbal comedy and there is a combination of both; there are comedies that are harshly satiric, and there are comedies that are mild and gentle. There are comedies that are singular films, funny or satiric or bizarre but unique, unlike other comedies. And there are comedies that seem like familiar friends, which look and sound and feel like films we have seen before and will see again. These last films are genre comedies, and like all generic forms they share certain similarities of structure and content; their **formula plots** are recognizable, and so are their conventions and icons.

Slapstick Comedy

The earliest comic genre (and perhaps the earliest genre of any kind of film) is slapstick comedy, a comedy based on physical activity (especially assaults) and accelerating momentum (especially chases). The silent motion picture derived this action-oriented comedy from burlesque, vaudeville, and music hall entertainment and brought it to a new height, especially with the slapstick comedies produced by Mack Sennett and the Keystone Studio (Figure 5-7).

Rational continuity and narrative continuity are *not* part of the formula of slapstick comedy. Indeed, the very lack of such coherence of logic and plot is part of the slapstick formula. Nor is there always the continuity provided by a single protagonist. A single character is usually the center of interest in most other genres, but as slapstick events slip from one to another, the events' initiators and victims change too. Types (rather than characters) move through the world, doing battle with whatever obstacles present themselves. These obstacles are either inanimate objects — food that will not stay on the plate, pianos that have to be moved through small spaces, doors that will not open or swing back and forth inopportunely, cars that break down or break apart — or people who stand for the pressures of society — policemen, headwaiters, rich, and/or pompous social figures. The episodic, almost musically connected, nature of slapstick comedy also determines that those obstacles be varied, and that the desired goal be relatively unimportant. Sometimes, in fact, the goal is actually forgotten. We may forget, for example, that the protagonist is on the way to a new job because we are taken up with the comic adventures (an escape from a dog, an encounter with a drunk) that take place on the way.

The formula resides primarily in activity, in the commotion resulting from attempts to overcome obstacles and obtain goals, whether the film is an early slapstick silent like one of Sennett's Keystone Kops shorts or his *Tillie's Punctured Romance* (1914) or a more modern attempt at slapstick such as *National Lampoon's Animal House* (John Landis, 1978), *Police Academy* (Hugh Wilson, 1984), or parts of *The Gods Must Be Crazy* (Jamie Uys, 1984). Motion and its acceleration through performance, camera manipulation, and editing are the key characteristics of classic slapstick comedy — and the resolution of the nonplot occurs most usually through exhaustion. The car/train/motorcycle chase finally involves the entire city, including the fire department and all of the dogs that have escaped from the pound; the pie fight moves from the confines of a restaurant or bakery into the street and the world, but eventually the car collapses, and the pies give out.

The basic formula, thus, of slapstick comedy is based on an episodic structure in which highly undifferentiated character types (when one cop is outwitted, another appears) struggle with one another in situations that emphasize physical movement and accelerating momentum (the food fight in *Animal House* is a good example), and the conventions of the genre can be identified by such units of action as the car chase, the pie fight, the dignified being undone, and also by such formal devices as fast motion and the long shot (the latter crucial as a convention of slapstick because it shows crazy actions expanding spatially as far as they can go) (Figure 5-8).

5-8 Slapstick comedy continues to be a prime form for sound films. *National Lampoon's Animal House* (John Landis, 1978) began a new cycle in which physical movement and accelerating momentum provide the bulk of the humor through the standard conventions of the genre: the car chase, the food fight, and the dignified being undone.

Romantic Comedy

Romantic comedy arises from the literary tradition called *new comedy*, a form (developed in ancient Greece and Rome) with a relatively rigid structure: a male and female (naive ingenues) fall in love and must overcome various obstacles (usually at least one parent objects) so that they can be united in marriage. In the ancient plays, most often, the couple is helped by someone who is worldly, especially a wily slave or adviser. Within the formula, certain conventions arise that play upon various sorts of reversals: mistakes of identity, of timing trysts and meetings, of male/female dress. A modern film example of the classic new comedy (which also happens to be a musical), first written for the theater and then adapted to the screen, is *A Funny Thing Happened on the Way to the Forum* (Richard Lester, 1966).

Romantic film comedy can only rarely, of course, include wily slaves or even feuding families, but in its classic form it nevertheless retains more than merely the spirit of new comedy. Feuding families are sometimes turned into family obstacles of quite another sort: one of the lovers (or both) is married, *Irreconcilable Differences* (Charles Shyer, 1984), or the couple is already married and has created its own obstacles based on sexual misunderstandings, as in *Wife vs. Secretary* (Clarence Brown, 1936), or the couple is recently divorced and one of the partners is about to remarry as in *The Philadelphia Story* (George Cukor, 1940) or *His Girl Friday* (Howard Hawks, 1940). Often the wily slave has been transformed into an urban domestic servant in the person of a butler or a maid or has become a shrewd, wisecracking neighbor (either a bachelor or a spinster who keeps discussing his or her bad luck with the opposite sex) or one member of an older and happily married couple.

A more far-reaching change in formula does away with the wily slave or adviser completely and allows one of the lovers to serve the dual function of naive ingenue in matters of love and wise and shrewd mentor in matters of life. Thus, one of the partners is usually more aggressive and more influential in effecting the desired outcome of new comedy — the marriage. Sometimes this role falls to the male; in *It Happened One Night* (Frank Capra, 1934), Clark Gable's newspaperman is the romantic protagonist who falls in love with Claudette Colbert's willful socialite, but he is also the shrewd educator whose knowledge of the world outstrips that of his romantic interest, and so he is able to teach her a thing or two and bring about their eventual union. Usually, however, it is the female romantic protagonist who performs the function of the wily slave, cleverly coping with the various obstacles placed in the couple's way (very often the obstinacy of the male) and bringing about the desired marriage. In *Bringing Up Baby* (Howard Hawks, 1938), for example, although Katharine Hepburn plays a scatterbrained ingenue who seems to be constantly getting herself and others into hopeless trouble, she is really an artful young woman going about getting her man and educating her naive paleontologist (played by Cary Grant) to an acceptance of the chaos inherent in life and to an acceptance of his love for her (Figure 5-9). In *Mr. Smith Goes to Washington* (Frank Capra, 1939), *The Lady Eve* (Preston Sturges, 1941), and *Ball of Fire* (Howard Hawks, 1941), too, it is the woman who is the aggressor and who, even when the male protagonist is in love with her and needs no persuasion, educates the male to the realities of life. It seems hardly an accident that the male protagonists in these films are idealists or are isolated by their single-minded zeal and their professions (paleontologist, small-town senator, rich snake enthusiast, and professor working on an encyclopedia) — and that the female protagonists are women whose occupations have taken them into the real world: the socialite who deals with people rather than with dinosaur bones, the Washington secretary who

5-9 In Howard Hawks's *Bringing Up Baby* (1938), Cary Grant and Katharine Hepburn played the "new comedy" roles of the naive ingenue and the wily slave. Though the wily slave is sometimes a male, often (as in this film) that part is given to the female. Katharine Hepburn appears to be a daffy, scatterbrained young socialite, but in fact she is a shrewd young woman overcoming all obstacles in her pursuit of her man.

knows the ropes, the card-sharp con artist, and the stripper. Perhaps one of the chief pleasures of the romantic film genre (and one that explains its appeals to women viewers *beyond* the supposed satisfactions to be found in the marriage or reunion at the end) is that it is a form in which it is safe for the female protagonist to wield power and to pursue goals usually open in genre films only to male characters. Because the desired end of romantic film comedy is marriage and the creation of a family within an accepted social structure, the female aggressor can do no wrong, cannot be, perhaps, too strong or too threatening; further,

5-10 The convention that a romantic comedy end with a reconciliation or a marriage to display the theme that love conquers all obstacles is carried to an extreme in *Splash* (Ron Howard, 1984) when the male protagonist, having fallen in love with a mermaid, magically is transformed into a merman in order to follow her back to the depths of the ocean where it is presumed they will live happily ever after.

the comedy and comic inventions of the romantic film comedy make it a decidedly closed film form, safe because it is distinctly separate from real life.

The romantic comedy usually will end with a reconciliation or a wedding — either on-screen or off (after the credits have ended). In *Splash!* (Ron Howard, 1984), there is a transformation instead of a wedding, as the human protagonist finds that love has given him gills so he can swim off with his mermaid forever (Figure 5-10). In all the films, whether the hero and heroine are ingenues or a married couple, an education will take place, obstacles will be overcome, and the couple will be united or reunited to affirm marriage, home, and the continuation of an institution crucial to society as we know it. Within the basic formula, many conventions signal the genre: the gallery of male suitors who surround the female, who are patently inappropriate mates, and who are made to seem asexual or ridiculously vain; the predatory female who stalks the protagonist but who loses out to the domestic potential and intent of the heroine; misunderstandings involving identity, intent, marital status; role reversals, fairly often including female impersonation when the male is caught in a situation in which he must don female clothing. Such sexual role reversal is much more pointed and political — addressing feminist issues — in two more recent versions of this genre,

Victor/Victoria (Blake Edwards, 1982) and *Tootsie* (Sydney Pollack, 1982) where the motivation for impersonation is economic. The protagonists find the only way they can get jobs is by masquerading as the opposite gender. These are still romantic comedies, however, since the impersonations do lead to romantic misunderstandings. The formal conventions of the genre include fast pacing: not only frenetic action, but also swift dialogue between hero and heroine, indicating their appropriateness for each other; their ability to match each other verbally or expressively indicates sexual and psychological compatibility. The conventional settings for the romantic comedy are interiors or obviously artificial exteriors, confirming the artificiality of the world of romantic comedy and enhancing its unthreatening aspects.

Musical Comedy

Although not every comedy with music is a musical comedy, musical comedies seem readily indentifiable as a genre. In a musical comedy, most characters sing or dance, and those who do not, or who do so badly, are suspect morally, ethically, emotionally. In *Singin' in the Rain* (Gene Kelly and Stanley Donen, 1952), Lina, the silent movie star, has a horrible voice, which, with the advent of sound, must be dubbed by the newcomer Kathy. Lina's impossible voice is important to the plot, but it is also crucial thematically, a key to the genre as a whole, which sees good and bad characters in terms of their ability to entertain. Many films, of course, use a great deal of music either in the background or in the foreground, but if the music in these films does not serve to tell us *about* the characters, the films are usually not considered musicals.

The musical comedy is a kind of romantic comedy, and it is interesting to note that whereas the nonmusical romantic comedy has tended to replace one of the two naive ingenues of new comedy with a shrewder, more engaging protagonist, the musical comedy has often kept up the tradition of bringing two equally naive ingenues together. What a naive young couple might lack in audience appeal, however, can be supplied by music, dance, and spectacular sets. Thus, it is not important that Ruby Keeler and Dick Powell are fairly dull and saccharine and overly familiar and predictable in such films as *42nd Street* (Lloyd Bacon, 1933) and *Dames* (Ray Enright, 1934), or that Judy Garland and Mickey Rooney almost browbeat the viewer with their youthful enthusiasm in Busby Berkeley's *Babes in Arms* (1939) and *Babes on Broadway* (1941). And because of the return to the new comedy tradition of the naive romantic pair, often there is a return to a contemporary version of the wily slave or adviser: the character Donald O'Connor plays in *Singin' in the Rain* or the father figures in the Mickey Rooney–Judy Garland movies, or Eric Blore in the Astaire films.

The musical, of course, as a romantic comedy may also use the more contemporary treatment of the hero and heroine in which either one or both are knowledgeable rather than naive. In some ways, the Fred Astaire–Ginger Rogers musicals are equivalent to the romantic comedy in which two rather sophisticated married people are parted through a misunderstanding revolving around some sexual/marital matter and are finally reunited with a true knowledge of the depth of their relationship. Although in these musicals the couple begin the film as separate entities, in their sophistication and self-confidence they are much like the married couple in the nonmusical romantic comedy. Through dance rather than snappy repartee their emotional difficulties are resolved and their reconciliation realized. Their difficulties come from similar sexual/marital misunderstandings and involve mistaken identities and motives; one need only examine, for example, *The Gay Divorcé* (Mark Sandrich, 1934) and *Top Hat* (Mark Sandrich, 1935).

One of the major distinctive formulas of the musical comedy film is the backstage musical or show business plot. From the early 1930s through the 1950s, the putting on of a show was equivalent to the courtship of the film's central characters. The show's problems were clearly related to the conflicts between the romantic protagonists, and the final successful opening night, including the audience's applauding at the finished production, was equivalent to the romantic union of the protagonists. Calling for production numbers in the finished show, the show business plot in *Dames* allows the songwriter hero and the aspiring actress heroine to join together — through the show itself — to convince the disapproving and ridiculously prudish uncle that show business and their romance are really good clean fun. In *The Band Wagon* (Vincente Minnelli, 1953), the romantic difficulties between the characters played by Fred Astaire and Cyd Charisse are personal equivalents to the difficulties that jeopardize the show in which they both become involved. In *Singin' in the Rain*, the introduction of sound to the movie industry is paralleled by the introduction of Kathy (a singer as well as a dancer) into the life of silent screen idol, Don Lockwood; her emergence and replacement of Lina (the female star) is also the emergence of Don's emotional commitment — and the emergence of a new form of entertainment, the sound film. In recent years the backstage musical has been revived, but its look at show business is less naive than it once was. *All That Jazz* and *A Chorus Line* (Richard Attenborough, 1985) display some of the difficulties and hardships of theatrical life, rather than suggesting it is just good, clean fun.

Several other musical formulas also are variations of the new comedy and romantic comedy formula. One variation is the musical biography, represented by films like *Night and Day* (Michael Curtiz, 1946) and *Funny Girl* (William Wyler, 1968); in both, there is less interest in biographical accuracy or completeness than there is in the film's presentation of music. Another variation, popular in the thirties and forties, was the revue film, a sort of grab bag of musical numbers, vaudevillian turns, forays into opera and ballet, all brought together under the very loose rubric of a follies: *The Great Ziegfeld* (Robert Z. Leonard, 1936), *The Goldwyn Follies* (George Marshall, 1938), and *The Ziegfeld Follies* (Vincente Minnelli, 1946). Although the romantic comedy provides the basic formula for most film musicals, other genre formulas have occasionally been employed. Generally when the settings, formulas, and character types from noncomic genres are added to a musical, they are treated comically. In the 1930s and 1940s Bing Crosby and Bob Hope made a series of road pictures, which were essentially musical parodies of the adventure genre: the spy thriller, the safari film, the swashbuckler. *Bugsy Malone* (Alan Parker, 1976), using preteens playing the conventional adult roles, is a comic musical gangster film and *The Rocky Horror Picture Show* (Jim Sherman, 1975) spoofs horror and science fiction films in songs, music, and dance.

As in all other film genres, conventions of both content and form can be found in the musical. One can point (for content) to the conventions of the audition, the discovery of new talent, the initial dislike between the two romantic protagonists, and the culminating production numbers. Among the conventions of form, one can point to the almost obligatory romantic love duet, rhythm song (which is more important for setting up momentum and pacing than it is for its emotional content), comic song (generally relegated to the leading supporting player or players), and so forth. But there are also certain formal conventions that viewers are less aware of: the way in which screen lovers sing to each other and to us so that the emotion and intimacy between the principals is maximized but artificial enough so as to include the audience, and the way in which the long shot and the long take are used so that we marvel at a dancer's endurance and defiance of gravity in what seems an unbroken space and time, and the way in which modern musicals have minimized the dancer and maximized the dance by creating motion through editing rather than through performance. Icons are relatively few in the musical compared to those in the horror film or the western, but the nightclub or the stage itself in a musical is iconic, as are the dressing room and various other objects and places associated with the theater. And certain objects, though not icons, are used iconically:

5-11 Because musicals are so expensive to produce, film musicals have been made from Broadway hits to insure an audience. *Cabaret* (Bob Fosse, 1972) was made from such a source. The Broadway *Cabaret*, however, was adapted from an earlier stage play, *I Am a Camera*, which had been made into a nonmusical film in 1955 and was itself based on a collection of Christopher Isherwood short stories.

certainly, when a dance number is about to begin, we in the audience *know* that the mop in the corner and the dummy on the couch will become part of the choreography.

The musical, once the most popular genre, has suffered the greatest decline. Musicals are extraordinarily expensive to produce compared to other film genres and it is almost a contradiction in terms to think of a B musical — although there were B westerns and B horror films and B gangster films. True, one can point to the handful of fairly inexpensively produced beach party pictures, but most musicals cost so much that filmmakers came to rely on the musical that had already proven itself financially on Broadway: *West Side Story* (Robert Wise, 1961), *The Sound of Music* (Robert Wise, 1965), *Hello, Dolly!* (Gene Kelly, 1969), *Fiddler on the Roof* (Norman Jewison, 1971), *Cabaret* (Bob Fosse, 1972), *Hair* (Milos Forman, 1979), *A Chorus Line* (Richard Attenborough, 1985). These musical films have become classics, but in general their conventions and variations on formula are those of the musical theater rather than those of the musical film (Figure 5-11).

5-12 Musical comedies take many forms. In the past it was traditional to create a fantasy world in which the character sang and danced and found "true" love. Sets frequently were clearly made of plaster and paint, as in the "Kissing Rock" number from Frank Borzage's *Flirtation Walk* (1934). Contemporary musicals have not only adopted more realistic settings (doing much location shooting), but as in *Hair* (Milos Forman, 1979), the story line has come to grips with more serious human problems, such as the relationship between the generations over lifestyles and the Viet Nam war.

Musical film today greatly differs from what it used to be. Whereas once all musical films could be comfortably placed under the rubric of genre comedy, today there are musical melodramas, including such films as *Saturday Night Fever* (John Badham, 1977), *Fame* (Alan Parker, 1980), and *Flashdance* (Adrian Lyne, 1983). Barbra Streisand's *Yentl* (1983) seriously depicts the problems of a Jewish woman of the nineteenth century who has to pretend to be a boy so she can get an education. *Pink Floyd-The Wall* (Alan Parker, 1982) probes a rock star's mental breakdown. Contemporary musicals do not always end in weddings; often, they end in death. The final sequence of *All That Jazz* depicts the protagonist's demise. Although filled with song and dance, these musicals also depict a narrative world constructed within the conventions of realism rather than according to the fantastic world of earlier musicals (Figure 5-12). Indeed, *Pennies From Heaven* (Herbert Ross, 1981), takes as its very subject matter the gap between the ugliness and disappointments of the mundane world and the beauty and grace of the musical's world where all desire is fulfilled. The psyche of character is explored, motivations seem realistic, and the obstacles the protagonists must overcome are often nearly insurmountable.

Nevertheless, some modern musicals simply celebrate contemporary music. Martin Scorsese filmed the last concert of The Band in *The Last Waltz* (1978), Jonathan Demme featured the Talking Heads in *Stop Making Sense* (1984), and Michael Apted showcased Sting in *Bring on the Night* (1985). Even when a plot of some sort is used — the sequences dramatizing the life of Prince in *Purple Rain* (Albert Magnoli, 1984) — the primary emphasis in these concert films is on the performance of the music.

GENRE MELODRAMAS

In a comedy, the protagonist must overcome obstacles of one sort or another in order to achieve success, a success the audience is certain will be achieved. One way to allow the audience to relax and pleasurably feign suspense is to make certain that the obstacles facing the protagonist are never taken seriously by the film itself — and so are not taken seriously by the viewer. The comic protagonist's problem or conflict is never actually a matter of life and death — although on occasion it may pretend to be. For example, the audience *knows* that Harold Lloyd in *Safety Last* (1923) will not fall to his death while climbing up the side of the skyscraper, no matter how close he comes to losing his grip, not only because it is Harold Lloyd climbing the building, but also because the film has been structured in accordance with comic conventions. Even if he slips and appears to fall out of one shot, in the next he will be saved by his suspenders or a convenient scaffold or an awning. The audience knows this because it is a convention of comedy that real death cannot exist in the comic world. Thus the suspense generated by Lloyd, Chaplin, or Keaton's antics is only a feigned suspense. In effect the exaggerated obstacles in comedy, and the exaggerated solutions, distance the viewer from the plight of the comic protagonist. The activities are seen as outside ordinary experience. For instance, when a person loses his job in a comic film, he is often literally kicked out of the office; he will then not only regain his job, but be elevated to an executive position by producing some outlandish publicity stunt that will include wild animals or a stunt plane or a trip in a barrel over Niagara Falls.

Even minor breaches of etiquette are treated with exaggeration. The average viewer is likely to feel self-conscious and to act awkwardly in certain tense real-life social situations, but is not likely to stumble and fall down several times, to douse herself or himself with liquids, or cover herself or himself with spilled food as does the male protagonist in *The Lady Eve*. The exaggeration distances us from the comic hero's *feelings* and makes us look instead at the funny elements of the action itself. We laugh because the situation we are watching is removed from reality.

In melodrama, however, even though we know that the protagonist will triumph in the end or that a satisfactory solution will be found to the central conflict, we also know that the dangers which threaten the protagonist are life-and-death matters, problems which matter to the audience as well as to the protagonist. Unlike genre comedies, genre melodramas construct the illusion of real mental and physical pain, suffering, and death: characters dodge bullets, not custard pies. In fact, it is because of this sense of the seriousness of physical danger that the hero's eventual triumph or failure matters. Nevertheless, one must be aware that this sense of seriousness is as constructed as the sense of lightheartedness is in comedies. It is a primary convention of the genre melodrama.

It is possible to consider all melodramatic film genres as based on a single structure — although that structure can accommodate a wide range of variation. Much as we can place the romantic film comedy in the tradition of new comedy, we can place the genre melodrama within the context of the romance in medieval literature. The romance (not to be thought of merely as a love story) follows a basic pattern: a society is found to be in grave trouble and a hero must be located who has great and special skills; with few exceptions traditionally male, he is charged with the task of saving the society by overcoming obstacles and solving problems, and he does so in a series of encounters that often culminate in one big struggle, at which point the society is returned to a state of harmony. Though we can clearly distinguish separate types of genre melodrama (the adventure film, the western, the horror film, the crime film), this basic romance formula can be found in nearly all of them. The few exceptions (such as the gangster film and family melodramas) in which the protagonists subvert the formula are still based on the romance formula, though perversely as in a mirror image. Although each of the major genre melodramas contains plot formulas, conventions, and icons, which distinguish it from another, the primary struggle of a hero who embodies good against the forces of evil pervades nearly all the melodramatic genres. The hero's eventual triumph ends not only in personal glory, but also in the resolution of social unrest (Figure 5-13). The harmony and rest at the end of the romance are common to all classic genre melodramas, including films as different as the western

5-13 One of the major plots found in the swashbuckler genre concerns the restoration of a proper and just authority to the throne. After being imprisoned unjustly, Errol Flynn escapes and turns pirate in *Captain Blood* (Michael Curtiz, 1935). Eventually he uses his powers to unseat the tyrannical governor of the island where he was held captive.

Shane (1953) and *Star Wars* (1977), a science fiction film. In fact, *Star Wars* is truly classic in its adherence to the romance formula. The young Luke Skywalker is rather like the young King Arthur (even developing special skill with a futuristic version of Excalibur). Aided by a wise and humane magician akin to Merlin, Luke's struggle against Darth Vader and the forces of evil is not only personal but also social; the destruction of the Death Star is crucial to the salvation of the film's world. *Star Wars*, in fact, is so attuned to the tradition of the classical romance that it simultaneously can absorb the characteristics of a number of genres: the adventure film, the science fiction film, the western, and the war film. Although the generic inclusiveness of *Star Wars* is, perhaps, atypical, it should be stressed that melodramas often overlap several genres. Although specific icons and conventions within the melodramatic formulae separate groups of films from each other, an overriding formula links them and, on occasion, allows us to consider a specific film as representative of more than one kind of melodrama.

Adventure Films

The adventure film is a particularly broad and all inclusive genre. It can, however, be broken down into smaller groupings such as the swash-buckler, the war movie, the safari film — and a group that might be called *survival stories,* including the disaster films. All of these subgenres have more in common than one might at first think. The distinctions are chiefly matters of their particular topographies, recurrent objects, specif-ic modes of costume, in short, their iconography. But beneath the abundant surface differences there are only two major variations within the adventure genre. One focuses on a relatively solitary hero, the swashbuckler, and the other focuses on a hero interacting with a microcosmic group, for example, a platoon in the war movie or a boat-load of castaways in the survival film (Figure 5-14).

In the swashbuckler, the hero — at heart a good citizen and a mem-ber of society, and in no way an anarchist — has been turned into an outlaw because the society in which he lives has been corrupted from within: a tyrannical regent has bent law and order to his own selfish ends in Michael Curtiz's *Captain Blood* (1935) and *The Adventures of Robin Hood* (1938), or some social injustice puts the hero in an adversary position to the prevailing social order as in *Scaramouche* (George Sidney, 1952) and in the three sound versions of *The Prisoner of Zenda* (John Cromwell, 1937, Richard Thorpe, 1952, and Richard Quine, 1979). The hero's role (even as he may initially reject it) is to restore order to society, not to destroy it. Sometimes this restoration of order means actually restoring an absent (or kidnapped) ruler to the throne as in both *Robin Hood* and *Star Wars.* Sometimes it means the hero must remind the society through his actions that it is time to reexamine its institutions and the people who have become responsible for them.

One of the most interesting conventions of the classic swashbuckler (and one that separates it from the other major adventure film variant) is that the hero is aristocratic. Although there are, of course, exceptions to this convention, it is recurrent enough to deserve consideration. In these costume dramas, the hero is at first set apart from the masses, either by virtue of his high birth or his profession. After facing evidence of the injustice of his society, he chooses to separate himself from alliance with the ruling order, and allies himself with the poor and downtrodden. This occurs not only in a classic film like *Scaramouche* but also in a much more contemporary and morally problematic film like *Rambo: First Blood Part II* (George P. Cosmatos, 1985). The hero dramatically moves from aristocracy to democracy (although he is never so democratic as to lose his flamboyant individuality or special skills). Thus, Robin Hood merges with his band of merry men and stresses egalitarianism. Scaramouche becomes an actor, a member of a profession that absorbs all talent

5-14 Though the adventure film is a broad genre, it can be broken into smaller, more clearly defined units. *The Adventures of Robin Hood* (Michael Curtiz, 1938), starring Errol Flynn, is a classic swashbuckler — a subgenre comprising sword fighting and elaborate costumes. The war film is another obvious subgrouping. The scene above of men in combat, though taken from *Rambo: First Blood Part II* (George P. Cosmatos, 1985), could have appeared in any number of other war films.

equally and allows passage through all sectors of society. Captain Blood becomes a common prisoner aboard a slave ship and mixes with men he might not otherwise ever have come to know.

A related convention in the swashbuckler affects the heroine. She is generally aristocratic, initially repelled by the crudeness of the disguised hero, and unable to respond to his democratic approach. By the end of the film she has come to realize that moral value and social value are represented by spirit and intent and action rather than by the superficial trappings of title, wealth, clothing, and manners (conventional manners, that is — for the swashbuckling hero never lacks manners or style). Once the heroine has realized this and made a commitment to the hero in his democratic guise, he in turn is able to reveal himself and to reenter the aristocracy. Together, it is implied, the couple will recreate a better society, one that retains all the best of the old rules and maintains the tried and true status quo (there are no real revolutions in genre films), but one that also will make sure those old rules are being administered justly and benevolently.

The classic swashbuckler is especially interesting in its emphasis on the individual hero. In this it adheres to the romance formula. It shares, too, certain elements with new comedy and with musical comedy, because it usually ends with a wedding and the hero is defined as much by his physical expressiveness as he is by his good deeds. It is no accident that some of the directors who were particularly productive in making Hollywood musicals were also productive in making swashbucklers — and it is useful to see dance numbers and sword fights as film sequences similar in their function and structure. George Sidney, for example, directed musicals like *Anchors Aweigh* (1945), *Showboat* (1951), and *Kiss Me Kate* (1953) — and swashbucklers like *The Three Musketeers* (1948), *Scaramouche* (1952), and *Young Bess* (1953). And Vincente Minnelli, the director responsible for many of Hollywood's best musicals, directed the musical swashbuckler *The Pirate* (1948). Indeed, in *Singin' in the Rain*, Gene Kelly plays both a song-and-dance man and a swashbuckling hero; the relationship between the two roles is made comically evident when the film-within-the-film Kelly is making, changes its title from "The Dueling Cavalier" to "The Dancing Cavalier." What links dancing and swordplay is not mere choreography; as physical activities they also have in common their emphasis on style. The dancer in the musical and the swashbuckler in the adventure film share a self-consciousness of their own artistry, and the viewer tends to judge their moral character on the basis of how well they physically perform.

Unlike the hero in most other adventure films (who takes himself and his function quite seriously), the classic swashbuckling hero, like the hero of a comedy, will often abstract himself from his actions and situation so he can evaluate or regard events ironically. Because he is often in disguise, in essence he is a performer giving a performance, partly for his own entertainment. Richard Lester's remake of *The Three Musketeers* (1974) can be viewed as a spoof of George Sidney's version with Gene Kelly — and yet Sidney's film and its characters are as self-conscious and purposefully amusing as Lester's. Gene Kelly's d'Artagnan, for example, in the middle of a deadly serious duel will turn a particularly acrobatic somersault and land neatly in a stance ready to parry another thrust; it is done not only for the viewer's amusement but also for the character's. Thus, personal style and self-consciousness are as characteristic of the swashbuckling hero as swords, plumed hats, sailing ships, and caskets of jewels are characteristic icons of this subgenre.

Contemporary versions of the swashbuckler like *Raiders of the Lost Ark* (Steven Spielberg, 1981) have tended to transform or blur the moral distinctions made obvious in earlier examples. Indiana Jones claims to be in pursuit of archeological treasures for the museum, for science, for the community of scholars — presumably making him more moral than his arch rival Bellocq who will sell to the highest bidder. Throughout the action of the film, however, Jones seems merely obsessed with winning the prize just as much as Bellocq is. There seems to be no ulterior purpose. In the end, of course, the ark is secured, even if inadvertantly, for the good side. The United States has the power of the ark behind it and Hitler does not: the Allies go on to win the war, the disordered world is brought back to order. But the audience is never quite sure of the hero's true motives as we are of a Robin Hood, for example, who announces in a conventional speech early on in the movie that he has dedicated himself, though an outlaw, to the restoration of the rightful ruler to the throne. Indiana Jones remains a question mark. Is he merely out for himself? Is he working for the good of society? The role of women in the modern swashbuckler is also more ambiguous. Since the modern hero no longer has to represent the triumph of the democratic spirit, the heroine is not required to represent the aristocratic woman who comes to her senses. And yet, Marion, in *Raiders,* like a shadowy version of earlier heroines, changes from an imperious, fiesty, independent woman enraged by the hero's callous treatment of her, to a limp, soft, clinging vine who needs rescuing. It is unclear at the end of the film whether this is a permanent condition for her or not: wedding bells for the happy couple are not ringing. In *Romancing the Stone* (Robert Zemeckis, 1984), the woman writer of fantasy adventures eventually discovers that she can actually be adventurous in real life. And yet, she seems to need the adventure hero to complete her life. Thus, it is unclear whether, in this film, as in the traditional adventure film, she is the prize for the male hero's success, or whether she has earned him through her conquest of her own fears.

A second variant of the adventure film can be called the survival film; its most obvious forms are the war movie and the disaster film. Generally grimmer than the swashbuckler, perhaps because it usually is more contemporary and less costumed and thus is less distant from the audience, the survival film nevertheless shares the basic characteristics of the adventure film and is strongly linked with the romance formula. The survival film's major emphases, like the romance's, are on the heroic triumph over obstacles which threaten social order and on the reaffirmation through individual action of predominant social values such as fair play and respect for merit and cooperation.

Survival films (including safari films as well as war movies and disaster epics) deal with a microcosm of society rather than with society in its largest numbers. Isolation, in the survival film, allows society to test itself and its components in a circumscribed and easily identified arena, and it allows all the obstacles facing society to be represented by one large and dramatic obstacle. A group is isolated in the desert in *The Flight of the Phoenix* (Robert Aldrich, 1966), because of an airplane crash. An overturned ocean liner contains the microcosm of *The Poseidon Adventure* (1972), the top floors of an office building isolated by an unreachable fire contain the group in *The Towering Inferno* (John Guillerman, 1974), prison barracks isolate the American soldiers of *Stalag 17* (Billy Wilder, 1953) and *The Great Escape* (John Sturges, 1963). In *Uncommon Valor* (Ted Kotcheff, 1983), a small group of Vietnam veterans must depend only on each other as they mount an expedition into Northern Laos in search of MIAs. In the war movie, separation into regiments or platoons creates a real and democratic microcosm embodying a wide spectrum of character types and ethnic groups, organized to fulfill clearly defined objectives.

After initially presenting its various characters, its *individuals*, in a normal situation without life-and-death stress, the survival film separates those characters from the society as a whole and causes them to confront the problem of survival. The major portion of the survival film is spent watching the process by which the group becomes an effectively functioning unit, and this process is marked by emphasis on the various kinds of behavior available to the individual character types. The viewer, therefore, is presented with a range of personal qualities (courage, cowardice, humor, intelligence, selfishness, self-sacrifice, and so forth), a range of ethnic, religious, and economic types (the Jew, Catholic, black, Native American, Chicano, rich snob, poor punk, and so forth), and a range of skills, either professionally acquired or amateurishly cultivated (the engineer, the electronics technician or radio ham, the Olympic swimmer, the priest, the hunter). This breadth of social representation allows the viewer to watch a range of behavior, to see played out on the screen all the possible ways in which the average social being (supposedly like the viewer) might respond to a life-and-death situation in a group. Obviously, all the skills and qualities that help the group rejoin the larger society are considered positive; those that serve only the individual are seen as negative.

5-15 Until recently the western was a popular genre. Setting, formula plots, and icons of this genre have remained generally constant. Even though *The Wild Bunch* (Sam Peckinpah, 1969) takes place around the time of World War I — there are machine guns and early automobiles in it — the story of a group of men avenging the death of one of their own is very familiar.

One of the primary, if submerged, lessons of the survival film is that crisis creates its own democracy; all sorts of people from all sorts of backgrounds and practicing all sorts of professions (socially acceptable under normal circumstances or not, as witness the hooker in *The Poseidon Adventure*), are important and crucial and *worthy* if they expend themselves to benefit the group and to reaffirm the value of social order. In all survival films, some members of the microcosm will end up sacrificing themselves for the good of the group. In contrast, the villain in the survival film is usually the group member who is too concerned with personal welfare, or too intellectual to act swiftly, or too cynical, or too neurotic, and who thereby threatens the success of the group's goal of reuniting with the larger society. On the other hand, the hero of the survival film emerges from the small group because of his skills, but once the group reenters the larger society from which it has been isolated, he is ready to disappear into the crowd. He has none of the personal style and idiosyncrasies, which mark the swashbuckling hero. In fact, personal style and idiosyncrasies are seen as undesirable qualities in the survival film, for they threaten the group and its goals in their individualistic, antisocial implications. Unlike the swashbuckler, the survival film is less interested in the lone heroic figure than it is in the ways in which individuals hinder or contribute to the creation and preservation of social order.

The Western
The western is perhaps the most clearly, visually identifiable film genre (Figure 5-15). Although it often shares certain characteristics with the

5-16 Though depending on repetition for its success, the genre film has always been responsive to changes in society. Thus the early western, for example, nearly always used Native Americans to represent a savage force facing the settlers of a hostile wilderness. Since the 1960s, however, westerns have depicted the Indian with far greater sympathy. In *Cheyenne Autumn* (1964), John Ford revealed the suffering and hardship of Native Americans forced to move to reservations.

adventure film (such as plots revolving around group survival, or conventions emphasizing personal style), it possesses its own specific landscape and geography, specific costuming, and, significantly, specific time — say, between 1850 and 1900. Although currently in decline, the western has a long tradition, and has been the genre most responsive to changing thematic concerns despite — or possibly because of — its limited geography and time. There is a great difference in the notions of heroism displayed by films such as *Stagecoach* (1939), *Shane* (1953), *The Man Who Shot Liberty Valance* (John Ford, 1962), *The Wild Bunch* (1969), and *The Long Riders* (Walter Hill, 1980), and yet the topography and costumes and certain objects (guns, stagecoaches, barbed wire) have generally remained constant (Figure 5-16).

The basic situation of the western concerns the change in the frontier region of the United States from a wide-open territory in which an individual male could find self-definition (through acts of violence and crime or through the possession and practice of prized individual skills) into a civilized and structured society with its foundations in family stability and group effort. This change did, of course, actually take place in America from Colonial days up to the beginning of the twentieth century, but the movie western (following the tradition of the pulp novel) has focused primarily upon the last fifty years or so of the nineteenth century, a period that included the opening up of the Oregon Territory and the movement of wagon trains westward, the Gold Rush, the Indian wars, cattle drives, and the beginning and completion of the transcontinental railroad. The iconography of the western film establishes the west as a place of deserts, wide-open plains, or badlands, full of wild Indians and equally wild and lawless white men, the former living in tepees, the latter in shantytowns, ruthlessly gouging the earth for gold, or buying up land and water rights for profit, setting up and running saloons with dance hall girls and gambling, or bounty hunting from town to town. Everywhere in the western, justice or the lack of it has been embodied in the presence of the gun. Although ordinary townsfolk and peace-loving settlers and farmers and ranchers appear in the western film, the central figures of the genre are the gun and the men who use it.

The gun is to the westerner what the sword was to the knight of the Arthurian romance. The weapon can be used by both good men and bad men — but in the romance, the good man is just a little bit quicker and a little bit more accurate. His agility and accuracy, which combine to become a personal style, define his place in the film morally and socially. The protagonist of the western, or at least of the older western, lived by a code; he never shot a man in the back or drew first, and even in fairly recent films the protagonist never kills a man merely for sport. The gun is an extension of the man, a physical representation of power and individual style.

Other recurrent objects (or icons) of the western are familiar modes of transportation, each carrying its own significance, its own cluster of dramatic associations and potential action: the horse, the stagecoach, the buckboard, the wagon train, the railroad. Costumes, too, are iconic, although films have come a long way from the simple representation of the good guy wearing a white hat and the bad guy wearing a black hat. One can identify dramatic roles and patterns of behavior by the clothes characters wear: the tin star, the string tie, the low-cut dress, the high-necked dress, the holster — even the various hats, which identify characters and their social and narrative functions.

Like other genre films, the western ends with an affirmation of the prevailing social order. At the end of the traditional western movie, the lawless town has been cleaned up and women and children can walk the streets in security, and schools and churches will spring up as signposts of civilization; the hero, who has lived by the gun and used it to clean up the town, will marry the girl at the end of the movie or promise to return to her as Wyatt Earp promises to return to Clementine

Carter in *My Darling Clementine* (John Ford, 1946). Or range wars and disputes between farmers and ranchers will be settled by a hero who has no place in the pastoral life that he has helped achieve, and he will ride off into the sunset, no longer needed, a melancholy, solitary, vestigial figure like Shane, the ex-gunfighter. The only other end for the man who has lived by the gun and used it to define himself is, of course, death; the death of the hero-gunfighter in a film like *The Gunfighter* (Henry King, 1950) is the death of a way of life, which cannot in its extreme forms be integrated into civilized society. The western is, above all, a nostalgic genre, for it shows men with one foot in the wilderness (with all its associations of freedom and individualism) and one foot in civilization (with all its associations of constraint and social contracts). And, while the western nostalgically celebrates the individual determining his own destiny, it simultaneously celebrates the growth of civilized society. Watching the western genre, we may mourn the passing of the past and at the same time feel pride in the emergence of the future; the conflicts between the benefits and disadvantages of both the wilderness and civilization are balanced and resolved on the screen.

Perhaps one of the reasons for the decline of the western as a viable genre in recent years is that audiences can no longer invest nostalgia in the circumscribed formula of the filmed western, can no longer believe in the myth of a glorious past, which inevitably led to a glorious present. Whether Americans as a group are more cynical about the present or more aware of the harsh and brutal history of the past is unclear. But attempts to revive the western — *Silverado* (Lawrence Kasdan, 1985), *Pale Rider* (Clint Eastwood, 1985) — have not met with unqualified success (Figure 5-17).

Fantastic Genres: Fantasy, Horror, and Science Fiction
Although it may be true that in some westerns, guns fire dozens of shots without being reloaded and that some heroic escapades stretch the limits of probability very thin indeed, the world of those genre melodramas previously discussed follow the conventions of realism. Someone, for example, who leaps out of a window goes down, not up. Some genre melodramas, however, invent their own worlds in which patently made-up events occur and in which fabricated physical laws operate. These genres are the fantasy film, the horror film, and the science fiction film. While each of them has a great deal in common with the others, each is distinctive in the way it uses its fantastic premises (Figure 5-18).

Fantasy films, for example, often drawn from mythology and fairy tales, are generally not meant to seem realistic at all. They deal with patently impossible occurrences and beings and, in fact, revel in their

5-17 The western, like other genres, has an historical life of growth, change, and decay. After a lapse of several years in which no westerns were produced, the form returned with two films in 1985. Clint Eastwood directed himself in *Pale Rider* and Lawrence Kasdan wrote and directed *Silverado*. Whether this indicates a resurgence of the genre remains to be seen.

use of special effects magic to create the impossible on-screen. The viewer is never asked by the film to believe in the armed skeletons who attack Jason in *Jason and the Argonauts* (Don Chaffey, 1963) or in the giant cloven-footed Cyclops in *The Seventh Voyage of Sinbad* (Nathan Juran, 1958); indeed, part of the enjoyment of such films is a recognition of the skills of the special effects technicians — for even children, the chief audiences for such films, are clearly able to distinguish between the everyday world and the world on the screen in which skeletons and Cyclops roam. Moreover, though the fantasy film often deals with the kinds of adventures and quests found in *The Odyssey* and in Arthurian legend, it deals less than any other film genre with the theme of the breakdown and restoration of social order. Because of the utterly strange context in which the adventure of the fantasy film's hero takes place, little emphasis is placed on the social effect of the hero's triumph. *Dragonslayer* (Matthew Robbins, 1981), *Conan, the Barbarian* (John Milius,

5-18 Some acts of heroism in the western and the adventure film frequently stretch the limits of belief, but to a large degree the world of genre melodramas resembles the world the viewer lives in. For example, when a person leaps out of a window, he goes down, not up. Fantasy genres, on the other hand, invent their own laws. Superman can, indeed, leap out of a window and fly in *Superman* (Richard Donner, 1978).

1982), and *Ladyhawke* (Richard Donner, 1985) simply revel in fantastic special effects and swordplay. Even when the fantasy film is set in the present and is less flamboyant in its use of special effects — as in *The Red Balloon* (Albert Lamorisse, 1956), in which the viewer hardly thinks about the effects or editing required to construct the relationship between a little boy and an anthropomorphized balloon — the fantasy film genre, more than any other, removes its protagonists and their adventures from a social context. In its exuberant presentation of the unreal, its lack of social and moral relevance, the fantasy film is perhaps the most escapist of genres.

Both the horror film and the science fiction film, in contrast, are usually concerned with moral and social realities, even if they have been set in a fantastic context. Both genres, like more conventionally realistic melodramas, are concerned with the conflict between individual desires and needs and community desires and needs. The horror film's plot, for

5-19 The monster in *Frankenstein* (James Whale, 1931) is seen in moral terms. The traditional horror film considers the desire for unlimited knowledge and power as sacrilegious, an affront to God and the natural order of things.

example, generally begins with a breakdown in the tranquil workings of a closed and traditional community. The moral breakdown usually involves an individual's Faustian rejection of human limitations and of God's singular power, and it is manifested physically with the appearance of the unholy creature whose very existence is an affront to natural and God-given physical law as well as a threat to the community (Figure 5-19). In *Frankenstein* (James Whale, 1931), man is guilty of trying to create life as if he were God — unnaturally, by himself — rather than in the normal, natural, and moral manner, within the social act of marriage and the establishment of a social unit, the family. Henry Frankenstein leaves his fiancée, his family ties, and his responsibilities to the community to bring forth his own child, the monster, secretively, antisocially, and blasphemously. Both *Dracula* (Tod Browning, 1931) and *The Wolf Man* (George Waggner, 1941) are also physical manifestations of unnatural and antisocial impulses. Both the vampire and the wolf man threaten the simple moral universe of the films they inhabit. One of the chief themes, thus, underlying the traditional horror film (and even those contemporary horror films, which attempt a certain psychological or surface realism) is the beast within — that unreasoning, primal, sexual, and selfishly asocial being, which may erupt through the thin veneer of civilized life and wreak havoc with all the good and moral social constructs upon which we have come to depend.

5-20 The modern horror film seems less concerned with moral issues. The fears represented usually revolve around totally unmotivated eruptions of violence from anonymous pathological killers or supernatural forces. In *Poltergeist* (Tobe Hooper, 1982), the spirits of the dead whose graveyard has been destroyed to make way for a subdivision are never depicted as "in the right," never credited with moral justification for terrorizing a family whose only crime was to live in the modern world, and be in the wrong place at the wrong time.

The horror film has readily identifiable conventions and iconography. In the films made in the thirties and forties, those conventions and iconography were more rigid than they are today, and some psychological horror films now have given up graveyards at midnight, garlic and wolfbane necklaces and garlands, silver-headed canes and silver bullets, wooden stakes, coffins, rats, and cobwebs. Yet almost all horror films, old or new, depend on the conventions of darkness, creaking doors, sudden noises, and surprise. The thematic concerns of the genre, too, are still the same. Whether one is dealing with old films like *Frankenstein*, *Dracula*, or *The Mummy* (Karl Freund, 1932), in which a fear of the irrational and bestial side of human beings actually takes a physical and monstrous shape and character, or whether one is dealing with modern films like Hitchcock's *Psycho* (1960), in which fear is manifested in the violence of a psychotic, or films like *Poltergeist* (Tobe Hooper, 1982), in which the fear of the irrational is linked to the supernatural but is treated realistically, almost all horror films share the same basic themes.

Many horror films also share certain conventions (Figure 5-20). The creature — whether Dracula, Norman Bates, or the poltergeist in a child's bedroom closet — is at first hidden from the rational world, which cannot conceive of or believe in unnatural beings and events; thus, the creature can initially operate without interference. As long as no one believes in it, it can menace, enslave, or kill many victims. And those victims, in a convention characteristic of the horror film, are morally or sexually linked with the monster; they have some intimate connection with it and their deaths never seem as haphazard and random as the deaths caused by the creatures in a science fiction film. The hero of the horror film is almost never the young and inexperienced male romantic lead, but instead tends to be an older figure, perhaps a physician or a priest, someone established and experienced in the irrational aspects of life and less libidinally distracted than the young male lead. Because this older figure is familiar with both the empirical world and the irrational world, when rational weapons do not work he is able to resort to mysterious means to defeat the evil and unnatural creature. He uses the laws governing the unnatural against the unnatural creature — hunting the vampire by day to drive a wooden stake through its heart, exorcism, psychoanalysis. In *Fright Night* (Tom Holland, 1985), the Van Helsing part is played by a television horror movie commentator. Obviously the most knowledgable person about horror lore in today's world. Usually, at the end of the horror film, the "children of the night" who threaten our civilized, social, moral everyday existence are subdued and society is returned to normal. The villagers can extinguish their torches, virgins can enjoy undisturbed sleep, and people can go to motels and take showers again — at least until the beginning of the next film in which the beast will erupt again.

Starting with *Halloween* (John Carpenter, 1978), a long cycle of horror films dubbed *slasher* films have become popular with young audiences. These films have shifted the classical horror film's focus. Fear of irrational, random, and spontaneous violence replaces the fear of evil within the human soul. In most of these films the attacks are perpetrated by an escaped psychopath (generally male) against young women who are sexually liberated (although anyone, young or old, male or female, who stands in the way may die a gruesome death). Although the assailants are seldom given any identifying characteristics, an authoritative figure in the film like a psychologist explains their actions as the result of severe sexual repression. But the explanations do not really explain anything at all, since the slasher is never a real character the audience cares about (as we once cared about the Frankenstein monster), only the personification of random violence. Hence the frequent use of masks to eliminate any human quality to the face of the killer. The settings of the new horror films are also more domestic than earlier films of this genre, taking place usually in suburbia and not the Carpathians, bringing the fear closer to home. The world of these films frequently depicts teen-agers quarantined in a world without adults who can save them. Or in some cases the actual threat is from within the family itself as in *The Shining* (Stanley Kubrick, 1980), where it is the father who menaces the wife and son.

Science fiction films, like horror films, often have creatures that threaten established order and society, but where the horror film emphasizes the moral and God-given order, the science fiction film emphasizes social and human-made order. The horror film tests the individual and her or his personal dealings with moral choice, but the science fiction film tests society and its institutions. The science fiction film is less about the conflict between good and evil in a closed community than it is about the workings of social institutions: government, the military, the public media, technology — and, more currently, the American family. The menace in the horror film is usually to the individual and the arena is usually small: a small town tucked away in the Carpathians, a tiny motel off an old highway, a bedroom in a Georgetown house. Particularly in the classic science fiction film, the threat is global and impersonal. While horror films are about the nightmare world that springs from within ourselves, science fiction films tend to be about the terrors of the daytime world, a world in which logic and the light of reason are as fearsome as those dark corners and the beast within. Reason, having not only produced the anxieties of the nuclear age, has extended to its disturbing extreme, disallowing the good as well as the bad expressions of human emotion. *Invasion of the Body Snatchers* (Don Siegel, 1956 and Philip Kaufman, 1978) is typical in its evocation of an alien invasion, which turns people into pods, unfeeling, unloving beings who look human but who all have the same bland and imperturbable expressions on their faces. In *Blade Runner* (Ridley Scott, 1982) and *The Terminator* (James Cameron, 1984), science has produced replicants who cannot be distinguished from humans. In *The Terminator* the figure is totally unfeeling, programmed only to terminate its target with a tenacity that is indeed frightening. But in *Blade Runner*, the fear is expressed that science could make replicas of human beings so like us that they would have fears, hopes, and desires, which might lead them to overthrow their masters. Or if not, that they would have to suffer from the knowledge of their own mortality just as we do. Whereas the horror film deals with our fears of our mysterious spiritual and animal origins, the science fiction film deals with our fears of our reason, a reason that has created the machinery of the contemporary world.

Science fiction films also have their conventions and icons, although the fact that they often deal with limitless space and time tends to make

5-21 Two kinds of images are contrasted in most science fiction films: the ordinary, familiar, the everyday; and the wondrous or strange created with models, makeup, or special effects. Both types of imagery are found in this shot from *E.T.* (Steven Spielberg, 1982) where the boy represents the familiar and the extraterrestrial creature the wondrous.

their conventions and icons a bit less constant than those of horror films. Various icons such as the spaceship, the topography of the desert or the seacoast (found with chilling regularity in the low-budget films of the fifties), and the laboratory (clean and well lit, in contrast to the musty and sepulchral labs in horror films) often appear in the genre. And certain visual conventions such as the cool, flat, third-person distance of the camera from its wondrous subject matter (aliens, starships, planets in space, mutants) are also constant, if less obvious (Figure 5-21). Always, however, the concerns and emphasis of the genre are more social than moral.

The fantastic aspects of the science fiction film, unlike those in the horror film, are meant to seem conceivable to the viewer. The laws that govern the world of science fiction are based on supposed fact, and they are regarded as extensions of the physical laws that operate in the real world. The films, in short, are meant to be credible in ways in which the horror films are not. Whereas the horror film confronts the terror of the unknown with the laws and rituals of magic and religion, the science fiction film confronts the terror or promise of the unknown with the laws and rituals of science.

In the science fiction genre, therefore, science is the basis of both the problem and its solution. As bad science, it is private, elitist, involved with knowledge for its own sake rather than for social good, and it is often represented by an obsessed individual (the familiar mad scientist) who speaks a private and undecipherable language — or, in many contemporary films, by a multinational corporation. As good science, it is public, democratic, involved with knowledge that will be employed technologically for the good of society, and it is often represented by a team of scientists, or by a scientist-hero who speaks accessible, plain English. In *The War of the Worlds* (Byron Haskin, 1953), for example, we first meet the hero-scientist on a fishing vacation, where he wears grubby clothing, attends a small-town square dance, and talks plain English. Open, democratic, and cooperative activity leads to a positive solution in the genre, just as lonely, secret obsession and solitary hysteria (even in a crowd) is shown to be ineffectual, if not downright dangerous to the social order.

Although often ambivalent about the uses of technology, the science fiction film emphasizes (through its use of special effects) the beauties of technology, the wonders of machinery, which nearly transcends human imagination: the sleek and ascetic flying saucer sitting in the middle of Washington, D.C., in *The Day the Earth Stood Still* (Robert Wise, 1951), the prim golden robot of *Star Wars* (1977) standing against a background of pale sand and sky, and the brilliant display of light that is the video game world of *Tron* (Steven Lisberger, 1982).

Science fiction films, however, do not have to use a great many special effects, and they do not have to deal with spaceships and extraterrestrial creatures. Science fiction has come to include films that extrapolate from present reality in politics, social problems, medicine, human relations; thus, *Privilege* (Peter Watkins, 1967), *Wild in the Streets* (Barry Shear, 1968), and *1984* (Michael Radiford, 1984) treat alternative political structures, *Soylent Green* (Richard Fleischer, 1973) treats the problem of overpopulation and food supply, *Blade Runner* (Ridley Scott, 1982) treats genetic engineering, which results in replicants who are more human than humans, and *Cocoon* (Ron Howard, 1985) treats the problem of the elderly. No matter what the time of the film (for science fiction can happen in the past, present, or future), no matter what the location (for the genre can take place in small-town America or in the middle of a galaxy), the films all have in common their attempt to astonish us, to cause us to wonder at the images we see. These images can be bizarre, like the Korova Milkbar with its sculptured nude drink dispensers in *A Clockwork Orange* (1971), or normally inaccessible to our human and physical perception, like the holistic vision of planets and moons in space in *Star Trek III: The Search for Spock* (Leonard Nimoy, 1984), or such images can be ordinary and familiar like the sports car turned time machine in *Back to the Future* (Robert Zemeckis, 1985). But because of the context, these images amaze us, fill us with wonder

5-22 America's fondness for the antisocial individual as a heroic figure is quite evident in western and gangster films. Jesse James and Billy the Kid have been subjects of many westerns, and the famous gangster of the 1920s, Al Capone, has inspired several films. Howard Hawks made the first version of *Scarface* in 1932, and the story was updated by Brian DePalma in 1983 with Al Pacino playing the lead.

rather than fear. We tend to anticipate what we will see next — rather than, as in the horror film, dread what we will see next.

Antisocial Genres: The Crime Film and the Family Melodrama

> In ways that we do not easily or willingly define, the gangster speaks for us, expressing that part of the American psyche which rejects the qualities and demands of modern life, which rejects "Americanism" itself.
> Robert Warshow [4]

Although all genre films end by reaffirming the value of unselfish devotion to the needs of society, a few genres flirt with the possibility that the desire to be different, to stand out from the group as an individual (Figure 5-22), to act out of self-interest, is heroic, if finally misguided and unprofitable. Although all genre melodramas end up by reaffirming the status quo and the predominant social order, two film genres deemphasize group and/or community needs — until near the end of the films — and concentrate instead on the individual who dares to oppose the values of society. These two genres are the crime film (and within that genre, particularly, the gangster film and film noir) and the film that chronicles the struggle of a woman to find happiness, a kind of film, which, for want of a better name, is called the *family melodrama*. Both of these genres focus on individuals who, by choice or desperation, become social outcasts. Although, at first, these genres may seem worlds apart in their concerns, they are similar in their exploration of independent and ambitious individuals whose attempts at self-definition are both heroic and tragically antisocial. In both genres, the protagonists believe they are superior to society, and in both genres, they pay dearly for that belief — either by dying or by becoming socially isolated. And, although both genres end by affirming traditional morality, showing the viewer, in effect, that crime does not pay or that women belong in the home, they also both spend most of their screen time on the progress of individuals who have dared to challenge the basic values of society.

The crime genre encompasses many variants. The gangster film, perhaps the most antisocial of all, was chiefly made in the 1930s in depression America. Examples include *Little Caesar* (Mervyn Le Roy, 1930), *The Public Enemy* (William Wellman, 1931), and *Scarface* (Howard Hawks, 1932). But it has been resurrected from time to time in films like *The St. Valentine's Day Massacre* (Roger Corman, 1968), *The Godfather*, Parts I and II (Francis Ford Coppola, 1972, 1974), a remake of *Scarface* (Brian DePalma, 1984), and *Once Upon a Time in America* (Sergio Leone, 1984). The gangster film originally came out of the newspaper headlines of the 1930s, headlines referring to real gangsters like Al Capone and Baby Face Nelson, who became figures of mythic stature, headlines referring to Prohibition and bootlegging and bad economic news for the average citizen. On one level, the gangster film of the 1930s can be seen as an antisocial, if covert, response to a society that was not adequately serving the average citizen. The gangster film's basic plot generally charted the rise and fall of an individual criminal within the ranks of a criminal organization, which closely resembled the corporate structure of business organizations. The film's protagonist starts, like a Horatio Alger character, green and raw on the bottom rung (often coming to the big city from a smaller town or from a rural environment), and through ambition, hard work, ingenuity, and perseverance he achieves success — defined in both the socially accepted world of big business and in the illicit world of organized crime, by becoming the head of the organization, the president or the big boss. The socially approved method of achieving success is, in the gangster film, directed toward antisocial ends. Moreover, the hardworking, ambitious, ingenious gangster also demonstrates the vile side of the American work ethic; winning out over the competition means machine-gunning them, advancement means killing those who stand in the way ahead of you.

5-23 Though there have been many changes in the gangster film, one of its consistent themes has been to assert that the struggle to reach the top ends in loneliness or death. In this shot we see the young, ambitious protagonist at the beginning of his career. Edward G. Robinson, in *Little Caesar* (Mervyn Le Roy, 1930), meets the gang for the first time. By the end of the film he will have taken complete control, but when he dies at the hands of the law, none of the gang members will be with him.

The eventual success of the central figure of the gangster film, too, is unattractive, because once all the opposition has been eliminated, once the big boss's chair has been attained and secured, the only rewards of success left are isolation, loneliness, and fear, for one by one the gangster's friends become his enemies (Figure 5-23). All that hard work, the gangster film seems to say, is for nothing, for emptiness, or for death. Success is really failure. In Part II of *The Godfather*, after Michael Corleone's final business success is ensured by the murder of his brother, and his wife and children are no longer with him, Corleone is shown in close-up, alone in the frame, isolated by all his massive effort. The other end of success in the gangster film is death; the gangster's rise to the top leads to his murder, either by an associate who emulates him or by the forces of the society. All in all, the gangster film deeply questions the basic value of success as Americans have defined it; it suggests that individual success (esteemed in our society) is inseparable from personal corruption. In the gangster film, it is not merely crime that does not pay — success itself does not pay. And, although the ending of the gangster film reaffirms legitimate society by bringing about the gangster's death or by focusing on his isolation, the major emphasis in the film is on this covert and subversive theme. The gangster thus stands as a heroic and tragic victim of his belief in a system that has no meaningful payoff (Figure 5-24).

5-24 One of the most famous moments in the history of the gangster film occurred in William Wellman's *The Public Enemy* (1931). James Cagney displays the extent of his irrational hostility by shoving a grapefruit into Mae Clark's face. Women in gangster films usually function to show off the status of the ambitious criminal. He may do with them as he pleases.

The G-man film was an offshoot of the gangster film of the 1930s. An outcry that movies (as well as the other media of the times) glorified criminals resulted in implementing the industry's Hollywood production code in the mid-1930s, and so films that previously had centered on the gangster shifted their attention to the law enforcer who battled the gangster. Often little else was changed; the films contained the same crimes — and, in fact, some of the actors who had played the gangster-hero before the code, like James Cagney in *The Public Enemy*, now played the law enforcer-hero in films like *G-Men* (William Keighley, 1935). Despite the similarities between the gangster film and the G-man film, however, the one basic difference was crucial; the underlying thematic complexity of the gangster film, which questioned the values of success in capitalist America, was severely simplified.

Another variant of the crime film is the private eye or detective film. Again, the protagonist of the story is on the right side of the law — but, more interestingly than in the G-man film, he is sometimes only just on the right side of the law and his social morality is often hidden from the viewer until the very end of the film when he places his social responsibility above his personal desire. Thus, the morally ambiguous Sam Spade (played by Humphrey Bogart) in *The Maltese Falcon* (John Huston, 1941) finally reveals himself as an adherent of a moral code that says that a man has a responsibility to his partner even if he does not personally like him, and he also turns in the woman he loves to the authorities because she is a murderess. Spade ends by affirming the social structure. Even though he recognizes the arbitrariness and unfairness of society's codes, their abuse at the hands of the selfish on either side of the law, he also recognizes that without them there would be unbearable chaos. The private eye is in some ways comparable to the gunfighter in the western; like the gunfighter, he moves between two worlds: the world ruled by violence, personal desire, and the gun, and the world ruled by sanctioned violence, social needs, and the law. And, like the gunfighter, the private eye is partially defined by his style, his cool responses, his resilience and readiness for the unexpected. Unlike the western genre, however, the private eye film tends to focus on the moral world of the protagonist. That world, urban and nightmarish, is peopled with characters who are not to be trusted, however attractive they may appear. This is as true of the lying Mrs. Mulwray (Faye Dunaway) in a film like *Chinatown* (Roman Polanski, 1974), as it is of the faithless Brigid O'Shaughnessy (Mary Astor) in the earlier *The Maltese Falcon*. The private eye must travel through this morally unstable landscape and escape with his principles intact; that is the best he — and the viewer — can hope for. Although the criminals in the film may be apprehended in the end, the private eye film depicts a world whose very foundations are weak and unstable.

Often, the private eye film is linked with a group of films identified by certain common themes and stylistic traits. These are called *film noir*, that is, "black film". *Film noir* is visually marked by its nighttime imagery, urban landscape, and thematic focus on ambiguously corrupt characters whose chief activity is double-dealing in a society that seems to have no redeeming members and no hope for a moral and civilized survival (Figure 5-25). Because the *film noir* was usually a low-budget film made in Hollywood in the 1940s and 1950s, it was generally shot in black-and-white. Today, however, hardly any films are made in black-and-white, and a contemporary *film noir* like *Body Heat* (Lawrence Kasdan, 1983) creates its aura of seedy decadence with color.

The caper film, chiefly concerned with executing an ingenious crime, on the other hand, is not particularly concerned with society; rather it focuses on process. In some ways, this variant of the crime film resembles the survival film (one of the two major forms of the adventure film). It chronicles a team effort to achieve a common goal — and most of the film focuses on the process of overcoming obstacles in the path of successfully robbing a train, or cracking a bank safe, or some such thing. Like the survival film, the caper film is interested in the ways members of the group respond to each other and to crises. But the isolation of the

5-25 The *film noir* is set in an urban landscape: cheap apartments, dreary streets, warehouse districts, crummy dives. This landscape is a metaphor for the corruption, dishonesty, and conniving that takes place in a dog-eat-dog world where survival is the only value. Even though set in the near future, *Blade Runner* (Ridley Scott, 1982), exhibits all the visual style and moral miasma of a typical 1940s *film noir*.

group in the caper film is self-imposed, and the group does not necessarily represent the larger society. Instead, the emphasis in the caper film is on the caper itself, on the human and mechanical processes involved in preparing the caper, in brilliantly overcoming the obstacles to success, and in finally attaining the goal: opening the bank vault, stealing the jewels. The caper film seems to be a wry and cynical celebration of professionalism and process; it is akin to a how-to film: how to make a crystal set, how to throw a pot. It is no accident that one of the great examples of the caper film — *Rififi* (Jules Dassin, 1956) — has practically no dialogue; we and the criminals are intent on accomplishing the caper, and the very lack of human interchange recognizes the degree to which a human group has become a well-oiled machine. Since all the participants in the caper film are involved in a criminal activity, nothing in the film moves the group toward integration with the main body of society from which they have temporarily seceded. Because watching the caper film is so absorbing, generally pleasant, and relatively nonviolent, it is easy to overlook the fact that the viewer wishes for the success of an illegal enterprise; so much film time and painstaking effort (by the characters and the camera) is lavished on an illegal activity that the viewer would be sorely disappointed by a caper that was not finally pulled off. In this sense, the caper film is antisocial in its thrust, although it tends to ignore the society of the world in which it takes place and is, therefore, often located in exotic places like Monte Carlo or indoors in what amounts to almost abstract space filled simply by chairs and a table spread with plans. Sometimes, too, the films end with a rather whimsical affirmation of justice: while the caper itself is successful, the loot turns out to be fake or, after the caper, the participants are double-crossed, or the wind blows the money away.

Most crime films are set in a city, generally contemporary with the time in which the film was made. But some modern films have focused on the gangster of the 1930s or have attempted to recreate the private eye film of the 1940s; examples are *Al Capone* (Richard Wilson, 1959), *Dillinger* (John Milius, 1973), the previously mentioned *Chinatown*, and *Farewell, My Lovely* (Dick Richards, 1975). *Blade Runner*, though set in a futurist city, evokes a sense of the film noir/detective film of the 1940s. The urban setting of modern life — even when that modernity is placed back in the late 1920s and early 1930s — is filled with objects that have become iconically significant to the crime film: telephones (candlestick and coin phones), radios (and later television sets) spouting news bulletins, machine guns, liquor stores, nightclubs, fast cars with screeching tires, newspapers, murky bars and cigarette smoke, cheap hotel (and later, motel) rooms marked by their anonymity, and neon lights. Clothing, as well, has had a particular significance to the genre: the snap-brimmed hat pulled down so as to hide a character's eyes; the private eye's trench coat, its collar pulled up for protection against some all-pervasive dankness; the expensive suits and cashmere coats of gangsters who have reached the top, and the cheap satiny flamboyance of women's clothes meant to convey notions of sexual availability and moral laxity.

It seems a big leap from the crime film to the family melodrama, that broadly defined genre of films supposedly made to appeal to female audiences. The family melodrama, however, has a great deal in common with the crime film, particularly the gangster film. Both focus on an individual who dares to oppose the law, which governs social behavior, charting that individual's initial naive optimism and ambition, the individual's rise toward what seems a desirable goal, and finally, that individual's fall and recognition that the goal carried with it the seeds of personal and social destruction. Indeed, if the gangster film shows the irreconcilable conflict between personal success and popular democracy in the traditionally male world of business, then the family melodrama shows the same conflict in the traditionally female world of the home. What is illegal in the family melodrama is the protagonist's desire to go beyond the socially approved limits of home and family — and when she succeeds, she must, like the gangster, pay dearly for her success, a success revealed as finally worthless and containing the seeds of her own destruction. (Even a modern film like *Kramer vs. Kramer* — Robert Benton, 1979 — reflects this classic moral in regard to its ambitious and errant mother.) In the family melodrama, woman's greatest crime is infidelity or its counterpart, home-wrecking. But the crime of personal ambition — even to benefit her family — is almost as bad. We watch the female protagonist in much the same way we watch the gangster: noting and even admiring that pathological determination to rise above one's peers, recording with ambivalent emotion how the fulfillment of personal drive leads to social death.

In *Mildred Pierce* (Michael Curtiz, 1945), for example, what seems to be a woman's innocent ambition to provide for her family ends in a horrendous act of murder. Mildred (Joan Crawford, who played many such ambitious women in the 1940s) is full of energy and hopes for her children, but in fulfilling those hopes she turns into a hardworking but cold and ambitious individual, both heroine and villainess together. The same drive for power (represented by both money and control over the men in a woman's life) is shown in *The Strange Love of Martha Ivers* (Lewis Milestone, 1946). Played by Barbara Stanwyck, another actress who was able to seem simultaneously heroic and castrating. Martha is constantly asserting herself; as a child, she kills (with audience sympathy) a vicious, power-hungry aunt and then grows up like that aunt, ruthless in her business dealings, contemptuous and manipulative of her husband. Finally, she even attempts to get her old love to kill her husband. Like the gangster, of course, both Mildred and Martha end up badly, the first isolated, and the second dead.

The family melodrama, which represents the dark side of domestic life in the way that the crime film represents the dark side of business life, was made primarily in the later 1940s — in the postwar period — representing, perhaps, in a melodramatic dream landscape the fear of what would happen to the economic power assumed by (and thrust upon) women during the war years. As the gangster film of the 1930s can be seen as a pessimistic response to the realities of the Depression, a nay-saying on an unconscious popular level to the positive American myth of success, so the family melodrama of the 1940s and 1950s can be seen as a pessimistic response to social changes initiated by World War II, a nay-saying on an unconscious level to the popular American myth of domestic bliss and willing female subservience.

✸ Genre as Myth

The fact is that each generation must create its own myths and its own heroes, or else regenerate those of the past. . . . We desperately need a renewal of faith in ourselves as Americans, as good guys on the world

scene, as men and women, as human beings who count, and so we return temporarily to the simpler patterns of the past. The old superheroes
rise again — *Wonder Woman* and *Superman* — and we get old-fashioned
genre films like *Rocky* and *Star Wars*.
Andrew Gordon [5]

When we think carefully about genre films, we see that they reveal
unconscious fears and desires beneath the surface plots. The makers of
most genre films over the past fifty years or so were not, of course,
deliberately trying to depict on the screen the repressed fears and desires of their audiences (they were not students of Freud or Jung or
even of genre film theory), but surely one can assume that genre films
are enormously popular because they fulfill some sort of psychological
need. It is too simple to say that these movies are only entertainment,
are just sheer fun, are escapist, and do not mean anything. Genre films
are popular films, the films most of us grew up with and the films most
people go to see. If we can understand their appeal we can learn
something important about ourselves as social beings, and about the
growth of our culture.

It is no accident that all of the films in each film genre tend to tell the
same basic story, with sometimes only the most minor variations. This
repetition is less a cause for criticism than for the recognition that each
genre deals with a certain basic conflict, which, unresolved in real life, is
comfortingly resolved on the screen. The genre film can deal, for example, with the conflict between the individual desire to be different
from others and the desire to be like others, with the conflict between
individual needs and group needs, and with the conflict between material success and spiritual success — and it can deal with such conflicts in
ways in which more intellectual and unique films cannot.

The filmmaker may have intended only to entertain his audience
when he made *The Wolf Man* (1941); he may, in fact, have had no
particular conscious reason for choosing his material other than that it
allowed Lon Chaney, Jr., to follow in his father's footsteps, put on
bizarre makeup, and perhaps make a bundle for the studio. Yet perhaps
the choice of material itself and the response of audiences to it was not
trivial. Right there, on the screen, is particularized the unnamable beast
we may try to keep hidden beneath our civilized skins. That animal
emerges on the screen bristling with hair and violence and sexual desire.
Through the process of identification with the protagonist — the wolf
man — we may act out our worst fears and desires in such a clearly
fantastic context, that they may be purged from our unconscious selves.
We may think we have just seen an inconsequential escapist fantasy, but
our personal and unconscious fears may actually have been transformed
from personal nightmare into a depersonalized and group myth.

It is not surprising that recent studies of genre films have tended to look at the films' structures as comparable to the structures of myth and fairy tale. Myth and fairy tale transform individual dreams into group dreams in which the problems presented and the solutions effected are seen as universally valid. Thus, one can draw strong parallels between the structure of what scholar Joseph Campbell calls the *monomyth* (the underlying similarity in myths) and the structures of all genre films, between the composite heroes of world mythology and their progress and the composite heroes of genre films and their dramatic progress. Recognizing that despite the infinite variation of locale and decoration there is only a limited number of human and socially supportable responses to life problems, Campbell illuminatingly reduces the mythological adventures of a host of heroes from a host of cultures to one great adventure experienced by one composite hero. This "Hero with a Thousand Faces" (to use the title of one of Campbell's books) responds to the call of adventure and separates himself from the society of which he has been a part. He is then confronted with a series of tests and trials in a process of initiation, which culminates in his successful completion of crucial tasks. He then returns and reintegrates himself with society and passes on the lessons he has learned, or he is rejected because of the threat to society his experience presents. Always, however, the hero is a person of exceptional gifts (Figure 5-26).

One can draw parallels not only between the genre film and myth, but also between the genre film and the folktale or fairy tale. The Russian Vladimir Propp's analysis of over a hundred fairy tales revealed not only certain basic plots, but also a certain basic cast of *dramatis personae*, defined by their function; under various guises, this cast is also basic to genre films. Propp names the hero, of course, and then goes on to identify the villain, who chases and engages in combat of some sort with the hero; the donor or provider, who gives the hero some magical device or agent that will aid him in accomplishing the major tasks imposed by his adventure; the helper, who performs various supportive roles for the hero and who may aid the hero in a crisis and who transfigures the hero by the contrast provided by his lesser gifts; the princess and her father (or one of them), who assigns the hero his task and who rewards him when it is accomplished; the dispatcher, who sends the hero off on his adventure and who is often an agent of the princess and her father in some fashion; and even the false hero, who counterpoints the real hero, aping the latter's search and being found wanting in his abilities and talents.

Campbell suggests a distinction between the myth and fairy tale: myth is microcosmic (a miniature representation of the world, analogous to the larger world) and the hero's resolution of problems carries

5-26 Genre films present many examples of what Joseph Campbell called "the hero with a thousand faces." Sometimes this mythic hero looks like Clint Eastwood in *Pale Rider* (Eastwood, 1985), but he can also look like Michael J. Fox in *Back to the Future* (Robert Zemeckis, 1985). Genres transform ordinary humans into mythic figures.

with it the possibilities of regeneration for his whole society; the fairy tale is macrocosmic (the larger world) and the hero's resolution is basically personal and particularized. In these terms the genre film can be considered both myth *and* fairy tale. On the surface, it is a fairy tale, concerned with a particular hero and adventure and with the resolution of a fairly circumscribed problem in the only world there is. Under the surface, however, it is mythic in its presentation of broad conflicts played out by participants who stand for forces in the larger world. In addition, on both levels its impulses are social: the hero returns the world to order.

In its dramatization of myth, the genre film can also be seen as a ritual. The viewer participates in a manner similar to attendance at other social and religious rituals such as baseball games or church services. Ritual activity, as defined by social scientists like Bronislaw Malinowski and Claude Lévi-Strauss, has several requirements and characteristics. It is, of course, repetitive. It is cumulative, in that action is built serially upon action and that power comes from the accumulation of action rather than from concluding action. (A classic example in the genre film would be the emotional power and weight accumulated by the rebellious female in the family melodrama, which far outweighs the moral ending of the film that demands her being cast out from the society.) Ritual is symbolic and uses various simple objects and signposts (for example, a cross) to evoke complex associations. Ritual is also nostalgic in that it celebrates the past, what has been done before and will be done again. Ritual is simplistic in that it presents a clearly identifiable and dualistic universe: light is in conflict with darkness, good with evil, male with female. This dualism is clearly seen in most genre films in the hero-vs.-villain plot structure, in the very simple but visually communicative use of light and dark clothing to separate the good guys from the bad guys in the early years of film melodrama, and in the paradoxical dualism of themes, which directly oppose notions of success and failure and of individual fulfillment and group satisfaction. All of the *Rocky* films have been so classic in their dualism — Rocky is good, the opponent is evil — that the appeal of such a satisfying ritual is almost universal. Another characteristic of ritual is that it is predictable; one knows what is going to happen next and what is going to happen at the end, and that knowledge, rather than producing boredom, is comforting and pleasurable. Finally, ritual is functional; it provides its practitioners with temporary psychological, emotional, and social ease: the purgation of personal anxiety and fear, a feeling of well-being, and a sense of belonging to a group with homogenous goals. The genre film is similarly functional, temporarily resolving what in the real world remains an irreconcilable or paradoxical conflict. The genre film assuages individual anxiety and, like ritual, does so magically and seemingly without effort, always affirming an established and socially acceptable order of things.

Genre Films and Society

> . . . The crucial factors which distinguished a *genre* are not *only* characteristics inherent to the films themselves; they also depend on the particular culture within which we are operating. And unless there is world consensus on the subject (which is an empirical question) there is no basis for assuming that a "Western" will be conceived in the same way in every culture. The way in which the term *genre* is applied can quite conceivably vary from case to case. *Genre* notions — except the special case of arbitrary definition — are not critic's classifications made for special purposes; they are sets of cultural conventions. *Genre* is what we collectively believe it to be.
> Andrew Tudor [6]

Genre films can also function as a cultural barometer. The viewer can look at the evolution of a particular genre, say the western, and see reflected in its shifts in attitude, changes that can be likened to shifts of attitude in the contemporary society which made and attended the films. It cannot be dismissed as mere accident that the western hero has changed from a figure like Bronco Billy Anderson, who bore some strong resemblance to his real-life counterpart, to a white-hatted hero on an intelligent horse, like Roy Rogers or Gene Autry in the 1930s and early 1940s; to the psychologically contemplative or disfigured hero-villains of the 1950s and 1960s; to the corporate hero-villains of the late 1960s and 1970s such as those in *The Wild Bunch* (1969); to those films of the 1970s which presented the hero as septuagenarian and outdated as in *The Shootist* (Don Siegel, 1976) or *Tom Horn* (William Wiard, 1980). Those shifts reflect the contemporary concerns of the culture in which the films were made, and while it may not be useful to assign a one-to-one correspondence between occurrences in the social and political and economic life of movie viewers and occurrences on the screen, it can be productive to examine genre films as a response to social history and contemporary concerns. Surely it is reasonable to see, in the changes in the hero of the western, from the single-minded Gene Autry and Roy Rogers to the pragmatic Bill Holden and Lee Marvin, a shift in the way in which America defines its heroes. In 1981 Michael Cimino tried to make a socially conscious western about labor strife in Wyoming. *Heaven's Gate* cost 50 million dollars to make and was a disaster at the box office. In that same year *The Legend of the Lone Ranger* also failed to make money. Until 1985, no serious westerns were made. This could mean that Hollywood was afraid of losing money on a form the audience no longer wanted. The lukewarm response to *Silverado* and *Pale Rider* in 1985 indicates the traditional value system associated with the western and its lone hero are no longer something the public wants to buy.

Seeing genre films as a barometer of popular and often unconscious tensions and moods can help explain why, for example, certain genres suddenly reestablish their popularity after lying dormant for a period of time, or why certain foreign countries adopt and transform as their own a particular American film genre and have little interest in others. Japan, for example, has made many science fiction films, Italy many westerns. Looking at genre films as a reflection of the culture that produced and responded to them can lead to the contemplation of such questions as whether the popularity of the disaster film was a natural response to contemporary ecological concerns — or whether it was popular because it appealed covertly as a fantasy drama in which contemporary people were the helpless victims of cataclysmic forces beyond their control and for which they could not possibly be held responsible, a cinematic response of sorts to a world already beset with famine, drought, and Watergate.

Genre Parody and Antigenres

In fact, the history of convention in American film has always been the history of successive exhaustions of convention. The exposure and elaboration of certain actors and actions pleases and solaces the audience but

then finally leaves it cold. When the genre conventions can no longer evoke and shape either the emotions or the intelligence of the audience, they must be discarded and new ones tried out. Genre films essentially ask the audience, "Do you still want to believe this?" Popularity is the audience answering, "Yes." Change in genres occurs when the audience says, "That's too infantile a form of what we believe. Show us something more complicated." And genres turn to self-parody to say, "Well, at least if we make fun of it for being infantile, it will show how far we've come."
Leo Braudy [7]

Generally speaking, film genres (at least up until fairly recent times) have been unself-conscious. Their styles have been relatively invisible; the viewer is conscious chiefly of the narrative rather than of the *way* the camera tells the narrative. Genre filmmakers, moreover, were intent on telling a story, and they were not particularly aware of the covert psychological and social content of the subtext of the films they were making. Today, however, both audiences and filmmakers have become more aware of the covert implications of genre films. Audiences are more cinematically sophisticated — and many of today's top film directors are keenly aware of the myth-making accomplished by film genres. The self-consciousness of both audience and filmmaker can best be demonstrated by the work of two contemporary filmmakers who have used genre films for differing purposes: Mel Brooks, calling the viewer's attention to the formal structure of genre films, to the delightful familiarity of generic plots, conventions, and **iconography,** has produced comedy; and Robert Altman, using and abusing audience expectations of familiar genre plots, conventions, and iconography, has subverted the genre from within, shaking the audience from a passive state of dream-viewing into an active state of thought.

Brooks's films pay homage to film genres rather than criticize them. He has parodied the musical in *The Producers* (1968), the western in *Blazing Saddles* (1974), the traditional horror film in *Young Frankenstein* (1975), silent slapstick comedy in *Silent Movie* (1976), and the Hitchcock suspense thriller in *High Anxiety* (1978). In all his films, he uses genre conventions and iconography to confirm — by the emphasis of exaggeration — the audience's knowledge and familiarity with the kind of movie it is watching. The surprises in Brooks's films are not disturbing, do not call into question the concept of genre or its possibly faulty notions regarding social values; instead, Brooks's surprises celebrate the limited world set forth by the genre. When the gunfighter in *Blazing Saddles* demonstrates the quickness of his draw by not moving his hands at all and then asks the sheriff whether he saw it, the humor stems from the audience's knowledge of westerns and their rules; when the monster marries at the end of *Young Frankenstein* and ends up sedately reading the *Wall Street Journal* in domestic bliss, the humor is a product of the viewer's past sympathy for the unloved misfit whose ugliness sent those around him into screaming paroxysms of horror. The humor of Brooks's movies is never at the expense of the genres he parodies; rather, it is derived from a loving extension of the familiar, from carrying all the laws and rules of a particular genre to their furthest extreme.

Robert Altman's films, on the other hand, subvert genre films from within. Those films he has made that at first seem to be traditional genre movies end up unsettling viewers, making them realize how passively they have tended to accept genre conventions and rules. *M*A*S*H* (1969) was Altman's first commercially successful film to play against genre, but its comic thrust somewhat softened the attack on the conventions and social affirmation of the traditional war movie. All the characters in the film are selfish rather than traditionally heroic; the Korean war (a thin disguise for the Vietnam war) is made analogous to a vicious football game in which nobody plays by the rules, and the practice of medicine is seen as a dirty and ridiculous business rather than as a heroic calling. *McCabe and Mrs. Miller* (1971) subverts the western; amidst a meticulously recreated northwestern town bathed in constantly nostalgic light, a drama is played out between a hero who is stupidly vain (if touching) and a heroine who is a prostitute with business acumen and a more literal than proverbial heart of gold. The classic gunfight at the end of the film fulfills audience expectation in that McCabe actually kills the bad guys, but it subverts audience expectation by leaving McCabe wounded and finally dead in the snow, the town and his true love withdrawn into their own pursuits. *Thieves Like Us* (1973) and *The Long Goodbye* (1973) both combine violence, serious and stereotypical characterization, and genre plotting with ironic elements purposefully used to distance the viewer from an emotional involvement with the film's created world. *Thieves Like Us* is a gangster film that emphasizes the ugliness of place and the plainness of its characters, as if in response to the glossy and gauzy beauty of its cinematic predecessor, *Bonnie and Clyde* (1967). At the end of *The Long Goodbye,* after private eye Philip Marlowe kills the friend who has duped and used him, the detective walks away, kicking up his heels in a long shot while the tune "Hooray for Hollywood" is playing. Unlike Mel Brooks's films, Altman's films refuse to cooperate with the audience; rather than congratulating viewers for their knowledge of genre convention and movie history as does Brooks, Altman assaults viewers by using that knowledge against them.

The films of Mel Brooks and Robert Altman are, of course, at opposite poles. Brooks perpetuates genre forms and mythology while Altman subverts or demythologizes genre forms. Brooks's films suggest that

5-27 The Mel Brooks' legacy of affectionate genre parody can be seen in films like *Airplane!* (Jim Abrahams, 1980) where audiences and filmmakers recognize the formulaic absurdities of serious versions of the genres being spoofed but share a fondness for the form. Robert Altman's antigenre legacy is visible in the films made by the Monty Python group. Their take-off of a musical in *Monty Python's the Meaning of Life* (Terry Jones, 1983), juxtaposing the destitute poverty of the lower classes supposedly brought on by over-population with the inane gaiety of a musical comedy, suggests that musicals, like other forms of romantic fiction, are simply an opiate for the masses.

audience and filmmaker share an affection for the familiar, that they are both party to an unwritten and congenial contract, which specifies what the audience expects and what the filmmaker will give it. Altman's films, however, are antigeneric; they deny the contractual agreement with the audience, suggesting that viewers make themselves potential victims of the film and its maker by expecting something never prom-ised. Despite their differences of purpose, however, Brooks and Altman are similar in that they both have made audiences aware of genre conventions, aware of their own previously unrecognized expectations.

Today, genres have become more self-reflexive and audiences more self-conscious. Both viewers and filmmakers are more knowledgeable about genre forms and their ritual function. Brook's legacy is clear in films like *Airplane!* (Jim Abrahams, 1980), *Love at First Bite* (Stan Dragoti, 1979), and *Lust in the Dust* (Paul Bartel, 1985), which fondly parody their respective genres. Altman's influence is harder to distinguish, but sure-ly *Monty Python and the Holy Grail* (Terry Gilliam, 1975) and *Monty Python's Life of Brian* (Terry Jones, 1979) deviously undermine the Ar-thurian adventure film and biblical epics (Figure 5-27). Herbert Ross's imitation of a Busby Berkeley musical *Pennies from Heaven* (1981) is neither affectionate nor nostalgic. It's dark and grim tone is much more reminiscent of Altman's disturbing works.

NOTES

[1] *Violent America: The Movies 1946–1964* (New York: Museum of Modern Art, 1971), p. 19.

[2] *Underworld USA* (New York: Viking, 1972), pp. 23–24.

[3] *The Immediate Experience* (New York: Atheneum, 1971), pp. 129–130.

[4] *The Immediate Experience,* p. 130.

[5] "Star Wars: A Myth for Our Time," *Literature/Film Quarterly 6,* no. 4 (Fall 1978): 324–325.

[6] *Theories of Film* (New York: Viking, 1973), p. 139.

[7] *The World in a Frame* (Garden City, New York: Doubleday/Anchor, 1977), p. 179.

6

NONGENRE NARRATIVE AND ITS MAKERS

Nongenre Narrative

Countless story films employ conventional, easily recognizable characters in familiar plots, which take place in familiar settings and use traditional cinematic techniques to achieve traditional dramatic momentum and resolution. The most familiar and recognizable of these films, the most patterned and repeated, we call *genre films*. The western, for example, is one genre, and the horror film another. But there is no recognized name for the other sort of story film, the film that presents unfamiliar characters and situations or that is always ready to surprise us (to either our delight or dismay). Because these films are often made by people who are more concerned with film as a serious art than a business, they have often been referred to as *art films*. Unfortunately, however, the term *art film* has also come to suggest only those films made by foreign directors for an elite audience. Since there are many American directors who make works of film art and because many artistic films appeal to large audiences, the term *art film* is problematic. For want of a better term, we use the term *nongenre films* for those narrative films that usually are regarded as individual works rather than as part of a group of films.

Nongenre films are extremely surprising and novel in their content and/or their form, are usually valued for their originality, their new way of *seeing*, for the unique vision of their creators. These films are often about philosophical issues, social dilemmas, politics, difficult moral choices and usually — even when they are politically or philosophically committed — the films find no ready or absolute answers to the questions they pose. Such films may be serious or comic or may alternate between modes. Serious examples include *The Seventh Seal* (Ingmar Bergman, 1956), *The Conversation* (Francis Ford Coppola, 1974), and *Tender Mercies* (Bruce Beresford, 1984). Comic examples, that is, films that although roughly called *comic* nevertheless go beyond the traditional formulas of genre comedy, include Charles Chaplin's *Modern Times* (1936), *Playtime* (Jacques Tati, 1967), and *Purple Rose of Cairo* (Woody Allen, 1985). And those films that are both serious and comic nongenre films can be illustrated by Stanley Kubrick's *Dr. Strangelove; or, How I Learned to Stop Worrying and Love the Bomb* (1964), Luis Buñuel's *The Discreet Charm of the Bourgeoisie* (1972), and Barry Levinson's *Diner* (1983).

Although all nongenre films achieve a kind of individual identity, they can be grouped into three general categories according to their dominant narrative strategies: realism, expressionism, and comedy.

CHARACTERISTICS OF NONGENRE FILM REALISM

> You have to strike a mean between naturalism and a certain thing which is artistic, which is selective, you see. If you get the right balance, then you have this strange feeling of being life-like, everything looking very life-like and natural. . . . I think the cinema is the only medium that challenges you to be naturalistic, be realistic and yet be artistic at the same time.
> Satyajit Ray [1]

Narrative art is always conventional. On the one hand, a narrative is patently a fiction, a story, and yet it creates a world meant to parallel that of the narrator and the audience in some way. Otherwise it would be incomprehensible. Every narrative has characters who act like humans (even in a fable or a myth, their behavior resembles ours) in situations that are as recognizable as possible, even if they might not actually be able to occur in the known world. Thus, at one extreme we can understand a tale about a godlike figure able to range instantly about the universe or make sense of a personification of a particular vice or virtue, or even the actions of some impalpable, bodiless energy mass that might express neither desire nor disgust, because even though not very common, such activities are imaginable to the human mind.

At the other extreme, we can construct a narrative in which the minute by minute actions and thoughts of an individual would be recorded in an attempt to render or present an image of a real person, living an actual life. If the object of the narrative is to re-present life, to imitate the space-time continuum shared by narrator and audience outside of the narration, then the recording of the minutiae of an individual's life would be more likely to achieve this impression than

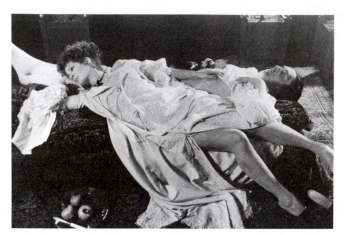

6-1   Realistic nongenre films do not have to be set in contemporary times, but when a historical era is depicted, it is never glamorized. The film does not revel in the charm, romance, and nostalgia evoked by the good old days; rather it usually demystifies, or demythologizes, the past. The eighteenth-century world revealed in *The Draughtsman's Contract* (Peter Greenaway, 1983) is as fragmented and unstable, full of sinister corruption and insidious terror, as any vision of our modern world.

presenting the activities of a handsome, well-formed god who could change into any animal at will. Narrators and audiences have come to agree on a set of practices for storytelling, a set of conventions, which when used by a narrator regulate the limits of the narration. Hence, what we mean by realism is not that the narrative is actually real, but that it follows certain rules or codes known to both makers and receivers of narratives, which gives it a realistic rather than a fantastic character.

Each kind of narrative — written or spoken, filmed or staged — will have its own subset of conventions that will fullfil the expectations audiences and makers of the medium have. In film the realistic non-genre film has a plausible plot — that is, events and actions are comparable to the viewer's experience in the world outside the theater. Usually this kind of film is set in contemporary times; the viewer's own experience brings an immediacy to the film. If, however, the film is set in the past, is historical, the filmmaker does not revel in the charm and romance and nostalgia evoked by the good old days; rather, the film usually demystifies, or demythologizes, the past. The re-creations of a past time in such realistically textured films as *The Seven Samurai* (Akira

Kurosawa, 1955) and *The Draughtsman's Contract* (Peter Greenaway, 1983) bear little resemblance to the re-creations of a somewhat sentimentalized past time in film genres such as the western and the musical (Figure 6-1). The Western adaptation of Kurosawa's film, *The Magnificent Seven* (John Sturges, 1960), presents its western gunfighters much more heroically than does *The Seven Samurai*, and the re-creation of an earlier era in Vincente Minnelli's *Meet Me in St. Louis* (1944) is patently nostalgic.

The characters in the realistic nongenre film usually act and speak in strict accordance with the rules of psychological probability. They also tend to be more complex and therefore less completely comprehensible to the viewer than the characters in genre films. Much as we respond to a real human being, never completely knowing or understanding all facets of another person, so we usually respond to the realistic nongenre film's characters. Those cinematic characters often perform little pieces of random, spontaneous idiosyncratic behavior, which do not advance the story but make the character credible and unique. Such characters also speak more naturally — and often, therefore, speak less communicatively than characters in genre films. Inarticulateness, the particular choice of vocabulary or of silence, is a convention of realism.

The stories and plots, too, of realistic nongenre films tend to be complex, untidy, open-ended. The happy ending in which the protagonist neatly triumphs over his problems is rare; such a pleasant wrapping-up of the story is generally reserved for comedies and genre melodramas. Tidy, sad, or near-tragic endings are also avoided. While the central character may come to some self-realization or solve some problems, the viewer is led to believe that the lives (and problems and triumphs) of the characters go on after the film has ended. Since life is continuous, the film's world, in a sense, is presented as continuous, even though the viewer has been privileged to see only a part of it. This, too, is a convention of realism (Figure 6-2).

Stylistically, the realistic nongenre film tends to reinforce this notion of the film frame as a window on the everyday world. Thus, space and time in the film approximate the viewer's personal experience of space and time. There is an emphasis, therefore, on invisible editing, on long takes (duration), and camera movements that preserve spatial unity. Settings tend to be ordinary and recognizable; events are staged in actual locations. Performers may be unknown or well known, but the realistic mode usually works better when the actors are not star personalities — or if they are stars, they are able to submerge themselves in the role (Figure 6-3). There is a great deal of difference, for instance, between Sally Field in *Places in the Heart* (Robert Benton, 1984) and Gene

6-2 The stories and plots of realistic nongenre films tend to be complex, untidy, open-ended. The film version of *A Passage to India* (David Lean, 1984) doesn't end with the protagonists neatly triumphing over their problems. Such a pleasant wrapping up of loose ends is rare in nongenre films. The viewer often gets the sense that the characters' lives go on after the film has ended, leading to more successes and failures, perhaps, but never a final resolution.

Hackman playing a professional wiretapper in *The Conversation*. Sally Field is a fine actress but her face is too well known and uncommon to allow the viewer to forget she is an actress playing a part. She brings her own persona to the screen and tends to negate the realistic texture of the film, turning it from a potential docu-drama into a genre movie. Gene Hackman, on the other hand, has a face that is somewhat anonymous in its ordinary features, and the viewer is able to forget the actor and believe in the tortured character living in a world where every human act may be under surveillance.

CHARACTERISTICS OF NONGENRE FILM EXPRESSIONISM

A lie is always more interesting than the truth. Lies are the soul of showmanship and I adore shows. Fiction may have a greater truth than everyday, obvious reality. The things one shows need not be authentic. As a rule, they are better if they aren't. What must be authentic is the feeling one is trying to see and to express.
Federico Fellini [2]

As Griffith is the great early creator of films using the conventions of realism, so Sergei Eisenstein is the great early creator of films using the conventions of expressionism. Although Georges Méliès first exploited the theatrical qualities of film to tell stories and is the progenitor of those films that are patently fantastic, Eisenstein nevertheless can be considered the spiritual father of expressionism, that style of filmmaking

6-3   The realistic film assumes that the frame is a window on a world. Actors who are not "star" personalities seem more appropriate to this mode, and nonactors fit even better. Haing S. Ngor was little known before he played the Cambodian journalist in *The Killing Fields* (Roland Joffe, 1983), and thus his portrayal seems true to life and not a performance.

which takes advantage of the formal properties of cinema. In his writings about the editing process, and in his films, Eisenstein demonstrated that meaning could be created by the filmmaker, that feeling or thought could be generated by the way in which the filmmaker juxtaposed images. Events could be created — in the mind of the audience — which were never really shown on the screen but which the audience invariably inferred; geography could be created, metaphors could be communicated by concrete images of objects, time and space were totally malleable, and film owed no particular allegiance to ideas of recording the everyday world.

A wide variety of expressionist conventions are employed by filmmakers in a variety of contexts. The expressionistic nongenre narrative film may or may not have a plausible plot (Figure 6-4); events within the film may or may not conform to the viewer's experience of the world outside the theater. Thus, Fritz Lang's German expressionist film *M* (1932), which tells of a city's search for a pathetic, yet horrible, psychotic child murderer (Figure 6-5), has a plausible plot, but other films have not so much a plot as a pattern of events, which seem to occur and recur as in a dream. Examples include Luis Buñuel's *The Discreet Charm of the Bourgoisie* (1972), Alain Resnais's *Last Year at Marienbad* (1961) or Martin Scorsese's *After Hours* (1985). Or the film may have a plot that is patently fantastic yet tells a story that is at least narratively coherent, like *The Man Who Fell to Earth* (Nicholas Roeg, 1976), *Pennies*

6-4 Federico Fellini, shown here checking the setup on a crane shot, has created films which are expressionistic; through color, costume, decor, and strange characters he reveals both his own and his characters' personal visions. If the plots and the sequences frequently appear illogical, no matter. Fellini insists: "What must be authentic is the feeling one is trying to express."

6-5 Expressionistic films often use objects to suggest actions rather than show them directly. Fritz Lang indicated the death of a little girl in *M* (1931) by first showing us her little ball rolling on the ground by itself and then her balloon rising freely in the air only to be caught by the utility wires. The balloon's drawn-on face and the fact that it looks like a doll further associates it with the child, trapped and finally murdered by the psychopathic killer.

from Heaven (Herbert Ross, 1981), or *The Fourth Man* (Paul Verhoeven, 1984). And, finally, the expressionistic nongenre film may have no plot at all to speak of, no usual story development or narrative movement to propel it forward in the ways most viewers have come to expect. Such films tell stories less through plot than through characterization and through the presence of the filmmaker (in his cinematography), exploring an idea or creating a mood. Michelangelo Antonioni's *L'Avventura* (1959) and *Red Desert* (1964), for example, tell stories about contemporary human beings lost in a cold, empty, modern world to which they have not yet adapted themselves and their emotional needs. The viewer who expects a traditional plot in *L'Avventura* will be disappointed, possibly even enraged, that the filmmaker never answers the question seemingly posed by the events that begin the film: Where has the film's original protagonist, Anna, disappeared to on the desolate volcanic island? A conventional realist story film would answer this question, but Antonioni never answers it because the answer has little to do with the story of his film. His story is not a conventional romance or mystery; rather, the girl's disappearance and her easy replacement in the lives of the other characters and in the film itself is what is important in conveying to the viewer the superficial relationships of modern people with even those they are supposed to love.

The American filmmaker Robert Altman also tends to reject traditional notions of plot, although the American cinema is the most plot-oriented in the world; in *Nashville* (1975), Altman has the thinnest of plots and a minimum of complex characterization, and yet the film is able to engage the viewer and to say something about the American experience, the discrepancy between our ideals and the reality of our lives. *Choose Me* (Alan Rudolph, 1984) is constructed almost like a piece of jazz. As modern jazz has no melodic line, *Choose Me* has no plot — and yet, like modern jazz, which *implies* a melody through counterpoint and harmony, the film implies a plot and central conflicts. Plot of a traditional nature is also missing from many politically oriented films, which must disguise their political content — either for an audience that would not sit still for polemic or for a government that might suppress the film or jail the filmmakers. Entertaining political films are made by Lina Wertmüller, whose bold and exuberant inconsistency and lack of traditional story appears in films like *Let's Talk about Men* (1965) and *All Screwed Up* (1974).

Some expressionist films attempt a Brechtian alienation by purposely distancing the viewer from the film, preventing identification with characters or emotional involvement with what is happening on the screen. By reminding the viewers that they are watching a movie, that they are being manipulated by the medium, such films usually cause the viewer to respond intellectually as well as emotionally. Such distancing can be achieved by films whose surfaces and random construction and interruptions produce an effect of artificiality. Such is the case with a good number of Jean-Luc Godard's films, among them *Le Gai Savoir* (1970), *Tout Va Bien* (1972), and *Passion* (1983), which use long, rambling interviews, interruptions of the action to bring attention to a particular issue, and the insertion of material that seems to have no connection with the narrative.

Characters in expressionistic nongenre films differ from characters in realistic nongenre films in many ways. Characters in these expressionistic films need not be at all like people in the real world. Death is a character (both chilling and comic) in *The Seventh Seal*; he wears black, plays chess, and literally chops men down in their prime. And Jean Cocteau's *Orpheus* (1949), set in the contemporary world, reenacts the legend of Orpheus in a nontraditional way. The messengers of Death ride motorcycles and wear black leather, but they are meant to be interpreted allegorically.

Because it need not present a credible world or probable characters, the expressionistic nongenre film can also manipulate dialogue and plot. Whereas the viewer of the realistic nongenre film expects characters to speak like people in the real world, characters in expressionistic films can speak unrealistically. Ordinarily inarticulate character-types, for example, may utter profound statements, characters may sing instead of talk, may speak in verse or in impeccable grammar. They may tell us about themselves with an awareness that really is the filmmaker's and not the character's. They may even step forward and tell us about what is going to happen next. For instance, *Days of Heaven* (Terence Malick, 1978) employs a narrator whose persona is that of an uneducated child. Nevertheless, she provides sophisticated commentary about the characters and action that not only belie her background, but also clash unrealistically with her usually limited vocabulary.

Similarly, whereas the realistic nongenre film is expected to be somewhat open-ended and untidy in its structure, the expressionistic film can hold an experience so highly structured it could not possibly exist in the real world. Films like *The Scarlet Empress* (Josef von Sternberg, 1934), *Tom Jones* (Tony Richardson, 1963), *One From the Heart* (Francis Coppola, 1983), and *Brazil* (Terry Gilliam, 1986) take place in a highly artificial world — and not merely because of settings or costumes. The balanced structure of the plotting and the formal developments within the film tell viewers they are watching a world on film controlled by the filmmaker (Figure 6-6).

Stylistically, the expressionistic nongenre film tends to emphasize its created nature. Time and space are more often broken down into separate units (shots) and reassembled (montage) than maintained in some prolonged and whole state (mise-en-scène). Thus, in the expressionistic film there tend to be more shots, and often cutting is highly visible, flamboyant, or disjunctive, flagrantly defying realist conventions of chronological time. Montage, rather than mise-en-scène, is the predominant editing pattern. Images are frequently filmed with distorting lenses or filters and color is used expressively rather than realistically (Figure 6-7).

Generally speaking, the expressionistic nongenre film is associated with European filmmakers; the realistic nongenre film is associated with American filmmakers, partly because the predominant Hollywood tradition of invisible filmmaking for all kinds of films tends to mask style in favor of action and story, and this tendency, in turn, has influenced American nongenre film style. *Heartland* (Richard Pearce, 1981) is a good example. Today, however, even American film has broken its allegiance to any particular mode. Because the highly structured Hollywood studio

6-6 Francis Ford Coppola used black-and-white stock, expressive lighting, time lapse photography, and superimpositions to fashion an expressionist style for his version of the S. E. Hinton novel *Rumble Fish* (1984).

6-7 The expressionist film makes great use of shadows. As the authorities wait in a dimly lit square for the appearance of Harry Lime, a wanted criminal in *The Third Man* (Carol Reed, 1950), a shadow of a man coming down a side street is thrown upon a wall. The suspense mounts as the shadow gets bigger and bigger. At last the man is visible, but it's not Harry Lime, only a balloon seller. The suspense is broken, at least for the moment.

6-8 Describing a film as "realistic" or "expressionistic" is often difficult and sometimes beside the point. Ingmar Bergman's *The Seventh Seal* (1956) combines the two seemingly opposed modes of storytelling with ease. On the one hand, Death is personified as a character with magical powers (expressionistic), and on the other hand, the re-creation of the life of the Middle Ages is documentary-like (realistic). The march of the penitents seems frighteningly real, what it might have looked like in those times.

system of the late 1920s through the early 1960s is no more, filmmakers working on independent productions can make a nongenre film that uses expressionistic conventions. We no longer demand that the art of film, the *artifice* of film, be invisible to the viewer. Francis Coppola's version of *Rumble Fish* (1984), for example, clearly displays its artifice in many ways: time lapse cinematography, sparing use of color in a black-and-white film, and artificial, symbolic dialogue.

The chief quality of the expressionistic mode is its artificiality and its chief effect is that viewers are constantly reminded — by the visible technique, the created structure, the manipulated characters — that what they are watching is a movie created by someone. An expressionistic film demands that we look *at* the frame rather than *through* it, that what we see contained in the frame is a world that does not attempt to imitate the everyday world. Obviously, few commercial expressionistic films are completely so. Just as the general ticket-buying public (both in the United States and abroad) does not usually patronize the most extreme examples of cinematic realism — the **uncontrolled documentary** — so too the public does not patronize the most extreme examples of cinematic expressionism — the independent **avant-garde** film. Although we have thus far separated realistic and expressionistic films in terms of their chief characteristics, it must be remembered that most films use *both* expressionistic and realistic techniques (Figure 6-8). There are no set rules that say a film *must* be one thing or the other. Sometimes, in fact, a blatant mixture may result in a movie that is for that very reason innovative. *The World According to Garp* (George Roy Hill, 1983), for instance, mixes realism and expressionism in its construction, use of music, cinematography, and characterizations. This combination creates an unsettling disequilibrium.

CHARACTERISTICS OF NONGENRE FILM COMEDY

> I not only plan for surprise in the general incidents of a picture, but I also try to vary my individual actions so that they, too, will come as a surprise. I always try to do the unexpected in a novel way. If I think an audience expects me to walk along the street while in a picture, I will suddenly jump on a car. . . . Figuring out what the audience expects, and then doing something different, is great fun to me.
> Charles Chaplin [3]

Most comic films repeat conventional comic plots (say, the early films of Laurel and Hardy, or musical comedies), but there are comic films that organize their material in such a way as to exhibit characteristics similar to those found in nongenre films. They are seriously concerned with important human issues, their humor intends to instruct as much as entertain, and their moral centers will frequently be critical of the status quo. Renoir's *Rules of the Game* (1939), Chaplin's *Monsieur Verdoux* (1947), Allen's *Purple Rose of Cairo* (1985), and Albert Brooks' *Lost in America* (1985) are notable examples of comic nongenre films.

Many of the most recognizable comic nongenre films are satiric, but even films without **satire** can be funny without conforming to any traditional formula or structure. François Truffaut's *Small Change* (1976), for example, depicts the odd and amusing behavior of children and their parents, but never condemns either group or holds them up to ridicule. The structure of the film is episodic — we see incidents in the lives of a group of children, some from this family, some from that — and the unpredictability of the events arouses surprise and amusement.

Most comic nongenre films, however, are satires. Even though one might be able to recognize certain conventional patterns of exposition in some of these films, the fact that they satirize a particular element in human nature or some specific aspect of society tends to make them unique. Jacques Tati's *Monsieur Hulot's Holiday* (1953) derives its structure from the picaresque tradition — following one person as he moves from one absurd encounter to another — but the picture of life at a French seaside resort is so specific that the film is one of a kind.

The fathers of silent comedy, Max Linder in France and Mack Sennett in the United States, never concentrated primarily on satire and social commentary, yet both inevitably used comedy to comment upon society and its foibles. In the comic world rich people are stuffy, cops are clumsy, merchants are stingy, and so these early makers of formula comedies can still be seen as the progenitors of cinematic satire, the comic form most found in nongenre films. By its very nature (think, for example, of the political cartoon in a newspaper making us laugh at the absurdity of inflation or the arms race), satire is concerned with important human issues. Its structure and its targets are complex. Indeed, criticism of social and political institutions has traditionally been refracted through satiric comedy.

Thus, satire always has some connection with the real world, the world inhabited by the viewer, though that connection can be weak or strong. Woody Allen's *Bananas* (1971) and *Sleeper* (1973), for instance, are satires which have referents to the real world in which we live but are finally so grotesquely exaggerated in incident and character that the films strongly resemble fantasy. On the other hand, although Allen's *Annie Hall* uses unrealistic devices and incidents that arise out of fantasy, the film's connections with real characters and real human problems make it more clearly satiric. Whether satiric plots are realistic or probable as in *Annie Hall* or Tati's *Playtime*, or whether they are unrealistic and improbable as in *Dr. Strangelove* or *Eating Raoul* (Paul Bartel, 1982), they share a serious underlying purpose, which is to reveal the audience and the society to itself (Figure 6-9).

Whether the comic films are satiric or not, whether they are superficially realistic or blatantly grotesque, almost all will end in a happy resolution. In the few that do not, for example, *Dr. Strangelove*, in which the world is blown up at the film's end, the distancing techniques of the film (chiefly exaggeration) will keep the viewer from feeling distressed. Because the usual comic film ends happily, its structure will be much more tidy and balanced than the structure of a realistic nongenre film.

Characters in the comedies are also likely to be exaggerated in some fashion. Even when they are relatively realistic, they can be drawn rather broadly, without the complexity of real people. The gay couple who live together in *La Cage Aux Folles* (Edouard Molinaro, 1981) are quite realistic, but their behavior (for example, their flamboyant displays of affection and grief) are out of the realm of fairy tales; we are pleased at their happy ending, but we are also aware that such happy endings are unreal.

Stylistically, the comic nongenre film borrows from the conventions of both realism and expressionism. Because satire is so large a part of the comic nongenre mode, however, exaggerated lighting, acting, dialogue, compositions, and camera technique are commonly used. Thus, one can point to three rather different sorts of satire — *Dr. Strangelove, Zero for*

6-9 Nongenre comedy usually has some connection with the world outside the theater, no matter how bizarre the plot. In *Eating Raoul* (Paul Bartel, 1982), the protagonists murder sex perverts in order to accumulate capital for their dream project, opening a charming little country restaurant so they don't have to live and work in the dirty, crowded, and dangerous big city. This implausible plot satirizes the American drive for success as well as reflecting the real problems of metropolitan existence.

Conduct (Jean Vigo, 1933), and *À Nous la Liberte* (René Clair, 1931) and find exaggerations in characterization, lighting, decor, and costuming in all three. The furthest extension of this kind of stylization and exaggeration is, of course, the animated **cartoon** — the film that is all stylization and exaggeration. In animated films adherence to common laws of time and space is as unnecessary as is adherence to normal human behavior. Characters may be flattened by cars, but a moment later they pop up and resume the chase. Although the typical cartoon tends to fall into various generic forms (one Roadrunner cartoon is much like another in plot and characterization and incident), some animated films, such as those made by the Zagreb Studios in Yugoslavia, are quite innovative in concept and structure.

THEMES AND AESTHETICS OF THE NONGENRE FILM

The classics in any medium have a particular quality of transcendence through which they outlive the fashions and tastes of the times in which they were made. A play by Shakespeare, a painting by Renoir, an opera by Mozart all deliver rich aesthetic satisfactions to generation after generation. In each instance, the artist's work is marked by a complexity of organization (whether it appears simple or not) coupled with meaning that speaks to humanity's basic and recurrent problems directly.

6-10 John Ford's *Stagecoach* (1939) is an example of a popular film which not only meets the requirements of the western genre but also exists on the level of high art. Critics who ordinarily dismiss genre films have lavish praise for its complex treatment of moral issues and its superior handling of visual material.

Individual or nongenre films, insofar as they use the cinema directly to explore important human questions, must be considered serious art, even if they are comedies. Serious art need not be viewed grimly, but it is always taken seriously (this is not the same as solemnly) by both the artist and the audience.

Many nongenre films are not popular; they are considered difficult, slow-moving, not entertaining. Of course, even the most difficult and esoteric of films must appeal to some relatively large group of people to earn back the large investment made in film production, but in comparison with the millions of people who go to more generic films for their entertainment, the number of people interested in viewing innovative films is relatively small. These films, though usually not distributed widely across the country in commercial theaters, nevertheless are often considered the most important films of any year. They are the films talked about by influential critics and reviewers and scholars and students. They are the films that win awards at film festivals around the world and, though they may not be big box-office hits in the year of their release, will continue to be shown long after their more financially remunerative counterparts have been forgotten. These nongenre films are usually considered intellectual fare parallel to modern poetry, opera, painting, fiction, and drama. Yet lest one imagine a vast dichotomy between nongenre films and genre films, it is important to remember that some exceptional genre films such as *Stagecoach* (John Ford, 1939) may, by virtue of their freshness or imaginative power, be high art as well as popular art (Figure 6-10). Conversely, some excellent nongenre

6-11 Ingmar Bergman, always the serious and committed film artist, has been probing the relationship between man and God and religion in films from the 1950s to the present. *Fanny and Alexander* (1982) explored the harshness of a nineteenth-century Swedish parson whose belief in man's fallen nature makes him a tyrant to his young second wife (above), played by Ewa Froling.

films have been made in Hollywood and have achieved great popular success, winning praise from both the movie critic and scholar and the average filmgoer. Films like *The Birth of a Nation* (D. W. Griffith, 1915) and *2001: A Space Odyssey* (Stanley Kubrick, 1968), and *Annie Hall* were commercial as well as artistic successes.

The great themes found in these films are very general when stated outright: What are human beings' relationships to each other? to environment? to God? to mortality? (Figure 6-11). In fact, abstracting these themes from the work in which they are embedded and elaborated upon often reveals clichés: "Art is long, life is short." "Man must suffer to win redemption." "Heroes are made, not born." "Man is always alone in an empty universe." Nongenre films express the primary paradox inherent in lived reality: you can love and hate the same thing at the same time — a person, the job, living itself. And it is in this way that nongenre films, whether or not their surface textures are fantastic, realistic, or expressionistic, are more true to the complexities of lived experience, i.e. more real, than genre films. Genre films often seem unrealistic, in this sense, because they separate things and people into that which we hate and that which we love. We hate the villains, we love the heroes and heroines. We hate injustice and bureaucracy, we love forthrightness and getting to the bottom of things.

In the working out of these themes, in the specific ways in which a particular nongenre film visualizes and gives dramatic statement to these themes, they resonate beyond clichés and catchphrases. It is not, however, simply a matter of a film addressing itself to great themes that deserves our attention; it is also a matter of the ways the film has used the materials, the way its techniques and structures have rephrased those old and answerless questions. Sheer technical brilliance alone is not enough. The perennial questions must permeate a film that moves and touches its viewers. In general, stories and narratives can encompass only a limited amount of variety in their basic themes, but each new treatment's use of the materials and techniques of the cinematic medium may be excitingly different.

Personal Visions

> I know that I have the ability to articulate images that sit deeply inside us, that I can make them visible. It is an athletic endeavor, like life itself. Things work inside of me for a long time, images become clearer, and at a certain point I just sit down and write the script in three days. There is always a key image; everything emerges from that, physically, not by analysis.
>
> Werner Herzog [4]

One characteristic of the nongenre narrative film is that it tends to make the viewer sense that it is the work of a unique artistic consciousness. This is true even when we know that filmmaking is a collaborative art and that films, like great cathedrals, are the work of many hands. In literature, painting, or music, the artist who created the work is usually easily identifiable. In drama or music, there are two kinds of artists: the writers or composers and the performers. The film artist, however, is more elusive. Not only does a film have a writer (perhaps several), and a director and performers, but it also has a producer, a cinematographer, an **art director,** and an editor (perhaps several). A film that is unified by an overall conception and execution may be attributed to the strong personal force of any one of these figures as much as it is the actual result of their combined efforts. The elaborate business of developing a movie from its inception to its release makes it extremely difficult to know who contributed what to a particular film, whose personal imprint on the film was the strongest. Screen **credits** are dictated more by

6-12   Rainer Werner Fassbinder was a significant contributor to the New German Cinema's examination of how the Nazi experience influenced the shape of life in Germany after World War II. In *Lili Marlene* (1980) he analyzed the way in which innocent and politically unaware individuals could be drawn into the Nazi web and what choices might be possible when they finally realized what they were doing.

tradition (and by union regulations) than by accuracy; they reflect only those people who last worked on the film before its release. Thus, although many writers may have contributed to the finished **script** at various points in its development, although directors may have been changed in midmovie — as was true, for example, with *Gone with the Wind* (1939), attributed to Victor Fleming — usually only the last person associated with a particular function gets the credit.

Attempting to unravel the intricate fabric of the collaborative effort that goes into the making of any film is an interesting, if sometimes hopeless, activity. Though most people tend to talk about *Citizen Kane* (1941) in terms of Orson Welles, its director and star, it is also possible to discuss the film's artistry in terms of Gregg Toland's cinematography, Robert Wise's editing, and Herman J. Mankiewicz's **screenplay;** all of these film artists have shown their artistry and the strength of their personalities in other fine films, and they all played important roles in the realization of *Citizen Kane*. On the other hand, there are directors like Federico Fellini and Ingmar Bergman who write their own scripts, supervise the camera work closely, oversee the editing, and so dominate the making of their films that they may be easily and clearly identified as the primary creative forces behind their works.

Because of the influence of these kinds of directors, critics and scholars have tended to focus on the director as the key person in control of the creation of the finished work (Figure 6-12). But one could almost as easily focus on a performer, a cinematographer, a writer, or an editor whose presence is the dominant factor in the film's artistic success. To illustrate these difficulties, we will discuss the director here. This does not mean, however, that the other members of the film production unit are less important — merely that they are usually less visible.

Film directors can be separated into three major categories: first, **film artisans,** who, though they make highly acclaimed and well-wrought films and thus must be considered good directors, never develop an individual and consistent body of work either stylistically or thematically; second, **film auteurs,** directors who, even though the script, the performers, and the production crew are imposed on them, establish their authority and stamp their films with a recognizable style or vision; and third, **film artists,** who are in nearly total control of every aspect and phase of the filmmaking process and the film itself.

THE FILM ARTISAN

> I don't *seek* to interpret, to put my own stamp on the material. I try to be as faithful to the original material as I can. This applies equally to Melville as it applies to the Bible, for example. In fact, it's the fascination that I feel for the original that makes me want to make it into a film.
> John Huston[5]

The first group of directors (for example, Michael Curtiz, Henry Hathaway, Sydney Pollack) might be considered fine artisans rather than artists; chameleonlike, they thoroughly match their style to the given material. In the past, these directors almost always worked for a studio. They were given scripts by the producers, which they were to transform into a completed film using a certain number of dollars and a certain amount of time. Almost all of these directors were committed not to personal visions but to bringing out the values of the script in the most effective and economical way possible. Camera work and editing were usually left to subordinate or equally powerful collaborators who had the same commitment to the story. These directors would film a gothic tale of horror with the appropriate music, the proper number of creaking doors, dark shadows, and odd camera angles. They would film a detective story with an appropriate sense of pace and an eye on the denouement, a biblical epic with a cast of thousands and the right number of spectacular scenes. Such director-artisans seemed most at home filming genre films, films whose very conventions are the familiar mainstays of commercial cinema.

A case in point is John Huston, who, over the years, has handled every genre of film there is and done them all well. His suspense films include *The Maltese Falcon* (1941) and *The List of Adrian Messenger* (1963). He has done adaptations of such literary works as *The Red Badge of*

6-13 John Huston is a master craftsman among American film directors. He has worked in a wide variety of genres and has adapted his style to the requirements of his stories. *Treasure of the Sierra Madre* (1948) is an adventure genre film, telling the classic tale of "three men and the gold." *Prizzi's Honor* (1985) is an offbeat blend of gangster and romantic comedy genres in which the star-crossed lovers are both paid killers for the mob.

Courage (1951) and *Moby Dick* (1956), *Fat City* (1972), *The Man Who Would Be King* (1976), and *Prizzi's Honor* (1985). He has made period films such as *Moulin Rouge* (1953) and *The Barbarian and the Geisha* (1958), and adventure films such as *The Treasure of the Sierra Madre* (1948) and *The African Queen* (1952). Despite this large body of work, including films that have become classics of American cinema and, like *Treasure* and *African Queen*, have attributes of both genre and nongenre films, no one of Huston's films bears a distinct relationship to the others (Figure 6-13). Without his name on the credits, no one of Huston's films can be recognized immediately as such from its style or form. The films have in common only their emphasis on narrative and their efficiency and competence; even moments of artistry in the individual films, moments of extreme brilliance, do not add up to communicate a sense of the director's personality, his stamp, imprint, or personal seal.

THE FILM AUTEUR

> Certain scripts you get, of course, you just feel hopeless. So you must try to do something with lighting, acting, décor, pace . . . all those elements. Or else the material is too usual, so you try to find an element of strangeness.
>
> Douglas Sirk [6]

6-14   Alfred Hitchcock is one of the few film auteurs whose name is familiar enough to mass audiences that people speak of going to see a "Hitchcock picture." Here he is shown in distinctive profile working with Janet Leigh on the set of *Psycho* (1960).

Directors of the second group — those who worked for Hollywood studios, but who transcended their routine assignments to create a body of work stamped with a distinctive style or vision — have been labeled *auteurs* by French critics. Although there has been a good deal of writing about such directors as Howard Hawks, Alfred Hitchcock, and John Ford, they are almost unknown to the general moviegoer. Only Hitchcock, because of his appearances on television, could be said to be a household word (Figure 6-14). The director's imprint in American films has never been as obvious as in many European films. The work of such directors as Fellini, Truffaut, and Bergman is, in fact, so distinctive that one can recognize their films without benefit of the director's credit at the beginning of the film.

Most American directors' films, however, seem not to be so clearly identifiable as those films made by European film artists. At first glance, most American films from the late 1920s to the present seem to be made from the same cloth; they all look like Hollywood films. They came from studios like MGM, Paramount, and Warner Brothers and they featured performers who were familiar stars. The actual physical look of the films seemed determined less by a single individual artistic consciousness than by the studio; Warner Brothers movies looked contemporary, were rapidly edited and scripted around social problems; MGM films looked rich and glossy, with high production values. These films were usually advertised with the star's name above the title; Warner Brothers gave us Bette Davis movies or Humphrey Bogart movies, and MGM gave us Greta Garbo and Elizabeth Taylor. Until quite recently, the names of American directors were seldom featured in advertising copy or on movie marquees; D. W. Griffith, Frank Capra, Cecil B. De Mille, and Alfred Hitchcock were the chief exceptions.

Aside from the presence of stars in the American film, the most important part of an American film was its story, the good tale that seemed to slip effortlessly through the projector as if from the lips of some expert and omniscient narrator. And these good movie tales tended to fall into identifiable groups dealing with similar subject matter. There were westerns, romances, mysteries, and war movies. Not until the French film critics of the 1950s began to look closely in admiration at American films was it remarked that beneath the homogenized surface appearance of the Hollywood film there were works of distinction and quality and that often these works were those of the same directors.

The names of such American directors as John Ford, Samuel Fuller, Nicholas Ray, and Douglas Sirk were added to the more familiar list of American film artists: Chaplin, Keaton, Capra, and Hitchcock. Still, it was apparent that these directors were not like the European film artists who had relatively complete control over their work and who could explore their personal aesthetic and thematic preoccupations with relative freedom. Rather, these Hollywood directors worked under studio rule, presumably as journeymen employees involved in the mass production of popular entertainment. They were assigned a script rather than choosing one. They were given a cast of performers and told by a producer to shoot the film in so many days. They did not have the right of **final cut** and so the studio and the producer could reedit and sometimes reshoot scenes and alter the film to their liking and their notion of what the public would like and pay money to see. Yet despite all these restrictions and enforced collaborations, somehow these directors, over the years, managed to make films that were stamped with their particular vision. Certain stylistic touches — like John Ford's use of the horizon line — or certain recurrent themes — like Douglas Sirk's exploration of the traditional roles of women — were consistently evident in nearly all the films of each of these directors. To be sure, they frequently worked, over the years, with one or two particular screenwriters or with a particular cinematographer or film editor — or they were able to specialize in a certain film genre, hence some of the consistency in their work (Figure 6-15).

Although the literal translation of *auteur* implies that the director is the author of the film in much the same way that a writer is the author of a book, the term is traditionally reserved for those directors who have *not* had complete control over their work, yet who have left a personal mark on their films. Alfred Hitchcock was just such a director — although from the mid-1950s he had relatively complete control over both the choice of script and the final version of the film by virtue of his enormous financial as well as critical successes. Hitchcock's films are all linked together by certain thematic and stylistic qualities. For the most part, he has made suspense thrillers. In most of his films, an innocent

6-15   Now revered by students and scholars of film, film auteurs like John Ford usually thought of themselves as people who made motion pictures in the entertainment business. They rarely discussed the theme or style of their films. Ford liked to refer to making pictures as just "a job of work." It was not until the French critics from *Cahiers du Cinema* "discovered" our American directors that we deemed them worthy of study.

bystander, an upstanding and law-abiding citizen, becomes involved in an extraordinary and often nightmarish adventure because his identity is mistaken (*The Wrong Man*, 1956 or *North by Northwest*, 1959); or he or she is in a certain place at the wrong time (*The Lady Vanishes*, 1938 or *The Man Who Knew Too Much*, 1935 and 1956); or he is falsely accused of a crime because of circumstantial evidence (*The Thirty-Nine Steps*, 1935 or *Frenzy*, 1972). Suspense is created to a certain extent simply by the nature of the plot, but through the years Hitchcock developed a style of editing and camera movement, which always created a high degree of suspense and viewer identification purely through visual means. The parallel editing in *Strangers on a Train* (1951), for example, which alternates the tennis match in which the innocent hero plays and the movements of the real killer who is attempting to frame him, builds an amazing tension primarily in the alternation and rhythm of the shots.

In addition to the major auteur directors like Hitchcock or John Ford, there are some directors like Anthony Mann who, although they have made many studio-inspired films that are hardly distinguishable from any other director's, have made a smaller group of films within their total body of work which does have a distinct and personal identity. Though Mann directed *The Glenn Miller Story* (1954), *God's Little Acre* (1958), *El Cid* (1961), and *The Fall of the Roman Empire* (1964), a varied and impersonal bunch, he has also made a group of westerns including *Winchester 73* (1950), *Bend of the River* (1952), *The Naked Spur* (1953), *The Far Country* (1955), and *The Tin Star* (1957). These latter films, although generically westerns, are also specifically Mann-made movies, exhibiting certain themes, which link them together as the work of one individual. All are studies of civilized men who go beyond the law and ordinary conventions of behavior in order to exact revenge for some past hurt, and yet who end up reliving the traumatic events that led to their initial separation from society. Mann's heroes travel through time, place, and experience, but the travel is cyclical, for they ultimately return to confront and accept their place in a social world.

A few auteur directors are valued less for their thematic consistency from picture to picture than for their cinematic style, their use of technique, which has remained visible and personal throughout their careers. Certain camera movements, particular kinds of visual compositions, what the camera "likes" to look at, can to the trained eye be seen as the distinctive elements in a Josef von Sternberg, Max Ophuls, Nicholas Ray, or Joseph Losey film. Though Joseph Losey's films, for example, have frequently focused on disturbed human relationships (*The Servant*, 1964; *Accident*, 1967; *Secret Ceremony*, 1968; *The Go-Between*, 1971), there seems to be no personal thematic vision; Losey also directed *The Boy with the Green Hair* (1948), *These Are the Damned* (1965), *Modesty Blaise* (1966), and *Don Giovanni* (1979). And yet, despite a lack of thematic clarity and unity, each Losey film seems marked by certain visual elements that are recurrent in film after film. Losey is fascinated with furniture and furnishings. His camera frequently moves obsessively around the interior of rooms, usually grand rooms, and it examines the details of the decor as if their texture and shape were more revealing of some reality and truth than the texture and shape of the room's inhabitants. In keeping with this desire to reveal the animate through the inanimate, Losey often focuses on mirrors, silver, and other polished surfaces, which reflect and distort the images of his characters (most effectively used and related to the film's theme in *The Servant*).

The typical auteur director, unlike film artists such as Fellini, Truffaut, and Bergman, seldom seems comfortable taking credit for those personal thematic and stylistic elements that critics have found in the films. The auteurs, tending to see themselves as storytellers, are somewhat embarrassed by the attention of critics. Unlike the film artists, these auteur directors do not see themselves as artists with a personal vision of the world, but rather as entertainers. Nevertheless, much like Shakespeare, who wrote his plays for a living, film auteurs may be "men for all seasons," people whose work appeals not only to the popular audience of its own time, but also to audiences and scholars and critics of later generations.

Young American directors whose work has been received with critical enthusiasm are peculiarly difficult to classify. Are they film artists or film auteurs? Most of their movies, appearing after the demise of the strong studio system in the mid-1960s, are the products of independent production companies. In this new kind of production, each film is treated individually rather than as part of a total studio output made by studio

6-16 Stanley Kubrick's *A Clockwork Orange* (1972) is an example of a non-genre narrative film that uses expressionistic rather than realistic elements to create a vision of the near future. Bizarre sets and costumes, ritualized violence, ironic music, distortion lenses, and rapid montage are some of the means used by this director who went from auteur to film artist.

personnel and geared to a studio look or reputation. Some contemporary filmmakers, of course, started within the studio system. Stanley Kubrick, for example, began making films in the early 1950s, working with such studios as Universal, MGM, and Columbia. Although he has always been intimately involved with the selection of his scripts, he did not form his own production company until after *2001: A Space Odyssey* (1968). Then he went on to make *A Clockwork Orange* (1971), *Barry Lyndon* (1975), and *The Shining* (1980). Thus, Kubrick went from being a film auteur to being a film artist who originates his own projects and keeps total control over them (Figure 6-16). Francis Ford Coppola has made big budget studio-type movies like *The Godfather* (1972) and *The Godfather, Part II* (1974), which are as personal as the smaller films he's made supposedly for himself, like *The Conversation* (1974) (Figure 6-17). *Apocalypse Now* (1979), Coppola's vision of the Vietnam war, is a hybrid: a big-budget film (reportedly over $30 million), but very unlike a studio film. It was made, rather, to express a private view, an interpretation of history and human nature. Coppola not only formed his own production company, but bought an old sound stage building in Los Angeles with the hope of reviving a studio production system. He hoped to have a number of films made on his lot (which he called Zoetrope Studios) by different directors each year. The plan went awry when his *One from the Heart* (1983), made entirely on a sound stage in imitation of the films made by Hollywood from the 1930s through the 1950s, failed at the box office and he had to sell the studio. In an effort to recoup his losses, he has directed and produced several films made from S. E. Hinton's

6-17 Francis Ford Coppola made big-budget movies like *The Godfather*, part I (1972) and part II (1974) for a studio (i.e., he was a film auteur) and then used the money he made from those films to finance more personal films like *The Conversation* (1974) (i.e., he functioned as a film artist).

teenage novels — *The Outsiders* (1983) and *Rumble Fish* (1984). Only the latter has the personal, stylistic flourishes one expects from this self-conscious filmmaker. Robert Altman, Martin Scorsese, and Woody Allen are only some of those contemporary directors who seem committed to making films that are personal statements.

Whether we identify these directors as film artists or film auteurs is, of course, open to discussion. In fact, the terms *film artist* and *film auteur* have recently been used interchangeably, auteur now generally meaning anyone (director, performer, cinematographer, screenwriter, or the like) who has stamped a film with his personality — whether or not he worked within or without a studio system. In any case, artist or auteur, these filmmakers are currently making films whose narratives share much of the novelty and artistic excitement formerly generated only by foreign directors.

THE FILM ARTIST

> Freedom is the absolute necessity. From the beginning, I've had total control over my films. . . . I can be very free even if I am surrounded by ten gorillas or one producer. And if I cannot feel free enough, then I will simply leave without making the film.
> Bernardo Bertolucci [7]

Though everyone who works on an aesthetically successful film may be considered an artist of sorts (including the cinematographer, composer, editor, and so on), the term *film artist* here refers only to directors who make a film to communicate their personal vision of the world. These directors belong to the third category of directors, artists in total control of the films they make. They are father, mother, and midwife to their films. They take themselves seriously, frequently writing aesthetic man-

ifestos, granting interviews, arguing theories, and supplying interpretations of their work. These directors do not see themselves merely as artisans, doing a job for an employer, but rather as individual
artists uncompromised by financial exigencies and marketplace demands (even if, in fact they are). Among these directors are Federico
Fellini (Italy), Andrei Tarkovsky (Russia), Akira Kurosawa (Japan), Satyajit Ray (India), Werner Herzog (Germany), and Susan Seidelman
(United States). It is notable that relatively few film artists are American.
In foreign countries, film production is heavily subsidized through taxes
on individual admissions, and in any case foreign films can often be
produced for less money than can American films. Foreign film production, moreover, has always been at some remove from the American
studio system, which was run by strong-willed producers such as Jack
Warner, Sam Goldwyn, and Darryl Zanuck, whose primary criterion for
filmmaking was financial success rather than artistic success. Finally,
however, foreign attitudes about film probably have helped foreign
directors to consider themselves film artists. Americans initially considered film lowbrow entertainment, but Europeans have long considered
film as serious art.

Especially since World War II, European directors have often originated an idea for a film, have gotten financial backing from banks,
independent sources, or government subsidy, and then have followed
the film through production to completion and release. This arrangement usually allows the director to include in his or her contract the
right to the final cut, the final decision as to how the actual release print
of the film will look. These directors most often work with a handpicked
production crew who stay together for picture after picture, forming
what amounts to a repertory production company, one knowledgeable
about and sympathetic to the director's style and vision. Thus, Werner
Herzog or Ingmar Bergman repeatedly works with the same crews and
often with the same performers. It is only recently that one can point to
an American equivalent in the production habits and films of such
contemporary directors as Robert Altman, Martin Scorsese, and Francis
Ford Coppola (Figure 6-18).

The work of these film directors often embodies such distinct personal characteristics that we often refer to the artist's vision — a term
familiar from literary criticism but especially appropriate here. This
vision can be either thematic or stylistic, but usually it combines both.
Bergman's films from his first internationally acclaimed hit, *The Seventh
Seal* (1956), to *Fanny and Alexander* (1983) all deal with such profound
questions as: Is there a God? What is reality? What hope is there for man
in an unresponsive world? How can one exorcise demons of the mind

6-18 Many of America's successful new directors grew up watching retrospectives of traditional Hollywood films. George Lucas and Steven Spielberg produced the *Star Wars* saga and *Raiders of the Lost Ark* (1982) in order to revive the adventure films they recalled from their childhoods. Martin Scorsese made *New York, New York* (1977) as an homage to the big band musicals of the 1940s. Brian De Palma makes thrillers in the style of his idol Alfred Hitchcock. Just as in so many Hitchcock films, the climactic scene of De Palma's *Blow Out* (1981), in which a protagonist must try to prevent a murder, takes place in a crowded public place.

and soul? Although these questions are chiefly embodied in Bergman's dialogue, which the characters speak, they are also embodied in the lighting and the color, the cinematography and the editing, and the acting, all of which Bergman supervises. All of these elements are distinctively Bergmanesque — in other words, recognizable from film to film — and are distinctively used to underscore and amplify the philosophical themes. Sound, or the lack of it in *The Silence* (1963), embodies ideas that Bergman wishes to express about communication; lighting in *The Magician* (1958) serves the thematic questioning of the difference between illusion and reality; color in *Cries and Whispers* (1972) weakens or strengthens in sympathy with the characters' emotional involvement in the events of the film.

The roll call of the names of such film artists is long; these directors come from all countries and appear throughout the historical development of the art. D. W. Griffith, Sergei Eisenstein, F. W. Murnau, René Clair, Orson Welles, François Truffaut, Akira Kurosawa, Satyajit Ray, Lina Wertmüller, Rainer Fassbinder — these are a few of the artists who have used film as their medium. These film artists can be obtuse, vague, argumentative, shocking, self-indulgent, ascetic, sublime. They

6-19 Werner Herzog, shown on location in the Peruvian Amazon during the shooting of *Fitzcarraldo* (1982), focuses all his films on men with powerful obsessions who often fail in their attempts to achieve the impossible. Herzog is just as obsessive about filmmaking as any of his subjects. Despite incredible setbacks in terms of accidents to cast and equipment, withdrawal of financing, and the impossible weather, he completed this film over a three-year period.

can present philosophic conundrums, they can ambush and attack the very audience that they are addressing — and yet, because of their individuality and their mastery of the medium, they are respected and loved by their relatively small but loyal audiences. Film artists such as Michelangelo Antonioni, Jean-Luc Godard, Bernardo Bertolucci, Robert Altman, Stanley Kubrick, and Terrence Malick see themselves creating art that has something important to say, which may potentially exist on a level with the works of da Vinci, Beethoven, and Dostoevski. This attitude toward the medium and its capacity for expression rests not so much on an inflated ego as on a personal obsession objectified and translated into the finished work of film art (Figure 6-19).

FILM AND LITERATURE: THE PROBLEM OF ADAPTATION

Although one of the reasons we admire film artists is their unique vision of the world, far more story films have been made from literary and dramatic sources than have been made from stories originally conceived for films. The economics of filmmaking and its reliance on mass taste makes its presence strongly felt in the choice of a story for a film. A novel or play or Broadway musical that has done well financially or is an established classic has a presold audience and advance publicity (Figure 6-20). Everyone who has been exposed to the original work or who has even heard about it will naturally be curious to see what the film version

6-20 In a famous essay, Sergei Eisenstein suggested the influence of Charles Dickens's narrative techniques on D. W. Griffith. It is no wonder, then, that Dickens has always been a popular choice as a source for film adaptation. David Lean, the noted English director, used rich shading and texture to depict the hard life of a poor boy in Victorian England in his version of *Oliver Twist* (1948).

is like. Some may come to scoff at the way Hollywood simplifies a reputable literary classic — for example, the two versions of *The Great Gatsby*, one made in 1949 by Elliott Nugent and the other in 1974 by Jack Clayton. Others may come to applaud the flesh-and-blood creation of characters and events hitherto only described on a printed page and imagined in the mind — as with *Gone with the Wind* (1939) (Figure 6-21) and *The Godfather* (1972). For many, the opportunity to see quality performers in great plays and musicals outside the major metropolitan areas provides the impetus; one can point to the superb performance of Sir Laurence Olivier in his self-directed *Richard III* (1956) or to Barbra Streisand repeating on film her Broadway performance in *Funny Girl* (William Wyler, 1968).

Granted that **adaptations** from previously successful sources are economically sound (and perhaps a great deal easier to script, for the characters are already drawn, named, and personalized, the setting chosen, the plot worked out), many serious aesthetic problems arise in translating a story effectively from one medium to another. Sometimes what works wonderfully well on the stage or on the page disappoints on the screen.

The main problem, of course, is that film is primarily visual communication; literature and drama are primarily verbal communication. Although literature and drama printed in a book use images or figures of speech, those images are constructed from language rather than from concrete objects. The language supplies information from which the

6-21 Though it is undoubtedly easier to make a good film from a book which has not been widely read, *Gone with the Wind* (Victor Fleming, 1939) is an example of a film which captured the spirit of the novel in such exciting images that the many readers of Margaret Mitchell's best-seller were not disappointed. Indeed, modern readers of the novel generally think of Rhett Butler as embodied in Clark Gable and Scarlett O'Hara as Vivien Leigh.

reader then constructs her or his own specific mental image. Film, on the other hand, by recording physical objects, gives every viewer the same set of images — and although each viewer may presumably interpret the meaning of those objects, the physical specificity of those objects is never in question. It is not unusual, therefore, that a film version of a favorite book or short story will not satisfy the viewer because the specific images chosen by the filmmaker — for example, the actor who plays Gatsby — will never be exactly the same as the images the reader conjured up from the printed word.

Dramatic Adaptation: Shakespeare as an Example

Even performed drama — theater — relies heavily on word pictures to create many of its effects. Since stage space is limited, other real and imaginative spaces must be conjured up through the magic of verbal metaphor and description spoken by the actors. In *Macbeth,* for example, King Duncan sets the scene for us when he says, "This castle hath a pleasant seat; the air/Nimbly and sweetly recommends itself/Unto our

6-22 When dramas are translated into films, stage space is often exchanged for "on location" cinematic space in order to heighten the sense of reality. Roman Polanski's version of *Macbeth* (1971) was filmed in an authentic old castle. Sometimes a director's choice of physical details may jar with our impressions of what such details should look like.

gentle senses." But when a filmmaker *shows* us a castle, it may jar with our impressions of what Macbeth's castle should be (Figure 6-22). Then, too, since the audience at a theatrical performance sits in a fixed position, usually a far greater distance from the performer than in the equivalent of the film's close-up, language is more often weighted to carry emotion and nuance than is the stage actor's physical presence. This is not to say that the actor's physical presence is not crucial to drama or that the various movements of the performer do not create emotion and meaning, but that language becomes extremely important when you are not able to see the speaker's eyes or watch the expression on his or her mouth from a close vantage point. Film, having both unlimited space and unlimited vantage points, is far less dependent upon dialogue than is theater. Adapting a drama from the stage to the screen may be more difficult than it first appears, for the filmmaker must find an appropriate cinematic space to match the imagined space in a particular play (and that does not always simply mean opening up the play so that scenes take place in a number of different locations). And she or he must find some way so as to neither merely duplicate nor unwittingly contradict the mental images created by the play's language.

Sir Laurence Olivier's film version of Shakespeare's *Henry V* (1945) provides examples of the various choices open to the filmmaker seeking spatial equivalents of the imaginative space created by the drama itself. In the beginning of the film we watch a production of *Henry V* taking place on the stage of the Globe Theater in London circa 1600. Since we are watching something that has the cinematic aura of a documentary reenactment — a re-created performance in Shakespearean England — we accept the fact that the camera has placed us in the subjective position of a spectator in the pit of the theater. We are there — the camera, our eyes — watching Shakespeare's play or looking up at the nobles and wealthy merchants in the boxes or at the orange sellers and then back to the play. This time and space in the film take on an existence that is undeniable: the construction of the Globe Theater and the weathered look of its texture; the costumes of the audience; the contrast between the audience and the players, the former moving randomly and the latter striking poses; and, most particularly, the rain that begins to fall and slightly distracts the players from the scenes they are playing.

Our interest is focused less on the play itself than on the re-creation of a performance in a historical period and in a particular geographical bit of space. To draw our attention to the play — Shakespeare's play, which is Olivier's true subject — Olivier breaks completely away from the performance in Shakespeare's England to cross the Channel to Henry V's fields of France and the battle of Agincourt. The documentary re-creation of an Elizabethan production is dropped in favor of re-creating the narrative, acting out not only the play but the story of Henry V as well. All the things that Shakespeare could only refer to briefly in words ("alarums and excursions") the camera gives us in full movement and color, in physical representation: hundreds of men in armor, banners fluttering in the breeze, the attack of the mounted knights, the hordes of English longbowmen with their showers of arrows. The film is doing what the movies do best — putting the viewer both imaginatively and visually right there in the actual place and in a time become present. In later sections of the film, however, the illusion of both the reality of the story as it is lived and of the documentary stage performance is deliberately broken; Henry woos Katherine of France in a patently cardboard castle and we find that Shakespeare's language is more dynamic and alive than the set within which it is spoken. Our own mental images created by the love play and poetry of the couple take precedence over the filmed images; the verbal metaphors are stronger than the visual accompaniments.

This effect can be reversed. In Olivier's *Richard III*, for instance, after Richard has been killed, his crown is kicked about in the dust by battling horsemen. The viewer sees it for a while, first rolling about like so much trash, ignored beneath the horses' hooves, and then rolling free and toward the camera, finally coming to a stop, which is then translated into the film's final image and credits. The viewer cannot quarrel with the literal reality of the crown and the appropriateness of its appearance in the scene; it fits the facts of the situation. And yet, because of the preceding events, and because the camera has kept it focused in the frame, and because the viewer has so much time to contemplate it on the screen, the crown takes on a metaphoric value as well as its literal one. Another example, among many, is in Akira Kurosawa's version of *Macbeth*, entitled *Throne of Blood* (1957). The Japanese director, taking up Shakespeare's references to Birnam Wood (never shown on the stage, of course), on the screen gives us Birnam Wood as a dark, mysterious labyrinth in which Washizu (Macbeth) is lost. This visible, actual forest becomes a metaphor for the state of Macbeth's mind; not only is he physically lost in the woods, but he is also morally lost. He cannot find the way out of the complex and conflicting desires he has for human power. This same kind of visible metaphor occurs in the Russian version of *Hamlet* (Grigori Kozintsev, 1964). Elsinore is a fortress-prison built on rocks; its drawbridge and portcullis are massive and forbidding, and we see them close on Hamlet as he rides from the freedom of the country-side back into a prison whose massive bulk literally blackens the screen and closes out the daylight. Hamlet is imprisoned in Elsinore just as he is imprisoned by his state of mind. Early on, after he has returned home for his father's funeral and his mother's wedding, he walks amid a crowded court and we hear a Shakespearean soliloquy as Hamlet thinks to himself. But the film's images do not merely duplicate the verbal metaphors; rather, we might say that the images match the metaphors, for we see the courtiers moving slowly in a clockwise circle, while the tragic hero, mentally isolated from them, moves more quickly, in sharper focus, counterclockwise.

In each of these examples, the geography becomes an integral part of the film's structure. In a movie, whether or not it is based on Shakespeare, the background is not just where the action takes place. The detective's tacky office or the sandy beach or the saloon is an intimate part of that action, sometimes even the cause of the action. And that background need not be highly conspicuous. Shakespeare set *Hamlet* in Elsinore, but what should Elsinore look like on a screen?

A comparison of the setting in three different film versions of *Hamlet* illuminates how much the background can affect the meaning and movement of the play. Olivier's version (1948) takes place in an undefined, labyrinthine space that is further removed from a connection with everyday reality because the lighting of that space creates separate

6-23 The setting selected by a filmmaker for an adaptation of a literary work can affect the meaning of the film greatly. This is especially true of drama, in which physical space is usually described only briefly, if at all. Sir Laurence Olivier set his *Hamlet* (1948) in an undefined, labyrinthine space, full of pools of light and heavy shadows. This Elsinore is elusive, inconcrete. The ill-defined setting creates a sense that Olivier's *Hamlet* is taking place as much in the nightmare world of Hamlet's mind as it is in physical space.

areas of light and dark and we cannot see the backgrounds against which the characters play. This Elsinore, then, is elusive; we cannot quite form a picture of it. Combined, of course, with the other elements of this particular version of *Hamlet* (the performers' interpretation of the dialogue, the director's decision to cut or rearrange certain scenes, and the Oedipal imagery of Hamlet's mother's bed), the space that we see, the backgrounds against which the action figures, makes Olivier's *Hamlet* take place as much in the nightmare world of Hamlet's mind as it does in concrete space (Figure 6-23).

In Kozintsev's *Hamlet*, as already mentioned, light is shut off by the massive and dark bulk of doors closing, of rock walls blotting out the sky and vertical barlike aspects of the background. Unlike the space in Olivier's version, however, the space in this Russian *Hamlet* is clearly seen and coherently connected, and we do not, therefore, feel we are being taken into Hamlet's mind.

Tony Richardson's version of *Hamlet* (1969) takes place in yet another setting, one that combines strategies of the previous two and yet creates its own meanings and sends its own messages. It is played indoors except for one scene, and that indoors is a claustrophobic, damp stone setting which seems to contain all the characters in such close proximity that it makes a viewer feel that (to quote from Jean-Paul Sartre's *No Exit*) "hell is other people." The backgrounds are seen clearly and so closely that the stone walls seem to sweat — as do the central characters. The background may sometimes be indistinguishable because we are watching the characters in such extreme close-ups, but when we see it, it is never unclear. The stones suggest the wetness and coldness of the place, and yet the flames and tapers that flicker through the film suggest a humid, sticky warmth; the disturbing contradiction parallels the similarly disturbing contradiction in Nicol Williamson's performance of the central character, a performance that emphasizes Hamlet's frenzied passion one moment and his cold and intellectual calculation the next. Because the camera stays quite close to the characters, the background at times complements Shakespeare's poetic imagery. While in the two other versions of *Hamlet*, Ophelia's death is shown to the viewer, Richardson, like Shakespeare, chooses to let us imagine it. But Richardson uses the background to help us *feel* Ophelia's death more strongly. As Queen Gertrude relates the description of how Ophelia died, she stands against a tapestry. Her shoulders are quite bare and her hair soft; the background of the tapestry is dull gold, against which we see the threads of dark green leaves growing from the branches of an artificial and woven tree. The contrast between the bare human skin and soft hair of the living Queen and the stiff gold and green of the false, dead tree is heightened by — and itself illuminates — Shakespeare's description of Ophelia's death by drowning. During the Queen's monologue we are forced to view an image, which, though appropriate, does not weakly duplicate the language; rather, the image comments upon the words.

Adaptations of Prose Fiction

As sources for films, novels and short stories seem in some ways to offer more flexibility to the filmmaker than do plays. For one thing, filmmakers are not usually expected to preserve all the dialogue in a novel; rather they can alter it, abridge it, or omit parts of it without the controversy that such modifications cause if a drama is similarly adapted for the screen. An audience regards a play as chiefly dialogue, and it expects to hear that dialogue, whereas it recognizes that a novel is not solely nor even primarily what the characters say. Narrative fiction abounds with descriptions of people, places, and things, which often can be easily translated into their concrete and representational cinematic equivalents. A description of a character's actions in a novel or short story often tells us more about the character than do her or his words,

6-24 John Ford's version (1940) of the Steinbeck novel *The Grapes of Wrath* changes the emphasis of the original. Instead of making a film attacking the social and economic ills that led to the displacement of thousands of Dust Bowl farmers, Ford shows us the enduring quality of the family and the way it can survive the worst of hardships. Ford deleted the interchapters that Steinbeck used to explore the political climate of the 1930s and instead concentrated on relationships within the Joad family.

and these actions can also be easily captured on film. Many characters in fiction, after all, are revealed as they go about their business alone, walking down streets, doing chores, peering into shop windows, looking at other people, puttering about the house — all without necessarily stopping once to have a conversation with any other character, something almost impossible to achieve in a play. Because a novel usually includes many characters and incidents (both major and minor) and because the novel is not normally read at a single sitting, it seems natural for the filmmaker to make a selection of what to keep and what to omit. This freedom creates problems as well. Omission of certain scenes or certain characters, or of secondary plots, is bound to disappoint readers who found those things important (Figure 6-24). And although some novels take very well to the screen, others depend for their power and development on their lengthiness, and they seem thin or abrupt on the screen.

The filmmaker is more likely to have success in adapting a lesser-known novel to the screen than a widely read one. Two films of Mike Nichols, a director who has adapted both dramas and novels for the screen, may be revealing. Nichols adapted a fairly unknown novel by Charles Webb, *The Graduate*. The book has very little physical or psychological description and its prose is unimpressive; in fact, the novel reads much like a movie script of dialogue without any of the camera angles indicated, thus allowing the director freedom to choose his or her own method of representation. In a way, it is a nonnovel, lacking the flesh that usually covers the basic skeletal structure of a single plot and few characters; it also lacks the longer form's rich language, which a writer normally uses to create various points of view, moods, tones, ambiguities. Nichols in *The Graduate* (1967) was able to provide the viewer with more than the novel provided: more details rather than fewer, more characterization rather than less, and more ambiguity and contrasting humor and pathos than did the book.

Nichols's adaptation of Joseph Heller's *Catch-22* (1970) was another matter. Heller's well-known novel is rich in word play, its best tools the absurdities of language. The theme of the book is not simply that war is stupid and crazy — something which does come across in Nichols's film — but that man lives in a quicksand of unintelligible meanings, symbolized by confused, inadequate, and unreliable words. Time and space are not presented chronologically; characterization is bizarre and stereotypical rather than realistic. The war and all its crazy participants are a complex literary metaphor, carefully worked out, word by word, pun by pun, paradox by paradox. Thus, a highly intellectual construct gives meaning to the comic-strip characters.

The film, however, must complete the subtle transformation of humor into horror not through the incremental accumulation and repetition of language devices, but through action shown on the screen. In Nichols's *Catch-22* we get real flesh-and-blood actors, we see real airplanes and have a real Orson Welles inhabit the fictional General Dreedle. These physical presences — people and things — detract from the power of the novel's central metaphor, which sets off a chain reaction of images in the mind. In the novel, for instance, the soldier in white, a soldier wrapped completely in bandages so that the men in the ward are not convinced there is anyone inside, works simultaneously as a comic device and as a powerful symbol. In the film, however, he is merely a plaster cast, an object we see, recognize, and know. He is a great deal less haunting and disturbing in the flesh than he is in the novel. He becomes merely a funny bit on the screen. In the novel, the bombardier Snowden and his wound achieve mythic proportions as Yossarian re-

6-25 In an attempt to transfer Franz Kafka's peculiarly claustrophobic vision of life to the screen, Orson Welles elected to use a variety of expressionistic techniques including *chiaroscuro* lighting, fog and shadow effects, and (as shown here) subjective close-ups filmed with a wide-angle lens to produce distorted perspective in *The Trial* (1962).

calls more and more details of an event we might really rather not find out about; in the film, the final revelation stops with the shocking picture of Snowden's entrails spilling out of the unzipped flak suit. The effect is certainly visceral, but it does not cause a great movement of the mind toward meaning. As it happens, the filmic treatment of Snowden is one of the best things in the adaptation. Because its images are bleached and cold and because its accumulation of small revelations as the scene recurs horrify and tease, it does create some of the suspense and mystical quality of its equivalent in the novel. But even so, the experience of Snowden in the film is too concrete and literal to create the cosmic horror of the novel's revelation of Snowden's secret — mortality.

Film and Literary Symbolism
Film literalizes what may function symbolically in literature. Unless the filmmaker is able to recharge the image with some cinimatically communicated richness (Figure 6-25) — in effect, to recharge the literal with its own mystery and symbolism — that literary symbol will not function successfully on the screen. In Melville's novel *Moby Dick*, the great white whale symbolizes the mysterious power of the universe, but in John Huston's movie version (1956), what we see is just a big mechanical fish. And the malevolent great white shark of *Jaws* (1976) is much more menacing when we see through its eyes than when we look *at* it, more

threatening as a symbol of mindless rapaciousness when we see its presence marked by two yellow floats, which bob up and down in the ocean, than when we actually see it present. Because film is necessarily representational, it is extremely difficult for objects to accumulate symbolic meanings; rather, they usually become increasingly ordinary and only physically meaningful. But because it is difficult does not mean that it cannot or has not been done.

Erich von Stroheim's masterwork *Greed* (1924) demonstrates how a filmmaker can transplant symbols and motifs from a novel to a film in a way that will not decrease their power. Although less than a fourth of the original (and unreleased) forty-two reels remain of *Greed*, this adaptation of Frank Norris's naturalistic novel *McTeague* succeeds in building a symbolic structure in the midst of incredibly realistic detail. For example, von Stroheim takes the novel's use of the characters' hands and transfers it to the screen in a way that adds force to the motif (Figure 6-26). From the first moment when we see the film's central female character — Trina — we are made aware of her constantly fluttering hands and her long white fingers. Von Stroheim emphasizes them by dressing Trina in dark clothing so that the movement of her white hands is constantly, but naturally, highlighted against a dark background as she touches the buttons on her dress nervously, or adjusts her dark hair. Our first awareness of those hands is their whiteness and their constant fluttering movement, which visually connects them to another motif in the film — the pair of caged birds, which, later in the film, are McTeague's wedding present to his new wife — Trina. Although the birds are not introduced until long after we have met Trina, von Stroheim has carefully prepared us to connect them with her, so that what happens to the birds will serve as a symbolic parallel to what befalls Trina and McTeague. After Trina marries McTeague, we see her growing obsession for money, as her miserly actions of counting money are connected to a sequence that ends with Trina sitting on her bed rubbing her hands with night cream. Again the context is realistic, but her actions make her look like a gloating miser rather than a woman preparing to go to sleep. Her hands are thus linked with her greed. After McTeague can no longer practice as a dentist, we see Trina whittling toys to sell and flexing her fingers in pain; her obsession is revealed not just by her actions as she counts and polishes and murmurs to the gold coins she is hoarding, but by images that show the gold in her hands; the coins lie across her palm in close-up or her long fingers hold a coin toward the light to see it sparkle. In the scene in which McTeague attempts to get Trina to give him some money by grabbing her hand and biting the fingers, the sadism of his actions is enhanced by all the earlier

6-26 Erich von Stroheim's *Greed* (1924) demonstrates how a filmmaker can successfully transplant symbols and motifs from a novel to film. Trina in the novel is characterized by her hands — the hands that make children's toys and also count hoarded money. Von Stroheim emphasizes Trina's hands by highlighting their pale, fluttery movement against the darkness of her clothes.

associations the viewer has had, the accumulation of emotion and experience, which makes Trina's hands more than physical appendages. The night that McTeague decides to leave Trina, they stand at the door of their hovel and Trina asks McTeague if he still loves her. Although Trina and her question are pathetic, we have seen Trina's sickening and unsympathetic stinginess and manipulation of her husband. It is therefore particularly horrifying when we watch Trina's long white fingers, now wrapped in scraps of bandage, slide insinuatingly and slowly up McTeague's dark jacket to embrace him around the neck. The image is ambiguous but powerful and carefully controlled: the hands have taken on an almost independent life of their own and yet they also belong to a simultaneously pathetic and repugnant Trina. Von Stroheim took the motif directly from the novel, but in visually representing the hands as hands he also was careful, by using techniques that add mystery and evocative power to the merely physical, to compensate for the photographic image's reductive concreteness.

The success of an adaptation from book or stage to screen will not depend on whether or not it is a line-for-line transfer from one medium to another, or on whether or not its metaphors, symbols, or motifs are the same in both media. A successful adaptation depends on how imaginatively the filmmaker is able to use the medium to convey what was conveyed in another medium. A film adaptation of a play or novel is simultaneously an individual *reading* of that play or novel and the actualization of that reading in moving images. The filmmaker must decide what the play or novel says, what it is about (a matter not only of plot and character but of tone and imagery), and then cinematic equivalents must be found. Many film adaptations have accomplished this difficult job, sometimes even surpassing their source material. (Some others, of course, have simply used the source as the basis for an entirely new and individual work.) As one does not criticize Shakespeare for not giving his audience a line-for-line adaptation of Holinshed's *Chronicles* or for not seeing that the essence of the *Chronicles* was historical rather than poetic, one should not automatically criticize a filmmaker who is fired into originality by the drama, short story, poem, or novel supposedly being adapted for the screen.

Acting: Actors and Stars

You can be trained to hell and gone, but if you don't have the imagination to conceive a performance, you'll be technically trained to achieve mediocrity. You have to tell the truth, with as much attention to detail as you can. I usually have a visual, visceral image of the character — I see

what he looks like and how he walks and talks immediately on the first
reading of a script; then I try to achieve that visual image. . . . My preparation seems to be much more subconscious than conscious.
Richard Dreyfuss [8]

The Hollywood film gave rise to the now faded star system, in which the
charismatic screen personalities of certain people were often used in
certain familiar roles. Douglas Fairbanks as the swashbuckling hero,
Joan Crawford as the forceful, independent woman, Jimmy Stewart as
the naive and sincere righter of society's ills, drew people into the
theater to see them reenact familiar personae. Hollywood's publicity
machine made sure the audience knew who the stars were.

Although audiences attended the first films to see movement of any
kind captured on the screen, and then next went to see narratives
dramatized, from the year 1910 — when the uncredited "Biograph girl,"
Florence Lawrence, joined the Independent Motion Picture Company
and was made a star and given screen credit — to the present, most
people have gone to films to see both a story and a star. It is only in
recent years that American audiences have been drawn into the theater
to see films of specific directors like Stanley Kubrick, Francis Ford
Coppola, or Steven Spielberg. Most often audiences still go to a movie
specifically to see a star like Robert Redford in *The Natural* (Barry Levinson, 1984) or Barbra Streisand in *Yentl* (Barbra Streisand, 1984). In
today's system of production, these stars are considered bankable.
Thought to have the power to bring patrons into the theater, no matter
what the story or the quality of the production, people with money
(distribution companies, private investors, banks) are willing to finance
a production in which they will appear. For a person trying to get a film
made, having a bankable star signed to do the picture is almost a surefire
guarantee that the money will be found. On the other hand, mistakes
can be made with this sort of thinking. Some investors found the team of
Sylvester Stallone (*Rocky* and *Rambo* hits) and Dolly Parton (well known
as a singer and quite successful in the film *9 to 5* (Colin Higgins, 1980))
ideal to create a box office success. For whatever reason — script, direction, poor marketing — *Rhinestone* (Bob Clark, 1984) was a bomb. The
individual popularity of the stars was not able to save the film.

Thus from Hollywood's perspective, performers (the talent) are a part
of the production materials and marketing system. But they can also be
viewed as an aesthetic element of any individual film. As the star system
developed in the United States, a peculiar division arose between **film
actors** and **film stars**. Some performers could play any part in any film
and play it well; yet no matter how often these actors appeared on the
screen, audiences seemed not to remember their names or their faces.

6-27 Many actors in films are neither recognized actors like Sir Laurence Olivier nor personalities like Jimmy Stewart. Their names are relatively unknown though their faces are familiar. Charles Durning played a middle-aged farmer who falls in love with the soap-opera actress Dorothy Michaels, who is in fact the struggling actor Michael Dorsey (played by Dustin Hoffman) in *Tootsie* (Sydney Pollack, 1982).

These actors did not have that charismatic quality or personality which somehow transcended the roles they played; since every role was different, the audience could never locate what seemed to be the person behind the mask, that consistent quality, that noticeable something, which for some performers was there, movie after movie. They were actors, not stars.

These actors usually fill the backgrounds, playing the lesser characters in films whose feature roles are played by stars. Sometimes their faces are recognizable after we have seen them perform often enough, but usually they so subordinate themselves to the narrative, they do not stand out apart from their roles; we tend to remember the movie character rather than the performer (Figure 6-27). In general, though there are exceptions, these actors are not likely to play leading roles in big movies, especially in America. American audiences — until recently — have for the most part paid their admissions to see stars, not simply actors. Foreign directors, on the other hand, have frequently used actors rather than stars for leading roles in their films — and they have, on occasion, even used nonactors, people off the streets, as in the Italian neorealist narrative films made toward the end of World War II.

Screen performers such as John Mills, Rod Steiger, Dame Edith Evans, and, more recently, Dustin Hoffman, Gene Hackman, Shelley Duvall, and Mary Steenburgen, occupy a middle ground between film actor and film star. They are not those nameless performers who are regularly **typecast** in specific roles (the sleazy landlord, the female barfly), nor are they — no matter how skillful, no matter how prominently advertised — personalities who dominate or transcend their characters, appearing on the screen as both the character they are playing and as themselves. Instead, they *become* any character the role demands, and we learn to know the character and to forget the actor (Figure 6-28). Gene Hackman, despite his featured status and the resultant familiarity of his face, becomes Buck Barrow in *Bonnie and Clyde* (1967) and later

6-28 Some actors and actresses occupy a middle ground between typecast character actors and stars. They are instantly recognizable, in voice and gesture, but they still make the audience forget the actor and remember the character. Jack Nicholson deteriorates into the psychopathic Johnny in *The Shining* (Stanley Kubrick, 1979); Diane Keaton is transformed into a nineteenth-century housewife in *Mrs. Soffel* (Gillian Armstrong, 1984).

becomes the quite different character of Harry Caul in *The Conversation* (1974). And Shelley Duvall has completely changed character from the hot-rodding opportunist of *Brewster McCloud* (Robert Altman, 1970) to the homely and shy Keechie, a young and pathetic gangster's moll in *Thieves Like Us* (Altman, 1973), to the attractive if vapid young wife who has stepped from the pages of *Woman's Day* in *The Shining* (Kubrick, 1981).

Film stars, however, are a different breed. These screen performers do not act in the customary theatrical sense of the word, and they should not be judged by theatrical standards. Although their names, costumes, and makeup change from picture to picture and though to an extent they do portray different characters, yet from film to film their own personalities are so strong that they can always be identified, even if like James Garner, the person is very indefinite, (a weak persona) that indefiniteness is always recognizable. They are always — to differing degrees — separate from the roles they play. From film to film Bette Davis, Joan Crawford, Barbara Stanwyck, Katherine Hepburn, James Stewart, Clark Gable, Humphrey Bogart, Cary Grant, John Wayne, Charles Bronson, Burt Reynolds, Barbra Streisand, and Robert Redford remain the same. They do not act to the point of submerging themselves in their parts; they are themselves as well as their parts. An actor or actress submerges his or her personality and creates a character; a star lets his or her own personality create the character. Sometimes this imposition of the personality onto the role is the result of typecasting. That is, an actress is chosen to play a role because she physically fits the part or the part has been written for her, and if she proves successful in the role, that role with variations will be given to her again and again. John Wayne was, of course, the classic example of this kind of type-casting; he was so successful in embodying the western hero that he was never readily accepted by audiences in other roles (except as the hero in World War II movies, which he played with some frequency).

More often than not, however, stars will be given a variety of roles to play in their careers, yet still they convince us, in film after film, that the surface distinctions in character are just that — surface; the stars are still the men or women we paid our admission to see *pretend* to be someone else. True, Humphrey Bogart was always best when he was playing the cynical tough guy (perhaps because those roles brought him stardom), and yet in such markedly different roles as Charlie Allnut in *The African Queen* (1951) and Captain Queeg in *The Caine Mutiny* (Edward Dmytryk, 1954), he was still unmistakably himself — Humphrey Bogart. In a comedy like *Beat the Devil* (John Huston, 1954) or in a light romance like *Sabrina* (Billy Wilder, 1954), Bogart was still the Bogey we knew and loved (Figure 6-29) in *The Maltese Falcon* (1941), where he made the character of Sam Spade forever his own, or in *Casablanca* (Michael Curtiz, 1942), where he made the cynical and world-weary Rick one of the most memorable screen characters of all time.

In a way, what we appreciate about stars such as Bogart is that they cannot act — or do not act. They return to us picture after picture, incompletely submerging their own selves in a characterization, and so they become familiar friends; we feel that if we met them on the street, we would have a fairly good idea of what to say to them, what they would say to us, how they would say it. Bogart's craggy face, his immobile upper lip, the way he spoke his lines, the mannerisms that so

6-29 Humphrey Bogart is a good example of a film star, one of those screen personalities who, year in and year out, in picture after picture, always seemed somehow to be the same. His own inimitable personality is never completely submerged, whether he is playing Sam Spade in *The Maltese Falcon* (John Huston, 1941), Rick in *Casablanca* (Michael Curtiz, 1942), or Charlie Allnut in *The African Queen* (John Huston, 1952). In fact, his personal qualities and screen presence made him the popular figure he was (and still is), rather than his ability to completely submerge himself in a fictional character.

marked his appearances on the screen, could never be taught in acting school. Bogart was what he was. He was himself in all of his pictures and, fortunately, he — not the character — was what the audience came to see. This star quality has, in a sense, the same appeal and interest that the genre film has. There is the consistent, recognizable actor who varies only slightly from movie to movie. In one film, Bogart is called Sam Spade, the detective; in another, he is Duke Mantee, a fugitive; in yet another, he is Rick Blaine, an expatriate who owns a bar in Casablanca during World War II: what we see is the constant persona only thinly disguised by the particular character he is playing.

This peculiar or distinctive quality that a star exhibits can be so pervasive that it may dominate a film, subduing the cinematography, the direction, and the editing (Figure 6-30). After seeing several movies in which such a particular star appears — perhaps Bette Davis, Cary Grant, or Marilyn Monroe — we can sense some unique element that firmly links these films; there is a special and constant tone to the films, the indelible imprint of a personality. Although viewers probably re-

6-30 Sometimes the distinctive quality of a star can dominate a film. Such an influence can be great enough to determine the performer as the true auteur of the film. No matter who the director, the Marx brothers' films seem to reflect their particular comic vision. They combined physical slapstick humor with verbal wit as they attacked middle-class values in their Paramount films, like *Horsefeathers* (Norman Z. McLeod, 1932). On the other hand, when they signed with MGM, this satiric thrust was tremendously muted as they became comic relief in typical musical comedy romances, showing the power of studios to shape their products.

member specific films and specific plots in which these stars appeared, they remember more vividly the star's physical imprint on the films: a particular face, a way of moving, a look, and an idiosyncratic and memorable voice.

This effect may be attributable to the studio and the producers who having found a successful combination (a money making one) are unwilling to change. That is, the film's producers may insist that a Bette Davis film reflect what they perceive as the package of characteristics that made the previous Davis films successful at the box office. In fact, something like this seems to have been the case, for during the 1930s, Davis complained and feuded with her studio, Warner Brothers, because they kept featuring her in the same kind of film over and over again, whereas she felt she had the skills to play a wider variety of roles. The Marx Brothers' films made at Paramount from 1930 to 1934 seemed to reflect their peculiar kind of comic vision, a combination of slapstick humor and zany verbal wit that attacked middle-class values. This thrust is tremendously muted when they signed with MGM whose penchant for musicals turned the Marx Brothers into comic relief for typical new comedy romances between popular boy and girl singing stars. Thus, the qualities observable in particular films that make us identify this film as a Clark Gable picture or a Rita Hayworth film may be as much the result of the studio's carefully tailoring the package as it is of the star's personality. There is enough biographical material to suggest that the conflict between performers and producers was widespread and occasionally so violent it ended in tragedy. The film *Frances* (Graeme Clifford, 1983) dramatized the true story of actress Frances Farmer and her struggles with the Hollywood system in the 1930s. Her conflicts with her studio produced severe mental problems and her career was cut short by an early death in an asylum. Nevertheless, film actors and film stars function in different but equally necessary ways — and it is important to remember that one group is not necessarily better or more inherently valuable than the other. Indeed, both kinds of screen presence are crucial to the story film and carry the burdens of characterization.

NOTES

[1] Interviewed by James Blue, *Film Comment* 4:4 (Summer 1968), p. 6.

[2] *Fellini on Fellini* (Boston/New York: Seymour Lawrence/Delacorte Press, 1976), p. 100.

[3] "What People Laugh At," in Donald W. McCaffrey, ed., *Focus on Chaplin* (Englewood Cliffs, New Jersey: Prentice-Hall, 1971), p. 52.

[4] In Gideon Bachmann, "The Man on the Volcano: A Portrait of Werner Herzog," *Film Quarterly* 31, no. 1 (Fall 1977): 7–8.

[5] In Andrew Sarris, ed., *Interviews with Film Directors* (New York: Avon Books, 1969), p. 257.

[6] In James Harvey, "Sirkumstantial," *Film Comment* 14, no. 4 (July–August 1978): 55.

[7] In Joseph Gelmis, ed., *The Film Director as Superstar* (Garden City, New York: Doubleday, 1970), p. 118.

[8] In Michael Goodwin, "Close Encounters with a Rising Star," *The New York Times Magazine* (January 15, 1978): 14.

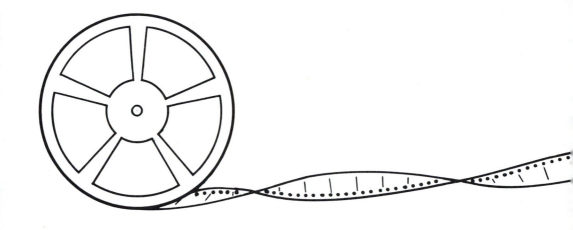

PART IV
THE
ALTERNATIVE
FILM

Historical Overview:
The Development of the
Documentary Film

FROM SILENCE TO SOUND

Influenced by the Industrial Revolution's emphasis on science and technology, Louis and Auguste Lumière made their first films in 1895 primarily from an urge to reproduce the everyday world, to record and document life around them. These filmed scenes from life (workers leaving the factory, a train arriving), however, could not indefinitely hold the imagination and attention of the viewing public. Although from 1895 to 1907 most films were documentary films — or, perhaps more appropriately, film documents — after 1907 such films were on the decline. Audience interest in film's ability to capture the everyday world was undercut by the growing production of fake documentaries, which were often much more exciting to watch than the film record of the real thing. The narrative film in which the emergent art of film editing *altered* precamera activity and created drama as it manipulated time and space appealed to audiences more than films of unstructured material. Although **newsreels** became a regular part of the movie program in 1910 when both Pathé and Gaumont in France released the first sets of composite documentary news footage, the public's chief interest in the movies had permanently shifted to the narrative film. As a result, although many documentary films throughout the century functioned as theatrical entertainment, the history of the form has generally been allied to noncommercial enterprise and has been developed by those filmmakers, governments, and social institutions who saw in the cinema a medium with the power to move people to social and political action.

After the Revolution of 1917, for instance, Lenin, seeing the need to educate people in remote areas of Russia to the purposes of the Revolution, asserted the alliance between film and the newly formed Soviet government. This educative

1 The trolley cars in Dziga Vertov's *The Man with a Movie Camera* (1928) are a good example of the difficulty of categorizing this film. Frequently (as here) the trolley cars are simply a mode of transportation recorded in normal time, with a normal lens. The image is documentary. At other times, however, the speed of the trolleys is increased, mirror images are used, and the trolleys turn into abstract forms, hurtling across the opaque frame.

function, along with the pressing political need to establish a sense of national unity and pride, became the basic motive for nonfiction filmmaking in the Soviet Union. Thus, the Soviet newsreel *Kino-Nedelia (Film Weekly)* was not only taken across the country on trains that screened films aboard for rural patrons but the films were also changed en route, as chief editor Dziga Vertov filmed additional material and, in a kind of ongoing process of documenting the world, incorporated it into subsequent screenings.

Vertov, a seminal figure in Soviet filmmaking and in documentary aesthetics, called for cinema to reject the artificiality of scripts, constructed sets, and actors in favor of its true subject: the lived world. Despite this call for cinema to avoid manipulating its subject matter before the camera, Vertov also believed it necessary that the cinematographer and the film editor illuminate unmanipulated and spontaneous life through full use of the camera's unique properties and through editing. Thus, in his own weekly newsreel, *Kino-Pravda,* which ran from 1922 until 1925, and in his later and highly influential *The Man with a Movie Camera* (1928), Vertov uses slow, fast, and reverse motion, animation, micro-cinematography, and **multiple exposure** as cinematic devices that revealed life as it was lived in ways physiologically unavailable to the viewer (Figure 1). Vertov's writings and films — though themselves limited to the period between two wars — have continued to influence both those filmmakers who wish to record life as it is lived with a minimum of mediation between that life and the camera, and also those filmmakers who wish to shape reality by participating in it during shooting and editing.

In America, after World War I, the documentary impulse manifested itself in the emergence of the feature-length **travelogue**. Americans were interested in seeing life as it was lived — but as it was lived elsewhere. Beginning with travelogue records of their explorations made as early as 1912, Martin and Osa Johnson pleased commercial audiences with exotic films from darkest Africa in which great white filmmakers unself-consciously patronized their native subjects. Although the Johnsons' films proved immensely popular, it was the success of Robert Flaherty's *Nanook of the North* (1922), a film about Eskimo life, which really initiated a concerted effort to film other cultures in other lands. Because of its artistry and its exoticism, *Nanook* excited a twofold interest: in what has come to be called the **ethnographic film,** and also in the documentary's commercial potential for dealing with real life in a dramatically satisfying cinematic structure. Flaherty dramatized as he recorded, using varying camera angles and distances that best showed the heroic qualities of a man using simple tools and great skill to survive in a beautiful but hostile landscape. The film gave rise to the term *documentary*.

Nanook began a trend in dramatic ethnography exemplified by the efforts of explorer-filmmakers Merian C. Cooper and Ernest Schoedsack in *Grass* (1925), which followed a mass migration of herdsmen through mountains in Turkey and Persia and in *Chang* (1927), a follow-up, which moved toward fiction in its dramatization of a Siamese family. These film explorers seemed bent on discovering spectacle (and finally created their own in a total fiction enlivened by documentary technique, *King Kong,* 1933). Flaherty himself was sent to Samoa by Paramount to make another *Nanook,* but returned instead with *Moana* (1926), a gentle film with little of the natural conflict between man and his environment found in *Nanook*. In commercial desperation, Paramount misguidedly advertised the film as "the love life of a South Sea siren" and the film, not delivering what was promised, proved a box-office flop. Flaherty's short association with Hollywood was terminated, but he continued making his documentaries under various nontheatrical auspices; his first sound film, *Man of Aran* (1934), was made in England, for example, and his *Louisiana Story* (1948) was sponsored by an oil company.

SOUND AND SOCIAL REFORM

Despite the relative success of exotic documentaries in the 1920s, it was not until the introduction of sound to the cinema in 1927 that the documentary form could begin to realize its potential as an educative, social, and political force. In America, Fox Movietone News in May of 1927 began releasing newsreels using the first optical sound system; such newsreels became part of nearly every theatrical exhibitor's programming. But, newsreel production aside, there was little interest in developing feature-length documentaries in the United States, where film was regarded as show business and movies were a commercial product.

The situation in England, however, was different. When the Depression hit Great Britain in 1929, a brash, inexperienced, self-taught student of media named John Grierson went to a governmental unit called the Empire Marketing Board and convincingly argued that film production should be one of the board's ways of informing the public about Britain's food supply. Thus, Grierson became the director of the board's Film Unit and in 1929 released the first of the only two films he ever actually made. *Drifters,* a classic example of the kind of film that was to exemplify British documentary's golden age, makes exciting and socially relevant the everyday dangers faced by herring fishermen in the North Sea. Filmmakers who joined Grierson's unit were instructed to make ordinary reality and peacetime as exciting and provocative on the screen as were extraordinary events like war. Grierson was intent on showing the British workingman to himself and educating him to the social realities around him.

These British documentaries at first were relatively straightforward in their glorification of the British workingman, but as time went on the productions became more complex and drew on the talents of such leading artists as poet W. H. Auden and composer Benjamin Britten to explore the dynamic possibilities of sound. *Night Mail* (Basil Wright and Harry Watt, 1936), for example, is intended on a factual level to show the process of mail delivery by train. Aesthetically, however, the film is an aural and visual poem to humans, machines, and the work they perform. Montage editing combined with Britten's score and Auden's chanted narration demonstrates the complexity and formal beauty of the British documentary of the 1930s at the same time that it demonstrates its basis in the everyday activities of British life. Although the Film Unit was terminated as part of the Empire Marketing Board in 1932, production did not cease; the unit was taken over by the General Post Office with Grierson still at its head.

The British documentary strongly influenced the emergent genre in Depression America. So, too, did a handful of documentaries made in various European countries, films that took social and political stands like *Borinage* (Henri Storck and Joris Ivens, 1933), which pled the cause of Belgian coal miners, or *Land Without Bread* (Luis Buñuel, 1932), which savagely and shockingly recorded poverty in Spain. By the early 1930s the Film and Photo League had been founded in New York City, and its various branches devoted themselves to the creation of socially significant documentaries addressed to the problems of Depression America. But it was not until 1936, when the Roosevelt Administration through its various work programs gave financial backing to filmmaking, that American social documentary had any real impact.

Pare Lorentz, a film critic with no filmmaking experience, was to symbolize the documentary filmmaker of Depression America. Backed by the Resettlement

Administration, he made a film depicting the conditions leading to the creation of the Dust Bowl, *The Plow That Broke the Plains* (1936). With the aid of talent culled from the ranks of the Film and Photo League, Lorentz implicated the whole United States in what might have been seen by some as merely a localized agricultural problem. Lorentz's second film, *The River* (1937), made for the Department of Agriculture, traced Mississippi River floodwaters from their beginnings in land depletion to their harnessing by the Tennessee Valley Authority. It so impressed President Roosevelt that he established the United States Film Service through presidential order, a service that was unfortunately short-lived because of criticism of its funding and the distracting conditions leading toward World War II.

PERSUASION AND PROPAGANDA

The production of documentaries in America during the Depression and prewar period was not, however, limited to governmental agencies. Thirties America, increasingly conscious of social and economic forces, was caught up by a documentary impulse. In 1935, an emotional, controversial, and blatantly editorial newsreel emerged — *The March of Time*. Practicing "fakery in allegiance to truth," it was so successful in theatrical release that it did not halt production until 1951, when television began absorbing the visual news function that had been performed by the movies. Supported by American partisans and intellectuals, *This Spanish Earth* (Joris Ivens, 1937) attempted to inform and influence American opinion against the Fascist cause in Spain. At the 1939 World's Fair in New York City, Willard Van Dyke and Ralph Steiner showcased *The City;* using various experimental techniques, it represented those kinds of films that dealt with problems on the home front like housing conditions, racism, unionization, and urban blight. And an offshoot of the Film and Photo League, Frontier Films, moved from national to international concerns as the world — and the United States — stood on the brink of war.

During this prewar period the word **propaganda** came into popular use. The white propaganda of social reform became the black propaganda of Nazi distortion. Hitler, long aware of the potential persuasive power of the cinema, named Joseph Goebbels as Minister of Popular Enlightenment and Propaganda in 1933, the year he came to power. Hitler also assigned Leni Riefenstahl, an actress turned filmmaker, to record the Nazi party rally in Nuremberg in 1934. The result was *Triumph of the Will,* a film that mobilized all the effects of the medium to cover an event staged as much for the cameras as for the Nazi Party members in attendance. Using simple content (clouds, church spires, flags, crowds, speeches, and marching parades), Riefenstahl so skillfully shot and edited her images and sounds that seen today — even with hindsight — *Triumph of the Will* attests to the awesome and frightening power the cinema can wield. Although Riefenstahl went on to make the epic *Olympiad* (1938) about the 1936

Olympic Games held in Berlin, she will be chiefly remembered for *Triumph of the Will.*

In England, the General Post Office Film Unit was renamed the Crown Film Unit. The efforts of the Grierson Golden Age came to fruition in the war films of Alberto Cavalcanti, Harry Watt, and Paul Rotha. In addition, new filmmakers appeared, most notably Humphrey Jennings, who became the leading filmmaker of the war period with *Listen to Britain* (1942), *Fires Were Started* (1943), and *A Diary for Timothy* (1945), films filled with human details that personalized the war effort and lifted morale. In the United States, films were needed for training military personnel and for explaining the United States to allies abroad. Impressed and chilled by familiarity with brilliant German film propaganda, Hollywood director Frank Capra borrowed enemy propaganda techniques to produce the *Why We Fight* series for the Signal Corps, the United States Army's filmmaking unit. Originally meant for distribution only to members of the armed services, the series was publicly released and shown in theaters around the United States. Other American-made films that portrayed the dreadful costs in human life caused by the war were victims of suppression; John Huston's *The Battle of San Pietro* (1944) and *Let There Be Light* (1945), for instance, were thought to be too pacifist or depressing in their implications to be shown even to their intended audiences, the men who were doing the fighting.

Although documentary production flourished during the war, it declined in the postwar period. The government's urgent need for propaganda and national mobilization had abated. Industry support also was not widespread. Perhaps, too, a nonfictional presentation of pressing social ills was not what a public weary of wartime deprivation wanted. Two other factors were also largely responsible for the decline of documentary. The first was the emergence of a new medium: television. In the early 1950s, newsreels began to fade from theater screens as television sets began to become part of the furniture of the American home. The new medium immediately proved itself more responsive than weekly newsreels in documenting current events while they were still current. The second factor contributing to the decline of documentary was cinematic technology, the heavy, bulky camera and sound equipment, which, as much as any aesthetic or moral philosophy, dictated the structure of documentary film. The lack of portable equipment meant that the documentary form had reached an impasse in its development. This did not mean, of course, that film documentaries were no longer being made. Several classics appeared, among them *The Quiet One* (Sidney Meyers, 1948), which, though scripted, documented a young boy's turmoil in the real context of Harlem, and *Night and Fog* (Alain Resnais, 1955), which explored time and memory in relation to the Nazi death camps (Figure 2). In addition, with John Grierson initially its head, the National Film Board of Canada was busy with documentary production given impetus by the need to define a national character.

2 In *Night and Fog* (1955), Alain Resnais intercuts long color tracking shots of the abandoned concentration camps, as they are over twenty years after the Holocaust, with black-and-white documentary still photos and captured films taken in the camps during the war. Music and poetic narration disturb the viewer's attitude toward the action and places shown in the images, asking the viewer to be aware of the tricks that time and memory play on the human mind.

DOCUMENTARY AND TELEVISION: NEW TECHNOLOGY AND NEW FORMS

It was television, however, which solved those technological problems and re-vitalized the film documentary. Initially, television documentary borrowed its social impetus from the tradition of the 1930s and 1940s. Its major form, per-fected by the veteran newsman Edward R. Murrow at CBS in the mid-1950s and still predominant today, combined a panoramic view of an American problem interspersed with humanizing interviews with people involved in the problem. Murrow's documentaries on such problems as the plight of migrant workers and hunger in America were emotionally affecting, and seemed hard-hitting at the time, exposing social ills and bringing them into the American living room. But despite some few exceptions, Murrow's belief that television documentary could become the conscience of its time was vitiated by the fact that it was also the conscience of its sponsor and its network; as the form evolved, it tended to take safe positions (for example, everyone is against hunger) and to ignore or avoid controversial ones. Nonetheless, early television contributed greatly to the changing form of nonfiction filmmaking. The interview was redeemed as a source of visual and aural interest, and this fascination with people revealing

3 D. A. Pennebaker, a key figure in America's modern documentary movement, captured the musically oriented youthful moviegoer's attention with
films like *Monterey Pop* (1968). Janis Joplin performs.

themselves led to the development of more improved, portable equipment,
which would be able to follow people about as they talked and lived their lives.
During the 1950s portable 16mm cameras began to replace the bulky 35mm
equipment; shoulders replaced tripods and often the old steady gaze of the
camera was sacrificed for hand-held immediacy. But the revolution in documentary filmmaking could not occur without wireless microphones and recording
units, a technological breakthrough accomplished by a film unit of Time-Life under the leadership of Robert Drew.

Organized in 1958, the Drew Unit consisted of filmmakers who were to become key figures in the modern documentary movement. There was D. A.
Pennebaker, who caught the contemporary and youthful moviegoer's attention
with his musically oriented documentaries like *Don't Look Back* (made with
Richard Leacock, 1966) and *Monterey Pop* (1968) (Figure 3) and began what
was to become a genre of theatrically released and commercially successful rock
documentaries, culminating in *Woodstock* (Michael Wadleigh, 1970). There was
Albert Maysles, who was to go on to make (with his brother David) one of the
enduring classics of modern **direct cinema,** *Salesman* (1969), which followed
four Bible salesmen on their rounds and into their motel rooms. And the Drew

Unit nurtured Richard Leacock, a filmmaker who had served an apprenticeship with Robert Flaherty and who had come to hate documentary narration that told him what to think instead of letting him think for himself. The unit was finally successful in liberating the camera and microphone and recorder in 1961. But the key film that conveys the excitement of that liberation and changed the look and sound of the documentary film actually was made a year earlier — before all the bugs had been completely ironed out. Made by Robert Drew and Richard Leacock, *Primary* was an on-the-spot record of a campaign for a presidential nomination in a primary election; no narrator acted as mediator between the events and the viewer, and the drama was found through camera movement rather than through emphasis on editing juxtapositions. This film marked the beginning of what was to be properly termed *direct cinema* — a form that seemed uncontrolled and minimally manipulated by the filmmaker/observer.

Although it was common practice at the time for television networks to commission and broadcast only their own documentaries, the innovative work of the Drew Unit caused ABC to contract for a series of films, making the Drew Unit virtually part of the network. As a result, television viewers became accustomed to a new documentary form that was as ambiguous and immediate as life itself. Public television has also supported the new documentary, commissioning yearly films from one of the direct cinema's leading practitioners, Frederick Wiseman. Once a lawyer, this prolific observer has let his camera record the complexities of public and private institutions like hospitals, high schools, juvenile courts, meat packing, the department store, and the fashion business. Anthology series like *Nova* and shorter series like *Nature* or *National Geographic Specials* continue to present scientific material to the lay audience.

The American development of direct cinema was not the only documentary response to the new technology, which allowed filmmakers to film and record sound with maximum mobility and minimal intervention. In France, the release of *Chronicle of a Summer* (Jean Rouch, 1961) heralded the birth of cinema verité — a form of documentary indiscriminately confused with direct cinema at first because of its similar rejection of traditional narration and manipulative editing and its use of the interview and the long take. Unlike direct cinema films, *Chronicle of a Summer* allows the filmmaker and his camera to play a part in the film, acknowledging their ability to alter and yet reveal life by their presence, letting them act as catalysts and provocateurs of action. Indeed, the term *cinema verité* — derived from *cinéma vérité*, the French translation of *Kino-Pravda* (literally film-truth) in homage to Dziga Vertov — is meant to describe the film truth generated and created by the filmmaker as well as by the subject matter itself. Practiced chiefly by European documentarists, the form has produced such classics as *Le Joli Mai* (Chris Marker, 1963), and it has strongly influenced such **epic documentaries** as *Phantom India* (Louis Malle, 1968), *The Memory of Justice* (Marcel Ophuls, 1976), and *Shoah* (Abe Stern, 1985).

4 Though Les Blank has used the direct cinema style to survey the eating habits and music of ethnic communities in Louisiana, Texas, and Wisconsin, his most well-known work is *Burden of Dreams* (1982) in which he documented Werner Herzog's making of *Fitzcarraldo*. Here he is shown with extras from the Campa and Machiguenga tribes and the steamship Herzog had to pull over a 40° hill in his film.

Today, documentary film has a number of traditions from which it can draw both its philosophical and aesthetic approaches. Most nonfiction films, of course, are created and absorbed by television, but the form still manages to survive independent of television as well. In addition to the popularity of rock-concert documentaries like *Stop Making Sense* (Jonathan Demme, 1984), there have been such relative successes as *Gates of Heaven* (Errol Morris, 1978) and *Burden of Dreams* (Les Blank, 1983) (Figure 4). The socially conscious documentary also has been popularly represented by *Hearts and Minds* (Peter Davis, 1974) which explores United States involvement in Vietnam, and *Harlan County, U.S.A.* (Barbara Kopple, 1976), which combines direct cinema with some cinema verité techniques in a film about striking coal miners. *Streetwise* (Martin Bell, 1984) and *Before Stonewall* (Greta Schieler and Robert Rosenberg, 1984) have also gained distribution in theaters, but many exhibitors are still wary of programming documentaries because most do not make money.

7

THE DOCUMENTARY FILM

When average moviegoers think of film, they think of narrative. Yet, the vast majority of films produced, shot, and distributed around the world are nonfiction films. Although some of these films are created solely for aesthetic reasons, most nonfiction films are produced for educational and promotional uses. Such films range from films for training insurance sales people and films urging viewers to go to Disneyland to films that explain a complicated scientific principle. Some of these nonfiction films are complex and aesthetically pleasing, yet compared to the fiction film, the nonfiction film has hardly captured the critical imagination as an object of study. Despite its numbers, the nonfiction film has been marginalized. In relation to the Hollywood narrative standard, it constitutes an alternative form of cinema. Whether seen on television or in a movie theater, the largest body of nonfiction films viewed by the general public is the **documentary,** a film that explores or documents the lived world. Documentaries, of course, differ widely in their philosophic, aesthetic, and technical approach to their subject matter and take many forms. This chapter will focus on this variety of documentary approaches and forms.

The Image of the Real

What I think they do is provide something that fiction films cannot provide, which is actuality, which is a sense that this is really happening. This woman is really having this baby. She is not an actress. She could die, right before your eyes. Or perhaps a cretin could be born, or perhaps her husband will kiss her and they'll be happy; but whatever is going to happen, it will really happen. Fiction films just can't do that.
Arthur Barron [1]

Documentary film, the representation of actual events and people on the screen, places its major emphasis on educating and persuading viewers. The fiction film places major emphasis on entertaining viewers (though it may also enlighten them). Because of these seemingly obvious differences, we all tend to know — or think we know — when we are watching a fiction film and when we are watching a documentary. On what do we base this assumption? After all, both documentary and fictional image and sound end up on the screen as only a *representation* of that reality we associate with daily existence in the lived world. What finally distinguishes them is their *presentation* of that representation. It is *why* filmmakers approach the events before their cameras and then *how* they present it to the viewer, which provoke our particular response to the representation. The basic premise on which the documentary film is based is that it is nonfiction — that what is seen and heard on the screen and sound track was not created expressly for the purpose of making a film — and that it bears a strong resemblance to what you or I would have seen and heard had we been at the scene of the filmed event.

Perhaps the most useful way to organize a discussion of the various kinds of documentary film is to look at the relationship the film assumes between its subject matter and the viewer. Does it primarily observe its subject matter? analyze it? shape it to promote or persuade? poeticize or dramatize it? In the process of looking at the films' primary functions we will, of course, also discuss their forms — for certain functions have an affinity for certain structures. But, given the prevalent connection that most viewers make between documentary film and some abstract notion of truth or reality, it is first necessary to examine some of the techniques and choices available to documentary filmmakers. These reflect the relationship between the filmmakers and the original subject matter and structure the finished film.

Form and Technique

Raw footage is the basic building block of documentary film. This footage is a document, a record of an event that has been minimally influenced by either the process of filming or the process of editing. All film, of course, is <u>subjective as well as objective</u>, but raw footage is the least influenced by the manipulations of the filmmaker. Thus, even though we occasionally regard the one-shot Lumière films of 1895 Paris as documentaries, they — like raw footage — are better considered documents: primary material that exists as a relatively unconsidered, unevaluated, unordered record. Indeed, therein lies their fascination and beauty; they bring the viewer as close to the primary experience they record as is humanly possible. And the presence and sensibility of the filmmaker who made the record is virtually invisible.

But the documentary film that is exhibited and seen by viewers is no longer raw footage. Indeed, the term *documentary* includes, in addition to its associations with recording actual events, the notion of filmic structure unified by a philosophy, ideology, and aesthetic, by an *ordering* of that material from a chosen human perspective. Thus, the documentary filmmaker acts as a mediator between the viewer and the event represented by the raw footage. That mediation may be highly visible or it may seem invisible because certain characteristics, which indicate the filmmaker's intervention between the subject and the viewer, such as narration, music, and montage editing, have become so conventional through frequent use that they have become invisible to the viewer. In some mediated documentaries, the filmmaker's role as manipulator is obviously revealed to the audience in an attempt at truthfully including the act of making the film as part of the event being filmed.

Whether or not viewers are consciously aware of the filmmaker's intervention between the subject and themselves, certain documentary techniques have evolved through the form's history and are available to the filmmaker who wishes to use them. Thus, the filmmaker can choose to make a film based on long takes, which preserve space and time and seem unmediated, or can choose to stress montage editing with its imposed juxtapositions. The filmmaker may use only synchronous sound, letting the subject speak for itself, or narration and commentary in voice-over explanations. Music might be used for uniting disparate images and for building drama, or the sound track might be kept the way it was recorded on the spot, or cleaned up through mixing. Events may be filmed only as they occur (from a suitable distance), or people confronted by the camera may be interviewed. The filmmaker may create an entire film from material shot by others, archival footage, which, when edited together, makes a compilation film. Or the line between nonfiction and fiction might be blurred by restaging and re-creating events, by combining actual events with fictional events, or by combining an overt poetic meditation with images of actual events. A few or many of these devices may be used, depending upon the filmmaker's philosophy of documentary and the film's ultimate function. And all will be embodied in a film structure, which is also responsive to the filmmaker's belief and goals. A documentary's structure may be dramatic, based on events that have a built-in or created crisis or culmination like an election or a big rock concert, or they may be organic and cyclical, based on the natural (and not necessarily dramatic) sequences dictated by the subject matter, such as the passing of seasons or the cyclical routine of an institution. They may be shaped so that events are revealed chronologically as they happen or have happened. Or the filmmaker may choose to use sound and images, together and separately, to evoke not only the present but also the past (and often both simultaneously). The filmmaker may even ignore time completely as an ordering device, so that we are not aware when the images we are watching happened.

Which techniques and which structures a filmmaker chooses for a given film tell us something about the filmmaker's relationship to the raw footage and about that filmmaker's relationship to the viewer and the film's intended function.

Documentary Functions

OBSERVATION

> I've been trying to make a series of films on contemporary American institutions, but each time I go out, it's a kind of voyage of discovery. I think if you knew what the film was going to look like before you started, then you'd simply be imposing a stereotype on a situation, and you wouldn't be learning anything or thinking about what you'd experienced.
> Frederick Wiseman[2]

The maker of a documentary chooses to be a certain kind of observer. The decision not to interfere in the event happening before the camera and not to impose more than a minimal structure in the editing process is not inevitable; rather, it reflects a specific documentary philosophy. This philosophy is based on three beliefs: (1) that the integrity of the event being filmed must be maintained, (2) that there is an inherent meaning in the event, and (3) that the camera can record and reveal this meaning to the viewer without explanatory mediation by the filmmaker. Two major forms of documentary generally adopt this philosophy of minimal intervention: the **ethnographic film** and **direct cinema**.

Ethnography, a branch of anthropology, attempts to describe the specific cultures of the various peoples of the world. Because traditional ethnographers emphasize description over analysis, and because their major arenas of study usually have been exotically located, those who have used the film medium for ethnographic purposes have also been able to create films that the general public finds fascinating. Thus, *Dead Birds* (Robert Gardner, 1963), made to observe the war-based culture of the Dani tribe of New Guinea, is more than scientifically gripping; its exoticism and pictorial beauty hold us, and our cultural collision with another system of war raises certain philosophical issues (Figure 7-1). The film, of course, is not sheer raw footage. It combines long takes and a moving camera, which preserve the integrity of time and space with some lyrical and suggestive montage, and it uses narration to tell us what the people we are watching are doing — and occasionally what

7-1 Ethnographic film attempts to capture a native culture as a record for anthropologists with as little interference as possible by the camera crew — either during the filming or afterwards in the editing process. Robert Gardner, however, in *Dead Birds* (1963), though describing aspects of the daily life and customs of the Dani tribe in New Guinea, focused on their peculiar formalized warfare system in order to make an implicit comparison with modern civilization's more brutal, spontaneous, irrational forms of warfare.

they are feeling. However, the film maintains a generally cool, scientifically observant position.

The same basic problems face today's ethnographic filmmakers that faced Robert Flaherty long ago when he made the first ethnographic feature, *Nanook of the North* (1922). Certainly, the technology has changed to allow today's ethnographers to follow their subjects and preserve that spatial and temporal continuity, which authenticates their observations and allows viewers the freedom to draw their own conclusions from the filmed material — and, of course, there is sound. But ethnographers must still find the structure that best represents their material. Flaherty chose a chronological one, showing the life and inherent drama of an Eskimo as he moves through the seasons of the year (Figure 7-2). Ethnographers must also consider and attempt to avoid or recognize and incorporate their own cultural biases and the way they influence what is looked at and from what vantage point. *Nanook* occasionally falls victim to cultural bias, as when a title equates an Eskimo baby with a Husky puppy, but it redeems itself by the fact that Flaherty enlisted the Eskimo's help in determining the events in the film. Indeed, some current practice harks back to Flaherty; today, ethnographers often teach the group to be filmed to use the camera and thus to make the film, so that the cultural bias exhibited is that of the culture under study.

Stylistically, ethnographic film is marked by plentiful use of long takes, the zoom lens, and a moving, often hand-held, camera — all of

7-2 Many of the same problems face ethnographic filmmakers today that faced Robert Flaherty when he made *Nanook of the North* (1922). Filmmakers must deal with their own cultural biases, and at the same time find a structure which best represents the material. Flaherty chose a chronological structure for *Nanook* based on seasons of the year.

which serve to maintain temporal and spatial continuity and thus preserve the integrity of the individual sequences. Both synchronous source sound and asynchronous voice-over narration are used, the first to authenticate the image and the second to explain what would otherwise be incomprehensible to the western viewer. Perhaps because ethnographic films so frequently record primitive and agrarian cultures, their editing is often based on seasonal cycles or on ritual events. Ethnographic films also may serve to record and preserve aspects of our own culture. Les Blank, although not an academic anthropologist, has made many films that document American regional, ethnic, and folk cultures: for example, Cajun life in southwest Louisiana in *Spend It All* (1975), Chicano life at the Tex-Mex border in *Chulas Fronteras* (1977), the musical traditions of New Orleans in *Always for Pleasure* (1978), and polka dancing in *In Heaven There Is No Beer* (1984).

In some ways direct cinema is very similar to ethnographic film. The aim of the filmmaker is to observe and record an uncontrolled situation — one neither controlled by the dictates of the camera or by the filmmaker's initial conception of the material nor influenced and changed by the act of filming itself. But whereas scientific observation motivates the ethnographer who films an alien culture, direct cinema filmmakers generally look at some aspect of their own and the viewer's culture and have no specifically defined or socially approved motive for their act of observation. What is considered respectable scientific observation in a film like *Dead Birds* may often seem like unethical voyeurism in a direct cinema film or series of films like *An American Family* (Alan and Susan Raymond, 1973), a series that raised extremely controversial questions about the presence of camera and crew as intruders and catalysts in the lives of a California family. (Albert Brooks showed the comic consequences of media invasion of an ordinary family in *Real Life* (1979), a fictional construction of a direct cinema documentary.) In direct cinema the very choice of subject matter often raises ethical and moral issues, issues dealing with distinctions between observation and voyeurism, with violations of privacy, and with the insidious or unconscious manipulation of events so as to create cinematic drama where there was none. All these issues seem to be heightened by the complex ambiguity of direct cinema, which, unlike the ethnographic film, uses no narration to explain itself or to distance the viewer (through the mediation of an intervening human voice) from the event being filmed.

One of direct cinema's leading practitioners, Frederick Wiseman, has to some degree circumvented some of these issues by choosing to observe and explore well-defined American social institutions supported by public taxes and therefore legitimately open to examination. In films like *High School* (1968), *Hospital* (1970), *Juvenile Court* (1973), *Welfare* (1975), *Model* (1980), and *The Store* (1984), Wiseman's aim — like the ethnographer's — is to present the everyday life of institutions rather than to compile a string of dramatic but exceptional moments. Like the ethnographer, he is interested in the ordinary process of the institution he records, and his films, therefore, take their shape from the recurrent and cyclical functions of institutional life. Although Wiseman talks about his work as a subjective exploration of institutions, he still sees his function as recording with as little polemic, rhetoric, and self-presence as possible the events themselves — so that the viewers are finally responsible for what they make of what they see on the screen. It is evidence of his success that many of his films have excited controversy and have produced opposing interpretations of their meaning; *Law and Order*, for example, has been viewed as presenting a very fair and somewhat positive portrait of the Kansas City police department — but it has also been praised (by groups unsympathetic to increasing police power) as an antipolice documentary, which emphasizes police ineffectiveness and brutality.

The ambiguity of another type of direct cinema is more problematic, raising those moral and ethical issues previously cited. Albert and David Maysles have been perhaps the foremost practitioners of films whose subject matter tends to bring both the filmmaker and the viewer into uncomfortable confrontation with the nature of their curiosity and with the purposes and implications of the act of filmmaking and the act of viewing. Although Wiseman seems socially justified in turning his cameras on public institutions, it is less clear what justifies the choice of a group of door-to-door Bible salesmen or two bizarre and eccentric relatives of Jacqueline Bouvier Kennedy Onassis as subject matter, choices made by the Maysles brothers in their landmark film *Salesman* (1969) and in *Grey Gardens* (1976). They initially avoided such issues by focusing their cameras on people who were already public figures: politicians in *Primary* (1960), performers in *Meet Marlon Brando* (1965) and *Gimme Shelter* (1970). Indeed, these public subjects not only helped the filmmakers sidestep the issue of an exploitative invasion of privacy, but they also helped to give the filmmaker a dramatic structure for the films: a political contest accelerating toward a climactic election, performers moving toward a moment of performance. Unlike the ethnographer and unlike Wiseman, the Maysles brothers look for the extraordinary and exceptional moments in ordinary life and for subjects that offer a built-in dramatic structure as they show crises, contests, and conflicts. Thus, their films avoid cyclic editing and tend to be shaped dramatically, emphasizing through camera movement and editing what has been called the *privileged moment* in which another human being does something extraordinarily personal or revelatory before the camera and the viewer. This tradition of seemingly unmediated, yet dramatically structured, documentary continues and enjoys some commercial success — particularly in certain performance and concert films, which allow the spectator a privileged backstage and private look at musical performers and culminate in the drama of some major public performance. While one thinks here of examples like *The Last Waltz* (Martin Scorsese, 1978) about The Band and *The Kids Are Alright* (Jeff Stein, 1979) about The Who, a film like *Say Amen, Somebody* (George T. Nierenberg, 1982) about gospel music also uses a direct cinema approach to the various performers and their performances.

Stylistically, direct cinema is much like ethnographic film in its use of the long take, zoom lens, and moving, hand-held camera. It does not, however, use narration, relying only on synchronous sound. Often the images and sound in early films were characterized by their technical crudity; unsteady, out-of-focus images, poor lighting, and flawed sound tracks were the result of inadequate technology in uncontrolled and spontaneous filming circumstances. Paradoxically, these flaws have come to suggest both immediacy and authenticity to the film viewer and even with today's technological advances, many contemporary filmmakers deliberately choose a crude style as proof of their film's unmanipulated and uncontrolled nature.

Direct cinema is an excitingly controversial documentary form. Often its unvoiced but omnipresent moral tensions are what make it so fascinating, compelling, and illuminating, and it has been praised as nonreductive in its approach, respecting rather than explaining life as it is lived. But such tensions have also led to criticism that the form is exploitative and voyeuristic. It has been charged with being overeager to catch people in private moments, with appealing to a suspect curiosity, and with pretending — through the effacement of the filmmaker's presence behind the camera — to offer an objectivity neither really felt nor practiced. In the final analysis, direct cinema is a film form and methodology only as ethical as the filmmaker behind the camera.

ANALYSIS

> I try to get all the facts from both sides, but I always accept the challenge to take sides. I don't even believe in the word "objectivity." I try to express my political views in my films. . . . But my views come out by means of irony and contrast and methods like that, not by editorializing or distorting the facts.
> Marcel Ophuls [3]

Documentary filmmakers who choose to analyze their subject matter rather than simply record it have also chosen to acknowledge their own mediation in the filmmaking process. Like ethnographers and the practitioners of direct cinema, documentary analysts believe both in maintaining the integrity of the reality being filmed and in the ability of the camera to uncover meaning in the doings of people. But unlike those documentarians, the analysts wish to explain and illuminate reality by finding and creating relationships between people and events rather than solely by observing them. Thus, the **analytic documentary** is rarely as scientifically detached from its subject matter as the ethnographic film or as ambiguous in its presentation as the direct cinema film. While analytic filmmakers admit their own presence as mediators, they depend on the integrity of the film record and the very scope and breadth of their presentation to give the viewer the feeling that the film is fair-minded even while it is not objective. Thus, analytic documentaries tend to use a broad canvas and to cover the same subject matter from a variety of sources and techniques. There are three major forms of the analytic documentary: the compilation film, cinema verité, and what might be called the *epic documentary*.

First developed in the 1920s by Soviet filmmaker Esther Shub who researched and compiled archival footage to create her classic *The Fall of the Romanov Dynasty* (1927), the compilation film is a documentary made solely from already existing footage. The filmmaker may never use a camera, functioning primarily as an editor, presenting and analyzing raw footage (made by others for other purposes) through juxtaposition and ordering of the material in the editing process. The most obvious kind of compilation film, and once the most plentiful, is the newsreel — although, strictly speaking, a great deal of its compiled footage was shot for inclusion in such a news magazine format. Key news events of national and international importance, incorporating footage often shot for other purposes (for example, battle footage), would begin the news-reel. This was followed by lighter material, which almost always included some footage about women (such as a fashion show or bathing beauty contest) and finally sports. The selection of material was determined as much by its ability to remain interesting and news, despite the weekly intervals between issues, as by its actual importance. Analysis was supplied primarily by voice-over narration and secondarily by headline titles between segments. Much more significant is the feature-length compilation film, which, through the juxtaposition of archival footage, attempts to analyze history through film records of events and people. Indeed, the compilation film generally makes history its subject matter, availing itself of raw footage found in national archives, news-reels contemporaneous with the historical events under scrutiny, and even home movies (Eva Braun and Hitler's have found their way into many compilation films about the Third Reich). Sometimes the resultant films are panoramic, and thus are often shown as a series of films as well as separate works; one can point to a twenty-six-episode series like *Victory at Sea* (NBC, 1952–1953), which analyzed United States naval action in World War II. Some, however, are feature length like *The Atomic Cafe* (Kevin Rafferty, Jayne Loader, and Pierce Rafferty, 1982) which focuses on the construction of American attitudes toward the bomb in the 1950s by compiling footage from educational films and films made by the United States government.

Stylistically, the compilation film is fairly easy to identify. It is composed of relatively short pieces of footage, which are linked, most commonly, by voice-over narration, occasional music, and by the editorial relationships imposed on the images by the filmmaker. Compared to other kinds of analytic documentary, the compilation film sometimes may function to mask the presence of the filmmaker-analyst; because the authentic raw footage often overwhelms the viewer, interpretive narration and editing seem almost invisible or simply true. Indeed, one contemporary practitioner of compilation film — Emile de Antonio — has done away with external narration completely in some of his films like *Point of Order!* (1964), which analyzes McCarthyism, and *Millhouse: A White Comedy* (1971), which presents a scathing and often funny analysis of Richard Nixon's political career. De Antonio depends on the juxtaposition of sound as much as he does on the juxtaposition of imagery; *Point of Order!* is austere in its use of synchronous source sound, but *Millhouse* goes so far as to use asynchronous music to shape our responses to the imagery. At one point, for example, the image shows us a head being reverently lifted into position atop a wax-museum statue of Nixon while the sound track plays "Pomp and Circumstance."

The second major form of analytic documentary, cinema verité, is a form unfortunately often confused with direct cinema because of many stylistic similarities between the two types of films. Both forms tend toward technical crudeness: **high-grain** images produced by fast film, which can record under poor lighting conditions, frequent use of the hand-held camera, haphazard composition, and flawed sound tracks. Both forms also depend primarily on a cinema of duration, on the long take and the moving camera (which preserve the temporal and spatial continuity of the event being filmed), on minimal manipulation through editing, and on a synchronous sound track. Indeed, there is very little stylistic difference between direct cinema and cinema verité — except for the fact that cinema verité makes extensive use of the interview and therefore contains many images in which talking heads address the camera. Philosophically and functionally, however, cinema verité is quite opposite from direct cinema. Verité filmmakers see themselves not as an observer but as catalysts and participants. Recognizing that the act of filming changes the event being filmed, verité filmmakers become an active part of their films; one can hear them asking their subjects questions and engaging in dialogue with them, and one can occasionally see them and their cameras reflected in mirrors or even in the action itself. Indeed, at times, verité filmmakers may even meditate on the sound track or before the camera about the making and meaning of their films. This notion of the filmmaker as participant rather than mere observer harkens back to Dziga Vertov, the Soviet theorist and filmmaker responsible for the newsreel *Kino-Pravda* (for which cinema verité is the French translation) and *The Man with a Movie Camera* (1929), in which the cinematographer is shown as an integral part of the action. This participatory function of the filmmaker explains the presence of the interview in so many verité films. The practitioner of direct cinema, dedicated to noninterference, can only observe an interview if it should happen before the camera; the verité filmmaker can cause it to happen and can be either the interviewer or the interviewed.

The function of cinema verité is analytic — to explore relationships among people and events and to understand them. Thus, as a way of dialectically countering its own admitted subjectivity, it may choose to focus panoramically on its subject matter. The titles of the films often indicate their attempt at breadth: *Chronicle of a Summer* (Jean Rouch, 1961) and *Le Joli Mai* (Chris Marker, 1963). *Chronicle of a Summer* — made by the originator of the modern verité movement and coiner of the term in homage to Vertov — asks Parisians on the street if they are happy, follows several of them about as they live their lives, interviews them on camera and also leaves them to their own devices in front of it, resulting at times in confession and moments of extreme emotion. In addition, Rouch screened the raw footage for the film's featured participants, provoking a discussion of the footage, which also became part of the film. And, in a final attempt at film truth, he and his collaborator Edgar Morin discuss — in the film — what they have learned from their experience making the film. This is far removed from direct cinema.

Indeed, sometimes the cinema verité filmmaker's own engagement with the material of actual events and people analyzes and transforms it to such a degree that film truth emerges as the documented truth of a personal meditation. The film becomes self-reflexive as it engages with its subject matter. In *Daguerrotypes* (1975), Agnes Varda combines direct cinema observation, cinema verité interviews, and her own poetic musings to give us a complete portrait of life and human relations in the small shops of a single Paris street. Jean-Pierre Gorin (who once worked in a filmmaking collaborative — The Dziga Vertov Group) makes his own engagement with the linguistic mystery of idioglossic twins who attracted wide media attention an opportunity to comment ironically on the surreal aspects of American culture and the American dream in *Poto and Cabengo* (1979). And Werner Herzog's voice-over meditations on both his own obsessions as well as those of his subjects turn his short documentaries such as *The Ecstasy of the Great Sculptor Steiner* (1975) and *La Soufriere* (1977) into philosophical explorations. These kinds of cinema verité documentaries are constructed as personal essays rather than as objective analyses, and they have become an increasingly popular form of documentary inquiry.

Both the compilation film and cinema verité come together in the third major form of analytic documentary, which because of its relatively

7-3 Marcel Ophuls, the foremost practitioner of epic documentary, attempts through over four hours of archival footage and interviews in *The Sorrow and the Pity* (1970) to understand occupied France under the Nazis.

recent appearance has no official designation. However, the form might well be called the **epic documentary** because it is characterized by its broad scope and its great length. Its combination of compilation film techniques (the juxtaposition of archival footage) with cinema verité techniques (primarily the interview) results in a unique structure; both past and present become temporal realities in the film when a piece of archival footage is juxtaposed with a contemporary interview of someone who had been present in that past event, or — even more complexly — when a piece of archival footage might be simultaneously accompanied by a past participant speaking in the present and with hindsight. The foremost practitioner of epic documentary has thus far been Marcel Ophuls. His *The Sorrow and the Pity* (1970) attempts through four and a half hours of archival footage and contemporary interviews to understand occupied France under the Nazis (Figure 7-3). Indeed, it is through its very breadth and duration that the complexity of the event is recorded with all its contradictory evidence. In another epic film, *The Memory of Justice* (1976), Ophuls similarly explores and analyzes the issues of individual and collective responsibility, focusing primarily on the Nuremberg war crimes trials of 1946–1947 but also making visual, aural, and thematic reference to France's relationship to Algeria and America's to Vietnam. The film runs more than four and a half hours in

7-4 Though documentaries can be made about any aspect of human life, the documentary impulse frequently is allied with a social conscience. The documentary filmmaker turns his camera on problems within the society. In *The Exiles* (Kent Mackenzie, 1959–1961) the life of Native Americans in Los Angeles is presented, showing the hardships and difficulties they face living in an alien culture.

its careful accumulation of human and historical documentation. Hours and hours of material from the past combined with contemporary interviews provided the basis for the multihour analysis *Vietnam: Ten Years Later*, which ran on television in 1983.

PERSUASION

> I sat alone and pondered. How could I mount a counterattack against *Triumph of the Will;* keep alive *our* will to resist the master race? I was alone; no studio, no equipment, no personnel. Commandeering a Hollywood studio for this effort seemed out of the question. Could I plan idea films and turn them over to the Signal Corps for production? Did they have the creative brains to cope with such propaganda blockbusters as *Triumph of the Will?* No. . . . The struggle for men's minds was too new, too highbrow, too screwball for old-line colonels who still referred to soldiers as "bodies."
> Frank Capra [4]

There are many kinds of **persuasive documentary** films, films which attempt to make a pitch, sell or promote an idea, change a point of view, make an appeal for some cause, incite the viewer to economic, social, or political action (Figure 7-4). Some of the films excite little controversy despite their manipulative techniques because the viewer already agrees with the position of the film, or because the film attempts to persuade by selectively emphasizing known characteristics of a given subject matter, or because the filmmaker's particular position is openly and unthreateningly announced. Some films on controversial topics are so insidious or so effective, however, that they are identified as *propaganda*. These films are seen as dangerous because the viewer disagrees with the film's position, or because the film distorts its subject matter, or because its method of persuasion is hidden or particularly meant to appeal to emotion at the expense of reason. Whether used for good or ill, the persuasive documentary can be extraordinarily powerful because it manipulates all the elements of film to make its point — a fact recognized by Adolf Hitler and Franklin Delano Roosevelt, by Leni Riefenstahl and Frank Capra.

Stylistically, persuasive films tend to be eclectic, using whatever means will accomplish their ends, whatever technique will best convey their messages. Thus, persuasive films may include archival footage, film shot contemporaneously, animation, reconstruction and dramatization, music, narration, synchronous and asynchronous sound, interviews, and so forth. Despite their variety, however, persuasive films have one element in common: they are all highly dependent upon the editing process for their power, and therefore they generally have a greater number of separate shots in them than do other documentaries. There are two major forms of persuasive documentary: the **exposé** and the **propaganda** film.

The documentary exposé owes its popularity to television and to the particular efforts of Edward R. Murrow, who pioneered the form for CBS and created a documentary series in 1951 called *See It Now*. The form uses analysis toward a persuasive end that is openly stated, usually by an on-camera narrator or reporter. The strategy is to lay bare what are assumed to be hitherto unknown facts to the viewer and, then, to appeal to the viewer as a reasoning and responsible person who, now aware of previously unknown or unavailable information, cannot do otherwise than take a position toward the subject matter similar to the filmmaker's. Once the evidence is exposed, the filmmaker's position seems rational and hardly controversial. But, on occasion, the subject under scrutiny may be extremely controversial. For example, Murrow's *Report on Senator McCarthy* (1954) not only exposed the Red Scare and the man who exploited it, but also called for America to censure his activities; and *The Selling of the Pentagon* (Peter Davis, 1971) both exposed the ways in which the U.S. Department of Defense promoted militarism with propaganda and also called for an end to such bureaucratic and dishonest manipulation of both the press and the American people. At other times, the exposé may shock or surprise viewers into awareness but the subject itself — and the position taken — is not controversial. Both *Harvest of Shame* (David Lowe, 1960) and *Hunger in America* (CBS, 1968) treat issues — the abominable living and working conditions of migrant workers and the widespread incidence of starvation and malnutrition in the United States — which, once presented, can only evoke the unanimous response that such conditions are socially undesirable. Thus, the exposés primary method is to educate viewers and then explicitly or implicitly exhort them to action. Filmmakers may play an overt role, acknowledging their mediation between reality and the viewer by presenting themselves or surrogate figures — narrators or onscreen investigative reporters — within the film. Although the selection of raw footage and the juxtaposition of shots in editing are usually made to seem relatively invisible, the purpose of the film (to reveal inequities) and the presence of the filmmaker (an informed and indignant guide) are made internally clear. Recently, the documentary exposé has been used not only to reveal current social problems, but also to expose and revise our dominant images of the historical past and its problems. The feminist filmmakers who made *The Life and Times of Rosie the Riveter* (Connie Field, 1980) expose the manipulative media imagery, which forced and persuaded American women into and out of factories during World War II, and they counter that imagery not only by revealing its internal contradictions, but also by letting women who lived the time speak for themselves and tell their own histories.

Since all films examining actual events are in some way social and political utterances that intend to influence the viewer, they all share elements of the most manipulative documentary form, propaganda. In *Mein Kampf* (1924), Adolf Hitler defined propaganda as an art that by using "appropriate psychological form" can "awaken the imagination of the public through an appeal to their feelings." This definition of propaganda describes all persuasive film that moves us emotionally — from the social propaganda films of the golden age of British documentary in the 1930s (made to instill pride in the viewer by celebrating the English workingman through driving editorial rhythms and emotionally stirring music and rhetoric) to the exposé documentary like *Harvest of Shame*, which shocked the viewer as it educated. (This film was shrewdly broadcast on Thanksgiving Day, so that Americans stuffing themselves with turkey might feel guilty as they realized the food they were eating came from the backbreaking and poorly rewarded labor of exploited migrant farm workers.) Although none of us likes to think that our feelings have been manipulated through the use of an "appropriate psychological form," nearly all persuasive films fit Hitler's definition of propaganda.

Propaganda — an extreme form of rhetoric — is not inherently evil. Nearly all forms of social communication are to some degree persuasive, rhetorical. (That is, following Aristotle, they attempt to find the most effective means to engage and persuade their audiences to a given end.) Rhetoric and persuasion, however, can be evil in its function if it persuades its consumers to perform unjust actions. Because the Nazis extensively used propaganda, certain Nazi assumptions have come to seem permanently linked to the notion of propaganda. Hitler assumed that people were fairly stupid and their memories short-lived. Based on these assumptions, Nazi propaganda found the appropriate psychological format in the reduction of reality to simple, easily remembered symbols and stereotypes and in outright distortion, so that it presented, as Hitler wrote, "only that aspect of the truth which is favorable to its own side."

Such was the method of two propaganda works (one German, one American), which are today considered classics of the form: Leni Riefenstahl's *Triumph of the Will* (1935) and Frank Capra's *Why We Fight* series (1942–1945). Although there are many differences between them, there are also many similarities, notably editing that stimulates the audience to sympathize with the cause being espoused. Thus, while it may seem shocking to link a film that promotes Nazi ideology with a film that promotes a democratic ideology, stylistically they have a great deal in common.

Both Riefenstahl and Capra (who studied Riefenstahl's films to combat them) juxtaposed relatively simple imagery to create emotional connections. The opening sequences of *Triumph of the Will* connect low-angle shots of Hitler with recurrent images of clouds and church and building spires, linking the man visually with stereotypical images connoting spirituality, loftiness, the deity; later sequences repeat images of marching parades, boots in step, flags flying in the wind — all edited together to amplify a feeling of exuberance and rhythm and joyful unity (Figure 7-5). In Capra's series, the editing arouses emotion more through contrast than accumulation and repetition. *War Comes to America* (1945), for example, juxtaposes shots of American children playing innocuous games with shots (which were staged) of Japanese children and German children playing war games. Neither Riefenstahl nor Capra was reluctant to create and stage the content of images that were presented in the film as reality. Riefenstahl's job was easier than Capra's because the Nuremberg rally of 1934 was itself staged as much for her cameras as it was for the Nazis in attendance; Hitler had planned on a film being made to glorify the event and to rally the German people to his cause. Capra went even further, since his film was primarily

7-5 Leni Riefenstahl created in *Triumph of the Will* (1935) one of the most talked-about examples of propaganda film ever made. This film depicts Hitler and his cause favorably, and the word *propaganda* has become associated with evil ends. During World War II, however, the Allies also relied upon propaganda films to persuade their populations that the war was morally and politically necessary.

a compilation film; not only did he stage certain sequences but he also intercut raw footage with fiction footage (never clearly identified as fiction) gathered from many sources. Capra also used animation geared to evoke a simple and visceral response from the viewer: the Axis powers' march through Europe is depicted as black ooze, which threatens to engulf a map of the world in darkness, or like an octopus, the march is represented by tentacles, which stretch to grasp anything within reach in a stranglehold.

Finally, both filmmakers use music and sound to sway the viewer's emotions. The sound track of *Triumph of the Will* is pervasively insidious in its insistent rhythms. There is no spoken commentary; rather, the sound track consists of martial parade music and patriotic songs mixed with the sounds of marching feet, cheering crowds, and the speeches made by Hitler and his associates at the rally. Again, as with the imagery, the effect is cumulative: Hitler becomes associated with constant cheering and the viewer, rhythmically caught up in the drumbeats and marching footsteps, becomes united with those at the rally. Although *Why We Fight* is word-dominated, music and sound effects are extremely important. Capra shows, for instance, images of Hitler touring a captured Paris juxtaposed with a sound track on which Judy Garland sings "The Last Time I Saw Paris." The narration is authoritative and exhortative; the language (for example, words like *free* and *slave*), strong in emotional associations; the individual sentences relatively short and phrased like slogans (easy to remember): the narrator, speaking over a triumvirate shot of Hirohito, Mussolini, and Hitler, orders the viewer to "take a good look at this trio. Remember their faces. If you ever meet them, don't hesitate." Elsewhere, the narrator assures the viewer that despite Axis aggression "free men are like rubber balls. The harder they fall, the higher they bounce."

Clearly, the methods used by both Riefenstahl and Capra are similar: there are few differences, if any, between the techniques of good and evil propaganda films. It is the cause they wish to persuade us to which is open to moral judgement.

AESTHETIC EXPRESSION: POETRY AND DRAMA

> From Flaherty I really learned almost feeling things instead of looking at things with a camera . . .; he conveyed to me what it's like to discover something visually with a camera. They're very, very subtle things, extremely hard to talk about meaningfully. Flaherty had a little line he was fond of: How in the world do you teach somebody to smell a rose?
> Richard Leacock [5]

John Grierson, founder of the British documentary movement of the 1930s, once said that documentary was the "creative treatment of actuality." Though he believed that film should always be used in the service of socially relevant subject matter, he recognized that applying the techniques of poetry and drama to documentary material could educate and illuminate the viewer in ways that a straightforward approach might not. The Grierson-produced *Night Mail* (Basil Wright and Harry Watt, 1936), for example, uses poetic devices (including a narrative poem on the sound track) and a highly aesthetic visual style to communicate the energy and excitement inherent in what might be considered the commonplace train delivery of mail from England to Scotland (Figure 7-6). Although style and poetry are used to reveal the subject, the film's subject is still the mail delivery, not its own style.

Robert Flaherty, too, although he has been criticized for forsaking social concerns, always subordinated his visual poetry to the existential claims of his subject. Generally considered the foremost, as well as the first, practitioner of the poetic documentary, Flaherty had a sense of beauty that was an integral part of his vision. Flaherty has produced monumentally beautiful images on the screen, but his subject matter,

7-6 *Night Mail* (Basil Wright and Harry Watt, 1936) used poetic devices (including a narrated poem on the sound track) and a highly aesthetic visual style to communicate the energy and excitement inherent in what might be considered the commonplace delivery of mail from England to Scotland.

the "noble savage" who struggles and wins against the forces of nature, is always primary. (One could argue, of course, that the very notion of concrete human beings as noble savages is hardly a subordination of poetry to real existence.) Flaherty simultaneously recorded nature as a harsh reality and as a metaphor for human life. The arctic wastes and drifting snows of *Nanook of the North* awe us with their visual beauty. The image of a sleeping sled dog, for example, its coat covered with falling snow as it sleeps outside an igloo, transcends the literalness of its content to function as a metaphor for human sleep, rest, and death. In *Man of Aran* (1934), Flaherty used natural sound to heighten the thrilling images of giant waves crashing against the rock shelves of an island during a storm; the waves are photographed and the film constructed so that the sea becomes personified, seeming in its anger to climb the rock face as if to pursue and destroy the vulnerable family, which dares to struggle against its might (Figure 7-7). Whatever the environment, Flaherty found beauty and preserved it in his images: the gentle curves of South Sea palms and beaches in *Moana* (1926), even the majestic carriage of an oil derrick in the Louisiana bayous moving through a natural environment more like a stately dinosaur than a mechanical invader in *Louisiana Story* (1948).

The poetic documentary may also be the mode of the filmmaker who wishes to record the beauty, patterns, and rhythms of small events and taken-for-granted phenomena such as a rain shower. Joris Ivens' *Rain* (1929) is structured like a lyric poem or a piece of music — but from

7-7 Many documentaries seem little interested in detailing the facts about a place, a happening, or a culture. Instead they attempt to give the viewer an emotional experience related to the subject. Robert Flaherty, for instance, used natural sound to heighten the thrilling images of giant waves beating against the shore as frail humans attempt to live in an inhospitable landscape in *Man of Aran* (1934).

images of actual rain, wet city streets, and real puddles. The poetic mode can also be used to document the small, personal voice of an individual, to evoke the mood and tone of a particular life. Asian-American filmmaker Arthur Dong paid homage to both his mother and to the Chinese immigrant experience in his short and lyrical *Sewing Woman* (1982). An autobiographical monologue (in English and Chinese) provides the aural accompaniment for evocative images from past and present edited in a poetically suggestive rather than rhetorically expository manner (Figure 7-8).

Along with lyric devices, the documentary will often use dramatic devices to engage its audience with the actual events recorded in the individual shots. Indeed, almost all documentary films, from the least mediated forms of direct cinema to the most mediated, use drama to varying degrees and from varying sources. Drama may be found in front of the camera as part of the life being recorded, or it may be created, constructed by the editing process.

Perhaps the most widely seen documentary dramas photograph the natural world. Footage of animals and exotic landscapes becomes the raw material of films that tell stories. These films create characters from

7-8 Sometimes the lyrical documentary can illuminate the small personal voice of an individual. Asian-American filmmaker Arthur Dong evoked the mood and tone of his mother's experience as well as that of other Chinese immigrants in his short, poetic *Sewing Woman* (1982).

their animal subjects, and the script and editing create dramatic action. Walt Disney Studios has long been the foremost producer of such films, generally geared for family audiences. Sometimes the footage of unstaged material is combined with staged scenes in which actors perform — and these films really do not fit comfortably into the documentary category. But in many other films, drama is imposed on raw footage; while nothing is staged, the film is created, constructed through editing, to entertain in the manner of fiction. Thus, in *Charlie, the Lonesome Cougar* (Disney, 1967), the two central figures are a cougar named Goodtime Charlie and a terrier named Chainsaw and the funny and dramatic action takes place in a lumber camp in the Cascade Mountains of the Pacific northwest. The very fact that the animals are characterized by names indicates the tone and the attitude taken toward the subjects, and an amiable narrator further anthropomorphizes the creatures through word choice and by ascribing human feelings and motives to the animals. The very title of the 1984 rerelease of *Animals Are Beautiful People* (Jamie Uys, 1974) is a blatant announcement of this sort of documentation of nature. Films that do not anthropomorphize nature and that still use it for dramatic purpose are relatively rare, but do exist. *The Hellstrom Chronicle* (Walon Green, 1971), for example, imposes a science fiction narrative structure on a feature length documentary film about insects; the movie posited an ultimate battle between humanity and the insect world while it observed its subjects in scientific fashion.

Dramatic documentary uses dramatic structures (such as suspense) and devices (such as parallel editing and the compression and extension of time) to vitalize its content. Sometimes, the drama is found as the event is being filmed and does not have to be imposed through editorial structuring. This was true, for example, in *An American Family*, when during the course of the filming, Pat and Bill Loud began to reveal marital problems and decided, on camera (perhaps *because* of the camera), to get a divorce. Indeed, direct-cinema filmmakers who wish to minimize an imposed editorial structure will often choose a subject that is inherently dramatic, which is self-structured toward climactic resolution, which has a built-in crisis. *The Chair* (Drew Associates, 1963), for instance, asks and answers the question: Will a condemned man be executed or will the governor commute the sentence at the last minute? The film uses direct-cinema technique but with multiple cameras so that it can dramatically use parallel editing and cutaway shots showing the electric chair being readied, the defense lawyer hard at work, famed attorney Louis Nizer arriving to help. Indeed, the film opens with an introductory line of narration — "Somewhere in the city of Chicago there is a chair" — which parallels the fictive "Once upon a time." It has even been argued that the film exploits the real events and people in a stereotypically fictional manner: the hero is not the condemned man but his attorney, who, relatively untried, is working for nothing; and the prosecutor, made into the heavy, has the odds on his side. This kind of crisis structure informs many documentaries, from a minimally structured film like *Waiting for Fidel* (Michael Rubbo, 1976), which amusingly anchors its otherwise self-exploratory nature on the question whether Fidel Castro will show up for a promised interview with three Canadian filmmakers in Cuba to see him, to a highly structured work like *Pumping Iron II: The Women* (George Butler, 1985), which was advertised as "a story of strength, desire, courage . . . and a new definition of woman." The latter not only followed a female body-building competition, but also was the reason the competition was arranged — the filmmakers sure that documentary drama would result when traditionally feminine bodybuilders were challenged by the radical physique of competitor Bev Francis.

Re-Creation: The Ethics of Documentary

When Albert E. Smith returned to New York from Cuba with his San Juan Hill footage, he was worried: in spite of the Roosevelt posturing, it looked like a dull uphill walk, in no way fitting the "charge up San Juan

Hill" trumpeted by newspapers. Meanwhile theaters clamored for the Cuban material, already publicized. So Vitagraph held off its distribution until Smith and his partner J. Stuart Blackton had shot a table-top "battle of Santiago Bay" complete with profuse cigarette and cigar smoke, explosions, and cardboard ships going down in inch-deep water. Combined with the shots brought from Cuba, it became the hit of the war coverage.
Erik Barnouw [6]

The basic assumption most viewers make about documentary film is that it is about actual events rather than an imaginatively created fictional world, that it in fact documents, records, and preserves with a degree of integrity the world as it is commonly experienced. As this chapter has shown, however, it is possible to take images of reality and manipulate them, for example, to turn Hitler into a man-god moving against a staged background or to set up a body-building competition so that its somewhat determined drama might be recorded. The "creative treatment of actuality" can turn truth into a lie, non-fiction into fiction. As viewers, we have come to expect that the film which looks and feels like a documentary will show its subject matter like it is. In fact, however, it may show it as it is not. Because viewers expect truth, the documentary filmmaker must face ethical issues concerning the nature of the truth and reality which are less relevant to fiction film. And the boundaries between creative treatment and distortion, between fact and fiction, truth and lies, are frequently difficult to see clearly — particularly when *all* images are selective and partial representations of some unseen and larger context.

How should the filmmaker and the viewer regard the act of re-creation and reconstruction, for example? Flaherty's *Nanook of the North* and *Man of Aran* ignore many contemporary practices of the Eskimo and the Aran islanders. Moreover, old and no longer practiced methods of hunting and fishing were staged for Flaherty's cameras; that these episodes were re-creations was not announced to the viewer. The capture and killing of the huge basking shark in *Man of Aran*, for example, is accomplished by harpooners hunting from a small open boat, seeking to obtain the shark's fat for lamp oil. The method and purpose were facts for an older generation of islanders, but for most of the men we see in the boat it was the first time they had hunted that way; indeed, oil lamps were no longer in general use. Have we been deceived? And if we have, is the deception in the act of re-creation and staging — or is it not telling viewers that they are watching a re-creation? Some viewers might feel deceived, but others might feel Flaherty was justified in practicing what has been called *salvage ethnography* and that the islanders and their heritage were being served by the film. In *Nanook*, Flaherty wanted to record life inside the Eskimo's igloo, but both room and light were insufficient to allow his camera to function properly. To solve the problem, the Eskimo built a larger igloo than would have been normal and then cut away part of it to allow for more light. How do we regard this kind of staging for the cameras? Is it less or more deceptive than the Aran islanders' shark hunt? Today, if such films were being made to be screened on television, they would have to carry a message, either at their beginning or end, such as "Some of the events depicted are re-creations. But all are accepted as factual occurrences by naturalists." This explanatory line now appears on almost all of the nature documentary series on television, from *Wild Kingdom* to the remarkable documentary explorations of Jacques Cousteau.

Sometimes, in order for the viewer to decide what constitutes a film lie, it becomes useful to attempt to determine the filmmaker's intent. But evidence of good or bad faith may be hard to come by. We know that Flaherty, despite his re-creation or staging, was scrupulous in his attempts to show Eskimo truth because we have written records by and about him, and also because he related his reliance on Eskimo suggestions concerning footage. On the other hand, bad faith and the desire to make a commercial enterprise out of deceiving the viewer is evident in the many staged re-creations that passed as newsreels in the early days of film. Sometimes they combined the real and the fake. Indeed, sometimes an entire news film was faked from totally irrelevant and already existent footage. In 1899, Frances Doublier (once a Lumière cameraman) reconstructed the famed Dreyfus case for audiences around the world, identifying shots of an anonymous French captain as Dreyfus, a Parisian building as the scene of his court-martial, and even a long shot of the Nile delta as Devil's Island (really off South America), where Dreyfus was imprisoned; the irony of all this was that Dreyfus was court-martialed in 1894, a full year before the cinématographe and the first films were shown in Paris. Although considered good business by its practitioners, this kind of reconstruction was clearly deceitful.

Some films, however, are honest about their acts of staging and reconstruction, announcing through various conventional means like film credits or disclaimers that the images were created for the film and did not merely happen. Paradoxically, the best of these films are made in such good faith and are informed by such an honest desire to illuminate reality through the act of staging that often the viewer sees them as documentaries and remembers them as documentaries, despite the various disclaimers. Such is the case, for example, with *The Quiet One* (Sidney Meyers, 1948). With a script written by James Agee, and using subjective as well as objective cinematography, the film follows a fictional character, a young black boy named Donald, in his turbulent and moving emotional odyssey from sickness to the beginnings of mental health as he moves from the isolated ghetto of Harlem to the Wiltwyck School for disturbed children. Donald's problem was real and the film was shot against real backgrounds and in the real school, but Donald himself was an actor, the narrative was a fictional construction, and the credits admitted the fiction. Nonetheless, perhaps because of the sincerity and low-key tone of its dramatization, the film remains permanently associated with documentary film.

This same kind of association occurs with a quite different kind of recreation and staging, one which has had far-reaching political implications. Adopting the techniques and style, the very look and sound and feel of newsreels, direct cinema, and cinema verité, *The Battle of Algiers* (Gillo Pontecorvo, 1966) might, by analogy with analytic documentary, be called analytic fiction. The film makes no pretense at deceit. After its initial credits, which indicate the presence of a story and screenplay, the following caption appears alone on the screen: "Not one foot of newsreel has been used in this reenactment of the battle of Algiers." The film that follows then appears to document the Arab uprising against the French in Algiers during the 1950s. The film, despite its disclaimer, is so much like a documentary in style and structure that it seems real and true. Stylistically, it uses hand-held camera, high-speed film, which results in grainy and often overexposed images, and an imperfect sound track. Structurally, it seems to have the randomness of actual experience, beginning in the middle of an unexplained action that becomes comprehensible only as the viewer accumulates more data. It uses no single hero and it avoids an omniscient psychology of its characters; what we know about the people in the film is what we see and hear. That such an announced fiction can convince us we are watching documentary should make us aware of the degree to which documentary film is a *style* we have learned to recognize and not a truth in itself. *The Battle of Algiers* has had tremendous impact, particularly on third world filmmaking, which has found it politically effective to combine elements of documentary and fiction in one film. An interesting variant on Pontecorvo's film exists in the powerful Bolivian film *The Courage of the People* (Jorge Sanjines, 1971); the film re-creates and stages an army massacre of striking miners that occurred in 1967. Smoothly shot and in color, the film lies somewhere between fiction and documentary not only because of its historical specificity, but also because many of its actors were actual participants in and survivors of the real massacre and were called upon as advisers and collaborators in the filming.

What, then, are the boundaries of documentary? At times, they are flexible, bending to accommodate Flaherty's salvage ethnography, al-

7-9   Viewers generally believe they can distinguish between documentary and fiction films. In a fascinating exploration of viewer expectations, Mitchel Block's short film *No Lies* (1973) appears to be a cinema verité interview in which a film student films and talks to a friend who reveals that she had only a few days before been attacked and raped. The setting, the young woman, the hand-held camera, the poor sound quality, the out-of-focus shots all combine to give the impression of a real, unrehearsed moment of intensity which accidentally was captured on film. At the end of the film however, credits indicate that the woman was a professional actress and that the whole film had been scripted. Viewers are forced to rethink their attitudes toward the woman's plight, since now they realize that the rape didn't "really" happen — and yet they may feel cheated because they didn't know that they were in fact being lied to by the filmmaker.

lowing the polemic reconstructions and total distortion of the Nazis so long as they are labeled propaganda, accepting the association with the kind of fictional document represented by *The Quiet One*. There is only one certainty about documentary and film truth. And that is that documentary film — like fiction film — is composed of two-dimensional images and thus presents an illusion of substance and reality. Whether what we see on the screen reflects or distorts a particular truth, whether we are watching an eyewitness account of uncontrolled situations or a staged re-creation, cannot always be ascertained from the film itself (Figure 7-9). Its truthfulness, its reality, must be corroborated by other sources, a corroboration that is sometimes difficult to obtain.

Most documentaries do not evidence their authenticity or lack of it as does surrealist Luis Buñuel's purposefully outrageous travelogue, *Land Without Bread* (1932). This filmed document of the poverty-striken Hurdanos increasingly provokes our suspicion as the narrator objectively describes the film's subjects as barbaric, announces a choir of idiots, and overtly lies to us (his words disproved by the image we see on the screen). Ultimately, if we seek truth and reality in the documentary film, we are dependent upon the good faith of the filmmaker and our own constructive skepticism. Although it is perhaps the moral responsibility of documentary filmmakers to remember that the film form within which they have chosen to operate has become inextricably connected with truth and reality, it is also the responsibility of viewers to remember that they are, after all, watching a film. Every documentary is merely an interpretation of reality, an interpretation of events mediated by filmmakers, whether individual, industrial, institutional, or governmental. It is finally the option and the responsibility of the individual viewer to question and test the validity of that interpretation of reality through whatever means possible.

NOTES

[1] Quoted in G. Roy Levin, *Documentary Explorations* (Garden City, N.Y.: Doubleday, 1971), p. 308.

[2] Thomas R. Atkins, ed., *Frederick Wiseman* (New York: Monarch Press, 1976), p. 34.

[3] "Why Should I Give You Political Solutions?" *Film Critic* 1, no. 2 (November–December 1972): 56.

[4] *The Name Above the Title* (New York: Macmillan, 1971), p. 329.

[5] Quoted in G. Roy Levin, *Documentary Explorations*, p. 210.

[6] *Documentary* (New York: Oxford University Press, 1976), p. 24.

Historical Overview:
The Development of Experimental,
Independent, and Animated
Filmmaking

BEGINNINGS: THE BREAK WITH REALISM

One can distinguish between, on the one hand, the recording function of cinema and, on the other hand, its creative or expressive function even at its earliest stages of development. The Lumière brothers were interested in the every day world, pointing their cameras at relatively uncontrolled subjects in natural surroundings without any thought of altering those images through the cinematic apparatus itself. Georges Méliès, however, immediately recognized the cinema's ability to create illusions, to present images that defied the physical laws of the real world. Thus, while the Lumières simply pointed their camera and turned it on, Méliès painted elaborate backdrops and created artificial sets and then further manipulated his staged fantasies in the camera itself, running the film backward and forward, stopping and starting it up again to create magical appearances and disappearances. Although his films depended chiefly on narrative, and so led the way to the creation of the popular and commercially successful fiction film, Méliès can also be regarded as the father of the avant-garde and experimental cinema, for he was the first to stress film's dissociation from reality rather than its connection to it. His films were the first to demonstrate the aesthetic autonomy of which the medium is capable. It has been to this possibility of film that artists from other art forms have been drawn, and thus the history of the avant-garde, experimental, independent, and animated film has been peopled with filmmakers who were also artists, sculptors, architects, and musicians.

The first attempts to create motion pictures antedated photography, and resulted in mechanisms like the Zoëtrope, which animated drawings on paper frames; it is not surprising, then, that the animation of drawn figures was one of the first kinds of fanciful film art. Indeed, the earliest creators of the film cartoon delighted in the magic of the medium and its power to make the imaginable visible. Although the animated cartoon appeared as early as 1900, Emile Cohl, a French cartoonist who found in the new medium an outlet for his fertile imagination, was the first filmmaker to adopt the form wholeheartedly. Between 1908 and 1918, Cohl specialized in cartoons that transformed drawn objects from one thing to another in a surreal world in which nothing was stable; a man turns into a window and the window then turns into something else, defying logic and physical law and delighting the viewer with the unexpected. In the United States, Winsor McCay, already a noted cartoonist, made his first animated film in 1909; its protagonist was his famed comic-strip character Little Nemo, and his cartoons were extraordinary in the complexity of their drawings and their use of perspective. In Russia, Ladislaus Starevitch began a long career in model and **puppet animation.** The fact that he used 3-D figures in no way made his work less imaginative and more realistic than drawn animation; his *The Revenge of the Kinematograph Cameraman* (1912), for example, animates insect models to tell a story of a love triangle. And, in the United States during the 1920s, Max and Dave Fleischer combined animated drawings with live action in their popular *Out of the Inkwell* series, the cartoon figures materializing literally out of the inkwell of the live cartoonists and wreaking havoc until they were returned to the ink bottle. In all of these animated works, what is seen on the screen owes more to the artist's imagination, of course, than it does to the laws of physical reality. The world shown in the frame is an independent world, governed by its own laws. To be sure, these early cartoons were not considered seriously as art by the audiences who saw them: they were entertainments and hardly to be linked to such weighty art movements as expressionism or surrealism. Yet, in fact, in its creation of worlds in which logic and cause and effect do not operate as they do in the real world, the cartoon is the first avant-garde film form — and perhaps the only avant-garde film form readily appreciated by mass audiences.

While imaginative film artists in the United States submerged and popularized their expressionist and surrealist impulses in the animated cartoon, more overt experiments with the medium went on in Europe, a Europe caught up in artistic ferment in the 1920s. Movements such as German expressionism, **dada,** and surrealism were all radical artistic responses to modern life. These movements rejected traditional notions of reality and representationalism, and this rejection found its way into literature, painting, theater, and film. Thus, the seminal film of the German expressionist movement, *The Cabinet of Dr. Caligari* (Robert Wiene, 1919), used painted sets, deliberately distorted into perspectives that imitate not what the eye sees but what the tormented soul experiences. The sets were designed by Hermann Warm, who declared that "films should be living paintings." This important notion of film as a canvas also underlies the work of the German abstract painter Hans Richter and his Swedish collaborator, Viking Eggeling. Interested in adding the dimension of time to abstract painting, they turned to film. In *Rhythmus 21* (1921) and *Symphonie Diagonale* (1921), they experimented with abstract forms and gradations of black and white to explore geometric shapes. These were the first consciously artistic abstract and avant-garde films; their creators were not concerned with presenting reality or telling stories, but rather with making film works analogous to paintings and music of the day. Richter continued using both drawn and photographed forms to create what he called *absolute* or *pure* films with no actors, no plots, and no allegiance to the external world, films bent only on creating abstract patterns out of the plasticity of the medium. But he also was later influenced by the French avant-garde filmmakers and went on to make anarchic dada films.

SURREALISM AND THE AVANT-GARDE

The most dynamic contributions to the history of avant-garde film came from the French. It was to Paris in the 1920s that artists from around the world went to join with other artists in that explosion of aesthetic sensibility called *modern art.* Expressionists, **constructivists,** cubists, **futurists,** dadaists, and surrealists argued and practiced their aesthetic philosophies, each in its own way a response to the complexity and ambiguous nature of reality in the modern world. They wrote manifestos and outraged the conservative bourgeois public with their unconventional art, in a reaction against the excesses of World War I. They were also inspired by the daring and controversial work of Sigmund Freud, which dealt with such taboo subjects as sex and power, the fantasy and nightmare worlds of the unconscious. Because of its ability to realize the impossible in images and to add the dynamic elements of time and transformation in and through space, film seemed a highly appropriate medium through which to explore and represent the human unconscious as well as the configurations of abstract patterns. And, above all, it seemed to offer the opportunity to shock viewers into a new awareness of their relationship to the world.

Both the dadaists and the surrealists used film to attack and upset bourgeois notions of art and reality. Indeed, the dadaists based their creative efforts in acts of destruction meant to emancipate the visual imagination from any dependence on bourgeois tradition — and that even meant a rejection of Freudianism because the new psychology was inextricably linked with a bourgeois unconscious. The dadist films thus rejected any kind of logic, dream logic included. Man Ray, an expatriate American photographer, for example, destroyed notions of traditional filmmaking in *Retour à la Raison* (1923) by sprinkling salt and pepper and tacks and various other objects on unexposed film and developing the resultant images as a film made to insult his fellow dadaists. And René Clair, who went on to direct feature films made a short film to serve as an intermission for a ballet, entitled appropriately enough *Entr'acte* (1924). It is full of the anarchic, absurd, and illogical images and occurrences so loved by the dada movement: a ballerina turns into a bearded gentleman with a pince-nez, a game of chess is played on the rooftops of Paris, a man is shot and carried about in a coffin, which becomes the object of a wild funeral and a chase led by a camel, and when the coffin is finally recovered, the dead man jumps out unharmed. Performing these zany antics were artists whose work soon became world famous: Darius Milhaud, Marcel Duchamp, Erik Satie, Man Ray, and Francis Picabia. This film movement, however, came at the end of the dadaist movement in general, which by 1925 consumed itself in its most extreme manifestations and was finally absorbed by the surrealists.

The surrealists, like the dadaists, believed in the liberating qualities of illogic and shock. But the surrealists adopted Freud's view of the illogic of dream and the hidden aspects of human consciousness. Thus, the surrealists valued psychic automatism, the free, shocking associations made by an unconscious liberated from the control of reason, morality, and a planned aesthetic. These associations, according to the surrealists, were a reality superior to the reality apprehended by a reasoning, socialized, and constrained consciousness — thus the term *surrealism*. One of the first clearly surrealist films was *The Seashell and the Clergyman* (1928); made by a French woman filmmaker, Germaine Dulac, it linked Freudian imagery with sex and religion. It was shortly followed by the film that has since come to be regarded as the classic of surrealist cinema, *Un Chien Andalou* (1928). A collaborative work of painter Salvador Dali and filmmaker Luis Buñuel, and titled meaninglessly (translated, the title is *An Andalusian Dog*), the film is loosely structured along the free-associational paths taken by a Freudian dream. In its images of a cloud passing across the moon, an eyeball slit by a razor, a hand from which insects emerge, priests pulling a piano that serves as a coffin for dead animals, rational connections and cause and effect are inoperative. The film turned many stomachs and became a cause célèbre. Buñuel's next film, *L'Age d'Or* (1930), used shocking imagery to attack both capitalism and Catholicism and was received even more violently; rioting broke out in the theaters when it was shown.

Not all experimental and avant-garde films were quite so aggressively threatening. French cubist painter Fernand Léger, for example, used ordinary objects like pots and pans to construct a rhythmic ballet in his *Ballet Mécanique* (1924), believing that a new drama could be created that would allow man "to be free and yet not . . . lose touch with reality." Oskar Fischinger in Germany continued in the tradition of Richter's absolute film, beginning in 1925 his series of film studies which were based on mathematics. Also in the 1920s a group of relatively popular avant-garde films known as **city symphonies** emerged, so called because of their urban subject matter and their attempts at a musical structure. As early as 1921, Paul Strand and Charles Sheeler in their *Manhatta* impressionistically recorded New York City, but the city symphony reached maturity in films like *Rien que les Heures* (Alberto Cavalcanti, 1926), *Berlin: Symphony of a Great City* (Walter Ruttmann, 1927), *Rain* (Joris Ivens, 1929), *The Man with a Movie Camera* (Dziga Vertov, 1928), and *A Propos de Nice*

(Jean Vigo, 1930), films which all used fragments of real life as the basis upon which to construct abstract film poetry.

Most avant-garde and experimental filmmaking was centered in Europe, but there was some avant-garde filmmaking in the United States, although the American films tended to be more aesthetically conservative than their European counterparts. Three films appeared in 1928 representing the range of these efforts: *The Fall of the House of Usher* (Melville Webber and James Watson), which used expressionistic techniques to adapt Poe's story; *The Life and Death of a Hollywood Extra* (Robert Florey), which used expressionist techniques to spoof *The Cabinet of Dr. Caligari* in its tale of a Hollywood extra whose dreams of fame and fortune are frustrated; and *Steamboat Willie* (Walt Disney and Ub Iwerks), which introduced Mickey Mouse and sound to the animated cartoon in a totally surreal evocation of barnyard life. Although there were a few other experimental films, like Ralph Steiner's H_2O (1929), which abstracted images of light on water into patterns, it was primarily the animated cartoon that kept experimentation alive and well in the United States until the 1940s.

DECLINE: SOUND AND THE WAR YEARS

With the introduction of sound to the cinema in the late 1920s — a technological advance that coincided with the economic step backward of worldwide depression — avant-garde and experimental filmmaking fell into decline. Part of the problem was caused by the difficulties the new technology presented; the independent filmmaker could not afford to use sound, and the artist working within commercial production systems had to undergo the difficult and frustrating process of rethinking and readapting his art. In addition, the same kind of political and social commitment that drove the European avant-garde to make shocking, untraditional, and abstract films in the 1920s provided the impetus for their acceptance of a style more relevant to the social, economic, and political ills facing Europe in the 1930s. Although there were rare instances of personal films like poet Jean Cocteau's *The Blood of a Poet* (1930) (Figure 1) or Len Lye's experiments with drawing and painting directly onto the film stock as in *Colour Box* (1935), most filmmakers were in some way committed to the effort to end the Depression, and subsequently to help win the war.

Although avant-garde and experimental filmmaking declined during the war years, those years stimulated the development and widespread use of 16mm cameras and projectors both abroad and in America. This equipment became readily available and was relatively inexpensive (much of it was war surplus), allowing for the growth both of independent filmmaking and of an audience (chiefly organized in small film societies) for the independent, personal, avant-garde film. During the mid-1940s, then, the conditions supported a resurgence of independent film production in America.

1 Jean Cocteau uses representational images — houses, humans, animals, automobiles — in his films, but as in *Blood of a Poet* (1930) the way in which he uses them is surreal. People become poetic symbols through their stylized acting, dialogue, and costumes.

RENAISSANCE: THE RISE OF THE INDEPENDENT FILMMAKER

Maya Deren, a modern dancer, almost single-handedly originated the new American avant-garde. In *Meshes of the Afternoon* (1943), a film made with her husband, Alexander Hammid, she created a world in which reality and dream merged into a stream of consciousness communicated by imaginative cinematic techniques and personal symbolism. Deren was important not only as an artist and as a filmmaker, but also as the creator of an audience for avant-garde films. In 1945, she toured university campuses across the country with *Meshes of the Afternoon* and two of her other films, *At Land* (1944) and *Choreography for the Camera* (1945). The tour successfully tapped a hitherto unidentified audience, and film societies began to spring up in urban and educational centers to offer showcases for this new form of personal cinema. The Museum of Modern Art in New York expanded its circulating film library, making experimental and avant-garde films more available. In 1946 the San Francisco Museum of Art began its "Art in Cinema" series, stimulating avant-garde film production in the Bay area. And in 1947, Amos Vogel founded the Cinema 16 group in New York with the express purpose of exhibiting unusual films, whether modern or classic, documentary or experimental.

From that time to the present, the output of experimental films has continued unabated. Indeed, as filmmaking equipment has become less expensive and more portable, and filmmakers have experimented with distributional film co-operatives to rent their works for exhibition, independent filmmaking has increased. Every type and kind of film has been made, the only common characteristic uniting them being their independent mode of production and the idiosyncratic vision of their creators. Still, the influence of their predecessors can be discerned.

The absolute and pure cinema of early artists like Richter can be found in the work of Norman McLaren, one of the great contemporary animators, who also paints directly on film, as demonstrated by *Begone Dull Care* (1949) (Figure 2). Pure cinema can also be found in the works of the avant-garde structuralists, who believe that a film's shape is determined by the mechanics of the cinematic apparatus. Michael Snow's *Wavelength* (1966–1967), for example, is a 45-minute slow zoom through a room into a photograph on a wall; whatever occurs in front of the camera lens is recorded with equal lack of emphasis: a possible death, the changing of filters and focus, empty space, the occasional presence of people. The desire to make of film a nonrepresentational art is reflected in such contemporary works as *Permutations* (John Whitney, 1968), which uses computers to create abstract forms, and *Corridor* (Standish Lawder, 1968–1970), which combines stroboscopic light patterns so as to simulate brain waves.

The influences of the dadaist and surrealist movement continue in an active **underground cinema,** geared to shock the viewer into examining her or his culture and her or his notions of art. Both Kenneth Anger and Andy Warhol have been key figures: Anger with his series of films, culminating in *Scorpio Rising* (1963), *Lucifer Rising* (1966–1967), and *Invocation of My Demon Brother* (1969), which explored machismo and homosexuality, and Warhol with his experiments in minimal cinema like *Empire* (1964), which focused a static camera for an 8-hour look at the Empire State building and outraged audiences accustomed to drama and things happening in film. In a more humorous vein, Bruce Connor has used old movie footage to satirize an audience's dramatic expectations in films such as *A Movie* (1958).

Personal cinema has flourished in the work of Yvonne Rainer, Stan Brakhage, Ed Emshwiller, James Broughton, Bruce Baillie, Jonas Mekas, and Shirley Clarke. Brakhage, particularly, has been a key figure with his epic avant-garde work

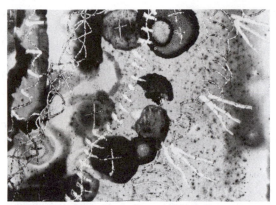

2   Norman McLaren's *Begone Dull Care* (1949) is representative of the abstract, nonrepresentational film. This frame enlargement shows the scratches and globs of paint that have been applied directly to the film stock.

Dog Star Man (1961), combining representational images with painting and scratchings on the film stock.

The term *independent film,* synonomous with underground film, once reflected the filmmaker's desire to be independent of the Hollywood system of institutionalized production, distribution, and exhibition. Independent filmmakers were individual artists making films not for gain, but for personal expression, specifically making films that would not be suitable for mainstream theatrical release because of their subject matter, style, or length. Today, the term is frequently applied to a group of films and filmmakers with exactly the opposite aspirations. These films are feature length fiction films that aspire to theatrical distribution, but are normally produced outside of the mainstream sources of funding, because the project is considered unbankable. Usually it is because the filmmakers have no track record; they are not known to those in the business. These independent filmmakers raise money through foundation grants, public television, and other private sources frequently assembling only enough to arrive at a completed release print, which can be shown at festivals with the hope of attracting a distribution deal. *Heartland* (Richard Pearce, 1981) followed this route to eventual theatrical screenings.

Northern Lights (John Hansen, 1979), *The Return of the Secaucus Seven* (John Sayles, 1980), and *Stranger than Paradise* (Jim Jarmusch, 1984) are other examples of films that were able to gain high critical praise and eventual distribution through the festival network. Now sometimes called the *Off-Hollywood* film movement, the independent feature movement is well established with a loosely affiliated group of small distributors and theaters around the country whose audiences respond to the latest from this group of filmmakers, hoping to see a new talent before that person is elevated to working in the Hollywood establishment. For some who have made the crossover, however, the rewards of success are not always unalloyed. Susan Seidelman made *Smithereens* (1982) for very little money, but it was so highly thought of, she was able to raise more money, more quickly for her next picture *Desperately Seeking Susan* (1985). Unfortunately she found that having a distribution deal and a union crew infringed somewhat on her personal sense of independence. Although she fought and won the right to make the film she wanted to make about a woman who was trying to find herself in the modern world of uncertain sex roles, the studio distributing the film tried to sell the film as a teenage musical film because the rock star Madonna had a part in it. The film did not sell well to the teenage audience because Madonna does not play herself in the film. After a couple of promotional test screenings with the teenage pitch, the studio admitted its mistake and revised its marketing strategies. The film did much better under the new advertising because it found the audience that would appreciate the film's contemporary concerns.

ANIMATION

Finally, of course, the animated film has remained the most popular and widely seen form of experimental cinema. In America, during the golden age of animation in the 1930s and 1940s, Disney Studios, Warner Brothers, and MGM created enduring cartoon characters like Mickey Mouse, Bugs Bunny, Roadrunner, and Popeye. Seeing the world with surreal vision, animators like Bob Clampett, Tex Avery, Chuck Jones, and Max and Dave Fleischer made the American cartoon an art that explored the collision between matter and space at the same time it entertained and delighted a large public. In Europe, contemporary animation has been greatly influenced by the work of Jiří Trnka's sophisticated puppet films in Czechoslovakia and the formation of the Zagreb Studio in Yugoslavia (1956); animated films were made for adult audiences and were often intellectual and satiric in their treatment of thematic material like war and modern society. Since the golden age, American animation has found new voices in the work of Ralph Bakshi and Robert Crumb, whose *Fritz the Cat* (1972), using animated characters in a feature-length film far removed from Disney, dealt with contemporary issues like sex, violence, and drugs. Further, many experimental filmmakers like Robert Breer use animation to give a liberated form to their exploration of cinematic time and space.

Many of the techniques of experimental and avant-garde cinema have been absorbed and popularized by filmmakers of mainstream theatrical films. Indeed, some experimental filmmakers have gone on to become theatrical filmmakers. But many prefer the total control the individual artist has over a single small work, independently produced for noncommercial purposes. These independent filmmakers, working in isolation or in groups, are creating what they believe is true film art, an art that has little to do with the narrative film as we know it in theatrical release or on television. They view their films not as commodities meant to appeal to a mass audience or as the results of collaborative effort. The camera and film stock are their equivalent of paint and canvas, of pen and paper, a medium of individual expression.

8

EXPERIMENTAL, INDEPENDENT, AND ANIMATED FILMS

Film as Film

> You must set aside the existence of the commercial films. You must forget the arts in general. But what is left, you may ask? My reply is simple. What is left is film as film. Film which contains as much of metaphor, simile, and allusion as any of the basic poets which you have studied.
> Gregory Markopoulos [1]

The films grouped in this chapter do not share easily identifiable characterstics. Indeed, the very fact that the films are called by a variety of terms is a sign of their diversity. *Experimental, independent, avant-garde,* and **underground** have been used synonymously, but each term also carries its own distinct meaning and emphasis. Experimental film, for example, suggests a film made for the purposes of trying out some new technique, some new aesthetic, some new structure, or some new apparatus. Independent film suggests a film made outside the traditional system of commercial theatrical production; generally, such filmmaking is characterized by its extremely low budget, its small crew, and its lack of access to widespread distribution, promotion, and exhibition. The term *avant-garde film* (literally "advance-guard") implies that the film is ahead of its time, in the forefront of an aesthetic movement, that it is a film not concerned with traditional means of communicating traditional content. And the term *underground film* seems given to films that are potentially shocking to traditional moral and aesthetic values, films that are subversive in their intent and effect. Some of the films considered in this section merit all these names, while others are best described by only one of the terms.

Even the animated film, despite its relatively clear distinguishing characteristics, needs some qualifying terminology. Animation can be applied to live action, 3-D models, and two-dimensional drawings, or it can be accomplished through computer graphics. And the animated film may be a traditional narrative feature, a surreal but commercially made cartoon, or an experimental, independent, avant-garde, or underground film.

Still, we can see some resemblances. With the exception of the Off-Hollywood independent feature and the animated film produced for theatrical release, most of the films discussed in this section do share some general characteristics. First, the films are usually made by a single artist or a small group, aiming not at commercial success but at artistic expression. Second, these films tend to be short, generally running anywhere from 1 minute to $\frac{1}{2}$ hour. Although a few films run 1 hour or more (feature length), both financial and structural considerations tend to curtail the length of the films. Third, financing for the films generally comes from institutional grants and from patrons, friends, and relatives of the filmmaker. Fourth, and last, almost all production is 16mm, although recently super 8mm and videotape have become popular.

For the most part, the filmmakers mentioned in this chapter are singular artists, who, with a few friends, a few dollars' worth of raw film stock, and a haphazard collection of equipment, attempt to create a personal piece of cinematic art determined more by their own vision than by the demands of a prospective audience. These filmmakers, of course, make their movies for an audience, but they envision this audience as a small, specialized group of viewers who might appreciate the ingenuity, the invention, and the creativity of the artist working with limited resources to make a personal statement. The audiences for such films are generally college and university film societies, museum members, student and professional filmmakers, and the intellectual avant-garde usually found in urban centers. For the most part, the viewer who wishes to see these films must seek them out. Although major metropolitan areas like New York and San Francisco frequently have relatively well-publicized showcase and retrospective screenings at museums and little theaters, screenings elsewhere are generally scarce and are likely to occur not in auditoriums regularly used for films but anywhere a screen and projector can be set up. The films must be rented from filmmakers' cooperatives and 16mm rental companies. Finally, whether the films are shown in large cities or small towns, because of their brevity and because audiences are accustomed to buying tickets for film programs running at least 1 hour, the films are exhibited in packages. Thus, although each was conceived individually, the films are almost always shown (not always to their advantage) in groups.

Because these films are diverse, and because terms like experimental, independent, avant-garde, and underground film are fuzzy, it is best to discuss the films according to their basic aesthetic approaches.

The Representational Film

Many independent films use images that closely resemble the world outside the film frame: human beings, animals, objects, landscapes. Things represented on the screen are the stuff of which the film is made. In some films they are cinematically treated without distortion and tell short narratives in a fairly traditional, realistic mode. Indeed, sometimes only the film's brevity keeps the film outside of the mainstream of commercial theatrical cinema. One example is *An Occurrence at Owl Creek Bridge* (Robert Enrico, 1961), a film that imaginatively tells a story about recognizable characters but, because its running time is less than an hour, is too short for normal theatrical distribution. Most of the Off-Hollywood regional independent features, like their standard Hollywood models, also ascribe to the conventions of realism. Joel Coen's *Blood Simple* (1985) detailed a story of misunderstanding, suspense, and murder in a contemporary small town in Texas. The ordinary setting — scenes take place in bars, tract houses, motels, cars on freeways — is made bizarre only by the quirky, but authentic people who inhabit it. Such films can easily make the crossover from festival circuit to shopping mall multiplex exhibition because they follow the standard narrative conventions. Other independent features, however, are somewhat more innovative, creating a different kind of realism. The story line of *Stranger than Paradise* (Jim Jarmusch, 1985) revealed a Hungarian immigrant's initiation into American life with wry humor in situations that appear very authentic. But the film's narrational method, a parody of long take, static camera set-ups with long fades to black between scenes, is hardly what one expects from contemporary, conventional Hollywood realism. Though the film received high praise from national critics and some distribution in mainstream theaters, its slightly offbeat form made it less accessible and hence less popular with average audiences.

Other Off-Hollywood feature films dare to take more chances and often so blatantly violate the canons of acceptable realistic convention that they can only achieve exhibition in cult theaters — small houses in metropolitan communities that play the more adventurous independent features, foreign films, documentaries, and cult films like *Eraserhead* (David Lynch, 1977) and *Rocky Horror Picture Show* (Jim Jensen, 1975) that appeal to a narrow segment of the population (Figure 8-1). *Liquid Sky* (Slava Tsukerman, 1983), for example, combined elements of the

8-1 Some off-Hollywood films blatantly violate the canons of acceptable realistic convention, which usually limits their exhibition to cult houses — small theaters that specialize in films that appeal to a narrow segment of the film-going public. But like *Rocky Horror Picture Show* (Jim Jensen, 1975), they may play there endlessly and be seen by more people than if they were regularly shown.

science fiction film, perverse sexuality, violence, and documentarylike images of New York City's punk music world in such odd proportions that mainstream audiences could not be enticed to accept it. But cult audiences have found it to their liking. *Imposters* (Mark Rappaport, 1979), like other Rappaport films, a surreal blend of stylized characters, plots (there always seems to be more going on than you can track in a Rappaport film), and settings, never assumes any of the configurations of conventional realism. Though some festival goers have raved about the film, finding it grotesquely funny and ultimately moving, even cult audiences have not jumped on the Rappaport bandwagon: his films, like other experimental and avant-garde work, seems relegated to film society, classroom, and festival exposure.

The most traditional short representational films are narratives comparable to short stories. There are many such films and they vary tremendously both in subject matter and in style, but they are united by their attempt to tell a complete story, marked by a fairly identifiable beginning, middle, and end, and by their introduction of and final resolution of a dramatic conflict. Some are simply shortened versions of the kind and variety of narrative films one might expect to see in regular theatrical release. Thus, highly imaginative and personal films like *The Red Balloon* (Albert Lamorisse, 1956) and *An Occurrence at Owl Creek Bridge* are understood and appreciated by the mass audiences that have had a chance to see them. The story of a young boy and his magical and anthropomorphized friend, a red balloon, and the story of a man mentally living a split-second of wish fulfillment, which takes the form of an exciting escape from his soldier captors, are completely comprehensible and conventional in their structure and drama.

Other short narrative films, however, are less traditional in either their structure or their cinematic treatment of representational subject matter. It is not their length alone that separates them from the mainstream of commercial narrative cinema. Roman Polanski, for example, made several such short story films during his student and apprentice days in Poland and France before he emigrated to Hollywood and turned to theatrical filmmaking. Although his cinematic techniques were fairly straightforward (his characters were filmed with little distortion, against real landscapes), his stories were unconventional in subject, structure, and theme — strange parablelike tales reminiscent of absurdist drama in the mode of Eugene Ionesco and Samuel Beckett. In *Two Men and a Wardrobe* (1958), for instance, the camera rather straightforwardly follows two men who appear from out of the ocean carrying a wooden wardrobe on a strange odyssey through a town whose inhabitants seem oblivious to either the charm or oddness of their strange burden. After several misadventures and many rejections, they finally return to the sea, carefully maneuvering their way across a beach covered with regimented sand castles made by a little boy, and they march into the ocean with their wonderful and evocative burden to disappear in the waves. This kind of film is hardly a traditional narrative; its human characters enact a combination of realistic and fantastic actions in order to make a philosophical point.

A short film narrative also may make relative sense, that is, its characters are recognizably human on an emotional as well as a physical level and its actions are generally determined by comprehensible causes. What may be untraditional is the film's form, the way it is narratively and visually constructed. For example, one of the key films of experimental American cinema is Maya Deren's *Meshes of the Afternoon* (1943), a film about a woman who, returning home in the afternoon, falls asleep and *dreams* about her return home, her feelings of isolation and unhappiness, and in the dream (or is it the reality?) finally commits suicide. Deren does not see her film as divorced from connection with reality: "This first film is concerned with the relationship between the imaginative and the objective reality. . . . It is a whole creation out of the elements of reality — people, places, and objects — but these are so combined as to form a new reality, a new context which defines them according to their function within it."[2] A different kind of short narrative film which makes sense, that is, tells a traditionally comprehensible story, is Chris Marker's *La Jetée* (1962). A short science fiction film, it creates images of a post–World War III France from which the film's hero is sent into the past and future. What is completely untraditional about this science fiction exploration of time travel, however, is that the film, except for one brief moment, is entirely composed of still photographs that freeze motion and destroy the distinction between past and present as we usually perceive it in the ongoing immediacy of the *motion* picture. Thus, the entire film, a complex study of time and its relationship to human memory, goes far beyond the traditional concerns of its basic narrative story.

Even more removed from the narrative tradition to which mass audiences respond are those films that use a combination of cinematic tricks and bizarre occurrences to turn recognizable people and objects and places into a work of cinema that bears only the slightest resemblance to the everyday world as it is normally experienced. One of the classic surrealist films — *Un Chien Andalou* (Salvador Dali and Luis Buñuel, 1929) — is not abstract in its images. Indeed, the shock the film elicits is derived from its very representational quality: an actual eyeball is slit by a razor for no comprehensible reason, live ants crawl out of a wound in a man's hand, a dead donkey is wedged into a piano, which is being towed by two live human beings in an actual room. Thus, the film uses the material of the everyday world as we normally perceive it but puts it to incomprehensible, shocking, and funny use. And in addition to the bizarre relationships established between actual things, places, and people, as well as a structure that lacks an allegiance to cause-and-effect narrative, *Un Chien Andalou* uses cinematic magic in images which give the illusion of being strictly representational: hair in a woman's armpit is suddenly transformed by a dissolve into a man's beard, a face lacks a mouth, a book turns into a gun. The film has less a story than a purpose. Using representational images, it subverts causal logic; indeed, inserted titles mock traditional narrative expectations, beginning as they do with "Once upon a Time" and moving to a sporadic and unrelated "Eight Years Later," "Towards Three in the Morning," "Sixteen Years Before" and, finally, "In the Spring." In the surrealist tradition, the film embraces the illogical logic of dreams. It uses reality as the base from which to liberate the human spirit to a better and higher reality, a surreality. Thus, almost all of the dadaist and surrealist films are representational, aiming to shock audiences into new perceptions of the world, to criticize repression and the lack of imagination, and to give a stale and civilized society a kick in the pants. As Buñuel himself puts it:

> The sources from which the film draws inspiration are those of poetry, freed from the ballast of reason and tradition. . . . This film has no intention of attracting nor pleasing the spectator; indeed, on the contrary, it

attacks him, to the degree that he belongs to a society with which surrealism is at war. . . . The motivation of the images was, or [was] meant
to be, purely irrational! They are as mysterious and inexplicable to the
two collaborators as to the spectator. NOTHING, in the film, SYMBOLIZES
ANYTHING.[3]

With similar aims, some contemporary filmmakers have made films
using the images of real life. The most representational and the most
aggressive in his attack on traditional perceptions of art has been,
perhaps, Andy Warhol, a painter turned filmmaker. Much as he gave
the bourgeois art world a jolt with his painting of Campbell's soup cans,
he has enraged audiences with his minimal films: movies taken of real
events from a fixed vantage point, of an often interminable length dictated by the event being filmed, and minimally edited — if at all. *Eat*
(1963), for example, is 45 minutes of a man eating mushrooms, *Sleep*
(1963–1964) is 6 hours of a sleeping subject who occasionally moves or
turns in the bed, and *Empire* is an 8-hour record of the Empire State
building seen from one location. Crucially dependent upon their representational qualities, Warhol's films are aimed less at documenting
reality than at mounting an assault on the viewer's complacent perception of and relationship to reality and art.

Most recently feminist filmmakers have chosen alternative film practices to communicate the message that mainstream, conventional narrative film form and content is dominated by male attitudes and ideas.
Thus, for them, the very act of making an experimental or avant-garde
film, one that denies ordinary narrative expectations and pleasures, is a
specific political statement. Yvonne Rainer, for example, has developed
a technique in her short films — *Film About a Woman Who . . .* (1974),
Journeys from Berlin/1971 (1980) — of presenting images of actions of
people and a voice-over narration that lacks identity. That is, the narration does not represent a traditional narrator commenting on the images
nor the interior monologue of one of the figures in the frame. This
clearly violates audience expectations of narrative continuity and prevents emotional identification with either the characters or the narrator.
Rainer, describing a film she is working on, says that here the female
voice-over will be identified as the estranged wife of the man Jack Deller
whose activities will be pictorialized on the screen, but to continue her
disruption of normal narrative expectations, the man will be played by
three different actors indiscriminately.[4]

Sometimes the attack on the norm is funny as well as shocking.
Filmmakers such as Bruce Connor and Robert Nelson use humor and
satire to criticize the social world external to the film. Again, there is an
intimate connection between representational images and the world in

which the viewer lives. In his important short film appropriately entitled *A Movie* (1958), Bruce Connor uses found footage from old narrative movies, newsreels, and educational films. This footage is representational in content, and at first we laugh at Connor's odd juxtapositions of tanks, submarines firing torpedoes, cowboys, and starlets in various states of undress, but soon we realize, with the insertion of increasingly violent imagery, that Connor is saying something about our easy acceptance of violence because it's only a movie. In a similar tradition but using his own footage, Robert Nelson attacks our culture's racial stereotypes with a watermelon as his protagonist in *Oh Dem Watermelons* (1965), a film that plays with the cliché connecting blacks and watermelons. After an initial static shot of lengthy duration showing a watermelon, which, isolated on the screen with no function, becomes an increasingly funny object, the first moving footage of the film shows a group of black males pushing and rolling a watermelon down a steep incline in a park. Intercut with this material are images of watermelons being squashed, kicked, exploded, rubbed over a woman's breasts, animated into a rocket, and found to have intestines. Over all this outrageous, funny visual material, a chorus of voices sings the phrase, "Oh, dem watermelons" again and again and in such a rhythm as to evoke primitive tribal drumming. Finally, the initial footage of the watermelon being rolled downhill in front of the boys is run in reverse at high speed, the watermelon now chasing the boys, who are scuttling uphill backward. The entire film is ridiculous, ebullient, and funny, but in its way it is also serious, for anyone seeing it would have great difficulty in ever again taking seriously clichés about blacks and watermelon.

The major difference between the films of Connor and Nelson and those of Polanski and Warhol is that Connor and Nelson have used highly manipulative editing and optical trickery. Thus, Connor's editing imposes relationships between representational images (tanks, cowboys, starlets), which were never filmed for such a purpose, and Nelson's close-ups of watermelons, combinations of animation and representationalism, and use of reverse and fast motion are cinematic techniques that change the meanings implied in the straightforward cinematography of individual shots. Polanski's and Warhol's films, on the other hand, maintain a recognizable space-time continuum; they visually achieve their special quality through the distortion of narrative tradition. Polanski's men carrying a wardrobe move inexplicably through a series of actions, which make little sense and must be interpreted symbolically, and Warhol's films of the Empire State building or a sleeper have neither characters nor dramatic action.

8-2 Norman McLaren used an optical printer to show each increment of movement of two dancers in *Pas de Deux* (1969). Using a dark background and vivid side lighting on the figures, McLaren created abstract patterns within the two-dimensional frame.

These two approaches to the representational image may be combined in a single film that often lies somewhere between a documentary and an abstract film. In Norman McLaren's *Ballet Adagio* (1971), the major impulse seems documentary, for the camera records as an observer the difficult pas de deux performed by two dancers; there is no editing of the dance, and the film is shot in slow motion, which reveals the dancers' craft and artistry. On the one hand, the film seems to duplicate — but much more pleasantly — the minimal cinema of Warhol, with its preservation of space and time. On the other hand, the fact that the film is in slow motion places *Ballet Adagio* closer to films which optically or through editing distort the space-time continuum. Another of McLaren's films, *Pas de Deux* (1967), is more spectacular in its effects and seems more the result of an aesthetic than of a documentary impulse (Figure 8-2). *Pas de Deux* uses multiple exposures to record two dancers, so that their movements are seen broken down into tiny movements of normally imperceptible time. On the one hand, the representational images of the dancers are transformed into black-and-white patterns of light and movement. And yet, on the other hand, the dancers performing the dance are also represented. *Pas de Deux* is generally regarded as an experimental or avant-garde film; it is less obvious, however, how one categorizes *Ballet Adagio*.

Dance films, nature films, and sports films often combine a documentary preservation of space and time with abstracting techniques, creating

8-3 Trick effects can be created when two different images are printed separately on the same frame. In this image from *The Man with a Movie Camera* (Dziga Vertov, 1928), it appears as though the cameraman has mounted his tripod atop a giant camera. This film uses a host of editing techniques to reveal the rhythm of life in post-Revolutionary Russia. Thus it might be called a "city symphony."

a form that, through optical effects and editing, imposes rhythm on representational images. Such films often use slow motion, superimpositions and dissolves and multiple imagery, graceful camera movements, kinetic and rhythmic editing to document and to convey a sense of beauty. Indeed, they often create events that never occurred. A sports film called *Solo* (Mike Hoover, 1971), for example, seems to document a particular climb up a mountain; cinematic manipulation seems confined to the use of sun flare off the lens and certain extremely lyrical camera movements. Actually, however, the climb we see never took place — for it is a combination of many different climbs in twenty-one separate locations. *Solo* is not a document of a mountain climb; it is a celebration of mountain climbing, a personal evocation of feeling rather than an objective recording of an activity.

Along with dance and athletics, objects and particular geographical locations have lent themselves to this rhythmic transformation from representational image to abstract image. At one end of the continuum, a filmmaker using images from life makes documentaries. At the other end, a filmmaker may use the images of the world chiefly as abstract patterns of light and motion. Somewhere in the middle are those filmmakers who create lyrical celebrations of events, of experiences, of places with representational images (Figure 8-3). Sometimes it is difficult to categorize those films in the middle range. *Rien que les Heures* (Alberto

Cavalcanti, 1926) and *The Man with a Movie Camera* (Dziga Vertov, 1928), for example, are more socially oriented and thus closer to the documentary pole of the continuum than either *Berlin: The Symphony of a Great City* (Walter Ruttmann, 1927) or *Rain* (Joris Ivens, 1929), whose documentary images are primarily used for their form and as a base for a musical editing structure. Ruttmann, for example, inspired by Vertov's writings on editing, got "the idea of making something out of life, of creating a symphonic film out of the millions of energies that comprise the life of a big city."[5]

Despite the difficulties of attempting to categorize noncommercial representational films, the process of categorizing can be illuminating. We can learn about the nature of film by asking questions, even if the questions have no definite answers. In what ways is, for example, *Night and Fog* (Alain Resnais, 1955) a documentary about the Nazi holocaust and in what ways is it a personal and emotional film essay? Is Fernand Léger's *Ballet Mécanique* (1924) a celebration of everyday objects rhythmically edited — or is it really abstract and nonrepresentational in approach, because it takes those objects out of their connection with a 3-D reality and makes them seem two-dimensional?

What unifies the films discussed in this section is a cinematic attitude on the part of their creators. Despite the variety of their techniques, whether subtle or brazen, a certain respect for three dimensionality is observed, a respect that acknowledges the film frame as a window rather than as a canvas. The images *represent* things in an acknowledgment of a world that exists outside the film frame, a world that has dimension and substance (Figure 8-4). Thus, the representational film, no matter how experimental, is not totally self-contained or independent, for its reference point is the ordinary world — outside the frame — in which all of us live.

The Abstract Film

Imagine an eye unruled by man-made laws of perspective, an eye unprejudiced by compositional logic, an eye which does not respond to the name of everything but which must know each object encountered in life through an adventure of perception. How many colors are there in a field of grass to the crawling baby unaware of "Green"?
Stan Brakhage[6]

The second category of experimental, avant-garde, or independent films refuses an alliance with the real world outside the film frame. The film frame is not used to refer to and represent the 3-D world in which we move. It is regarded as a sort of canvas that can be adorned with various

8-4 Robert Wood deftly plays with the sound track in
Etude (1972). A young man in an overcoat carrying a
small case trudges through the woods until he comes to
a roaring creek. There he sets up a music stand and begins to conduct an imaginary orchestra. The sound
track, which up to this point had included only natural
sounds, abruptly shifts to the music being conducted.
The audience hears what is in the mind of the young
man. From then on both the natural sound track and
the music sound track are intercut with the images of
the conductor and the falling water to create a beautiful
interplay between image and sound.

combinations of shapes and forms and colors and movements to create
independent, autonomous works of art. Rather than functioning as a
transparent window *through* which the viewer looks into a third dimension, the frame and the film become opaque. No longer do we look
through the frame to the world outside — we look *at* it. In such an
opaque film, the film artist assumes that images constitute meanings in
themselves, that the form of the film is similarly meaningful, and that
both form and content are not used to *refer* to or *represent* something else.
Even when real objects are photographed, they lose their reference to an
external world, becoming pure forms and colors and movement. Thus,
real objects and places and beings are removed — abstracted — from a
connection with reality, and they become as autonomous in their function as a design composed by a computer.

These films are often meant to stir the viewer intellectually, and to
stimulate the eye, but not usually to rouse emotions. Indeed, in many
abstract films the viewer becomes a participant in an intellectual and

perceptual drama whose theme is aesthetics. We may, for example, begin by looking through the frame and end by looking at the frame — the entire film thus serving as a lesson in perception. Such is true of Michael Snow's *Wavelength* (1966–1967), a 45-minute film structured around a single zoom shot taken from a stationary camera position in a large loft-type room. The viewer is first exposed to the room in a long shot: it is bare except for some shelves along the sides and a desk, chair, and telephone at the far end; there are three long windows, also at the far end of the room, through which light from the street enters. For the entire duration of the film, the camera zooms slowly and constantly toward the far wall, taking 45 minutes to transform the long shot of the room into an extreme close-up of a portion of a photograph of waves tacked up on the wall. The film thus explores, by demonstration, the structure of the zoom — and it also explores and plays with the viewer's perception and expectation. At the beginning of *Wavelength* the audience sees the representational image of a room — but as time passes, no one enters and nothing seems to happen. When some people at last do come into the room (they move a bookcase and then leave), the audience is teased into having certain dramatic expectations. Such teasing occurs again late in the film when a man walks into the frame and then collapses out of it, presumably dead, and when a woman, discovering the body (an act we do not see), makes a telephone call. A tension is thus created between the viewer's perception of the film as transparent, as a window through which one looks at something real, and the perception of the film as opaque, as a canvas that explores its own created space. Although nothing happens if one regards the frame as a window, a great deal happens if it is seen as a canvas: throughout the film, the light changes as the daylight comes in the window, and as the filmmaker adds artificial light and uses filters; exposure settings are changed as well, sometimes allowing the viewer to see clearly out the windows and at other times confining his or her vision indoors. *Wavelength* is frustrating, boring, tantalizing, and intellectually exciting in its exploration of cinema, aesthetics, and perception. It is also — like many other abstract films — a teaching film, for it teaches the viewer an alternative way to experience a film: to look at the frame instead of through it.

Another example of this kind of abstract film that explores its own devices, its own construction, and engages the viewer in active intellectual participation, is *Zorn's Lemma* (Hollis Frampton, 1970). The 1-hour-long movie is divided into three sections: the first shows the viewer a black screen while a voice reads couplets from an eighteenth-century alphabet primer, the second introduces a series of 1-second shots of alphabetically organized street signs, which are replaced letter by letter with more random imagery as the pattern is continually repeated, and the third is one long, static shot of a snow-covered landscape against which a medieval text on light and form is read by various voices in a repetitive rhythm. Basically, *Zorn's Lemma* is a film about learning, about reading (letters and images). Its first section presents us with the abstraction of words and letters heard from a reading primer. The second and most engaging section is a reading lesson, for the viewer attempts to learn the visual alphabet being set forth in place of the more familiar but equally arbitrary system of characters of the written alphabet. The viewer is quick to recognize that Frampton's choice of street signs is presented sequentially and each begins with a corresponding letter from the familiar alphabet (although there are some letters missing, among them most appropriately "I" and "U"). Thus, when random images of animals, objects, and places begin replacing the lettered signs, the viewer begins to equate them with alphabetical characters and tries to remember their signification as they are repeated. The entire section demonstrates the arbitrariness of language and the conventional demands of learning to read; it is also, perhaps, the most entertaining part of the film, for it gives the viewer something to do, an active role. The third section of the film seems frustrating and boring by comparison — and perhaps its very difficulty is the point. The viewer is confronted by a static long shot; if it is to be read, then rote learning and alphabetical or visual signification will have to be abandoned and a new means of reading applied. Thus, *Zorn's Lemma* explores an intellectual and perceptual problem by demonstration and it is, in its own way, as rigorous and admittedly difficult as a written essay on a similar subject.

Not all abstract films are difficult in the manner of *Wavelength* and *Zorn's Lemma*. Films like these two, concerned with structure and perception, tend to be the most frustrating and hard to understand for an untutored audience. Many abstract films, however, like such works of art as paintings, sculpture, and music, are meant to give aesthetic pleasure or to produce a physical sensation. Such films are conceived less to be understood than to be felt, sensed, and experienced. These abstract films do not play with audience expectations or create shifts of perception of the film frame from transparent to opaque. They simply begin as opaque films — exploiting all the tools of cinematic technology to create art objects made from two-dimensional images, which move on the canvas of the screen. Design and color become dominant elements in such works, much as in painting, but of course movement is an additional and unique element.

This sort of abstract film was one of the first forms of avant-garde and independent cinema. Indeed, some of its practitioners were artists in another medium. In the early 1920s, for example, Hans Richter and Viking Eggeling were painters who turned to film because the new medium offered opportunities to explore plastic expression and to add time to the kind of abstract works they were doing on canvas. Thus, in their *Rhythmus 21* (1921) they explore the form of the square, and in *Symphonie Diagonale* (1921–1924) they experiment with diagonal lines over a period of time. Similarly, Oskar Fischinger explored geometric forms and created abstract patterns based on musical structures and forms; he used shapes in time the way a composer uses notes in time. Usually quite short, this kind of absolute and abstract film has been made from film's early history to the present, and it has been particularly popular when combined with music. Fischinger, for example, was delighted when sound film made music an integral part of cinema, and further removed his absolute film studies from a connection with everyday reality: "Under the guidance of music . . . there came the speedy discovery of new laws — the application of acoustical laws to optical expression was possible. As in the dance, new motions and rhythms sprang out of the music — and the rhythms became more and more important."[7] The influence of Oskar Fischinger's work can be seen in the Bach "Toccata and Fugue in D minor" section of Walt Disney's *Fantasia* (1940), and many of Norman McLaren's films — paint directly applied to the film stock in rhythm to appealing music — have delighted audiences who might not enjoy other experimental films. McLaren's *Begone Dull Care* (1949), for example, uses bright colors and has a fluidity that gaily expresses a piece of jazz played by the Oscar Peterson Trio.

During the 1960s and 1970s other kinds of abstract cinema came into being, aided by advances in contemporary technology. In some films the images are quite beautiful and the film is a pleasurable experience; in other films the images are abrasive and assaultive, experimenting with the viewer's physiological responses to light and color and duration and sound. Jordon Belson's *Allures* (1961) uses subtle superimpositions to transform a pulsating globe of color and light into beautiful variations, in what he has called *cosmic* cinema. John Whitney's work depends upon computer graphics; the designs of a film like *Permutations* (1968) demonstrate Whitney's contention that the computer's ability to detail and repeat precisely with the minutest incremental variations a particular image, allows individual film images to function like musical notes. And many of the abstract films of Standish Lawder, dependent on stroboscopic lighting and a knowledge of human physiology (particularly brain-wave patterns), are literally physical assaults on the viewer; *Corridor* (1968–1970) and *Raindance* (1974) are difficult to watch.

Finally we come to the nonrepresentational and abstract film, which also, paradoxically, attempts to make a personal statement. What occurs on the screen insists on the opaqueness of the image. Yet what emerges is a personal vision rather than an abstract design. The greatest practitioner of what we can call humanist abstract film is surely Stan Brakhage, an independent filmmaker who has been making films that combine representational and nonrepresentational techniques for over 25 years. His first masterwork, *Dog Star Man* (1961) attempts to convey the idea of the creation of the universe, through personal and subjective images. As in many of his subsequent films, Brakhage uses color filters, hand-draws images, paints on top of photographs, makes holes in the film, and uses distorting lenses, hand-held camera, and multiple exposures. He is fascinated by the act of seeing, and in his films he attempts to capture the subjective, physiological, and social nature of vision. He wants the viewer's vision unfettered by the conventions of seeing; he wants to make us see freshly, rather than as we are *supposed* to as dictated by conventions of painting and optics. In a collection of his writings called *Metaphors on Vision*, Brakhage explains the philosophy behind his work: "I suggest that there is a pursuit of knowledge foreign to language and founded upon visual communication, demanding a development of the optical mind, and dependent upon perception in the original and deepest sense of the word."[8] Films such as *The Act of Seeing with One's Own Eyes* (1971) and *Text of Light* (1974) continue Brakhage's personal exploration of vision and perception.

Though its subject matter, structures, and techniques are so various as to make even broad classifications extremely difficult, all abstract, nonrepresentational cinema explores the film medium as plastic and expressive. Film and the cinematic apparatus function like the canvas, paints, and brushes of the modern painter, like the score and instruments of the modern composer. The abstract film is a self-contained experience and expression. It is referential chiefly to itself. Its form is its content; its content comes into being in its form.

The Animated Film

Animation is an animated film.

A protest against the stationary condition.

Animation transporting movement of nature directly cannot be creative animation.

Animation is a technical process in which the final result must always be creative.

To animate: to give life and soul to a design, not through the copying but through the transformation of reality.

> Life is warmness.
> Warmness is movement.
> Movement is life.
> Animation is giving life; it means giving warmth.
> . . .
> Take one kilo of ideas (not too confused if possible), five dkg of talent,
> ten dkg of hard work and a few thousand designs. Shake it all together
> and if you are lucky you will not get the right answer to the question.
> Collective statement of cartoonists of the Zagreb studio[9]

Although most animated films are generally associated with mainstream commercial cinema and thus seem far removed from difficult and shocking experimental, underground, and avant-garde films, it is appropriate to discuss animation in the same chapter as these other, less accessible, works of film art. On the one hand, many avant-garde, abstract films are animated — from the work of early abstract filmmakers like Eggeling and Fischinger to contemporary film artists like Norman McLaren and Robert Breer. On the other hand, even commercial narrative animation is removed from reality, since the figures are drawn and not photographed. Couple this with animation's penchant for the fantastic transformation of space and matter, and you have a form that is closer to the abstract film than to the documentary.

All animated films — whether using pictures, models, or live actors — are based on **single-frame cinematography.** During the shooting process, instead of the continuous and automatic movement of the film stock through the camera at the rate of twenty-four frames per second, the film moves through the camera at a rate controlled by the filmmaker. Because the filmmaker can photograph three frames of a subject or twelve frames or twenty-four, how long a particular image will be seen on the screen can be varied and controlled. Controlling the time an image occupies the screen also controls the speed of its movement in space. A cartoon rabbit can be made to appear as if its movement were human and natural; a human being can be made to appear as jerky in movement as a doll or puppet. How smooth or how disconnected the animation will seem is determined by how many single frames are shot of the movement in question or how many are eliminated.

Imagine, for example, that it takes 1 second for a person in real life to raise his hand above his head. In a nonanimated film, that action would be recorded through the course of twenty-four frames as they move automatically through the camera; one increment of movement of the arm would be contained in each of those twenty-four frames — 1 second of film time. If a filmmaker wanted a drawn animal or a model puppet to seem lifelike in its movement, ideally twenty-four different

8-5 Directing animator Ollie Johnston makes faces in a mirror to help him capture subtleties of expressions for drawing characters for Walt Disney's *Robin Hood* (1973).

drawings would be made corresponding in their increments to human movements or move the puppet twenty-four different times — each change recorded on one frame of film photographed singly (Figure 8-5). When that film was ready for projection, it would be moved automatically through the projector, like any other film, at the rate of twenty-four frames per second and the action on the screen would appear lifelike, smooth, and unbroken. Because of the monumental labor involved, no human animator attempts this ideal — although computer-created animation can achieve it. It has been generally recognized that relatively smooth and lifelike animation can be accomplished if that 1 second of real action is translated into eighteen increments of movement, single-framed, and then projected at twenty-four frames per second. Less smooth but still acceptable as lifelike are nine increments of movement, each photographed two times and comprising two frames (double-framing). And often student filmmakers whose time and resources are limited may settle for six increments of movement, each photographed three times and comprising three frames (triple-framing). How many separate drawings or movements a filmmaker uses finally depends, however, on how lifelike he wishes the movement to be, how representational of real movement. While some animators wish their drawn characters or puppets to move like humans, other animators may wish their subjects to move like drawn characters or puppets. Just as with any other kind of filmmaking, the art of animation may be shaped by an urge to realism or, on the other hand, by an urge to fantasy. Indeed, the history of animation leads in two directions — the one taken by Walt Disney in the 1940s and after, in which the drawn figures become more and more lifelike, and the other taken by abstract artists like Robert Breer, a contemporary animator whose work makes no attempt at realism. Yet, despite these two divergent impulses, all animated film is to a fairly great degree unrealistic, for it uses the screen as a world disconnected from the one in which the viewer moves continuously and smoothly through time and three dimensions.

What unites all animated film is its basis in single-frame rather than continuous cinematography. What separates different kinds of animated film is the material to be animated and how that material must be manipulated before the camera to achieve movement. There are basically two sorts of material: two-dimensional and three-dimensional. Two-dimensional animation can consist of drawings or paper shapes and cutouts or pictures, photographs, and paintings. Three-dimensional animation uses as its material such diverse subjects as clay, puppets, miscellaneous objects like a pack of cards or pieces of fruit, and human beings. Each kind of animation, although based on single-frame cinematography, has its own requirements determined by the material.

TWO-DIMENSIONAL ANIMATION

> Animation is a chorus of drawings working in tandem, each contributing a part to the whole of a time/space idea. If a single drawing, as a drawing, dominates the action it is probably bad animation, even though it may be good drawing.
> Chuck Jones [10]

The most popular and oldest form of two-dimensional animation is made with drawings. Drawn animation requires that many separate drawings be made of an object or character's consecutive movements. In simple animation (a single stick figure, for example, against a blank background), the drawings may be done on paper and the changes made (for example, an arm is drawn a trifle higher, and in the next drawing, still higher) after the basic shape has been generally traced. Then two or three frames of each drawing are photographed; when the film is run continuously, movement is achieved. More complexly drawn animation requires another method, for if there are several drawn figures who will move against a drawn background, which will also change to correspond to their movements, the task of making entirely separate sketches would be prohibitive in time and therefore in cost. Instead, an efficient method of complex drawn animation has been devised called **cel animation.** An individual scene in the script is broken down into its background, middle ground, and foreground components, each of which is painted on an individual sheet of transparent celluloid. Together — one on top of the other — they form a sandwich. Without having to draw the same background again and again, animators may simply move their middle-ground cel containing cartoon figures across it, single-framing as they move. Those figures may be complete but for a few crucial omissions of feet and hands. Those parts of their anatomy that indicate movements of walking or pointing and so forth will be drawn on the foreground cel so that they contain all the tiny variables of movement to be seen in the finished film. Thus, for some portions of the film, animators may be able to use the same drawing of a background and the same drawings of their characters and will only have to alter the top layer of the sandwich. Although cel animation is efficient compared to the process of making individual drawings, it is still complex, time-consuming, and expensive, and thus the range and aesthetic complexity of cel-animated film varies widely, dependent upon how many layers exist in a given sandwich and how many drawn items move simultaneously. Cartoons made in the 1930s and 1940s, the classic Walt Disney features and short cartoons of artists like Max and Dave Fleischer, Walter Lantz, Paul Terry, Bob Clampett, Tex Avery, and Chuck Jones, for example, used many more individual drawings with a great deal more movement than the current animated cartoons made expressly for Saturday morning television viewing.

From film's beginnings, the animated drawing has been associated with the cartoon; it is the moving version of a comic-strip narrative. Drawn human or anthropomorphic animal characters enact a short and simple tale, in the process usually violating physical laws that govern the external and undrawn world. A mouse, for example, may flatten a cat with a hammer and a moment later the cat resumes its usual shape. These cartoon stories are almost always fantasy creations, their humor derived from the visual articulation of the impossible: animals talking and moving like human beings (Figure 8-6), the subversion of natural laws of gravity and cause and effect, the fluid transformation of the physical from one object to another, and the removal of pain and mortality from physical violence. Animal protagonists from the earliest Gertie the Dinosaur, who made her screen debut in Winsor McCay's 1910 cartoon, through Felix the Cat, Mickey Mouse, Bugs Bunny, and Roadrunner live in a world in which violence and mutilation are carried to extremes but never lead to permanent disfigurement and death. In Chuck Jones's *Rabbit Punch* (1947), for example, Bugs Bunny is a boxer. Confronted in the ring by a huge opponent who literally is transformed into a speeding locomotive as he charges Bugs, the resourceful and self-conscious rabbit disintegrates the film space and destroys the cartoon by "cutting" the film and facing the audience in triumph. Like live slapstick comedy, though carried much further, such cartoons let us laugh with delight at an impossible world liberated from mortality. We almost never feel sorry for the victims in a cartoon. Thus, it is extremely

8-6 Through the years Mickey Mouse became less animal-like and more human, a general trend to greater realism taken by the Disney Studio until they moved into making live-action films. Above left, *Steamboat Willie* (1928); above right, *The Dognapper* (1934); below left, *Fantasia* (1940); below right, *Mickey's Birthday Party* (1942).

8-7 It usually is a given of the cartoon in which animals act like human beings that sex and death do not exist. But Ralph Bakshi's *Fritz the Cat* (1972) is an example of a cartoon feature made for adults in which both sex and death are an accepted part of his creatures' world, just as they are of ours.

surprising and unsettling when an animator introduces death into his film, whether it be in a Disney film like *Bambi* (1942) or a modern animated feature like Ralph Bakshi and Robert Crumb's *Fritz the Cat* (1972) (Figure 8-7). Although the social milieu in which the animated animal protagonist moves during much of this film is realistic, treating as it does sex, drugs, greed, and opportunism, its violence is still cartoon violence and characters are quickly resurrected to act again. At one point in the film, however, one of Fritz's friends and advisers — a crow — is killed. In intense and surreal images, drops of its blood turn into billiard balls and are sunk into pockets on a pool table, which fills the screen. Once they are gone, we find that the crow has died and there is no resurrection to meet our cartoon expectations. The result is disturbingly

8-8 Greater and greater realism in animation both in story and in drawing has not meant the end of fantasy. *The Yellow Submarine* (George Dunning, 1968) is full of outlandish sequences where queer creatures spring to life from the pens and the creative imaginations of the animators.

effective, for the viewer is thrown back into a real world, one in which violence and murder lead to expected ends.

Putting aside such an unusual introduction of the laws of the real world, cartoon animation follows not the causal logic of human experience but, instead, creates its own logic (Figure 8-8). There is, however, another major impulse in the animated cartoon, particularly evident in its feature form, which sustains its length by depending on a more highly structured narrative. Begun by Disney and his studio in *Snow White and the Seven Dwarfs* (1937), a range of animated narratives has pretended to a certain kind of representationalism and verisimilitude in the midst of fantasy stories and drawn worlds. Along with animals who have been anthropomorphized, the films begin to feature human characters who are meant to seem real and who, thus, seem to function in a less imaginative sphere and according to more comprehensible physical logic than the liberated animal characters of the cartoon short. Despite this urge toward greater realism, however, the animated cartoon — no matter how narratively logical or how anthropomorphic — is drawn, and so it is patently unreal. Indeed, part of the wonder and pleasure the viewer feels toward such attempts at verisimilitude is the

8-9 Frank Mouris created a visual and aural biography in his *Frank Film* (1973). With the use of multiple sound tracks and a dazzling collage of images (11,592 in nine minutes), the film depicts the complex continuity of a mind recalling the past and free-associating in the present.

skill of its execution, the wonder derived from how lifelike an obviously drawn figure seems.

Drawn animation goes beyond the short or feature cartoon geared to youngsters and theatrical entertainment. A great deal of drawn animation is used for social, political, educative, and aesthetic ends. Often, political satire and social commentary can find an outlet in the animated film where it would be suppressed in a potentially too real live-action film. The rise of a full-scale animation movement in eastern Europe in the mid-1950s probably stemmed in part from this fact. Zagreb, Yugoslavia — the home of the Zagreb Studio, founded in 1956 — has become the center of that movement and the site of an international animation festival held every year to screen and honor short animated films from countries all over the world. Like many of their independent live-action counterparts, these animated films are politically and socially conscious. In their brief, humorous and witty, and occasionally grim stories, they frequently satirize the conventions and traditions of modern society, attack not only capitalism but complacent communism, promote ecology, and warn against the perils of automation, dehumanization, pollution, and overpopulation.

Serious animation can be used, too, by the avant-garde or experimental filmmaker to explore film structure, perception, the nature of film and its ability to create illusions. Robert Breer, for example, a leading American avant-garde animator, combines representational photographs with exact drawn duplications, which then change to something else, which move and then stop. In a relatively accessible cartoonlike *A Man and His Dog Out for Air* (1957), Breer has drawn lines that romp across the screen to the accompaniment of natural sounds, and only at the end of the film's 3 minutes do the lines coalesce to form the subjects of the film's title. Breer uses animation quite differently, however, in *Fuji* (1974), which bases an animated exploration of color and line on Mt. Fuji's initial representational presence in a piece of raw footage Breer took from a train window when he was traveling through Japan. The former painter was instrumental in pioneering rapid and assaultive **collage films** in which single-frame animation techniques are used to capture a different image in each frame; the effect when such images are projected is dizzying, and certainly visually stimulating. Breer is chiefly interested in the artistic possibilities of animation: "Animation implies making something inanimate appear to be animate; though single-frame filmmaking can include that, it isn't necessarily confined to that. A lot of my films don't involve the illusion of motion at all but are constructed out of time intervals and space changes."[11]

In addition to drawn animation, there are other kinds of two-dimensional animation. Many animated films regard the screen as a flat canvas upon which paper shapes and cutouts may be made to move. The results may be simple, or they may be extraordinarily complex. In the 1950s Stan Vanderbeek began making animated collage films using cutouts from magazines, line drawings, and photographs; other filmmakers, influenced by his work, expanded the possibilities of the form. In an amazing work called *Frank Film* (Carolyn and Frank Mouris, 1973), the filmmaker animates, through single-frame cinematography, cutouts from advertisements of consumer goods, pinups, magazine pictures of all sorts, and presents them to the viewer as an autobiographical accumulation of images stored in his consciousness (Figure 8-9). Frank Mouris sees the materials he uses in his films as "found objects, found images, which I rework into my own kind of universe which they make completely from scratch through drawings."[12] Combined with multiple and overlapping sound track, the images overwhelm the viewer with their rapid movement and patterning so that the sensory overload of stimuli the filmmaker speaks of is actually experienced by the person watching the film. A similar technique has been applied to photographs and paintings in the work of Charles Braverman, who has used single-frame cinematography to make visual collages like his *An American Time Capsule*. Originally released in 1968 as a 3-minute film, it has since been brought more up to date — to 1975 — and another minute added. In the film, Braverman creates an accelerating collage of secondary source materials — the face of an American president on a piece of currency; a painting by Frederic Remington, the great painter of cowboys; magazine and newspaper photos — to relate the history of the United States visually. The technique of animation not only allows him to show a great deal of material in a very short time, but also allows him a very tight control over the rhythms of the editing so that he can simulate in film form the increasing tempo of American life as it becomes more compressed and complex. Finally, a trend in two-dimensional animation is now being created by advances in computer technology. The computer is able to draw figures as well as to help animators work out their increments of motion more exactly and efficiently. In addition a number of computer animations have been filmed that resemble the most absolute and abstract avant-garde and independent films. *Tron* (Steven Lisberger, 1982) a commercially made science fiction film about existence inside a computer, used many of the new techniques in computer animation to make some of its more spectacular sequences. The Xerox camera (a variation of the one used in copying machines) was used to animate the feature length *The Fox and The Hound* (Art Stevens, Ted Berman, and Richard Rich, 1981).

THREE-DIMENSIONAL ANIMATION

When George Méliès first realized that stopping the camera, changing the position of a single object within the frame while leaving the other elements in the frame constant, and then starting the camera up again would result in the magical illusion of that object popping out of one spot and reappearing in another, he laid the groundwork for live-action and three-dimensional animation. Any inanimate object could be given the appearance of motion simply by manipulating it and photographing it exactly in the manner of two-dimensional animation. Projected, the object would appear to move. In 1910, the great French animator Emile Cohl delighted audiences with *La Chambre Ensorcelée (The Automatic Moving Company)*, in which the entire furnishings of a house pack themselves away without any assistance. Spoons disappear into drawers, knives march themselves into racks, beds make themselves up. This same technique is used today — sometimes to amuse, sometimes to perturb. A noted Polish animator, Walerian Borowczyk, animates objects to create surreal visions that sometimes evoke the illogic and terror of nightmares. In *Dom (House)*, made in 1958, for example, a wig inexorably and sinisterly climbs a table and consumes everything on it.

While there is a particular fascination attached to seeing common objects take on an animated existence of their own, three-dimensional animation is also a form for animating what are essentially sculptures. Modeling clay is therefore a particularly attractive medium in which the animator can work and many films use it in humorous and interesting ways. There has been, for example, a children's series of clay-model animation featuring a clay figure named Gumby and his clay horse Pokey. Little pieces of modeling clay join themselves together and turn into fantastic monsters who eventually metamorphose into Man in *Clay: Origin of the Species* (Eliot Noyes, Jr., 1964). Will Vinton and Bob Gardiner won an Academy Award for their clay animation film *Closed Mondays* (1974), and have gone on to do more elaborate films with what they call *claymation*. Dolls also provide a popular material with which the 3-D animator can work. There was, for example, a whole commercial series of doll animation films, called "Puppetoons," made by George Pal beginning in the 1940s. And the foremost pioneer of doll animation, Jiří Trnka, began making his unique films in Czechoslovakia in 1946. He used his figures to explore space, to mimic or create elaborate operatic effects, ballets. And, as well, Trnka used his animated dolls for satire and allegory; in *The Hand* (1956) his combination of cutouts and little animated dolls produces an absorbing allegory of repression in a totalitarian state. Yet another 3-D form of animation is relatively rare: pin animation. Here hundreds of pins are pushed up and down on a mounting so as to create shadowed areas. The effect is very beautiful, and subtle — a play of light and shadow the defining features of the finished work.

Three-dimensional animation can also take the form of live-action animated film. Again, based on the principles of pixilation, which Méliès discovered (stopping and starting the camera after every few frames), animating a live-action subject differs in its aesthetic implications from other forms of animation. Consider that all animated film, whether two- or 3-D, confers movement on a normally inanimate subject — a drawing, a doll, a wig. It brings to life — to motion in space and/or time — that which has no life. When the animated subject is already a living creature, however, the process seems to work in reverse. Instead of adding motion, the live-action animator takes it away — literally cutting time (and increments of motion) away through the process of single-framing, so the resultant motion of the live subject will seem jerky and artificial. Basically, this technique makes live people and animals abstract, unreal, and they are able to function not as credible characters but as cartoon figures. Thus, Norman McLaren in *Neighbors* (1959) is able to make an extremely violent parable about two men destroying each other over possession of a flower. The actors are pixilated and what would have been impossible to watch in live action is reduced to cartoon action through the process, McLaren is able to animate his pacifist message quite effectively.

Animated films range from serious to comic, from simple to complex, from witty and irreverent to subtly beautiful or surrealistically disturbing. They can range from the wonderful and anarchic characters dreamed up by the great Hollywood animators for a mass market to those personal visions seen and appreciated by a small, elite audience. No matter which, the animated film will always be with us — for it is a form through which artists with an interest in color, mass, and movement, with the belief that a film is a canvas, can express themselves.

And perhaps this urge to personal expression allows us to sum up the entire group of alternative films surveyed in this section: experimental, independent, and animated films. For the most part these films are made by individual artists, even when made in collaboration with others. Certainly, we have seen that Hollywood studio cartoons bear the stamp of their creators. And non-studio-produced films are even more usually singular works by singular artists. Creating this kind of cinema, the filmmakers closely resemble the traditional artists practicing in a more private medium: painters, sculptors, composers. They can say exactly what they want to say in moving pictures whether they photograph people or objects, animate drawings or clay, use a script to tell a story, crack a joke, or share a cosmic vision. It is a matter of avoiding commercial pressures to maintain artistic freedom.

NOTES

[1] "What Are You Ready For?" *December 7*, no. 1 (1965): 150.

[2] *Art in Cinema* (San Francisco: San Francisco Museum of Art, 1947), p. 58.

[3] *Art in Cinema*, pp. 29–30.

[4] Yvonne Rainer, "More Kicking and Screaming from the Narrative Front/Backwater," *Wide Angle*, Vol. 7, No. 1 and 2. (1985), pp. 8–12.

[5] Georges Sadoul, *Dictionary of Films* (Berkeley: University of California Press, 1972), p. 31.

[6] Interviewed by P. Adams Sitney, "Metaphors on Vision," *Film Culture* 30 (Fall 1963), unpaged.

[7] *Art in Cinema*, p. 38.

[8] Interviewed by P. Adams Sitney, "Metaphors on Vision."

[9] Ronald Holloway, *Z is for Zagreb* (London: Tantivy Press, 1972), p. 9.

[10] "Animation Is a Gift Word," *AFI Report* (Summer 1974), p. 29.

[11] "Animation Is a Gift Word," p. 35.

[12] "Animation Is a Gift Word," p. 36.

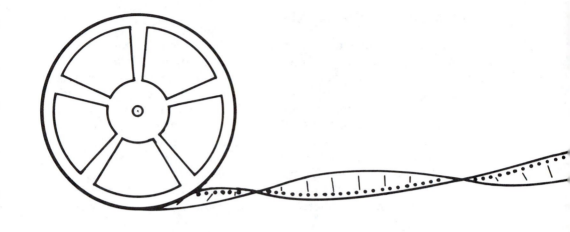

PART V
A GUIDE
TO FILM
ANALYSIS
AND
CRITICISM

⊛ Reading and Writing About Film

We all like to talk about the movies we have seen. Sometimes the talk is simple, an evaluation or a recommendation: "I hated that movie. Don't waste your money." Sometimes, however, the talk is more complex, an attempt to increase understanding of a cinematic experience and to share perceptions: "What'd you make of Harry Dean Stanton in *Repo Man?*" "He was just weird, man, plain weird." "But he kept talking about integrity in a corrupt world, just like one of those detectives in a film noir, didn't he?" "Yeah, sure, but that doesn't mean anything. It was just a weird movie, you know, like *Harold and Maude.*" Whether simple or complex, these conversations take place almost anywhere — in dorm rooms, at cocktail parties, over a lunch, while riding a bus to school or work, or, as Woody Allen humorously demonstrated in *Annie Hall* (1977), in lines outside movie theaters. These conversations about films, though often chiefly social, usually become more organized and specific in a classroom. And, of course, at their most structured, these expressions of ideas about film become written discourse taking the various forms of student papers, published critical articles, film reviews, and books on film theory and criticism.

Basically, writing about film can be divided into three kinds: film reviewing, film criticism, and film theory. Each kind presupposes a specific audience and a specific aim. A film review, for example, is written typically for someone who has not yet seen the film in question, and it aims at offering a recommendation to see or avoid the film. A piece of film criticism on the same movie, however, usually assumes that the reader will be familiar with the film, and it aims at analyzing the film. In the review, description of the film will often be quite general; it will say what the film is about, who is in it, what kind of movie it is. The critical article, however, examining a film familiar to both writer and reader, will be more specific and will tend to concentrate on a particular aesthetic, historical, cultural, or ideological issue. Indeed, in the third kind of film writing — film theory — aesthetic, cultural, historical, and ideological issues themselves become the focus, and specific films may not even be mentioned. The aim or function of film theory is to explore the nature of the film medium rather than the particulars of specific films, and such writing assumes a cinematically literate and sophisticated reader.

Though conversation about films can be stimulating and rewarding, reading and writing about films can provide a more coherent and contemplative pleasure. A thoughtful, well-argued book or article can open up the reader's experience and understanding of particular films, film history, film's relationship with other arts, film form and aesthetics, film and its relationship to social, economic, and political realities. Such writing can bring little-known films to the public's attention, resurrect interest in a director or performer or a period of film history, generate new ideas about form.

Students sometimes express irritation at having to read about films they have or have not seen. They may feel that simply watching and talking about the work is enough. Yet for a more than casual understanding of the art and history and mechanisms of cinema, it is necessary to read and write about film. Perhaps especially because the film experience is so transient — we watch the images pass quickly before our eyes and usually we cannot say, "Stop, I want to see that part over again" — the act of reading and writing, which is slow, deliberate, and contemplative, adds a proper balance to the study of film. This section of the book will provide an introduction to the many ways film has been and can be written about. The Historical Overview will treat professional writing about film. Chapter 9 will focus on student writing about film and offer suggestions about the planning and writing of a college paper about film.

Historical Overview:
The Development of Film
Reviewing, Criticism, and Theory

THE FIRST REVIEWS

The first English-language article printed about a projected film screening appeared in the New York *Times* on April 24, 1896, the day after the first Projecting Kinetoscope exhibition at Koster & Bial's Music Hall. For the next decade, professional film writing did little more than announce a new program of film releases and synopsize their plots. There was no attempt at evaluation or critical analysis, no recognition of film as a new art form. In fact, the first extensive writing about film that appeared on a regular basis recognized it as a money-making business. As the motion picture industry grew, trade journals and papers devoted exclusively to film were founded: *Views and Film Index* in 1906 and the *Moving Picture World* and *Moving Picture News* in 1907.

Individual films (nearly all one-reelers, lasting about 10 minutes) at first received hardly more than a plot summary in the trade journals. Yet, surprisingly, it was in the trade journals rather than in daily newspapers that longer, more thoughtful articles began to appear. On September 19, 1908, for example, the *Moving Picture World* carried an article that compared acting styles for the moving picture drama with the acting styles used in theatrical live drama. And the piece began this comparison of the two acting styles with a recognition of the film as art: "That the moving picture drama is an art, is a proposition as yet not well recognized by the public at large."

Thus, writers within and without the trade began to see and note the artistic potential of film, addressing themselves to discussions of aesthetic, moral, and social values in the new medium. Between 1908 and 1912 Frank E. Woods, for example, wrote a weekly film column under the by-line of "The Spectator" for the New York *Dramatic Mirror*. His thoughtful commentary, going beyond mere plot description to offer his readers evaluative responses, earned him a place in film history as the first major American film critic. He influenced to some degree the viewing habits of his readers, foreshadowing the kind of popular influence enjoyed today by a number of widely read (or seen and heard) film reviewers like Pauline Kael, Rex Reed, and Gene Shalit. Daily newspapers, however, saw no need for specialized film reviewers or critics. Instead, they assigned their regular drama critics or other staff reporters to cover those few films thought to be noteworthy.

D. W. Griffith's *The Birth of a Nation* (1915) was one such newsworthy film. By establishing the possibilities of cinema as a form of highbrow art as well as lowbrow entertainment, Griffith's epic created a subject for serious critical concern. With the release of *The Birth of a Nation,* the movies began to be worth discussion. After their initial discussions of *The Birth of a Nation,* journals like the *Nation* and the *New Republic,* which had hitherto seen the movies as mass entertainment for an uneducated populace, and therefore of no interest to their highly literate readership, began to review films on a regular basis. And from 1915 to the present day, regular film columns and reviews of current releases have been an integral part of daily newspapers and general magazines. Specialized film reviewers have gradually replaced the drama critic gone slumming or the available reporters who, at the moment, had nothing better to do than review a movie for their newspapers.

With the exception of *Photoplay,* founded in 1912 and an extremely literate fan magazine, it was not until the 1920s that specialized magazines treating film subjects seriously and aimed at the general public appeared. The National Board of Review (established in 1908 as a regulatory film censorship organization) founded the first such publication in 1920 with *Exceptional Photoplays.* This magazine provided reviews and analyses of current films and aimed at informing the general public of worthy and exceptional entertainments.

The end of the silent era of film began a new era in film writing. It was as if viewers, having lost the great art of the silent film to the crude and noisy stumbling of the early sound film, felt the need to write and to read about the passing of something they suddenly realized was important. Two periodicals chiefly concerned with the theory and the artistry of films, *Close-up* and *Experimental Cinema,* began publishing in 1929. Since then, both in the United States and abroad, journals devoted solely to film subjects and directed toward a readership of nontrade people have enjoyed considerable success.

THE EMERGENCE OF FILM THEORY: AMERICA AND EUROPE

Appropriately, coincidental with the year in which *The Birth of a Nation* was released, 1915, the first book-length study of film was published, *The Art of the Moving Picture,* by the American poet Vachel Lindsay. This book, the first major work of film theory, attempted both to distinguish the properties of film from those of other arts and to synthesize the properties of other arts within the one art of cinema. The second major book about film, Hugo Münsterberg's *The Photoplay: A Psychological Study,* appeared in the following year, 1916, the year that also saw the release of Griffith's second masterwork, *Intolerance.* In this book Münsterberg, an eminent German psychologist on the faculty of Harvard University, explored the psychological relationship between the film viewer and the screen image. Both of these theoretical books argue that cinema deserves a place alongside of the time-honored arts. Both Lindsay and Münsterberg had to deal with the supposedly unartistic mechanical quality of film: its ability to record a representation of the everyday world. Thus, both theorists stressed the ways in which the film medium changed and restructured the normal and lived flow of life into something new and artificial, that is, artful. They viewed and praised film as artifice, as formal construction, as material shaped by an individual artist's mind and hand.

Similar theoretical arguments appeared in essays all during the 1920s as intellectuals sought to validate as art what appeared to most people to be simply a highly profitable form of show business, and later as appalled critics saw the highly developed art of the silent cinema abandoned for the merely representational qualities of the infant sound movie. Not surprisingly, most of this serious theoretical writing about film thrived in Europe, where intellectuals had been attracted to filmmaking from the birth of the medium. (France, for example, had initiated the extensive filming of classic stage plays and famous novels well before World War I.) It was also in Europe during the 1920s that intellectuals and artists devoted to all the arts gathered and talked and put their aesthetic ideas into position papers and manifestos. In America, however, in the 1920s and early 1930s intellectuals scarcely took part in theorizing about film. There were, of course, some thoughtful reviews of specific films in the major periodicals of the time by critics like Edmund Wilson, Aldous Huxley, and Robert E. Sherwood, but no native major theorists or theories developed between the two world wars. After Hugo Münsterberg's book of 1916, the development of film theory and criticism became chiefly a European activity.

Although two theoretical works by Frenchman Louis Delluc appeared in 1919 and 1920 (*Cinéma et Cie* and *Photogénie*), the first major European work of theoretical importance was a book called *The Visible Man, or Film Culture.* This important book, published in German in 1924, was written by Béla Balázs, an expatriate Hungarian filmmaker and theorist, and is said to have greatly influenced the ideas and work of the Soviet filmmaker and theorist V. I. Pudovkin. It is one of the few pieces of theoretical writing before World War II that sees no contradiction between the representational properties of film and its existence as an art, thus making it essentially a realist theory. It was, moreover, the first of a number of important theoretical works written by Balázs, which are now available in English translation, foremost among them *Theory of Film: Character and Growth of a New Art,* written in 1945 and translated in 1952. Balázs's views on the medium of film seem remarkably modern, particularly his discussions of the potential of asynchronous sound and the power of the close-up.

Perhaps the most prolific and influential Europeans writing film theory during the 1920s were the Russians. Limited by their lack of access to the photographic materials needed to make films of their own, the early Soviet filmmakers argued, theorized, and wrote in various journals and newspapers about the particular qualities and properties of the cinema, paying special theoretical attention to the editing process. V. I. Pudovkin in 1926 published *Film Technique,* first issued as a series of pamphlets in a group of technical handbooks on film. These essays developed the linkage theory of film editing and montage. In a later work, *Film Acting* (1935), Pudovkin examined film performance in one of the few major works exploring the subject. Although Pudovkin insisted on the primacy of the emotional content of the film narrative, he was essentially a formalist in theory, for he emphasized the artistic control of cinematic devices and technique, that is, he employed cinema not as representational or realistic, but as a reshaping of material into an artistic form. Sergei Eisenstein also began publishing during this period, many of his essays provoked by friendly if vehement argument with Pudovkin's editing theories. Eisenstein outlined his theory of montage editing, based on conflict and dialectic, in a series of essays that appeared after his installation as a faculty member in the State Cinema Technicum in 1928. These were later collected, translated into English, and published as the two major theoretical works, *The Film Sense* (1942) and *Film Form: Essays in Film Theory* (1949). Pudovkin's work also eventually was translated into English and collected into one volume, *Film Technique and Film Acting* (1958). The theoretical writings of these important Soviet filmmakers, though long unavailable in English, were widely circulated and discussed throughout Europe and strongly influenced formal and manipulative approaches to the film medium.

TECHNOLOGY AND THEORY: FROM FORMALISM TO REALISM

The transition to sound at the beginning of the 1930s seemed to emphasize the literal, representational, and mechanical potentials of film at the expense of its abilities to communicate figuratively and artistically. Sound, both because it made greater realism possible and, at the same time, seemed crude, implied that the art of the cinema was based less on creativity than recording. For many critics and theorists sound appeared to be the enemy of art; for them, the art of cinema was the art of *silent* cinema, an art found not in film's ability to take representational photographs of life that happened to move, but in film's *inability* to reproduce and represent life. This inability to represent life meant that the film artist had to create an imaginative alternative. The critics of sound felt that it had destroyed a *visual* art form and that filmmakers now merely engaged in the representational filming of verbal dramas.

Although several of the great Soviet filmmakers and theorists like Eisenstein and Dziga Vertov wrote of the possibilities of expressive sound montage, and Bálázs in Germany argued in *The Spirit of Film* (1930) for the use of asynchronous sound as a counteractive to the literal quality of early sound film, Rudolf Arnheim, a German aesthetician, was thoroughly pessimistic. In a small book called *Film as Art,* published in 1933, Arnheim argued that film was a visual art in which the representation of reality was a minor element. Like other formalist theoreticians before him, he argued that film is art if the artist manipulates the plastic materials of film. The artist, not reality, determines the making of a film, for the artist, by editing and by selecting focal lengths and shot compositions, creates the rhythm and the visual patterns. Indeed, nearly all experimental and nonstory films owe their aesthetics to Arnheim's position, as do many narrative films. *Film as Art,* which codifies the formalist theoretical position, has been until recently the most widely read book of film theory ever written.

Less rigid film writing continued on its own course through the 1930s and 1940s, acknowledging and embracing sound and color and other technical advancements, which allowed the medium to achieve greater visual and aural fidelity to reality. After World War II, the emphasis on the formal qualities of film lessened and the emphasis on humanistic and contemporary subject matter that had been caught on the screen, rather than manipulated onto it, increased. Indeed, following the war, major works of theory and criticism attempted to justify this new realism by asserting that it took full advantage of the unique properties of the cinema. The ability of film to be socially relevant in ways denied to the other arts was much praised and discussed. Critical writing published in Great Britain arose out of the strong documentary movement of the 1930s and the influence of John Grierson, whose work — both practical and theoretical — was concerned with the primacy of the raw material of life from which films were made. In the United States, film critics like Harry Alan Potamkin, Otis Ferguson, Robert Warshow, and James Agee discussed film from political and sociological perspectives; although their work tended to discuss specific films rather than the theory of cinema, they suggested paths that today's theoreticians are only now treading. And, finally, in postwar Italy, **scriptwriters** like Cesare Zavattini and film directors like Roberto Rossellini — identified worldwide as Italian neo-realists — in their films, theoretical writings, and manifestos promoted a new realism in films.

This shift in theoretical emphasis from **formalism** to **realism** was fully realized with the founding, in 1951, of the *Cahiers du Cinéma,* the noted French film journal. The major force behind the magazine and a constant contributor to its pages was André Bazin, a film critic who has since been recognized as the first of the significant realist theoreticians. Ironically, Bazin, who wrote essays rather than books, really did not develop a codified theory of film like Eisenstein or Arnheim. Bazin's essays, however, were theoretical in their arguments about the nature of the film medium, and he clearly identified those properties of cinema that have since been linked with realist film practice: deep-focus cinematography and the opposition between montage editing and mise-en-scène editing. Bazin's essays were eventually collected and translated into English in a two-volume work called *What Is Cinema?* (1967–1971). By then, however, his work had long since influenced the French new wave films and filmmaker-critics like Jean-Luc Godard and François Truffaut. Indeed, as early as 1956, Godard reacted to realist film theory with an essay prefiguring current theoretical practice, which sees the division between formalist and realist aesthetics, between montage and mise-en-scène, as arbitrary and possibly irrelevant to the viewing experience.

Despite Godard's article, the major emphasis through the 1950s and most of the 1960s was on realist aesthetics. The second most influential work of realist theory was published in 1960 by Sigfried Kracauer, a German who had emigrated to America before World War II. His *Theory of Film: The Redemption of Physical Reality* argues that film is a photographic art, which, by capturing and organizing images of life, allows viewers to see more of that world than they could merely with their eyes in their ordinary life. The film frame to Kracauer is a window on the world, and the camera eye is able to see not only what we see under usual circumstances but also what is overlooked or imperceptible to the human eye.

CONTEMPORARY THEORY AND CRITICISM

By the late 1960s, the distinctions between formalism and realism, between Eisenstein and Arnheim and Bazin and Kracauer, seemed less illuminating than they had been. In actual practice, films used both formal and realist technique, and little theoretical writing seemed to deal with this contradictory fact. Emphasis in theoretical discourse moved elsewhere. In the United States, attention was directed at first toward the auteur theory, formulated in France and transformed into something slightly different by its American proponent, Andrew Sarris. Less a theory than a methodology, the auteur theory and practice, as set forth in Sarris's *The American Cinema: Directors and Directions, 1929–1968,* initiated a huge number of studies of directors, and it resurrected previously unknown films. It was also responsible for perhaps the only major publicized theoretical debate between two American film critics. Pauline Kael dismissed the auteur theory, and Sarris countered in what proved to be a series of fascinating essays. Eventually, the attention to film directors also extended the auteur theory to consideration of screenwriters, cinematographers, and performers. Critics in the United States and elsewhere also turned their attention to film genres; this inquiry into defining groups of popular films had been largely nontheoretical, but that changed in the 1980s.

Perhaps the greatest shift in theoretical emphasis occurred in 1968 with the publication in France of Christian Metz's *Film Language: A Semiotics of the Cinema.* The work was immediately controversial. Although it has since been amended and argued about and rejected for various reasons, it must be considered an important work of contemporary film theory. Metz's book, initiating an entirely new approach to the study of film, suggested that the theoretician study the viewer's understanding of specific cinematic devices in an attempt to find out if and how film comprises a language (analogous to verbal language) through its structures and codes. This work introduced the application of linguistic sign theory to the study of film. It argued, too, for the study of film as a science, and it promoted close textual analysis of specific works. Metz's position angered and threatened those critics, scholars, and theoreticians who felt that film study was not a science, that the interpretation of visual images could not be codified, and that **semiotics,** lacking a comprehensible terminology and methodology, was a dead end.

After the initial furor over Metz's approach had subsided, his work was attacked for other reasons. His attempts to understand signification in film were criticized by Marxist film critics, who pointed to the contradiction between Metz's theory and his unwillingness to recognize that sign systems are culturally and ideologically based. Since 1975, then, semiological theory has moved into more culturally and politically defined discourse and has, as well, attempted to incorporate psychoanalytic principles into its study of the relationship between film and viewer. Other theoretical positions, too, are currently popular in the United States and abroad: phenomenological, structural, anthropological, perceptual, and even physiological. Indeed, the explosion of interest in the study of film as an art and a scholarly discipline since the 1960s has led to a boom in the publication of journals and books that treat film from an extraordinarily wide variety of theoretical positions.

Today many magazines and journals devoted to film provide a platform for critical discourse on any aspect of film one might imagine. There are journals devoted to popular film, silent cinema, national cinemas, and interdisciplinary aspects of the medium. And, of course, television programs, daily newspapers, and magazines for a general audience continue to feature the work of practicing film critics and reviewers. Films are seen, examined, dissected, analyzed, studied, and written about by buffs, collectors, archivists, historians, teachers, scholars, journalists, critics, and theoreticians. At its best, such writing can help the viewer and student of film to understand the medium, its art, and its artists more fully.

A selected list of reading materials designed to help students and viewers expand their general knowledge of film history, theory, and criticism appears immediately following Chapter 9. It is important to recognize that all the ideas about film explored in *An Introduction to Film* are part of the tradition of film writing produced in the past (and in the present) by historians, theoreticians, and critics. In turn, every student asked to write a paper about a film subject becomes a part of this tradition, and adds to the continuing discourse on film. Thus, an investment of time reading some of the works suggested will not only help you complete a current assignment, but will also serve as an introduction to the on-going tradition of film analysis and criticism.

9

WRITING COLLEGE PAPERS ABOUT FILM

Classes in film study frequently require essays. The reasons are both obvious and significant. Although factual and technical knowledge about film can be tested in short-answer exams, films arouse feelings and opinions, and these, as well as facts, should be open to discussion. Only in a paper can a student demonstrate her or his ability to analyze responses.

Writing a paper helps a student to think. Papers force the student to confront the vagueness of unarticulated ideas and therefore to clarify unconscious assumptions. Of course, this kind of confrontation and clarification is hardly ever easy. Writing is not easy — even for those people who do it well. Putting the self on paper is putting the self on the spot, putting the self in possible peril. Even so, getting an idea actually articulated — *said* — so that one understands one's own feelings and communicates them to someone else, can be exhilarating. It is one thing simply to like or dislike a film and leave it at that, but to find out *why* one likes or dislikes it, to puzzle it out logically, is to deepen one's understanding and is a source, finally, of satisfaction.

There is a difference, of course, between writing a review and writing criticism. A review attempts to inform the reader about a film that has not been seen by the reader. Thus, it should say something about the content of the film as well as the reviewer's feelings about the viewing experience so that a prospective film goer can make an informed decision about going to see the film. An instructor may assign reviews, particularly of films to be seen outside of class. Most papers assigned in class, however, will require writing criticism. A critical paper on an individual film or a group of films or on a director or a movement will assume that the reader *has* seen the film. Therefore, what is required is some analysis of film structure or relating the current film to other films of a similar kind or identifying trends or interpreting themes or noting cultural and social contexts observable in the film.

Papers also serve as a dialogue between student and teacher. Because film study is a relatively new discipline, every student should feel encouraged by the possibility that he or she may be able to come up with an insight that has never been expressed before. The good film paper may very well instruct the instructor, helping him or her to see a film in a new way. But to say that students should approach the writing of a paper seriously is not to say that papers should be dull, solemn, or unimaginative. Rather, papers should reflect the way in which the student has interacted with the film in a lively, human, and vital manner. After all, along with close textual analysis and careful research, there is also a place for liveliness in film criticism. Here are two highly readable passages taken from student papers:

> One of the best episodes in the whole film [Citizen Kane] is the breakfast table sequence in which Welles details (in miniature) the demise of Kane's first marriage -- from endearment to estrangement -- in 120 seconds.

> In My Man Godfrey, William Powell makes as good a disguised prince as any character from the Brothers Grimm. The film loses nothing for beginning in an East River dump rather than in an enchanted castle in Far Far Away. The inhabitants of this dump are kindly, intelligent, and decent, but they have been put under a spell by the evil witch Depression. Fortunately for all, the almost divine being Godfrey is living in their midst having descended from Boston and his wealthy family.

When one goes to see a film, one is carried away by romance, brought to tears or laughter, made tense through suspense, or moved to a recognition of the joy and despair of the human condition. One makes judgments too — consciously and unconsciously — about how well the film did what it seemed to set out to do. Writing papers about film extends this natural human critical act. Transforming one's initial reaction into an organized written commentary can lead to a greater awareness of both the self and the medium. Indeed, at times it is only after writing about a film that one really gets to know exactly what that particular film experience has meant personally. The significance of that first impression — rapid and immediate — only becomes clear in the quiet of the study afterwards. All experience of film is valid as long as it can be communicated.

The Critical Act: How to Start

Whenever we share our experience of art, whether in conversation or on paper, we are engaging in a critical act. Even so simple a phrase as "I liked the movie" or "That film was a waste of money" implies that the speaker has transformed earlier raw and unarticulated emotional response into a critical judgment. Such simple expressions of like or dislike, however, usually fail to communicate satisfactorily the total mass of undifferentiated feelings and ideas provoked by the experience of viewing a particular film. One really means, "It was a waste of money — except for that funny scene when . . ." or "I liked the movie because . . ." and so forth. Writing about the film, on the other hand, forces the writer to think *specifically* — to recall specific scenes, specific pieces of **dialogue,** specific camera movements or editorial techniques. Writing about a film lets the writer relive it, feel it again, see it again — but all at a distance from the original experience. Borrowing from the English poet William Wordsworth, one might say that criticism is "emotion recollected in tranquillity." The recalled experience of the film allows one to reflect on the film's structure, **tone,** and meaning, and the *reasons* for one's reactions to a film.

Writing about film, like writing about any subject, is not as easy as talking about it. The opinions quickly and enthusiastically offered in casual conversation often are pitifully weak on paper. They are unsupported, inconsistent, vulnerable to attack; they reveal that the writer has not thought enough about the subject, has jumped to conclusions that have no visible means of support. Writing, in fact, is not the most difficult part of creating a paper. What is difficult and demanding is the act of thinking and defining, much of which should occur before one word is put on the page. But writing is also an aid to thinking; as you put down words in your first draft, you will see where you must do some further thinking.

Writing about film is especially difficult because, unlike a novel, a poem, a reproduction of a painting, or a recording of a musical performance, a film is not always readily available for extensive study. Usually one cannot see a film again and again and again. Even during the screenings one does have a chance to see, it is usually not possible to stop the continuous movement of images on the screen to study one image thoroughly as we might stop our reading of a poem to study a written image. Taking notes in a darkened theater is, unhappily, not the answer. If at all possible, a student should see a film at least twice. The first viewing of a movie should be experienced the way it was intended to be experienced — straight through from beginning to end with the viewer's attention on the screen. Scribbling in the dark alters and undermines the cinematic experience; one cannot give a film full attention while taking notes. (*After* the initial screening, impressions, details, and key scenes should be written down.) During the second viewing, some note-taking might, of course, occur during the screening itself. One might also read through critical articles and reviews and go to star and **genre** picture books on film, for these often contain plot synopses and production information. Remembering a movie is difficult and requires practice, but the ability to remember generally increases in proportion to the number of films seen.

Today with the availability of video recorders, the problem of recalling the details of a film is lessened. And the film can be stopped and started, run forward and backward, even freeze framed on some VCRs, so that particular passages can be looked at very closely. Though an aid to scholarship, the viewing of a film on a television screen does not reproduce the exact film experience. Making statements about composition, for example, may not be accurate because the original film may have been composed in a wider ratio. Cinemascope films suffer the most; films made before the 1950s, the least, since their ratios (1 to 1.3, the Academy ratio) approximate the dimensions of the television screen. There is also the problem of finding certain titles in the cassette format. Foreign films, silent films, 1930s and 1940s films may not be carried by every video outlet. Nevertheless, access to a recorder and tapes will help when it comes time to write papers.

Another problem that confronts the beginning film student and writer is, paradoxically, the liveliness of the flat screen. With many films, one does not seem as much to *see* them as to *live* or *dream* them. How, some students ask, can one begin to encompass in words that emotional and physical experience of a movie. How can one translate the simultaneous bombardment of the senses of sight and hearing into words that are strung, one after another, along the page? Although it may be difficult, and certainly it does not duplicate the experience itself, the attempt to find the right words and put them into order is the only way the fleeting moments of the film experience can possibly be captured. If the experience is valuable, then preserving that experience is also valuable. Though words may fail to record the exact shape and sound and feel of the film experience, they come a great deal closer to that end than a grunt of approval or disdain.

What to Write About: The Individual Film

The first step in writing is not taking a pen to paper, hauling out the typewriter, or leaping to the word processor. The writer first must mentally preedit the raw material (that jumble of feeling and thought

Content -
themes,
characteryation
moods

form -
cinematography
Sound
editing

connected with the film) much as the filmmaker mentally preedits the material to be photographed by first selecting the subject matter. Thus, the writer must first select a topic, a focus, an emphasis. Just as it is impossible to make a film about everything and anything, so it is impossible in a short paper to discuss usefully all elements of a film. Just as a filmmaker chooses the subject matter, decides where to place the camera and what will eventually be caught in the **frame** and what will be left out, so must the writer choose a specific subject and position herself or himself before the material. The writer, too, must limit the focus, decide what should be contained in the paper and what should be left out of it. The writer must decide whether to write about a particular film's content — its **themes, characterizations,** moods — or whether to focus on the film's form — its cinematography, sound, editing. Or the writer may choose to combine the two in a particular way for a particular critical purpose. One might write, for example, about the ways in which editing expresses the theme, or the ways in which sound supports characterization.

An individual's encounter with a movie, of course, is a total experience and not chopped up into potential topics. And, of course, the distinction between form and content is arbitrary. It is difficult to talk about one without also discussing the other; form creates meaning just as meaning dictates the form by which it is expressed. Orson Welles's *Citizen Kane* (1941), for example, might be no more than a pedestrian semibiographical fiction if its form were merely a chronological narrative of the events in magnate Charles Foster Kane's life. It might have drama but it would not have the same meaning it does if the camera viewed its subject objectively and omnisciently. It is just because Welles reveals the character nonchronologically — Kane dies at the *beginning* of the film — and nonobjectively — through a newsreel, through the reminiscences of several people with vested interest, that the viewer is intrigued beyond the mere facts of Kane's life. The form, in fact, creates the meaning. A fine paper could be written on the subject of how narrative structure contributes to the film's theme.

Since the split between form and content is arbitrary, since the two combine to create the films on the screen and to affect the viewer, the writer must in some degree deal with both, but can *emphasize* an aspect of one or the other. To emphasize theme, the writer may need to describe how the camera moves, how the images are illuminated, how the film is edited. Similarly, if the writer wishes to discuss a formal element like editing in a particular film, he or she may have to briefly discuss the plot, the characterizations, and what the film is trying to say. All the parts of a film work together to create a total effect. The best papers, however, select one specific element to emphasize, examine that element in detail, and use other cinematic elements of the film only as supportive material. If a topic is assigned, stick to it. If a topic is not assigned, try to write about something that genuinely interests you. Your interest will help you be more specific in details and elaboration of your points.

Below, isolated under the headings of *Content and Structure* and *Form*, are specific filmic elements which might be the focus of a paper on a given film. In addition, some questions are presented to stimulate intellectual responses to the particular film the writer may wish to deal with. If the questions seem irrelevant to the film in question or simply uninteresting, look for another area of emphasis — or better, generate your own questions, for one of the best ways of getting ideas is to ask yourself questions.

CONTENT AND STRUCTURE

Plot and Story

One can distinguish between the **plot** and the story of a film. The story is *what happens* in a film — the sum of the events in which the characters are involved, the situations in which they find themselves or from which they try to extricate themselves. The plot is not only the events but the *order* of those events as presented on the screen. Thus, two films may tell exactly the same story — say Little Red Riding Hood — but if one uses flashbacks or flash-forwards the plots are different because the order of the episodes differs.

Summarizing the plot of a single film does not make a critical paper. A summary of what happens in a movie does not require much thought; at best, it requires a good memory. It is no substitute for a discussion of *how* the plot reveals the story. A discussion of *how* the plot occurs (through the use of flashbacks, **jump cuts,** and so on) focuses on the film's narrative techniques, its form. A discussion of *what* the plot reveals or says focuses on the film's theme.

Statement of the plot of a film, then, is usually subordinate to a topic (such as a film's narrative structure or theme), which allows the writer to exercise his or her critical faculties. Therefore, events of the plot should be used selectively in nearly all papers to *illustrate* and *support* the critical thesis of the paper and to remind the reader of specific events relative to the discussion. The following excerpt from a student paper on *Citizen Kane* demonstrates how plot details in the film are used selectively to support a critical statement:

> This feeling of distance from Kane is enriched by
> the photographic techniques. The long shot comes
> into play many times: Kane sits down miles away
> from Susan in his castle, he is a small figure in

the street shot from his newspaper building, Xanadu
is often dark and in the distance, and Kane's nurse
in the beginning comes out of a very distant door.
Even when he is shot from relatively close up (out
of dramatic necessity), he seems to be distant.
We see a portion of his leg as we watch the drunk
Leland after the lost election, Kane looks like
Frankenstein as he wrecks Susan's room in the castle, and a hundred empty Kane shells appear in the
mirrors in the hall as he walks by.

Theme

The theme of a film is what the film is about, what the *whole* film communicates to the viewer. It is the statement the film makes or the question(s) it raises. Unlike the plot, it cannot be seen because it does not happen. The theme of a film is abstract — an idea. It is extremely important for the writer to understand this distinction between plot and theme so the two are not used interchangeably. In Ingmar Bergman's *The Seventh Seal* (1956), for example, the plot consists of the wanderings of a knight and his squire recently returned to their plague-ridden native land after a crusade. They meet various people in various places and the knight asks them a question to which he can find no answer: Is there a God? The theme of *The Seventh Seal,* on the other hand, is man's search for certainty, for knowledge concerning the meaning of his existence, for faith.

The theme of a film, then, is an idea, an abstraction. It cannot be photographed. François Truffaut, for example, identifies the theme of *Day for Night* (1973) in abstract terms: "*Day for Night* revolves around one central question: 'Are films superior to life?' It gives no definite answer. For there can be none."[1] The abstractness of Truffaut's statement cannot be photographed, but it can be expressed through the visible moving images of the film and through the audible sound. It is through selection of images and sounds, their arrangement and their internal rhythms that the filmmaker communicates a theme. Since words, unlike images, can express abstract ideas, sometimes themes are actually stated; the dialogue of a film may forthrightly say (through narrator or character) what the film is about. The viewer must select what appears to be the film's emphasis from all the verbal evidence given and must support that selection. And sometimes a speech that seems crucial to the identification of a film's theme may nevertheless be cryptic.

In Dennis Hopper's *Easy Rider* (1969), the single most important line of dialogue seems to be Wyatt's remark to Billy: "We blew it." But what does that mean? And, of course, a character might make a statement that seems to reveal the theme, but the character may be unreliable, or such direct statements may be thoroughly contradicted and subverted by other, nonverbal, cinematic elements. In effect, discovering a film's theme (or themes) is like doing a piece of detective work. Clues may be everywhere — in the images, in the dialogue, in the juxtaposition between the two. The clues may be obvious, they may be hidden; they may even be red herrings that lead the viewer down a blind alley.

The theme or statement of a film can be large and universal: people's inhumanity to each other, in Kon Ichikawa's *Fires on the Plain* (1960); the individual naif as a force for good against the corrupt and cynical, in Frank Capra's *Mr. Smith Goes to Washington* (1939); the exploration of reality and illusion, in Szabo's *Mephisto* (1982). The theme can also be narrow and specific: that the Russian Revolution of 1917 was good for the country and the people, in Sergei Eisenstein's *October/Ten Days That Shook the World* (1928); that the American people will elect anyone to higher office if he is properly packaged and sold, in Michael Ritchie's *The Candidate* (1972). Sometimes the theme of a film may be so simple and obvious that it does not bear much consideration. In *Star Wars* (George Lucas, 1976), for example, the theme is that goodness will triumph over evil. This is so simple a theme that it is hardly worth writing a paper about. *Star Wars* itself is an interesting film, but this interest is derived from elements other than its theme.

These three thesis statements from student papers identify the themes of several films:

> Bertolucci's The Conformist is a complex analysis of the causes and effects of fascism, postulating sexual insecurity and guilt as the cause, and debauchery and mindless conformity as the ultimate end.

> The final closing shot of Anarene in The Last Picture Show draws together the theme of the movie into a single, grainy, black-and-white photographic expression of emptiness, nothingness, and paralysis.

> In Deliverance, a film based on the novel by James Dickey, three basic themes are continually expressed through the actions of the four main characters: Humankind's struggle against Nature, Humankind's confrontation with other men, and Humankind's constant battle with the self.

The viewer may be able to piece the theme together using all the film's elements as evidence, but may then reject the theme because of personal bias. This is particularly true when a viewer sees a film whose theme is personally painful or distasteful. Two of the major themes of Luis Buñuel's *Viridiana* (1961), for example, are that too much piety is neurotic and corrupting, and that Christianity depends upon human suffering and poverty to keep itself valid and alive. The images of the film are as strong and controversial as the film's themes. One key scene shows us a group of beggars seated around a table in a parody of da Vinci's painting of *The Last Supper;* their conversation and actions are gross and sacrilegious. A devout viewer who disagrees with the film's thematic statements might dismiss the film as blasphemous and reject any further critical interaction with it. However, because the film reveals its theme masterfully, one should be willing to recognize the artistry of the work even if one does not agree with its message. Acknowledging the effective artistic realization of a disagreeable theme does not mean that one has betrayed one's principles or compromised one's moral standards. It is possible to appreciate the artistry of Leni Riefenstahl's *Triumph of the Will* (1936) without being a Nazi, just as it is possible to appreciate Stanley Kubrick's *A Clockwork Orange* (1971) without condoning violence.

There are a few simple questions the viewer can ask after seeing a puzzling film. These questions should, in fact, be asked even if the film is not puzzling, for their answers will help clarify the film's theme. They are a part of the thinking process that occurs before the act of writing begins.

1. Is there any clue to the film's emphasis in its title?
2. Does the dialogue offer any obvious expressions of what the film is about?
3. Do the characters themselves suggest the theme — through their names, their personalities, their clothing, their occupations, their situations?
4. If the characters are inarticulate, do their actions indicate the theme?
5. Are there any discrepancies between what the characters say and what they actually do?
6. Are there any discrepancies between what the dialogue indicates the theme is and what the form and structure of the film indicate the theme is?
7. Do the characters' relationships with their surroundings have any meaning?
8. Does the form of the film (the **lighting, composition,** the abruptness or lyricism of the editing, the sound other than the dialogue) reveal the theme?

Characterization
Characterization in a film is effective if a character's actions and dialogue convince the viewer of their appropriateness, so that the character as a

9-1 Some students find it difficult to distinguish the character from the actor in a film. They may say, "John Wayne is a salty-tongued, gone-to-fat sheriff." But in *True Grit* (Henry Hathaway, 1969), Wayne plays Rooster Cogburn, "a salty-tongued, gone-to-fat sheriff." The distinction between actor and character should be made clear in a film paper.

whole is seen as credible. In other words, the character must be — no matter how fantastic her or his actions — a believable person *within the context of the film* for as long as it lasts.

A character, of course, is a created person who does not really exist. The actor who plays the character, on the other hand, is real and does exist. The difficulty in dealing with characterization in a film is that too often viewers confuse the actor with the character or see the two as interchangeable. When students see a film starring well-known actors (Paul Newman, Barbra Streisand, Dustin Hoffman, Jane Fonda, John Wayne), they may get confused when writing a paper about the characters in a film: "John Wayne is a salty-tongued, gone-to-fat sheriff." But John Wayne is not a sheriff; he is an actor. The writer has confused the actor with the character, Rooster Cogburn (Figure 9-1). What the writer *should* say is "John Wayne plays a man who. . . ." Even though the public persona of some actors appears to be identical to that of the characters they play, the student writing about a character in a single film should recognize the distinction between actor and character.

When writers have not made the distinction between actor and character, they may start to write a paper about characterization but end up writing about acting. To write about acting, even to recognize whether a person up there on the screen *is* acting rather than just being, the viewer has to have seen the actor in more than one performance, in more than one film, or in real life. The topic of acting can be dealt with effectively if one is writing about several films in which the same performer appears, but it is usually useless to write about a performance in a single film. What is discussable in a single film is the characterization — the created person. Occasionally, students find themselves writing: "Dustin Hoffman was really great in *The Graduate* (Mike Nichols, 1967)." What they really mean is that they liked the character of Benjamin, which Dustin Hoffman portrayed. Once they realize that it is Benjamin who interests and engages them, they can easily go on to discover *why* they like Benjamin (Benjamin sees the shallowness and hypocrisy of a plastic society; Benjamin is caught up in deciding what to do with his life and this is a very real problem facing all young people). The writer knows Benjamin through evidence in the film — and that is the stuff of which good papers are made. The primary source of this evidence is not Dustin Hoffman's acting ability, but what the character Benjamin says and does in this one film.

This excerpt from a student paper clearly treats the characters and not the actors:

> In <u>Jules and Jim</u> we find the imprisonment of both sexes. Each creates the other. Catherine is so idolized as the ultimate symbol of woman that she can do no wrong. It is because Jules and Jim define her as an "ideal" woman that they put up with her. She is expected to act the way she does. Hence, Jules and Jim are prisoners of Catherine's whims, while Catherine is bound to their desires.

Before writing about a character in a given film, the viewer should ask the following questions.

1. Is it clear that I am interested in the character rather than in the actor?
2. What is the character's function in the film? Is he or she the main character or is he or she a secondary or minor character? Is the film *about* the character or is the character a device through which the filmmaker can make a statement?
3. Is my interest in the character based on what the character represents? If so, what is it precisely that is represented?
4. Does the character stay the same or change and develop through the film? What is the significance of the lack of change or of development?

5. Where is the evidence *in* the film to support my interpretation of the character's significance? Is it in the dialogue, the actions, the relationships with other characters, the relationship to the environment?

Tone

The tone of a film is its prevailing atmosphere, such as joyousness or horror. This atmosphere can be created by many things, for example, the setting, the lighting, the color, the sound, the rhythms of the editing. Tone is not necessarily dependent upon a film's subject matter. There have been horror films in which the established tone is essentially lighthearted, as in *Love at First Bite* (Stan Dragoti, 1979). There have been comedies in which the tone has been quite grim, as in Woody Allen's *Zelig* (1983). The tone of a film is never created by just one filmic element; all the elements together give the viewer the feel of the film, which may, or may not, be supportive of its subject matter.

Not all films have a constant or consistent tone. The tone of Orson Welles's *The Magnificent Ambersons* (1942), for example, is at first lighthearted and affectionate, but then it becomes grim, dark, claustrophobic, and withdrawn. The tone in the film parallels the movement of the Amberson family from wealth and solidarity to economic decline and fragmentation. It is created by the lighting, the sets, the camera angles, and the editing. At the beginning of the film, for instance, the interior of the Amberson mansion is brightly lit, it seems large and gracious, characters and the camera move gradually down wide stairways, glide smoothly across the rooms. As the film progresses, the lights seem less bright, shadows encroach on the screen so that, eventually, the interior of the house becomes dark and forbidding; the shadows press in on the characters until it seems that space disappears. In *The Magnificent Ambersons*, Welles gradually shifts the tone to support and emphasize the thematic content of the film. More recently, however, modern filmmakers have used abrupt shifts in tone — to startle the audience or to subvert their expectations. Almost all the films of Italian filmmaker Lina Wertmüller keep the audience attentive and in a state of disequilibrium. She uses shifts in tone to subvert the customary passivity of the viewer who normally relies on the tone of a film for information about what sort of experience to expect.

Some elements that contribute to the tone of a film are discussed in this excerpt from a student paper.

> Despite the hard times of the 1930s in which it is set, The Sting's tone is lighthearted. The flippant acting combination of Paul Newman and Robert Redford and the jovial musical score contribute

> greatly to this mood. The insertion of storybook
> graphics to separate each portion of the film adds
> to its unreal quality. Because of the clever
> script, serious incidents such as gambling, cor-
> ruption, and murder are subordinated to the process
> of the con and its amusing ingenuity. The result is
> a joyous film, devoid of any hint of the problems of
> the Depression.

Tone, then, is the atmosphere of a film, created by the sum of several cinematic elements. To deal effectively with tone in a paper the writer must be prepared to deal with *how* that atmosphere and mood is created. Some questions the viewer might ask follow.

1. What is the tone of the film? (Romantic? Lyric? Claustro-phobic?)
2. Does the film's tone change or is it consistent?
3. If the tone shifts, where does the shift occur? Is it gradual or abrupt? Why does it shift, for what purpose?
4. How is the tone revealed? (Through the lighting? The editing? The cinematography? The music?)
5. What relationship does the tone have to the theme of the film? Is it supportive or contradictory?

FORM

The Image

The images of a film are what the viewer's eye perceives on the screen. The basic components creating an image are the **film stock,** composition, camera angle, lighting, and camera and subject movement. Because so many elements contribute to the film image, the writer probably will not wish to discuss all of them in relation to a given film. Probably the writer will discuss no more than two or three in one paper; in fact, often the best paper deals thoroughly with only one element.

The two basic properties of the film stock that might be discussed in a paper are **grain** and color. Contemporary filmmakers can choose whether they wish their film to appear grainy or smooth, in color or in black-and-white. Ideally, those choices will be relevant to both the subject and theme of the film.

High-speed film can capture an image with the least amount of available illumination, but the image is (or at least used to be) grainy. Because such film was used by newspaper and newsreel photographers, grainy images are most often associated with journalistic and documentary filmmaking and photography. As a result, such images evoke on-the-spot immediacy, a sense of urgency and gritty realism. In the

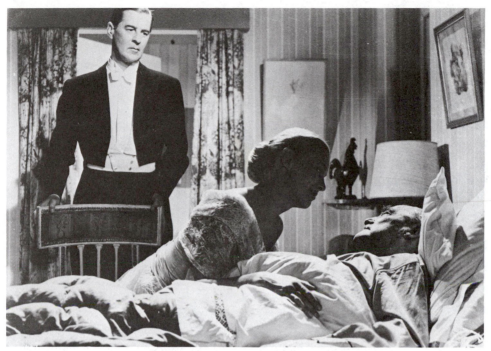

9-2 Black-and-white film can often emphasize details of texture. If this scene from Bergman's *Wild Strawberries* (1957) were in color, part of the viewer's attention would be occupied with the color itself, but without color the texture of fabrics — the woman's lace shawl, the man's evening clothes, the rumpled bedspread — stands out.

political film *Circle of Deceit* (1983), for example, director Volker Schlondorf uses high-speed color film, and the resultant grainy image confers an immediacy on the film that is consistent with its contemporary theme and narrative action. Most musicals, however, tend to be shot with slower-speed film, so that the images are closely textured, smooth, and controlled — in short, prettier.

Although most contemporary films are shot in color, black-and-white is still sometimes used to support both the mood and theme of a given film (Figure 9-2). For example, Woody Allen used it for *Stardust Memories* (1980), which alludes to Fellini's $8\frac{1}{2}$, a black-and-white film. Sometimes a filmmaker will alternate color with black-and-white in a film, using the shift to signal a change of mode; one can point to *The Wizard of Oz* (Victor Fleming, 1939) and, more recently, to *Rumble Fish* (Francis Coppola, 1984), both of which use color and black-and-white to differentiate between reality and fantasy. *Sophie's Choice* (Alan Pakula, 1983) uses black-and-white for memory sequences in the concentration camps.

9-3 Composition is the arrangements of objects in the frame. Antonioni indicates the distance that separates his characters emotionally by separating them on the screen physically, as he does here in *Red Desert* (1964).

Since almost all contemporary films are in color, the viewer tends to take the color for granted, as something real that the photographic image duplicates. Color, however, can be used expressively as well as mimetically, and there are now available all tones of color stock so that color images from film to film vary greatly. Color can be controlled — muted or exaggerated — either in the shooting process or in the laboratory so that it, too, supports or contradicts the subject and theme of a film. Jean-Luc Godard, for instance, has used primary and garishly flat colors to create a film image that resembles the comic strip or poster in its two-dimensional quality; his use of color is consistent with the structure and themes of his films, which explore media impact. The color in Robert Altman's *McCabe and Mrs. Miller* (1971), on the other hand, is muted and generally monochromatic in its scheme; it evokes both bleakness and nostalgia, the latter arising from the resemblance of the image to the brown tones associated with old photographs.

Composition is the arrangement of people and objects within the film frame (Figure 9-3). Even if the frame (the camera's vision) does not move, the rectangular space can be filled up in many ways. It can present pleasing and harmonious images or harsh and unharmonious ones. Those relationships may be achieved by the position of the subject

9-4 Composition of objects within the frame can also develop the notion of "offscreen" space when only part of an object is visible within the frame. The viewer presumes that the object continues, whether it be a wall or a forest or a person. In the case of a person like Dustin Hoffman in *The Graduate* (Mike Nichols, 1967), one can be sure that the lower part of his body does indeed exist below the frame, but without further information, say, shots from different angles, one cannot be sure that the glass upon which his hand rests continues beyond the frame as part of a real wall or whether it is simply a prop.

and of the camera (camera angle), and they are also affected by the actual size of the screen itself (Figure 9-4). Composition, one of the most important elements of the image, often provides a large enough topic for an entire paper.

Again, composition of the film frame — the use of film space — generally tells the viewer something about the nature of the film and its theme. Nobody in an Antonioni movie ever announces his or her state of alienation from other people, but the way the characters stand in relationship to other characters and in relationship to their environment dramatizes their alienation in visual terms. In his westerns, John Ford creates large vistas of open space where the human characters seem dwarfed by the vastness of nature, yet heroic in their attempts to civilize so vast and inhospitable an area. Carl Dreyer chiefly uses **close-ups** of faces to create the intensity in his *The Passion of Joan of Arc* (1928). Sergio Leone creates tension and suspense in the ways he uses both the close-up and the entrances and exits of characters on the wide screen of *Once upon a Time in the West* (1969). And the tilted angles of an entire **genre** of horror films complement the crazed and horrific action that generally occurs within them (Figure 9-5).

Lighting is another crucial element of the image. It is obviously important in creating the depth and quality of the black-and-white film,

9-5 Decor — the walls, the fabrics, the furnishings, the physical settings created for the film — can add an extra dimension to the image. In *The Cabinet of Dr. Caligari* (Robert Wiene, 1919), part of the response to the film is created by the tilted sets, the macabre lampposts, and the twisted cardboard trees.

but it is also important to the color film where it may seem less obvious in its uses.

To capture an image there must, of course, be sufficient light. Illumination, however, is not just a technical necessity; it is a component of mood, of drama, of an audience's emotional response to the image. A film heavy with shadows, a film in which there are dark corners, is likely to be somber, ominous, claustrophobic, frightening (Figure 9-6). Light comedy does not usually take place in shadow. Horror films do not usually take place in brightly lit settings. There are exceptions, of course, but artistic departures from the norm only prove the point that light or its absence creates certain definite expectations in the viewer. Alfred Hitchcock often lulls his viewers into complacency by shooting bright daylight scenes in which it appears unlikely that anything nasty will happen, but he tricks the audience by subverting its expectations; in his movies nasty things do happen in daylight and are doubly shocking for their unexpectedness. Light, and the way it is used, can also make objects and people and environments look beautiful or ugly, soft or

9-6 Lighting was used expressively and not realistically by Fritz Lang in *M* (1930). Peter Lorre's shadow appears against a "Wanted" poster at the exact moment he is luring his next victim, just offscreen. It is the first moment the viewer firmly knows that this unknown man is the child killer.

harsh, artificial or real. Indeed, illumination is perhaps the central element of the film image. All the other components of the image — film stock, composition, decor, camera and subject movement — can only be meaningfully employed when there is light.

The way in which the camera moves or does not move and the movement before it of the subject matter is also extremely important in establishing the effect the image will have on the viewer. Movement of the camera toward the subject (either by **tracking** or by using a **zoom lens**) draws the viewer into a closer, more intense relationship with the subject, and movement of the camera away from the subject creates emotional as well as physical distance. The effect will also vary in relation to the speed with which movement in or out is accomplished, creating surprise, suspense, tension. Movement across the subject, and the speed with which it occurs, also creates mood and establishes the viewer's relationship to the subject. A slow, leisurely **pan** across a landscape will feel quite different from a **flash pan,** which blurs the subject and tends to be dizzying. A camera mounted on a **boom** or a helicopter can produce liberating, swooping movements, or it can gaze at the subject coolly from a godlike distance. Moreover, the camera can move with a moving subject or lose it from the film frame, leaving behind an empty space. Indeed, subject movement in conjunction with camera movement creates complex spatial relationships, which are constantly in flux. Sometimes, as in the opening sequence of Orson Welles's *Touch of Evil* (1958), these relationships are extremely important to the thematic and narrative content of the film.

What we see on the screen — the film image — is the complex combination of the various elements discussed. Images can seem straightforward, showing us characters executing the maneuvers of the plot and not calling attention to themselves, while other images can be obviously flamboyant and expressive. The simpler the image, the more straightforward in its presentation of the subject matter of the film, the more difficult it will be to discuss it in a paper. These simple images, of course, are significant, but those images that fascinate the viewer visually and also relate to the film's subject matter in their formal properties usually provide the most interesting paper topics. This student writer calls attention to details of composition in an examination of *Jeremiah Johnson* (Sydney Pollack, 1972):

> The camera does not merely capture scenery
> through composition; it sees nature with human re-
> sponse. With human vision, the lens peers through
> soft hazy smoke in the campfire scenes and through
> tall reeds that web the beauty of nature. The image
> of a deer obscured by branches produces the effect
> of a human eye looking through a rifle sight --
> which is just what Jeremiah is doing.

The writer who wishes to explore elements of the images in a film might ask the following questions before starting a paper. These questions should also stimulate a wealth of other — more narrowly focused — questions.

1. Was the film's imagery particularly expressive?
2. What elements of the cinematography (film stock properties, composition, lighting, camera angle, movement, and so on) stood out, either because of their artistry or because they seemed inappropriate?
3. Did an awareness of the technique clarify the content and theme of the film — or did it obscure them?
4. With all the various aesthetic possibilities, why did the filmmaker choose to create the images just this way? How does choice of the stock, composition, angles, lighting, decor, and movement function?

Editing
Editing is the linking together of separate shots to form an entire and coherent film. This linking has some kind of narrative logic if it is a fiction film, some kind of intellectual logic if it is a documentary, and some kind of aesthetic logic if it is an abstract film. Whether accomplished within the camera, in the editing room, or in the laboratory,

editing provides the various kinds of transitions a filmmaker uses to get from one idea, time, place, or action to another. Editing — through its organization of time and space — creates the structure of every film.

The most common form of editing, **invisible editing,** attempts to smooth over the transitions from shot to shot so that they are not perceptible. Usually, the transitional sequence, cutting together a **long shot** to **medium shot** to close-up, goes unnoticed by the viewer who has learned to accept the cinema's ability to move through time and space effortlessly. Another common form of invisible editing is that accomplished by camera movement, the camera performing a quiet but essential selection process as it moves in for a close-up and then backs off into a two-shot and finally moves upward on a boom to photograph an overhead shot at a great height. This kind of **mise-en-scène** editing is — in one sense — not editing at all in that there are no physical separations (joined together at a later time) in the film material. Nonetheless, in another sense editing is going on — transitions in time and space are occurring and variety is being achieved.

The first kind of invisible editing is difficult to write about because it is both common and hard to see when one is viewing the film. Usually it is in the service of a narrative and little can be said about its use in a specific film that cannot be generally applied to other films similarly edited. Thus, the student may end up talking in generalities. Writing about mise-en-scène editing presents other problems. First, the student must recognize the presence of such an editorial style, and then remember and uncover what relationships are established in the frame by the movements of the camera. The context established by mise-en-scène editing must be read for its clues to the relationships it creates among people, objects, and environment and then those clues must be interpreted for meaning.

What is generally referred to as **montage** editing is a great deal easier for the beginning student to see and to write about. The meanings inherent in any particular shot are kept relatively clear (often through the use of close-ups) and the shots will usually be edited together quite rapidly — or obviously — in order to create a specific meaning or mood through their juxtaposition. Often other highly visible transitional devices will be used in addition to the **straight cut.** The **dissolve,** the **superimposition,** the **fade,** the jump cut call attention to themselves (Figure 9-7). It is much easier to recall Charlie Chaplin's commuters rushing for a train juxtaposed with a herd of sheep in *Modern Times* (1936) than to remember how, in Jean Renoir's *Grand Illusion* (1937), the camera movement created — in mise-en-scène style — the relationships between the men putting on the show in the prison camp.

9-7 The difference between mise-en-scène and montage images is visible in these two shots. In the montage shot, from the shower murder sequence in *Psycho* (Alfred Hitchcock, 1960), very little meaning can be gathered from this one image selected from the seventy-eight that make up the sequence. The character is clearly in the shower, but the opaque shower curtain cuts off any depth to the image, thus isolating the figure against a flat background. The viewer needs to see the images which come before and after to understand the relationship between the visible figure and the shadow behind the curtain. On the other hand, the image from *Citizen Kane* (Orson Welles, 1941), is extremely complete. The frame is full of information: in the foreground, the medicine bottle nearly empty suggests overdose; in the middle plane, Susan's figure on the bed, her face in shadow, suggests the deep sleep of death and recalls Kane's shadow as he towered over her earlier; and Kane himself, coming through the door in the deep background, reminds the viewer of his role in Susan's suicide attempt. Because information in all planes of the image is visible, the relationships between the planes can be seen.

Because most films combine montage and mise-en-scène or invisible editing styles, the student can contrast the use of both in a single film. A film like Michael Ritchie's *Smile* (1975), for instance, depicts a small-town beauty pageant, using both techniques for their respective effects. Mise-en-scène predominates, giving the film a realistic, semidocumentary atmosphere. Yet the film also uses montage sequences to make intellectual points and to create **satire;** short, rapidly cut shots of contestants responding with the same clichés to judges' questions are funny and thought-provoking. The student who chooses to write about the editing in a given film must be alert to the different editorial methods being employed and attempt to show how they work and what they mean. The dissolve, for example, is recognized in this excerpt from a student paper, which discusses Buster Keaton's *Go West* (1925).

> Keaton needs to show the time elapsing during a
> cross-country train ride. To compress time, he uses
> a series of dissolves on a sausage that show the
> meat slowly shrinking. The sausage is the only food
> Keaton has with him on the freight train, and its
> disappearance through the dissolves very tersely
> and effectively represents the long train ride.

In addition to addressing particular editorial techniques and devices, a paper on editing might also focus on the manipulation of time and/or space in a film. Editing controls these two basic aspects of film form. Time can be compressed or expanded or reshuffled into nonchronological arrangement. Space can be extended or abridged, can be relatively continuous or highly fragmented. The rhythms and mood of a film can also be established through the patterns of editing and this may serve as a good focal point for a paper. Films often strike the viewer as exciting or boring, lyrical or staccato in tempo and this response is most often primarily influenced by the rhythm of the editing.

Editing always conveys some kind of information about the film's intent and focus. If the editing is natural and unobtrusive, it tells the viewer to watch the other filmic elements. If the editing is, on the other hand, conspicuous, it has — or should have — a particular significance. Again, there are questions the viewer might ask about the editing in a particular film, before actually beginning to write a paper about the subject.

1. Was the editing noticeable?
2. If the editing was not noticeable, was it traditional invisible editing in service to the narrative? Or was it mise-en-scène, using camera movement and long takes to establish editorial relationships?
3. In those scenes in which the editing was noticeable, was it used as a signal, a signpost of something important?
4. Did the editing create meaning? How?
5. Did the editing contract or expand or distort chronological time? How?
6. What rhythm did the film have and how did the editing contribute?
7. What are some of the reasons the filmmaker might have had for editing the film the way he did?

Sound
Sound in a film falls into four categories: spoken dialogue and **narration, sound effects,** music, and silence. All of the aural elements in a film may

be used simultaneously or individually to create aesthetic effects and convey information about the film's content. All are as subject to editing as is the visual image. Sound can be **synchronous** with the onscreen image (source sound) or it can be **asynchronous.** It can have a temporal and spatial relationship coincident with the images on the screen, or it can evoke another time and space. It can be used to authenticate the images, lending credibility to what the viewer sees, creating an extension of the world seen in the frame into off-screen space, or it can make the images seem unreal, fantastic. It can change the entire tone of a scene, causing the viewer to regard the visual images on the screen ironically, comically, nostalgically, tragically, or romantically. Sound can subtly support what is in the frame, so that one is hardly aware of hearing it, or it can loudly contradict and act contrapuntally to what is seen, creating tension or humor or irony. The tension of a ski race in *Downhill Racer* (Michael Ritchie, 1969) is, in part, created by sound as this student paper demonstrates:

> The viewer is constantly reminded of the presence of the crowd by effective dubbing of the spectators' cheers. Cutting from cheers to silence to the sound of skis on snow and back to cheers on the sound track heightens the suspense of the race and helps to produce in the audience the drive and concentration that all competitors feel.

Certain films seem to lend themselves particularly to a discussion of sound not merely as technique but also as contributing to meaning. Indeed, a film like Francis Ford Coppola's *The Conversation* (1974) and Brian DePalma's *Blow Out* (1982) are about the creative and dangerous aspects of sound. And in Ingmar Bergman's appropriately titled *The Silence* (1963), a film about the difficulty of human communication, both sound and silence combine to convey the film's theme aurally as well as visually. In one scene, for example, the little boy Johann walks down the empty corridors of the decaying hotel in which he is staying and there is absolute silence — no footfalls, no background noise of any kind (Figure 9-8). The effect produced creates a sense of isolation and (despite the space on the screen) claustrophobia, communicating the psychic states of the film's central characters.

Here are some questions the viewer might answer before deciding to write a paper about the sound in a film.

1. Was the sound noticeable? (Did the viewer pay more than usual attention to it?)
2. What kinds of sound were used in the film? What were their separate functions?

9-8 In Ingmar Bergman's appropriately titled *The Silence* (1963), both sound and silence combine to convey the film's theme aurally as well as visually. In one scene, the little boy Johann walks down the empty corridors of a decaying hotel and there is absolute silence. The camera, mounted on the ceiling, looks down on the boy as he pauses before walking away from the camera down another corridor, making the boy almost an abstract part of the rug's pattern.

3. Did the sound support or complement the image? Was it synchronous or asynchronous? Did it authenticate the image or invalidate it?
4. Was sound at any time isolated, distorted, heightened, or obscured? If so, to what purpose?
5. Did sound serve as a transitional device? What images and/or scenes did it link and how did it function?
6. Was silence used to any special effect?
7. Was the use of sound of more than average importance to the film?

What to Write About: Multiple Films and Extrafilmic Issues

Thus far, this chapter has explored the various possibilities for paper topics involving one film, its content and form. This emphasis on the single work of art allows even the student with the most limited cinematic experience to write successfully about a film. This methodology rightly focuses attention on the experience of the work itself — not on other films, not on the film's place in film history or its place in a general historical and social context, not on its relation to other art forms.

Other critical positions, however, can be taken toward the film experience and the writing of a paper about film. Nearly all students have seen not just one film, but many. It is therefore natural and automatic that comparisons will be made between films, that films will be related to extrafilmic experience both personal and historical, and that films will be grouped together on the basis of their similarities of content and form.

Thinking about films in relation to each other and to personal and extrafilmic experience can give rise to fascinating questions, many of them answerable within the context of a written paper. The viewer may ask: Why do Alfred Hitchcock's films almost always sustain my interest? What is horror — and are horror films really horrifying? Why were there so many lavish musicals made during the Depression when people did not have jobs? What makes explicit violence and sex such a box office draw? Although it comes with different titles, stars, dialogue, and budgets, why do we go to see what seems to be the same movie again and again? All of these questions are best discussed with reference to several films. All of them imply relationships between films, between film and history, film and society, and film and the viewer's own personal cinematic history.

COMPARISON AND CONTRAST

Although most students have seen many movies, some may have seen only a handful of extremely popular contemporary films and whatever films are shown in class. A student who has not seen a great many movies may feel uncomfortable in trying to relate films to history, to cultural trends, or to film genres. The easiest and usually the most successful approach for such a student is to compare and contrast two films recently seen. That way the writer need not make any large generalizations that cannot be supported from firsthand viewing experience.

If an instructor's assignment is very specific — a list of topics such as "Compare the editing patterns in Eisenstein's *Potemkin* with those in Pudovkin's *Mother*" or "Select any two westerns seen this term and discuss the nature of the hero" — there is no problem. But if the student is required to select two films for comparison, then be certain that there are enough common elements to make the comparison sensible rather than farfetched. There is no sense in comparing a Marx Brothers film with *Citizen Kane*. Films do not have to be extremely similar or diametrically different to be suitable for a comparison, but they do have to have a reason for being compared. Since all films use light, for example, it is fairly safe to discuss lighting in any two films. A better and more selective focus would be to discuss the lighting in two horror films, because both films seek to elicit the same response in the viewer. Or one could discuss the lighting in two films directed by the same person or produced by the same studio. In each case, the range of discussion has narrowed, and the particular selection of the two films seems reasonable, the comparison for a purpose.

If the selection of films for comparison is appropriate and the focus is narrow enough, the variety of possible comparison-contrast papers is immense. One could compare the variations on a well-known plot using *Raiders of the Lost Ark* (Steven Spielberg, 1981) and *Romancing the Stone* (Robert Zemeckis, 1984). One could discuss the treatment of a common theme — the distinction between illusion and reality, for instance — in Ingmar Bergman's *Persona* (1967) and Luis Buñuel's *That Obscure Object of Desire* (1977). Any of the formal elements of film — editing, camera movement, composition, sound — are fair game for selective comparison. Social attitudes toward crime revealed in two gangster films of the 1930s might be interesting to compare — as would be the same attitudes revealed in two films from two eras.

One of the most intriguing and frequently assigned comparison-contrast topics treats a film adapted from some previous work of art, say a novel or a play or even an earlier film. Because the writer of a paper on **adaptation** is dealing with two works — the film and the source from which it was made — the most convenient form the paper can take is comparative, the identification of like and unlike things in the film and in its source. Essentially, comparing a film adaptation to its source raises basic theoretical issues about the nature of the film medium and its unique qualities that allow it to function better than or less well than other media. Some of the issues the writer might wish to focus on (and, again, one or two at most should be selected for a short paper) are: How are interior states of being communicated in both media? How and where does action occur in each? What is omitted or added in the adaptation process? Do the themes of the works differ or are they the same? This thesis statement from a student paper shows one specific focus a paper on adaptation might take.

> In Slaughterhouse Five, Kurt Vonnegut said,
> "Life is just a collection of moments." He went on
> to demonstrate this statement in his novel through
> the time transitions made by the main character,
> Billy Pilgrim, from one moment to the next. In the
> book, these transitions were instantaneous and
> made with great ease. Translation of the book into

```
a movie, however, caused unusual transitional
problems that demanded the director and editor find
new and effective means to convey the character's
time tripping.
```

Generally, the least interesting papers on adaptation pit one work against the other as if they were enemies; the writer then proceeds to take sides and judges one work better than the other. A much more productive and interesting way to deal with adaptation is to see each work as valid in itself; the comparison is being made not to settle a contest, but to raise and clarify questions about the nature of the two media. Thus, Anthony Burgess's novel and Stanley Kubrick's adaptation of *A Clockwork Orange* (1972) can be seen not as competitors but as complementary and different works of art. Similarly, Carlos Saura's *Carmen* (1984) is Bizet's opera and it is also something quite different.

Any comparison paper begins, of course, with at least two works. But one can add more titles and make comparisons within a larger group. What follows are suggested groupings of films into categories around which the student might shape a paper topic. Although the form of the paper will usually be less clearly structured than a comparison-contrast between two films, it will still depend upon choosing a topic that makes worthwhile the discussion of the films together.

GENRE GROUPINGS

Film genres are groups of films linked by similar subject matter, plotting, **conventions** of action and dialogue, and the use of particular objects, landscapes, and costumes, which through their familiarity take on **iconic** significance. Genres are also most usually *popular* films seen by a lot of people representative of the culture at large. The genres most clearly defined in terms of form and content and the ones most written about as genres are the western, the horror film, the science fiction film, the gangster film, the musical, and the adventure film. Within such genres other smaller groupings of film arise: the caper film (a kind of gangster film), the disaster film (a kind of adventure film), the suspense film (a kind of horror film).

Film genres are the most obvious groupings for a paper concerning multiple films (Figure 9-9). The writer can focus on the identifying marks of an established genre (**formula** plots, conventions, icons) or attempt to do the same for a less well-known grouping. Or, one can focus on a specific element of a genre — the western hero, the use of landscape, the theme of west vs. east — and use several westerns to illustrate similarities, differences, and/or the evolution of these elements.

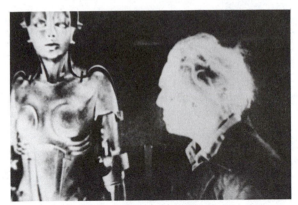

9-9 Fritz Lang's *Metropolis* (1926) might suggest a variety of papers that could be written about film groupings. It might be a part of a study of German expressionism, a look at the science fiction genre, an auteur study of Lang, or an examination of the historical and political climate of pre-Nazi Germany.

AUTEUR GROUPINGS

The **auteur** of a film is the film artist or personality whose force of vision or charismatic qualities dominate and structure the finished work. Initially, it was thought that only a **director** could be an auteur, but now critics speak of auteurism in relation to performers, **screenwriters,** cinematographers, and editors.

An auteur grouping of films is a natural way to link films. There is no need to explain why the films are being discussed as a group if they are all films by Alfred Hitchcock, if they all star Bette Davis, if they are all written by Dudley Nichols, if they are all shot by James Wong Howe or edited by Dede Allen. Thus, instead of spending a great deal of time and space explaining why the films are being grouped, the bulk of an auteur paper will focus on describing similarities of form and content in the work of a single film artist. One could write, for example, about John Ford's use of landscape in his many westerns, or one could shift the emphasis slightly and discuss the way in which Ford's landscapes accentuate his basic theme of man against the wilderness. One might look at a number of Hitchcock films in order to isolate his thematic concerns with guilt and authority, or to point out his skillful use of objective and subjective point of view to create audience identification and anxiety.

Again, it is advisable to narrow the focus to a single area, deciding in advance whether to concentrate on an auteur's editing or imagery or whatever. Too broad a focus will result in a paper far too general to be illuminating.

CONTEXTUAL GROUPINGS

The context of a film or group of films can include such broad areas as economic, social, and political history and such narrow areas as the role of women portrayed in 1950s family melodramas. Although it is possible (and sometimes even preferable) to discuss a single film in relation to contextual matters, most student writing about extrinsic issues relevant to film generally concerns a number of films. It is easier and safer to make sociological and political observations about films when talking about a group of films that show a trend of some sort, or that reveal the particular concerns of a culture at a given time. Writing about film and its relation to the world seems most successful when it deals with several films.

Because a film depends on a mass audience, it can often tell us something about the society that produced it: the attitudes prevalent toward certain subject matter, standards of normality, and morality. Because large numbers of people attend movies, social commentators have wondered to what extent the screen image affects the viewer. They have asked the question: Do films of a particular time in a particular place reflect the society or does the society respond to the influence of the films it sees? Although the answer to this question is debatable, the question points out the close relationship that exists between film and everyday life. This relationship can be the starting point for a paper that focuses on a selected area of this relationship (Figure 9-10).

A sociological analysis of film is always concerned with history — time and its passage and the changes it brings about. One may group films together to indicate some theory or to raise questions: What does the depiction of sex and violence tell us about ourselves as a nation? Do political films raise revolutionary consciousness, reflect something that already exists in the body politic, or are they really maintaining the status quo by substituting movie action for real action? Do pornographic films spur the latent sex criminal to overt action, or do they serve as a cathartic that keeps the potential offender off the streets and in the theater? One may observe a group of films and intelligently speculate on this relationship to the attitudes and emotional stresses of people at the time the films were made. Relating film to social and political history is a fascinating occupation, but one should recall that the generalizations offered, however plausible, cannot be proved. One cannot, for example, *prove* that people in the 1930s went to see James Cagney and Edward G. Robinson in gangster films because the very popular film genre perverted the Horatio Alger myth of American get-up-and-go and thus satisfied people's secret lack of faith in the American way of life. Certainly an analysis of gangster films and of the short and scrappy actors who

9-10 Contextual papers might investigate the relationship between the values represented in a film and the time when the film was released. Commentators have suggested, for example, that a film like *Raiders of the Lost Ark* (Steven Spielberg, 1981), despite its escapist entertainment-genre surface, exhibits conservative political attitudes held by the recently elected Reagan administration and which were present in the body politic at the time: American superiority over third-world countries, anti-Arab sentiments, anti-feminist views, and fundamentalist beliefs.

played their protagonists could offer such a thesis, which could be explored with supportive detail from the films, relating it to the Depression and other social realities of the times. Such a thesis is, however, impervious to proof; one could pose any number of other reasons for the films' success, some of which might contradict the one already suggested. The best sociologically oriented papers explore an issue by looking at a variety of potential alternatives.

Before assuming too patly that a film reflects the culture of which it is a part, one can check the assumption by studying the evidence offered by documents such as newspapers. D. W. Griffith's *The Birth of a Nation* (1915), for instance, gives a one-sided portrayal of blacks during the Reconstruction period after the Civil War, but before we assume that Griffith's view was the common view of the period, we should study the accounts of the reception of the film in newspapers of the time. Such a study will reveal that many reviewers strongly objected to Griffith's picture of blacks.

Films that deal overtly with social problems can also tell us much about changes in social attitudes over a period of time. The cinema's changing treatment of racial or ethnic prejudice, poverty, war, crime, capital punishment, alcoholism, drug addiction, and psychological disorders not only can reveal the social and historical context in which a film was made, but also can reveal to the contemporary viewer the history of an attitude. By watching a number of films made over a period of years dealing with alcoholism, for example, the student can see what is initially considered a bestial, if not criminal, habit turn into a disease, something for which its victims cannot be held morally responsible. Some films, however, do not display an evolving and progressive attitude toward socially relevant subject matter. This does not mean such films would not provide good material for a paper focusing on their *lack* of responsiveness to social changes. Some films about war, for example, may stress the horror and futility of mass aggression, while others made at the same time may underscore the honor involved in combat, the glory connected with the patriotic sacrifice of one's life for one's country. One has to look at the historical context of the particular films in question to arrive at any kind of intelligent analysis of the attitudes expressed: Was there a war going on at the time the film was made? Was it made after a war — or before one? What actual war was contemporaneous with the film? Was it generally thought of as a good war like World War II or a bad war like the Vietnamese war?

Films, particularly popular films, are inextricably intertwined with history, society, and politics, with a culture's ideology. The student who wishes to write a paper about some aspect relating film to culture must carefully narrow the focus as much as possible and must carefully select examples to support the speculations.

Research Papers

Although one may be required to do some research in connection with a short paper dealing with an individual film or group of films, generally the student will draw chiefly on her or his immediate experience of seeing the film and her or his memory of it. If, however, one chooses or is assigned to write about some aspect of the history of film, research is the essential first step.

Unfortunately, the films themselves are not often the student's primary resource material. Few students, for example, have seen enough early films to rely on their personal experience for the bulk of their source material. To write about the history and the development of film or about the history of a single film or film artist, one must use the library and its various source materials. The student must seek information in books; in memoirs and letters written by actors, directors, production people, and technicians; in biographies and autobiographies; and in newspaper stories, movie reviews, and magazine articles written at the time in which one is interested, histories of the cinema, and scholarly journals, which might have already printed material on the subject matter the student is researching. In the body of the paper, the student will organize and present material selected from the readings, combined with personal analysis of that material, appropriately citing sources through footnotes and a bibliography. (A section on manuscript preparation follows, but the student should consult a handbook like *The MLA Style Sheet* for detailed information and examples.)

The research paper ultimately depends on the careful selection and use of source material. But the evaluation, organization, and interpretation of that material is the student's own contribution to the paper. Indeed, a research paper can be creative from its inception, offering an interesting thesis that the research illustrates and supports. A paper which argues that MGM's success was largely due to the artistic control wielded by production head Irving Thalberg will be much more interesting to read than one which merely recounts the facts and figures surrounding that studio's eminence. A research paper should not be considered a dry demonstration of the student's ability to use the library and the correct annotations. Instead, the research paper should offer an interesting hypothesis, support it with evidence, and draw reasonable conclusions.

Manuscript Preparation

The material in this section — modified to reflect the differing subject matter — is taken from Sylvan Barnet's *A Short Guide to Writing About Literature*, 4th edition.[2]

The following suggestions can be taken as a guide for the preparation of the film paper unless your instructor specifies something different.

FORMAT
1. Use 8½ × 11 inch paper of good weight. Turn in the original, not a copy.
2. Write on one side of the page only. If you typewrite, double-space. If you submit a handwritten copy, use lined paper and write, in ink, on every other line if the lines are closely spaced.
3. Put your name and course number at the top of the first page. It is a good idea to put your last name on each page in case a page gets mixed in with other papers.
4. Give your essay a title rather than a number such as "Assignment No. 1." Place the title about 2 inches from the top of the

first page. Capitalize the first letter of the first and last words of your title and of all the other words except articles, conjunctions, and prepositions, thus:

The Light and the Dark in <u>Citizen Kane</u>

Notice that your title is neither underlined (indicating italics) nor enclosed in quotation marks, though material usually underlined or enclosed in quotation marks is so written, as is the film title in this example.

5.   Begin the essay an inch or two below the title. If your instructor prefers a title page, begin the text on the next page.
6.   Leave an adequate margin — an inch or an inch and a half — at top, bottom, and sides so that the instructor will have room for annotations.
7.   Number the pages consecutively, using arabic numerals.
8.   Fasten the pages in the upper left-hand corner with a paper clip or staple. Stiff binders, especially plastic, are unnecessary; indeed, they are a nuisance to the instructor, adding bulk and making it awkward to write annotations.
9.   Film titles like the titles of books are underlined (indicating italics). Do not use quotation marks.

REFERENCES

Avoiding Plagiarism

Though footnotes may sometimes be used to add material, which would not smoothly fit the movement of the paper, their primary function is to acknowledge the writer's debt to other sources for ideas that are not common knowledge. When in doubt about whether to give credit or not, do. Not to acknowledge such borrowing is plagiarism — the theft of another person's ideas. This means you must give credit not only for direct quotations, but also for an attitude, insight, or interpretation created by someone else. Suppose, for example, you come across Gerald Mast's statement in *The Comic Mind* that Fatty Arbuckle was "so quick on his feet he could outrace a matador." You cannot use these words without giving credit to Mast. Nor can you retain the idea but alter the words, say, to "Arbuckle was so nimble he could run faster than a matador," presenting the idea as your own, for here you are simply lifting Mast's idea. If you want to use Mast's point, give him credit, using his exact words within quotation marks. Following the new MLA guidelines for citations, you need only place the author's name and the page reference in parentheses after the quoted material:

> ```
> It is hard to believe that such a fat man was "so
> quick on his feet he could outrace a matador" (Mast
> 35).
> ```

Or if you mention the author in your sentence, you only place the page number in parentheses:

> ```
> As Mast said, Fatty Arbuckle was "so quick on his
> feet he could outrun a matador" (35).
> ```

If you wish to use an idea that appears in a longer passage, do not quote the entire passage, but summarize the idea and give the author credit. For instance, if you have read Stanley Cavell's book *The World Viewed* and want to use his idea that familiar stage character types are transformed into a whole new set of equally familiar film types, you might write: The Private Eye, the School Marm, the Swashbuckling Sea Captain, as Stanley Cavell points out, are only a few of the new types that film created from the old types found in popular theater (228).

Citing references in the body of a paper has been much simplified with this new system. Always mention the author's name, either in the sentence or in the parentheses, and the page reference. The complete publication information of the source — title, volume, publisher, and so forth — will be available to your reader in a list at the end of your paper under "Works Cited" (which replaces the old Bibliography). Simply follow common sense to avoid confusion. If you are using two sources by the same author, devise short forms of the titles of each book, e.g. (Mast, *History* 348), (Mast, *Mind* 173). If you have found two different sources whose authors have the last name, use a first initial, e.g. (J. Smith 62), (F. Smith 465). If the reference goes over several pages include them, e.g. (213–4), (162–83).

WORKS CITED

"Works Cited" is a list of works refered to in the piece of writing. Placed at the end on a separate page, "Works Cited" is arranged alphabetically by author; the author's last name is given first. If a work is by more than one author, it is alphabetized under the first author's name; the last name is given first, but the other authors' names are given in normal order. Put a period after the author's name, a period after the title of a book, and at the end of each entry. Page numbers are not given for books, though the page numbers that an essay spans in a journal or a book are included. Begin the entry flush with the left-hand margin and indent subsequent lines if an entry is long. Single space each entry and double space between entries. Here are some samples.

Butler, Ivan. <u>The Horror Film</u>. Cranbury, NJ: A. S. Barnes, 1967.

Dillard, R. H. W. "Even a Man Who Is Pure at Heart." In <u>Man and the Movies</u>. Ed. W. R. Robinson. Baton Rouge: Louisiana State University Press, 1967, 129–74.

Gifford, Denis. <u>Movie Monsters</u>. New York: Dutton, 1969.

Kinder, Marsha, and Beverle Houston. "<u>Rosemary's Baby</u>," <u>Sight and Sound</u>, 28 (Winter 1968–1969): 17–19.

Sypher, Wylie. "The Meanings of Comedy." In <u>Comedy</u>. Ed. Sypher. Garden City, NY: Doubleday, 1956, 193–255.

Helpful Hints for Writing Papers

SOME THINGS TO AVOID

1. *Do not* recount the entire plot of a film. Writing about what happens in film rather than what the film means or how its effects are achieved is *not* criticism. Summarize the plot in a sentence or two: "*Shane* is a western that concerns an ex-gunfighter who helps a family of sodbusters in a range war." Then, selectively use plot incidents to clarify, illustrate, and solidify points within the body of the paper.

2. *Do not* write generally about an entire film. In a short paper you cannot cover the acting, directing, editing, lighting, sound, and so forth and say anything significant. Focus on a single element and explore it as thoroughly as you can. It is better to exhaust an idea than to flit from one idea to another.

3. *Avoid* words like "great," "good," "effective," "emotional," "well-done," and "interesting" as simple adjectives in phrases like: "The use of location was very effective," or "Light was used in a very interesting way." Statements like these strung out on a page fill up the white space but do not say anything. If these words are used at all, they must be immediately qualified by more specific information, and supported by concrete details. In what way was the location used? And why was it effective? How was light used? What did it have to do with the story or characters that made it interesting?

4. *Do not* use examples from the films just to let the instructor know you have seen the film or because you merely want to pepper the paper with examples. Make sure the examples are relevant to the point you are making. Once the example is located in context to the rest of the film (for example, the scene

when the gunfighter first comes to town), be as selective and specific as possible with that material which relates to your argument.

5. *Do not* leave gaps in your thought and in the logical development of your paper. Be sure that your argument moves coherently and with appropriate transitions from point A to point B to point C. Do not move about from point A to point K back to point B or omit the interim points. Do not expect the reader to think the way you think or to fill in the gaps for you.

SOME THINGS TO DO

1. *Do* focus on a particular and relatively narrow topic suitable to the length of your assigned paper. Have a thesis — a one-sentence summation of what your paper is about — clearly in mind before beginning to write. Make sure the paper has a function: argue with a critical position, make a statement, and prove it.

2. *Do* use specific examples from the films to illustrate your points. Be precise and accurate in describing your example. General assertions such as "The acting was awful," "The cinematography was breathtaking," or "The editing was monotonous" have no validity without support by examples from the film(s) under discussion.

3. *Do* take the writing of the paper seriously. Consider that most instructors take time and effort to read and annotate your work. Regard your own mind and time as too valuable to waste simply filling up pages with bland material.

4. *Do* try to be imaginative in relation to your material. This does not mean inventing material simply for originality's sake, but it does mean that your views, your intuition, your insights can be valuable.

5. *Do* check your paper carefully for typographical errors, errors in grammar, and the like before turning it in. Finish the paper in advance if possible and put it aside. Proofread it a day later, and you may well be able to spot any inconsistencies in logic or any other problems not apparent in the heat of composition. For some people, reading the paper aloud is a helpful way to detect errors.

Student Papers

Several sample student papers follow. One draws a parallel between film form and content, showing how the alternating pattern of sound and silence reveals aspects of a protagonist's character. One describes the characteristics of a particular genre by focusing on a specific film which set the pattern for that genre. One examines the social and cultural context in which cult films operate using a single film as detailed example. This paper also quotes from research material. The papers were all written by students in introductory film classes. They are not completely free of problems and mistakes, but their success should be both relevant and encouraging to the student who is first beginning to write papers about film.

Focused title States topic.

SOUND AND SILENCE IN CITIZEN KANE

Citizen Kane is a masterful cinematic look at both the public life and the private life of the flamboyant main character, Charles Foster Kane. The film is almost universally lauded for the skill with which the director (Orson Welles) interwove the content and the form to create a synthesis of theme and style which epitomized all that had gone before. As part of his creative manipulations of cinematic form and technique, Welles used the sound in the movie to sharpen the contrast between the exterior and interior sides of Kane. Throughout the film, the scenes depicting Kane's public life are accompanied by upbeat tempos, rapid-fire dialogue, and generally loud volume levels; the scenes revealing his private life are underscored by slow, brooding tempos, echo-chamber dialogue, and much quieter volume levels -- even silence.

Moves from the general to the specific: thesis is implicit.

The film opens like a classic horror movie: the camera slowly approaches a dark castle on a hill at night, while somber, funereal strains of music set the mood of sinister foreboding. The camera eventually targets one of the few rooms in the castle that is lit. Once inside the room, the music stops abruptly and a moment of dead silence is broken by a man's last word: "Rosebud." This short but suspense-building moment of silence serves not only to ensure the viewer's rapt attention, but also to offer the first inkling of the utter emptiness and isolation that characterized so much of Kane's life. It is ironic that, even though it appears Kane died totally alone (no one else was in the room at the time), his final word would eventually be widely known and in fact become the focal point of a search to discover what Charles Foster Kane was all about. Again, the silence accompanying Kane's death is shattered by the rousing introduction to a newsreel clip on Kane's life. The announcer's voice blares facts about Kane's life over a melodramatic musical background. The clamor and din of the newsreel set the pattern for the way Kane's

Connection made between the silence of certain moments in the film and the emptiness of Kane's emotional life.

public life will be treated in the rest of the film.

The scenes showing Kane in the crowded office of the Inquirer are very lively and aurally complex; Bernstein, Leland, and Kane constantly interrupt each other and everyone else who tries to talk to them. They must yell to be heard over the dancing girls Kane hired to celebrate the Inquirer's success. Kane's gubernatorial election rally is punctuated by wild cheering and applause. Susan's short-lived opera career is summarized in a whirlwind montage of her screeching high notes, her voice teacher's yelling, and the orchestra's relentless minor and diminished chords.

> Loud passages of film are contrasted with quiet ones, furthering the main point.

Contrast these loud scenes with their private side counterparts. When Kane signs his declaration of principles, there is a brief lull in the usual bustle of the newspaper office, as if to signal that we are now being made privy to a more intimate facet of Kane. After his defeat in the election, Kane's talks with Leland in muted tones, with no interrupting, and we get a glimpse of what their friendship is really like. Following Susan's attempted suicide, Kane sits in absolute silence at her bedside waiting for her to recover, and when she does, finally relents and allows her to quit her singing.

> Metaphor of Kane as a "thunderer" in his public life is explored.

It is interesting to note how often thunder is heard throughout the film. Perhaps this represents Kane's megalomanic view of himself. Indeed, as Geddes is leaving Susan's apartment after delivering his ultimatum, Kane thunders, "I am Charles Foster Kane!" The whole of Kane's public life was accompanied by noise; everything he did he did to attract attention, to make the masses listen to him and hear what he had to say. But he, himself, would rarely stop and listen to what others were saying to him. His ideal audience would resemble his vast collection of statues -- always there, always attentive, but never able to think on their own or talk back to him.

> Again contrast is made between loudness of public scenes and private scenes in the film, linking noise and volume levels with the state of the character.

When Kane takes Susan on a picnic, they remain in their tent while the guests sing and party around them. As Susan raises her voice to Kane, he impatiently orders her to keep it down so the guests will not hear. This Kane is a far cry from the thundering opinion molder that his public side had cultivated. Whereas before he spurned what people would think of him because (as he told his first wife) "People will believe what I tell them to believe," now he is concerned about what a handful of oblivious guests will think if they hear them arguing. It was Bernstein who remarked that Kane "lost everything he had." Perhaps nowhere is this loss

better symbolized in the film than in this scene --
Kane had lost even his ability to "make noise," to
thunder out his views and ideals at others and make
them hear and agree.

The later years of Kane's life were spent far
away from the din of New York City, in his never-
finished palace called Xanadu. What few words were
spoken in the massive rooms and empty corridors
echoed hollowly, emphasizing the loneliness that
he experienced there, even while Susan was still
around. The whole tone of the film changes to reflect this loneliness. Whereas the first part of
the film was cheerful, jubilant, and full of noise,
the last part is somber, muted, and very quiet.

Conclusion restates thesis effectively and extends point about sound and silence to cover total reading of film. Film technique creates meaning.

This masterful manipulation of sound in Citizen
Kane is a subtle but effective way in which Welles
heightened the contrast between Kane's public life
and his private life. It is significant that Thompson was unable to discover the meaning of "Rosebud," because a man's life is too complex and mul-
tifaceted to be summarized in one word. And even
after the shouting and clamor of Kane's public life
died down, his inner self remained largely a mystery, shrouded in silence, and lost somewhere in
the decaying reverberations of Xanadu.

Straightforward title.

Opening makes good general points about the history of genres...

but final sentence should state that the paper will focus on The Maltese Falcon as proto- type of detective genre.

THE DETECTIVE GENRE

The making of a film with all of its components was,
and still is, a difficult task. Once films that
appealed to popular tastes had been produced, filmmakers discovered that the easiest way to sell a
picture and produce it rapidly was to imitate a recent success. There was little to do but repeat and
vary. The early 1920s saw the birth of this cycle.
Films that emerged because of the requirements of
mass production and their popularity, and had a
recognizable pattern, form what is called a genre.
Even though most films of a particular genre are
exceptional, it is generally true that the first,
the prototype, is the strongest and the best of all
these.

A genre, then, is a class or group of films that
contain similar characteristics, themes, plots,
and form. These films follow preset patterns of
narration and have stereotypical characters and
settings. An individual film need not contain all
of the elements of its genre, but enough that it can
be classified with the others. Each film, therefore, is a model or example of others in its genre.
Because of this, one particular member of a genre
may appear to be very familiar when seen, as if it
had been seen before.

Detective genre is shown to share characteristics of other genres.

The detective genre, like other genres, portrays a single concept of society rather than a true picture of life as a whole. This aspect of life is presented, however, as if life consisted of nothing more, giving the film a certain flatness. The aspect most common to the detective genre is greed or death. The study of the detective genre, as the study of any genre, can be divided into formula plots, conventions, icons, and stereotypical characters.

The concept of a formula plot can be thought of as a recipe for making a film. The formula of a detective film is surprisingly simple and is, almost without exception, the same. A person or group of persons hire a detective to locate a lost or missing object or person. The quest becomes complicated due to the nature of the object or person. During the course of the movie, the detective is caught by people opposing his goal. The detective takes that chance to ask his captor about the unclear details of the story, knowing that he will escape later.

Specific elements of the detective genre formula plot are elaborated.

The typical detective film ends with a meeting, in one form or another, with the principle characters involved. This is when the whole story with all its details is explained by the detective, the object or person is found, and the guilty are revealed. The Maltese Falcon has a similar plot.

The plot of a genre is unfolded and visualized through the use of conventions. Conventions are units of action, sometimes called episodes or scenes. The specific details of a convention are not identical, but vary from film to film. In this way suspense is created and the interest of the public is retained. The final meeting of all characters that was previously mentioned is an example. This scene, as portrayed in the detective film The Maltese Falcon is a classic example of variation. The missing parts of the story are all put together by the detective Sam Spade, played by Humphrey Bogart, and lead to only one other character, who is also the guilty party.

Detective genre conventions are presented and shown to be found in the prototype film.

The smallest item that has any specific meaning in a genre film is called an icon. An icon can be a sound, a scene, an object, clothing, an action, dialogue, or even a character. An icon can signify merely by its appearance a whole mood or environment. Icons get their special meaning from their repeated use in the same context in film after film. The Maltese Falcon has some excellent examples of the icons in detective films. Typical of the men involved in a detective film is their manner of dress: the long trench coat with upturned collar and bulging pockets, the dark suit and the

Icons of the genre are defined and examples from The Maltese Falcon are explored.

hat with the brim turned down on one side. The frequent scene of Wilmer leaning against a wall or reading a paper to hide his face is typical of someone trailing another person. The handgun is another icon of the detective film.

Stereotypical characters of the genre are enumerated in general and in the specific film under discussion.

The detective film has its share of stereotypical characters. Characters with flat personalities who represent a class of people, rather than real people with complex personalities. They are characterized by their dress or role in the film. The detective will usually have a partner whose powers do not match those of himself. The secretary of Sam Spade plays this role in <u>The Maltese Falcon</u>. This is Dr. Watson in the Sherlock Holmes films and the son of Charlie Chan in those films. The crook always has one, if not more, bungling do it men (Wilmer). Quite frequently, the actors who portray these stereotypical characters become the characters they portray in the minds of the movie public. These, then, become icons, whose mere presence tells exactly what character they will play. Humphrey Bogart as Sam Spade and Basil Rathbone as Sherlock Holmes are examples.

Conclusion repeats the basic elements found in the detective genre.

We have seen that the detective film follows a formula plot that has been used many times over in other detective films. This formula is visualized by conventions that vary to add interest and suspense. Particular items, called <u>icons</u>, are repeatedly used to create moods or tell untold stories. And stereotypical characters are used in the stories. These factors combine to relate one film to another in the detective genre, and although the film itself may die, the detective genre never will.

Title announces topic.

THE CHANGING ROLE OF THE CULT FILM

Clear statement of thesis and elaboration indicate direction of essay.

Originally an out-branching of the avant-garde film movement, cult films have arguably become a separate genre. Where simple genre films, such as westerns and musicals, aimed at and adhered to the heart of American values, the basic form of the cult film is to undermine, pervert, or at least be the catalyst for a personal inspection of those values. Undeniably, there are those cult films that try to do nothing more than be unquieting, even gross. But the aim of these films is not unlike the aim of many of the Marx Brother's comedies of the 1930s: to question and shake middle class values.

Probably the most infamous of the midnight movies is <u>The Rocky Horror Picture Show</u>. Released in the mid-1970s, this tale of Transylvanian, transsexual, science fiction has created one of the

Focuses on a well-known example to prove thesis. Uses quote from written source to bolster argument.

most unique cult followings ever. Depending upon where the movie is seen and the fanaticism of the regulars, the film can range from merely offbeat entertainment to a total audience participatory "rite of intensification" (Hoberman 38). Utilizing props, costumes, counterpoint dialogue, and in New York, whole casts that mimic the characters during the film, Rocky Horror regulars have reached a new high in cultism.

Good, concise synopsis of plot.

In this film, a naive midwestern couple, Brad and Janet, attending a friend's wedding in a rural church, have decided to become engaged. On their way to inform their high school teacher, Dr. Scott, of their betrothal, car trouble forces them to seek shelter in the castle of the androgynous, yet un-deniably male, Dr. Frank N. Furter. The castle is the secret headquarters of aliens from the planet Transsexual. The couple arrives just before the ceremonial unveiling of Furter's newest Franken-steinish experiment, a handsome blond male named Rocky. Furter seduces both Brad and Janet, captures Dr. Scott when he comes to investigate for the gov-ernment, and is eventually murdered by his second in command, Riff-Raff. Lacking suspense, the plot is basically a parody of science fiction plotting. The movie's main concern is the characters' sexual practices; but neither human nor sexual excite-ment adequately explain Rocky Horror's staggering appeal.

Good use of quoted statistics.

With almost 10 years of Rocky Horror cultism gone by, the fervor has quieted some, and scholars have been able to evaluate this phenomena. Surveys have been administered to RHPS goers, and have shown that the audience is equally male and female, white, young, single, high school or college age, politically uncommited, and heavy consumers of mass media. Of those that claimed a religion, 50% were Catholic, and 21.2% were Protestants (Austin 463). So the question must be asked, Why do seem-ingly average, God-fearing young people feel the need to attend repeatedly performances of this dis-turbing and bizarre movie?

The answer lies not merely in the status associ-ated with the attendance of the film, but in the movie's similarity to a modern day rite of initia-tion, and the current sociocultural struggle re-sulting from the introduction of openly homosexual and bisexual roles as options.

The majority of Rocky Horror participation is verbal. There is a constant dialogue between par-ticipants and the movie, similar to that of a Re-vival Baptist priest and congregation. This so-called counterpoint dialogue is not promoted by or

Very detailed
discussion of
what happens at
screenings.

called for in the movie script. The dialogue is
sometimes designed to add to the humor of the film,
but more often to show familiarity with the film's
timing and cutting. These calls are not used to
vilify, or display anger toward the film, but to
show participation in and acceptance of the movie's
contemporary values. Many of the interjections are
aimed at the repressed, sexually straight Brad and
Janet, and the figure of authority, Dr. Scott.

Parallel between
general rituals
and cult films
as rituals made
clear with
quoted material.

    In his book Rites of Passage, psychologist
Arnold Van Gennep describes the psychological development of a person as, "a series of transitions
from one stage of psychosocial development to another, and from one socioeconomic role to another."
More simply, he describes people going through what
are more commonly referred to as "experimental
stages." He goes on to explain that each of these
transitions or passages is accompanied by ceremonial behavior, "whose essential purpose is to
enable the individual to pass from one defined
position to another which is equally well defined"
(3). Rocky Horror potentially functions as this
ceremony, or rite of intensification by restoring
social equilibrium where the laws of social interaction are changing. It allows for gradual
change in the individual, or acts merely as a release; a harmless act of temporary role playing.

Details of ritual
behavior make
parallel precise
and specific.

    Rocky Horror shares with other midnight movies
the aura of participating in some ritual or gather-
ing, late at night, when the city is asleep. Van
Gennep has noted that the sacred and the profane
share the same physical dimensions, and the difference is in the individual's perception. Therefore,
"ceremonies often occur at night, a natural, symbolic transition after the ritual death of (separation from) the old day, and before the birth of
(incorporation into) the new day" (xvii). Thus,
another possible aspect contributing to the appeal
of Rocky Horror.

Further examples
extend the
argument.

    Parallels to rites of passage are found through-
out The Rocky Horror Picture Show. Brad and Janet
upon entering Frank N. Furter's castle, are re-
lieved of their clothes, and given new (sacred?)
outfits like Furter's, consisting of stockings,
corsets, and high heels. This is reminiscent of the
purification ceremonies performed before rites of
passage. These are used to begin the individual's
separation (cleansing) from the profane, and begin
his or her transition. The transition itself takes
place that night when Frank N. Furter seduces both
Brad and Janet in separate scenes. In the end,
Frank N. Furter is killed by Riff-Raff, and as the
castle (actually a spaceship) blasts off back to

Transsexual, Brad, Jane, and Dr. Scott are left still attired in Transsexual clothing, suggesting that the characters have been permanently, if incompletely, changed by this experience.

The role of the Transsexuals as a race is clearly symbolic. The fact that they are aliens suggests the notion that they are like the human sexual deviants they parallel in our culture; they are treated as though they had descended from outer space, while they have actually arisen from our very heartland, and have always been a part of our society.

Concluding paragraph summarizes and restates thesis.

Despite the subject matter of The Rocky Horror Picture Show and other cult films, they do not necessarily indicate that society is headed for complete bisexuality. Some commentators have suggested that they indicate a current trend toward psychological androgeny. Brad and Janet's night at Frank N. Furter's castle forces them into new sexual identities, in which they participate in novel new roles. The ambiguity of these sexual identities parallels our present confusion of how the current sex–role evolution will be resolved. The amazing success of The Rocky Horror Picture Show points to the fact that the film's audiences are using these showings to express their pent–up anxieties and confusion brought about by this changing and unresolved conflict over modern values and sexuality.

WORKS CITED

Austin, Bruce A. Portrait of a Cult Film Audience: The Rocky Horror Picture Show. Journal of Communications 31 (1981) 450–65.

Hoberman, J. and Jonathan Rosenbaum. Midnight Movies. New York: Harper, 1983.

Van Gennep, Arnold. The Rites of Passage. Chicago: University Press, 1960.

SELECTED SOURCES FOR FURTHER READING

The following selection of reading materials is intended to help students enlarge their general knowledge of film history, theory, and criticism, and to aid them in discovering further source materials that may be of help in writing critical and research papers. It is not meant to be a basic bibliography and includes only a few volumes that focus on auteur studies, individual genres, or other specialized subjects. Some of this kind of material is cited in appropriate sections of the text. For an introduction to specialized subject matter and to theoretical texts, consult some of the anthologies listed below in which excerpts from such original sources have been reprinted. Consult the "Historical Overview" before Chapter 9 for books most frequently cited as the seminal works of film criticism. The bibliography is divided into several sections for convenience: Theory and Criticism, Film History, Contextual Criticism, Guides to Film Information, Selected Interviews with Filmmakers, Bibliographical Guides, and Film Periodicals.

THEORY AND CRITICISM

Andrew, Dudley J. *The Major Film Theories: An Introduction.* New York: Oxford University Press, 1976.

———. *Concepts in Film Theory.* New York: Oxford University Press, 1984.

Cadbury, William, and Leland Poague, *Film Criticism: A Counter-Theory.* Ames: Iowa State University Press, 1983.

Grant, Barry K., ed. *Film Genre: Theory and Criticism.* Metuchen, NJ: Scarecrow Press, 1977.

Kaminsky, Stuart. *American Film Genres: Approaches to a Critical Theory of Popular Film.* Dayton, Ohio: Pflaum, 1974.

Kaplan, E. Ann. *Women and Film: Both Sides of the Camera.* New York: Methuen, 1983.

Kuhn, Annette. *Women's Pictures: Feminism and Cinema.* London: Routledge, 1982.

MacCann, Richard Dyer, ed. *Film: A Montage of Theories.* New York: Dutton, 1966.

Mast, Gerald, and Marshall Cohen, eds. *Film Theory and Criticism: Introductory Readings,* 3rd ed. New York: Oxford University Press, 1985.

Nichols, Bill, ed. *Movies and Methods.* Berkeley: University of California Press, 1977.

Perkins, V. F. *Film as Film.* Baltimore: Penguin Books, 1972.

Schatz, Thomas. *Hollywood Genres.* New York: Random House, 1981.

Sitney, P. Adams, ed. *Film Culture Reader.* New York: Praeger, 1970.

————. *The Avant-Garde Film: A Reader of Theory and Criticism.* New York: New York University Press, 1978.

Wollen, Peter. *Signs and Meaning in the Cinema,* 2nd ed. New York: Viking, 1972.

FILM HISTORY

Allen, Robert C., and Douglas Gomery. *Film History: Theory and Practice.* New York: Alfred A. Knopf, 1985.

Balio, Tino, ed. *The American Film Industry.* Madison: University of Wisconsin Press, 1976.

Barnouw, Erik. *Documentary: A History of the Non-Fiction Film.* New York: Oxford University Press, 1974.

Bordwell, David, Janet Staiger, and Kristin Thompson. *The Classical Hollywood Cinema.* New York: Columbia U. Press, 1985.

Brownlow, Kevin. *The Parade's Gone By.* New York: Ballantine Books, 1968.

Ellis, Jack. *A History of Film.* Englewood Cliffs, NJ: Prentice-Hall, 1979.

Fell, John. *A History of Films.* New York: Holt, Rinehart and Winston, 1979.

Fielding, Raymond. *A Technological History of Motion Pictures and Television.* Berkeley: University of California Press, 1967.

Jacobs, Lewis, ed. *The Documentary Tradition: From Nanook to Woodstock.* New York: Hopkinson & Blake, 1971.

Jowett, Garth. *Film: The Democratic Art.* Boston: Little, Brown, 1976.

Knight, Arthur. *The Liveliest Art: A Panoramic History of the Movies,* rev. ed. New York: New American Library, 1979.

Mast, Gerald. *A Short History of the Movies,* 4th ed. New York: Bobbs-Merrill, 1986.

Sklar, Robert. *Movie-Made America: A Social History of the American Movies.* New York: Random House, 1975.

CONTEXTUAL CRITICISM

Alloway, Lawrence. *Violent America: The Movies 1946–1964.* New York: Museum of Modern Art, 1971.

Altman, Rick, ed. *Genre: The Musical.* Boston: Routledge, 1981.

Bluestone, George. *Novels into Film.* Berkeley: University of California Press, 1957.

Gluckman, Andre, ed. *Violence on the Screen.* Translated by Susan Bennett. London: British Film Institute, Education Department, 1971.

Harrington, John. *Film and/as Literature.* Englewood Cliffs, NJ: Prentice-Hall, 1977.

Jarvie, I. C. *Movies and Society.* New York: Basic Books, 1970.

MacBean, James Roy. *Film and Revolution.* Bloomington: Indiana University Press, 1975.

Sobchack, Vivian. *Screening Space: The American Science Fiction Film.* New York: Ungar, 1986.

Wright, Will. *Sixguns and Society: A Structural Study of the Western.* Berkeley: University of California Press, 1975.

GUIDES TO FILM INFORMATION

Aaronson, Charles S. *International Motion Picture and Television Almanac.* New York: Quigley Publications, 1930 — . Annual.

Ash, Réné. *The Motion Picture Film Editor.* Metuchen, NJ: Scarecrow Press, 1974.

Bawden, Liz-Anne, ed. *The Oxford Companion to Film.* New York: Oxford University Press, 1976.

Cawkwell, Tim, and John M. Smith. *The World Encyclopedia of Film.* New York: A & W Visual Library, 1972.

Corliss, Richard, ed. *The Hollywood Screenwriters.* New York: Avon, 1972.

———. *Talking Pictures: Screenwriters in the American Cinema.* New York: The Overlook Press, 1974.

Cowie, Peter, ed. *International Film Guide.* New York: A. S. Barnes, 1964 — . Annual.

Enser, A. G. S., ed. *Filmed Books and Plays: 1928–1974.* New York: Academic Press, 1974.

Film Daily Year Book of Motion Pictures. New York: Film Daily Publishers, 1918 — . Annual.

Gottesman, Ronald, and Harry M. Geduld. *Guidebook to Film: An Eleven-in-One Reference.* New York: Holt, Rinehart and Winston, 1972.

Halliwell, Leslie. *The Filmgoer's Companion*, 6th ed. New York: Hill and Wang, 1977.

————. *Halliwell's Film Guide: A Survey of 8,000 English-Language Movies.* London, New York: Granada Publishing, 1977.

Higham, Charles. *Hollywood Cameramen.* Bloomington: Indiana University Press, 1970.

Kozarski, Richard, ed. *Hollywood Directors, 1914–1940.* New York: Oxford University Press, 1976.

————. *Hollywood Directors, 1941–1976.* New York: Oxford University Press, 1977.

Krafsur, Richard, ed. *The American Film Institute Catalogue of Motion Pictures Produced in the United States: Feature Films 1961–1970.* New York: R. R. Bowker, 1976.

Manchel, Frank. *Film Study: A Resource Guide.* Rutherford, NJ: Fairleigh Dickinson University Press, 1973.

Manvell, Roger, and Lewis Jacobs, eds. *International Encyclopedia of Film.* New York: Crown, 1972.

Monaco, James. *Film: How and Where to Find Out What You Want to Know.* New York: Zoetrope, 1976.

Munden, Kenneth W., ed. *The American Film Institute Catalogue of Motion Pictures Produced in the United States: Feature Films 1921–1930*, 2 vols. New York: R. R. Bowker, 1971.

The New York Times Directory of the Film. New York: Arno Press, 1974.

The New York Times Film Reviews 1913–1968, 6 vols. New York: Arno Press, 1970.

Roud, Richard, ed. *A Critical Dictionary of the Cinema.* New York: Viking Press, 1977.

Sadoul, Georges. *Dictionary of Film Makers.* Translated and edited by Peter Morris. Berkeley: University of California Press, 1972.

————. *Dictionary of Films.* Translated and edited by Peter Morris. Berkeley: University of California Press, 1972.

Sarris, Andrew. *The American Cinema: Directors and Directions, 1929–1968.* New York: Dutton, 1968.

Sitney, P. Adams. *The American Avant-Garde.* New York: Oxford University Press, 1974.

Thomson, David. *A Biographical Dictionary of Film.* New York: Morrow, 1976.

SELECTED INTERVIEWS WITH FILMMAKERS

Baker, Fred, with Ross Firestone, ed. *Movie People: At Work in the Business of Film*. New York: Douglas Book Corp., 1972.

Geduld, Harry M., ed. *Filmmakers on Filmmaking*. Bloomington: Indiana University Press, 1969.

Gelmis, Joseph. *The Film Director as Superstar*. Garden City, NY: Doubleday, 1970.

Higham, Charles, and Joel Greenberg. *The Celluloid Muse: Hollywood Directors Speak*. New York: New American Library, 1972.

Kantor, Bernard R., Blacker, Irwin R., and Kramer, Anne, eds. *Directors at Work: Interviews with American Film-Makers*. New York: Funk & Wagnalls, 1970.

Levin, G. Roy. *Documentary Explorations: 15 Interviews with Film-Makers*. Garden City, NY: Doubleday, 1971.

Samuels, Charles Thomas, ed. *Encountering Directors*. New York: Putnam, 1972.

Sarris, Andrew, ed. *Interviews with Film Directors*. New York: Bobbs-Merrill, 1967.

Sherman, Eric, and Martin Rubin. *The Director's Event: Interviews with Five American Film-Makers*. New York: New American Library, 1972.

BIBLIOGRAPHICAL GUIDES

Aceto, Vincent J., Jane Graves, and Fred Silva. *Film Literature Index*. Albany, NY: Filmdex, Inc. Quarterly.

Batty, Linda. *Retrospective Index to Film Periodicals 1930–1971*. New York: R. R. Bowker, 1975.

Bowles, Stephen E., ed. *Index to Critical Film Reviews in British and American Film Periodicals, 1930–1972*. New York: Burt Franklin, 1975.

———. *Index to Critical Reviews of Books About Film, 1930–1972*. New York: Burt Franklin, 1975.

Bukalski, Peter J. *Film Research: A Critical Bibliography with Annotations and Essay*. Boston: G. K. Hall, 1972.

Gerlach, John C., and Gerlach, Lana. *The Critical Index*. New York: Teachers' College Press, 1974.

International Index to Film Periodicals (FIAF Index). New York: R. R. Bowker, 1972 — . Annual.

Kowalski, Rosemary Ribich. *Women and Film: A Bibliography*. Metuchen, NJ: Scarecrow Press, 1976.

Leonard, Harold, ed. *The Film Index: A Bibliography. Vol. 1. The Film as Art*, reprint ed. New York: Arno Press, 1966.

MacCann, Richard Dyer and Edward S. Perry. *The New Film Index: A Bibliography of Magazine Articles in English, 1930–1970*. New York: E. P. Dutton, 1974.

Monaco, James, and Susan Schenker, eds. *Books About Film: A Bibliographical Checklist*, 3rd ed. New York: Zoetrope, 1976.

Rehrauer, George. *Cinema Booklist*. Metuchen, NJ: Scarecrow Press, 1972. *Supplement One*, 1974. *Supplement Two*, 1976.

Schuster, Mel. *Motion Picture Directors: A Bibliography of Magazine and Periodical Articles, 1900–1969*. Metuchen, NJ: Scarecrow Press, 1973.

FILM PERIODICALS

American Film. (Monthly). American Film Institute, Kennedy Center, Washington, DC 20006.

Cineaste,. 333 Sixth Avenue, New York, New York 10014.

Cinema Journal. (Semiannual). Film Division, Northwestern University, Evanston, Illinois 60201.

Film Comment. (Bimonthly). Film Society of Lincoln Center, 1865 Broadway, New York, New York 10023.

Film Criticism. (Three issues a year). Box 825, Edinboro, Pennsylvania 16412.

Film Culture. G.P.O. Box 1449, New York, New York 10001.

Film Heritage. University of Dayton, Dayton, Ohio 45469.

Film Quarterly. University of California Press, Berkeley, California 94720.

Film Reader (Annual). Northwestern University Film Division, Evanston, Illinois 60201.

Journal of Film and Video. Department of Communication Arts and Sciences, Rosary College, River Forest, Illinois.

The Journal of Popular Film and Television. Popular Culture Center, Bowling Green State University, Bowling Green, Ohio 43403.

Jump Cut. (Bimonthly). 3138 West Schubert, Chicago, Illinois 60647.

Literature/Film Quarterly. Salisbury State College, Salisbury, Maryland 21801.

Quarterly Review of Film Studies. Redgrave Publishing Company, 430 Manville Road, Pleasantville, New York 10570.

Screen. 29 Old Compton Street, London W1V 5PL, England.

Sight and Sound. British Film Institute, 81 Dean Street, London W1V 6AA, England.

Take One. (Bimonthly). Unicorn Publishing, Box 1778, Station B, Montreal H3B, 3L3, Quebec, Canada.

Wide Angle. Box 388, Athens, Ohio 45701.

SELECTED FILM GLOSSARY

The following concise definitions are meant as either quick introductions or brief reminders. For further information, consult the index, which will refer you to the pages that give a fuller discussion. Whenever possible, we have used the definitions (or parts of definitions) published by the University Film Association (Monograph No. 2) as *Glossary of Film Terms* (University Film Association, 1978). Compiled by John Mercer, this thorough glossary draws upon a previous work published in 1955 by the University Film Producers Association. When our definitions are derived from the *Glossary of Film Terms*, they are followed by the letters *UFA;* when that *Glossary* uses the 1955 definitions, it appends the letters *UFPA*. Because the *Glossary* is much more extensive than ours and also more technical in some respects, occasionally we decided to simplify or to write new definitions more appropriate to this book. For more complete terminology, we urge the reader to write to the editor of the *Journal of Film and Video* for information about obtaining a copy of the *Glossary of Film Terms*. As the editorship changes hands regularly, check a recent copy of the *Journal* for the name and address of the current editor.

A

abstract film A film that uses mass, line, and color to create shifting and changing patterns. Also, loosely, any nonrepresentational film.

Academy ratio The size of the frame mask in 35mm cameras and projectors as standardized by the Academy of Motion Picture Arts and Sciences (1 to 1.3). Used from the 1930s to the 1950s.

adaptation The movement to the screen of a story, novel, play, or other work suitably treated so as to be realizable through the motion picture medium.

ambiguous time   Time on the screen that is either inadvertently or intentionally unclear. Dissolves, fades, and other transitional devices are not precise in their indication of the extent of the passage of time. Superimpositions also reveal time passing, but do not indicate how much. Often, ambiguous time is used in montage sequences whose purpose is to create mood and atmosphere, or to convey general rather than specific narrative information, for example, the lovers have spent time together and their love has deepened.

analytic documentary   A form of nonfiction film that attempts to analyze its subject matter rather than simply to record it. That analysis involves the filmmaker's own interaction with the subject, within the film, or his or her purposeful juxtaposition of footage to make a point. Unlike the persuasive documentary, which is a sort of propaganda film, the analytic documentary tries to show many facets of the subject matter although it makes no claim to objectivity.

anamorphic lens   A lens that squeezes the material it perceives so that its wider than normal scope can be recorded on a normal size film frame. During projection the image will be widened and appear as normal in size on a wider-than-normal screen (2.5 or 2.85 to 1).

angle   See **camera angle.**

aperture   *1) Lens aperture:* The opening, usually an adjustable iris, which limits the amount of light passing through a lens. *2) Camera aperture:* The mask opening, (in 16mm motion picture cameras, 0.410 × 0.294 inches), which defines the area of each frame exposed. *3) Projector aperture:* The mask opening, (in 16mm projectors, 0.380 × 0.284 inches), which defines the area of each frame projected.

art director   The person who assesses the staging requirements for a production and arranges for and supervises the work of set design and preparation. *UFA*

aspect ratio   The width-to-height ratio of a motion picture frame as photographed. Also, the ratio of the frame dimensions as projected on a screen.

associational editing, relational editing, associative editing   The juxtaposition of shots in order to present contrast, comparison, similarities, or ideas. *UFA*

asynchronous sound   Sound derived from a source not in the image on the screen at the time it is heard, that is, sound not in synchronization with corresponding lip movement or object movement in the film.

auteur theory   A theory that says there is a person primarily responsible for the entire style and treatment of the content of the film. Generally used in reference to a director with a recognizable style and thematic preoccupation, the theory also covers other production personnel (writers, performers, cinematographers, editors) who are seen as the major force behind a given film. More particularly, film auteurs function within the boundaries of studio production systems and are distinguishable from film artists, who have nearly total control over all aspects of production.

avant-garde, avant-garde film (French, literally "advance guard") *1)* A movement toward innovation in the arts in the 1920s, encompassing such approaches as cubism, surrealism, and dadaism, and including experimentation in filmmaking. *2)* Any current innovative movement in the arts. *UFA*

B

background music Nonindigenous music that accompanies a film, usually on the sound track, but may be from a live performance of one or more instrumentalists, or from records or tapes. Most background music in nontheatrical films is not scored to fit the action; in theatrical films the music is usually written to reinforce and emphasize the action. *UFA*

backlighting Light coming from behind objects or performers being photographed. *UFA*

blimp A camera housing that, because it is soundproof, prevents the noise of the camera's operation from being recorded on the sound track. Once immobile or awkward and bulky, blimps are now light and portable.

boom, camera boom A sturdy vehicular support providing vertical, horizontal, pivotal, and translational movement for camera and operator, enabling them to assume, rapidly and conveniently, almost any desired angle in relation to the scene to be photographed. *UFA (UFPA)*

C

camera angle, angle The physical relationship between camera and subject. If the camera is low, tilted up toward the subject, the result is a low-angle shot. If the camera is high, tilted down toward the subject, the result is a high-angle shot. If the camera is tilted neither up nor down, the result is a normal-angle shot. If the camera is not tilted but is placed at the eye-level of a person standing or seated, the angle is called an eye-level shot. If the camera is tilted off its horizontal and vertical axes, the result is a tilt angle or dutch-tilt angle. *UFA*

camera movement Any motion of a camera during a shot, such as panning, tilting, dollying, craning, rolling, or wobbling. *UFA*

camera speed The rate at which film is run through a camera in frames per second (fps) or feet or meters per minute. The normal speed for sound film today is 24 fps, for silent 18 fps.

cel A transparent sheet of cellulose acetate or similar plastic serving as a support for drawings, lettering, and so on, in animation and title work. Usually, it is punched, outside the limits of the camera field, with holes that fit pegs similarly arranged to facilitate registration of successive cels during preparation and photography. *UFA*

characters, characterizations   The fictional people within a narrative film, not to be confused with the actors who play them.

CinemaScope, Scope   Trade name (Metro-Goldwyn-Mayer) for wide-screen films made and projected by the use of anamorphic lenses on camera and projector. *UFA*

cinema verité   (French, literally "film truth") A style of filmmaking begun in Europe in the 1950s involving the use of portable sound cameras and recorders, and the cinematography of interviews and events on location. Commentary, sometimes obtained from interviews and hidden recorders, was used as well as lip-synchronous sound. Cinema verité films usually sought strong, sometimes radical, opinion. Often one of the filmmakers asked questions. *UFA*

Cinerama   A wide-screen process that originally used three cameras, three corresponding projectors, and stereophonic sound. *UFA*

city symphony   A type of nonfiction film that uses images of cities both lyrically and socially. Often structured around a dawn-to-dusk movement and edited rhythmically.

close-up shot, close-up, CU, close-shot, CS   A shot in which the image of the subject or its most important part fills most of the frame. A close-up shot of a person usually includes the head and part of the shoulders. *UFA*

code   The rules or forms that can be observed to allow a message to be understood, to signify. Codes are the rules operating on the means of expression (and thus are distinct from the means of expression). *UFA*

collage film   A type of experimental or avant-garde film that uses single-frame cinematography to control the speed with which images of various objects, cutouts, and drawings are overlaid, animated, and presented to the viewer.

color film   Color film carries one or more emulsions in which, after processing, brightness values of a scene are reproduced in terms of color scales. *UFA*

color saturation   The measure applied to how vividly a color appears on the film, that is, whether it seems washed out or dense.

comedy   Generally, a work of literature, drama, or film that has a nontragic ending and creates a climate considered humorous by a majority of viewers. There are many different types of comedy (slapstick, parody, screwball comedy), and comedy may be created around any subject matter.

compilation film   A film made by editing together large amounts of footage shot for other purposes, that is, old movie clips, home movies, newsreels, and so forth.

composition   The distribution, balance, and general relationship of masses and degrees of light and shade, line, and color within a picture area. *UFA (UFPA)*

contextual criticism   A form of criticism that sees film in relation to the context in which it was created and in which it is shown. Considerations of specific films and groups of films touch on history, politics, sociology, psychology, and other disciplines.

continuity The appearance in a fiction film of an autonomous, temporal flow of events. Standard Hollywood editing practices to hide the fact that film scenes are built up out of shots which are normally filmed out of sequence.

contrapuntal sound, counterpoint Sound, especially music, that contrasts or conflicts with the action in a motion picture. *UFA*

convention A recurrent unit of activity, dialogue, or cinematic technique that is used in films and is familiar to audiences, for example, the shoot out in a western, the line "There are some things man was not meant to know" in a horror film, the editing of a chase scene.

counterpoint See **contrapuntal sound.**

crane, camera crane A movable vehicle that has a long boom on which a camera can be mounted and moved up much higher than on a small dolly. *UFA*

credits, credit titles Names of people responsible for script, costumes, art direction, cinematography, acting, electricians, carpenters, assistants to the assistants, and so forth.

cross-cut A cut from one line of action to another. Also applies as an adjective to sequences that use such cuts. *UFA*

cubism An art movement, beginning about 1910, in which people and objects were broken down into their geometric components.

cue sheets Sheet music available to accompanists of silent films. Cue sheets indicated moods or dramatic sequences like the chase and then provided appropriately paced music, which might be played for any movie.

cut *1)* The instantaneous change from one shot to another. *2)* A command used to stop operation of the camera, action, and sound recording equipment. *3)* To sever or splice film in the editing process. *(UFPA)* Also, to eliminate a shot, sequence, or some sound from a film. Loosely, to edit a film. *UFA*

cut-away shot, cut-away, CA A shot of action occurring at the same time as the main action, but not part of the main action. A cut-away shot may be preceded by a definite look or glance out of frame by an actor or actors. Conversely, it may show something of which actors in the preceding shot are unaware. Example: during a chase, a shot of what is going on back at the ranch. *UFA*

D

dada An art movement of the 1920s, which predated surrealism. Like surrealism, it promoted incongruity, illogic, and shock. Its aims were anarchic and nihilistic.

decor   The furnishings and decorations used in a motion picture action field, especially set furnishing and decorations. *UFA*

deep-focus cinematography, deep-field cinematography   Cinematography that renders objects in focus at both near and far distances through the use of small f-stops, short focal length lenses, or both. *UFA.*

depth-of-field, D/F   The distance in front of a camera and its lens in which objects are in apparent sharp focus. *UFA*

dialogue   Lip-synchronous speech in a film with the speaker usually, but not always, visible. *UFA*

direct cinema, uncontrolled documentary   A type of location, nonfiction, close observation cinema in which lightweight cameras and sound recorders are used to record action as it actually happens with indigenous sound only. The origin of the term, used to distinguish this kind of filmmaking from cinema verité, is attributed to Albert Maysles. *UFA*

direct cut   See **straight cut.**

director   The individual who interprets the script in terms of performances and cinematic technique, and who supervises all phases of the work involved in achieving a coherent, unified film presentation. *UFA (UFPA)*

director's script   See **shooting script.**

disorientation cut   Two pieces of film edited together for their disorienting or dislocating effect on the viewer. The cut is made to confuse the viewer as to content, space, or time.

dissolve, lap dissolve   An optical edit which results when one shot fades out at the same time that a second shot fades in.

documentary   A nonfiction film. It uses images of life as its raw material and may be of many different types with many different purposes.

Dolby system   Trade name for a noise-reduction system designed to reduce the noise level of a tape or optical recording and thus achieve better fidelity. *UFA*

dolly   *1)* A small, sturdy wheeled platform built to carry camera and camera operators to facilitate movement of the camera during shooting. *2)* To move the camera by means of a dolly while shooting. *UFA (UFPA)*

double exposure, multiple exposure   The photographic recording of two (or more) images on a single strip of film. The images may be either superimposed or side-by-side in any relationship, sometimes individually vignetted. *UFA (UFPA)*

double-system sound recording   The recording of sound on a recorder that is separate from the camera. The recorder is usually a magnetic tape recorder with sync-pulse capability or a magnetic film recorder. *UFA*

dramatization   The acting out and the realization of that acting out in images on the screen of a fictional or factual event. Narration tells us what happened, dramatization shows it to us as it happens.

dub   To transfer sound from one medium to another. Also, to put dialogue, sometimes foreign, into a film after it has been shot. *UFA*

E

edge numbers, edge numbering   Numbers placed on the edge film to facilitate matching (conforming) of original film and sound to edited workprints. *UFA*

editing, cutting   The process of assembling, arranging, and trimming film, both picture and sound, to the best advantage for the purpose at hand. *UFA (UFPA)*

effects, FX   Depending on context, either sound effects, optical effects, or special effects. *UFA*

elevator shot   A shot in which the camera moves straight up and down, not in an arc as on a crane. *UFA*

emulsion   The coating, consisting of gelatin and silver salts (unprocessed film), gelatin and metallic silver (processed film), or iron oxide (for magnetic sound) bonded to and supported by a film base. *UFA*

epic   A film that stresses spectacle and large casts, often with a historical or biblical plot. The emphasis is on scope, and so, appropriately, many epics have been filmed in various wide-screen processes.

epic documentary   A recent form of documentary distinguished by its great length, its combination of interviews and stock footage, and its attempts to be accurate and fair through its complexity and scope.

establishing shot   Usually, a long shot that shows the location of the ensuing action, but may be a close-up or even a medium shot which has some sign or other clue that identifies the location. Sometimes called a *cover shot*. *UFA*

ethnographic film   An anthropological film that combines visual raw data and analysis through commentary and editing. *UFA*

experienced time   The time the film seems to take to the viewer, generally felt as a sense of rhythm and pacing, that is, the film felt long and boring or excitingly fast. Not to be confused with subjective time, which belongs to a screen character rather than the viewer.

experimental film   An independent, noncommercial film that is the product of the personal vision of the filmmaker. *UFA*

exposé   An investigative documentary that presents factual material ignored or unknown, with an eye to effecting viewer action. Sometimes it approaches yellow journalism and is more exploitative than socially oriented.

expressionism, expressionist, expressionistic   Fantasy and distortion in sets, editing, lighting, and costumes used as a means of expressing the inner feelings of both filmmaker and characters.

extended image   Composition within the film frame that draws the viewer's eye and consciousness beyond the frame itself and suggests the completion of the image outside the camera field, for example, an image of half a face in the frame will provoke the viewer to complete the image mentally, and so to extend the face beyond what is shown in the actual image.

extreme close-up, ECU, extreme close shot, ECS   A very close shot of some detail, such as an actor's eyes or a small object. *UFA*

extreme long shot, ELS, XLS   A shot that shows considerable distance. Usually used only in reference to outdoor shots. *UFA*

F

fade   An optical or sound effect in which the screen or sound track gradually changes from black to an image or silence to sound (fade-in) or the reverse (fade-out).

fast film   A film that has relatively high sensitivity to light, usually an exposure index of 100 or higher. *UFA*

fast motion   Action which has been photographed at a filming rate less than normal, then projected at normal speed. Sometimes called accelerated motion. *UFA*

feature film, feature   Usually, a fictional narrative film lasting more than an hour, made for showing in commercial theaters. *UFA*

film   *1)* A strip of flexible, transparent base material, usually cellulose triacetate, having various coatings such as photographic emulsions and iron oxide, and usually perforated. *2)* To photograph a motion picture. *3)* The cinema in general. *4)* A movie, a motion picture.

film artisan   A filmmaker who realizes a given film on the screen competently and aesthetically, in accordance with production dictates of a studio, or other commercial considerations. Generally not the originator of the story and not preoccupied thematically, the film artisan does not develop a personal style, but matches his or her style to the needs of a particular production.

film artist   Generally, a filmmaker who has as much control over the idea, production, realization, and final form of a released film as is possible, given the collaborative nature of the commercial medium. Unlike the film auteur, who faces many studio-determined obstacles in realizing his or her personal vision on the screen, the film artist often works independently and with hand-chosen collaborators. (Often loosely used as a synonym for film auteur.)

film auteur   See **auteur.**

film criticism   The analysis and evaluation of films, usually in relation to theoretical principles including both aesthetics and philosophy. *UFA*

film movement   The films and filmmakers who constitute a cinema (usually national) at a given period of historical time. Most often, social and political factors cause a film movement, bringing together artists who have common aesthetic and political goals and who recognize themselves as a group.

film noir (French, literally "black film") The term refers to a group of films that share a common cinematic style and related themes dealing with corruption, generally in urban settings. Most often used in reference to a group of films made in Hollywood during the 1940s and 1950s.

film review, review A summary of the content of a film, usually accompanied by information about the cast and the production, and often by the reviewer's judgment as to the worth of the film, published in print media or delivered orally on radio or television. *UFA*

film speed *1)* The general term used to indicate a film emulsion's sensitivity to light; the higher (or faster) the film speed, the better it is able to record an image with low illumination. *2)* The rate of speed at which the film progresses through the camera and the projector, measured in frames per second or feet or meters per minute.

film stock Unprocessed film with various characteristics, for example, black and white, color, infrared, high speed, low grain, high contrast.

film theory General principles that explain the nature and capabilities of film. The ongoing discourse that attempts to uncover such principles.

filmic time and space The expansion, condensation, or elimination of time and space, as well as shifts from a film's present to past time, through flashbacks, and to future time, through flash-forwards, structured by lighting, color shifts, angle, framing, sound, and so on.

filter A device used both in sound recording and mixing and in cinematography to block out unwanted sounds, light, or color, or to change the natural quality of sound, light, or color.

final cut The editing of the film as it will be released in theaters. The filmmaker who has the right to final cut will guarantee that her or his version of the film is not tampered with prior to its release.

fisheye lens An extreme wide-angle lens that distorts the image so that straight lines appear bowed at the edges of the frame.

flash pan, swish pan An extremely rapid pan in which the subject becomes blurred.

flashback A shot or sequence (sometimes quite long) showing action that occurred before the film's present time. *UFA*

flash-forward A shot or sequence that shows future action or action which will be seen later in the film. *UFA*

flatbed editor, flatbed editing machine, horizontal editor A table on which there are upright spindles for film and sound tracks, sprocket drives, heads for picture projection and sound reading, provision for interlock and advancing or retarding sound, and other features, used in various ways in the editing of films. *UFA*

floodlight, flood   Any of various types of lights that cast wide beams of light.

focal length   The distance from the lens to the film plane when the lens is focused at infinity. A lens with a long focal length is a telephoto, a short focal length, a wide angle.

focus   *1)* The sharpness or definition of the image. *2)* To adjust the sharpness and clarity of the image by adjusting the lens or light source so as to create sharp or soft focus or to change focus.

foreground music   Often synchronous, music that finds its source within the actual narrative of the film. It can be heard realistically over the radio or from a television set, or performed on screen by the narrative characters (both major and minor) or by performers in the background.

formalism, formalist   A cinematic or critical approach to film which stresses form over content in the belief that meaning occurs in the way that content is presented.

formula   A pattern of dramatic actions or plot (for example, the reluctant hero of a western forced to take up his guns once more for the final shoot-out) that becomes familiar as it is repeated with minor variations from film to film.

frame, framing   *1)* One individual picture, as defined by the limits of the camera aperture, on a piece of motion picture film. *2)* To compose a shot. *UFA (UFPA)*

freeze frame, stop frame, hold frame   A frame that is printed repetitively so that although the projector is still operating, the image in the print can be seen without movement for a desired length of time. *UFA*

futurism   An art movement around the time of World War I, emphasizing speed and dynamism in its forms as a response to modern life in the machine age.

G

gate   A hinged support for projector or camera pressure plate. Also, loosely, the camera or projector film aperture. *UFA (UFPA)*

genre   A film type, such as a western or science fiction film, which usually has conventional plot structure and characters; loosely, a formula film. *UFA*

German Expressionism   A film movement in Germany from 1919 through the 1920s, peaking about 1925. Following earlier expressionist movements in fine art and literature, filmmakers used decor, lighting, and cinematic technique to express interior states of being and feeling rather than to record an objective reality.

glass shot   A shot taken through a sheet of glass bearing titles or other art work in order to superimpose titles or artwork on the moving background. *UFA (UFPA)*

grainy, graininess, grain An image is grainy if it appears to be made up of distinguishable particles or grains. Actually, this is due to the grouping together, or clumping, of the individual silver grains, which are by themselves far too small to be perceived under normal viewing conditions. *UFA (UFPA)*

H

hand-held Shot with a camera by a camera operator. Also, the somewhat wobbly image on the screen, which results from such shooting. *UFA*

high-angle shot, high shot See **camera angle.**

high contrast The appearance of an image in which tones grade quickly from white to black with few intermediate values. *UFA*

high grain See **grainy.**

high-key A quality of any picture in which the emphasis is distinctly on the lighter tones. Also, in lighting, a relatively high level of illumination of subject, with relatively short-scale tonal rendition. *UFA (UFPA)*

high-speed film *1)* Film that has extra perforations for use in high-speed camera. *2)* Film that is very sensitive to light. *3)* A film made using mostly high-speed cinematography. *UFA*

holography Photography using laser light instead of sunlight or conventional artificial light, producing 3–D images.

I

icon, iconography An object, landscape, or performer who accrues symbolic as well as particular meaning and conveys that meaning through recurrent presence in a group or genre of films. Not to be confused with a motif, which accrues such meaning in a single film only.

image (photographic) Any photographically obtained likeness in a processed photosensitive material. *UFA*

independent filmmaking Film production initiated by a person or persons not under contract to a commercial studio. Some independents may produce without making use of union personnel or commercial facilities, other than a laboratory. Others may subcontract the production to union personnel and commercial facilities. Off-Hollywood features made on low budgets. With the demise of the studio system in the 1960s, nearly all theatrical films today are independent productions.

insert shot, insert A shot of some detail of the main action or parallel action that can be made at any time during production, then inserted into the action during the editing process. *UFA*

intellectual montage An assembly of shots through editing that results in conveying an abstract or intellectual concept. A group of people being menaced and beaten by mounted police next to a shot of cattle being slaughtered in a slaughterhouse provokes the idea that the people in the first shot are being victimized and are helpless, considered no better than dumb animals by their oppressors. This idea is not pictured; it is suggested by the relationship of the two shots.

intercutting   Insertion into a series of related shots of other shots for contrast or other effect. *UFA*

invisible editing, invisible cut   A cut made during the movement of a performer, achieved either by overlapping the action, or by using two cameras and then matching the action during editing. Such cuts make shifts of camera position less noticeable. Conventional Hollywood narrative structure.

iris   A circular masking device, so called because of its resemblance to the iris of the human eye.

J

jump cut   An instantaneous advance in the action within a shot or between two shots due to the removal of a portion of film, to poor pictorial continuity, or to remind intentionally the viewer that editing is taking place.

K

key light   The light source that creates the main, brightest light falling on a subject.

L

lens aperture   See **aperture.**

light, lighting   *1)* Radiant energy. *2)* Illumination (the lamps) used in connection with filming. *3)* To arrange illumination for shooting. *UFA*

live action   The action of living things, as distinguished from action created by animation. *UFA*

location shooting   Shooting done away from a studio. *UFA*

long shot, LS   A shot that shows all or most of a fairly large subject (for example, a person) and usually much of the surroundings.

long take   A single shot (or take, or run of the camera) that lasts for a relatively lengthy period of time before it is juxtaposed with another shot. It reveals information within an unbroken context of space and time, and through camera and subject movement rather than through editing.

low-angle shot, low shot   See **camera angle.**

low contrast   Of a photographic image, having a long gradation of tones from white to black. *UFA*

low-key   *1)* Pictures in which the majority of tones lie toward the darker end of the scale. *2)* In lighting, a generally low level of illumination of subject, with relatively short-scale tonal rendition. *UFA (UFPA)*

M

magnetic tape, magnetic sound Thin tape bearing an iron oxide coating on which sound may be recorded and from which sound may be reproduced. *UFA*

mask A device used to block or limit the passage of light from one area while admitting whole or reduced illumination to another area. A mask is used to create a wider ratio image on 35mm film by cutting off the top and bottom of the original nearly square image.

master shot, master scene A long shot or moving shot that includes all of the action in a particular sequence, with the camera fairly distant. After it is made, if only one camera is being used, medium shots and close ups are made of the repeated action and are inserted into the master shot during editing. *UFA*

matte shot A shot in which a portion of the action field is masked off with action put in later either in the original camera, in a bipack camera, or in an optical printer.

medium shot, MS A shot that shows part of a person or object. A medium shot of a person is usually considered to be one which includes head, shoulders, chest, and enough additional space for hand gestures to be seen. *UFA*

melodrama In Aristotle's terms, a work of literature or film that treats serious subject matter (often life and death situations), but is distinct from tragedy because the ending is always happily resolved with the protagonist overcoming all obstacles to achieve his or her desired goal. In those cases where the protagonist does not fully have the audience's sympathy (that is, the socially unacceptable ambitious female of the 1940s or the gangster hero of the 1930s), the happy ending for society, not the protagonist, may be somewhat ambiguous. Also used as a term for women's pictures, that is, the family melodrama.

microcinematography Cinematography accomplished through the use of a microscope. Mostly used in scientific filmmaking, but also used in documentary and fiction films.

minimal film, minimal cinema A type of experimental film that attempts to reduce film to its basic properties (its recording of actuality in continuous space and time) with minimal intervention by the filmmaker.

mise-en-scène *1)* A term generally used to describe those elements of the film image placed before the camera and in relation to it, rather than to the process of editing that occurs after the interaction between camera and subject. *2)* Also, the images in which context and relationships are revealed in units that preserve continuous space and time.

mix, sound mix To combine sound from two or more sources into a single recording, usually with adjustment of tonal quality and/or relative volume level. *(UFPA)* Also, the completed recording itself. *UFA*

montage The assembly of shots, hence, editing, and especially the portrayal of action and creation of ideas through the use of many short shots. In the 1920s, the Russians formulated several kinds of montage styles. Later, in the United States, montage came to mean a series of shots, often with superimpositions and optical effects, showing a condensed series of events, for example, a crime wave in a city. *UFA*

motif An object or sound that becomes linked to a film's narrative in a meaningful way so that it becomes symbolically identified with a character or action. The glass paperweight in *Citizen Kane* and the attack music in *Jaws* are motifs. Not to be confused with icons, which function from film to film, motifs convey specific meaning in a single film only.

multiple exposure The addition of images to a strip of film after the initial exposure, done by rewinding and reexposing the film in the camera more than twice, or by combining images in printing. *UFA*

multiple image Having several images, not superimposed, within the frame.

multiple track, multiple channel More than one recording source for motion picture sound. For easier control in sound mixing, dialogue, music, and effects are recorded on separate tracks, which are then mixed into one track, or several tracks for stereophonic sound. As many as eight tracks can be used for the final optical sound track.

N

narration Commentary spoken by an off-screen voice. In informational films, the voice is usually that of an anonymous expert. In dramatic films, it may be the voice of one of the characters. *UFA*

negative image An image in which the light and dark areas in the original subject are rendered correspondingly as dark and light areas. In the case of a negative color image, the subject color values are represented in the film as colors complementary to the colors producing them, in addition to the usual inversion of the black-and-white tonal scale. *UFA*

Neorealism, Italian Neorealism A style of filming and kind of film content that became prominent in Italy after World War II, characterized by concern with human struggles against inhumane social forces, filmed mostly on location with untrained actors, and using unsoftened realism throughout. *UFA*

newsreel About 10 minutes of news film, edited with titles, music, speed, and commentary, formerly seen regularly in theaters, but now no longer produced in the United States. *UFA*

noise Unwanted sound in an audio pickup. *UFA*

nonfiction film Any film that does not use an invented plot or characters.

O

objective camera angle, objective camera Camera coverage that places the audience in the position of an observer of the action. *UFA*

objective time Time as it is recorded and revealed through camera movement and editing, unallied with any specific character in the narrative, or with a narrator. The camera functions as an omniscient third person narrator and the viewer is to perceive the time it perceives as undistorted by emotion or personality. Objective time often coincides with screen time.

off-screen space Space that is out of the camera field, but is implied by the film through the movement of the camera and subject movement into and out of the field of vision.

optical cut, optical effect, optical Any systematic progressive alteration of a motion picture scene, or transition from one scene to another, commonly made by the optical printer. Includes the fade, the dissolve, and the wipe, as well as a host of more spectacular effects. *UFA (UFPA)*

optical printer A printer consisting essentially of a projector and a camera. Light passing through the film to be printed subsequently passes through a lens system before striking the print stock. The lens system and associated devices permit reduction and enlargement and the making of various kinds of effects. *UFA*

optical sound Sound recorded on or reproduced from photographic sound tracks, as distinguished from sound recorded on or reproduced from disks, tapes, and magnetic film. *UFA*

out-take In general, any shot that is removed from a film. More specifically, shots that are not workprinted. *UFA*

overhead shot A shot made from a position directly above the action. *UFA*

P

pan, pan shot A movement of the camera from left to right or right to left along a horizontal plane. Unlike the tracking shot in which the camera moves with the subject, the pan is shot from a stationary point.

parallel editing, parallel action, cross-cutting The intercutting of shots of two or more simultaneously occurring lines of action. *UFA*

persuasive documentary A form of documentary that is aimed at convincing the viewer of a given thesis. Raw footage is assembled so as to make that point, and narration is not uncommon. At its most extreme, persuasion is attempted through dramatization presented on screen as actuality, or distortion of actual fact through editing or commentary; this form of persuasion is called *propaganda*.

pin spot A spotlight in which light is directed through lens and reflectors into an extremely narrow beam. Often used to add illumination to a performer's eyes.

point-of-view shot, p.o.v. shot, POV A shot made from a camera position close to the line of sight of a performer who is to be watching the action shown in the point-of-view shot. *UFA*

postsynchronized sound, dubbed sound Lip-synchronous sound recorded after film has been shot, either in the language used by the performers or in foreign language, which fits the lip movements of the performers. *UFA*

process shot   A shot made of action in front of a rear projection screen having on it still or moving images for the background. *UFA*

producer   The entrepreneur who initiates and/or manages film production activities. *(UFPA)* Also, the administrator who is assigned to manage the production of a contract film. *UFA*

propaganda film   A type of film used for persuasive purposes (often political) that tends to manipulate and distort actuality and to appeal to emotion rather than to rational thought.

puppet animation   Animation of puppet figures that often have numerous heads and body parts with slightly different expressions and positions. *UFA*

R

rack focus, pull focus, shift focus   To change the focus of a lens during a shot. *UFA*

raw footage   Exposed film that has recorded desired subject matter but has not yet been assembled into any kind of narrative or informative order, or selected on considerations of its satisfactory or unsatisfactory technical qualities.

reaction shot   Any shot, usually a cutaway, in which an actor reacts to action that has just occurred. *UFA*

realism, realistic film   The use of scripts, staging, costuming, and camera coverage that renders action as if it were real, not fantasy. Attending to the conventions of realism, that is, the promotion of ordinary human figures in lifelike situations concerned with everyday problems maintaining a high degree of plausibility.

reflector   A surface used to direct reflected sunlight (or artificial light) onto the subject matter to be photographed. It is used to either soften and diffuse harsh light or to enhance available light.

reverse motion, reverse action   Action that goes backward on the screen, achieved by shooting with the camera upside down, then turning the processed film end-over-end, or by shooting with camera rightside up and action reversed, or by reverse printing in an optical printer. *UFA*

running time   The time of the film's duration on the screen, its length, for example, $2\frac{1}{2}$ hours.

S

satire   A work of literature or film that ridicules or exposes the vices, follies, foibles, and shortcomings of its subject, most often society and its institutions.

scene   A dramatic unit composed of a single shot or several. A scene usually takes place in a continuous time period, in the same setting, and involves the same characters.

screen time, diegetic time   The time covered by the film's story, or narrative time, that is, a lifetime, a week, two days.

screenplay   See **script.**

screenwriter, script writer   One who prepares stories, treatments, and scripts for motion pictures. *UFA*

screwball comedy   A kind of American feature film that got its start in the 1930s, characterized by satire, sexual candor, romance, comically impossible and incongruous situations involving likeable people from different social classes, and fast-moving events. *UFA*

script   A set of written specifications for the production of a motion picture. *(UFPA)* There are several different kinds of scripts and they contain specifications for settings, action, camera coverage, dialogue, narration, music, and sound effects, in varying degrees of explicitness. *UFA*

selective focus   Rendering only part of the action field in sharp focus through the use of shallow depth of field. *UFA*

selective sound   A track in which some sounds are removed while others are retained. It can sound realistic, but it can also be so selective that its lack of ambient sound makes it seem artificial or expressionistic.

semiotics, semiology   *1)* The study of signification via codes or systems in texts. *2)* The general science of signs, of systems of signification. *UFA*

sequence   A dramatic unit composed of several scenes, all linked together by their emotional and narrative momentum. A sequence can span time and space so long as its dramatic elements and structure are unified.

setting   The location for a film or parts of a film. *UFA*

setup   One camera position and its associated lighting. Also, loosely, any arrangement of settings, lights, and cameras. *UFA*

shooting ratio   The amount of film shot compared to the length of the edited film, with the edited film having a value of one. *UFA*

shooting script   A final script that is followed by performers and the director during filming. *UFA*

shooting time   The time it takes to set up, perform, and record photographically the images and sound of a motion picture.

shot   *1)* A single run of the camera. *2)* The piece of film resulting from such a run. Systematically joined together in the process of editing, shots are synthesized into sequences, and the sequences in turn are joined to form the film as a whole. *UFA (UFPA)*

shot analysis   A careful and thorough recording of the separate shots that constitute an entire film or specific sequences. The analysis describes the visual images, camera movement, duration, sound, and transitions from shot to shot. Sometimes such an analysis is drawn as if it were a storyboard.

shutter In a motion picture camera, the mechanical device that shields the film from light at the aperture during the film movement portion of the intermittent cycle. Also, a similar device in projectors for cutting the projection light during the time the film is moving at the aperture. *UFA (UFPA)*

silent speed Originally, about sixteen frames per second, although camera operators varied their speed and projectionists were often instructed to crank more slowly for love scenes and faster for chases. Now, eighteen frames per second. *UFA*

simultaneous time Created by the parallel editing or cross-cutting of events that are narratively understood to be occurring at the same moment, for example, the heroine being tied to the railroad tracks, cut back and forth with the hero riding to her rescue. Can also be created through multiple image and split-screen technique, in which different events actually do occur in simultaneous running and screen time.

single-frame cinematography, single-frame shooting, single-framing Releasing the starting switch or release for each frame of film exposed. Often used to speed up greatly the normal motion of persons and objects, to give apparent motion to lifeless objects, and to speed up the growth and development of plants and animals (time-lapse cinematography), when the film is projected at normal speeds. *UFA*

slapstick comedy, slapstick Violent, acrobatic comic acting, generally depicting aggressive and destructive behavior.

slow motion Action that takes place on the screen at a rate less rapid than the rate of the real action which took place before the camera. This occurs when the camera is operated at a frame repetition rate greater than standard, but the projection frame repetition rate is maintained at standard or below. *UFA (UFPA)*

slow-speed film A film whose emulsion needs a greater or slower exposure to light to register an image satisfactorily. Compared to high-speed film (fast film), slow film produces a finer-grained, slicker looking image.

soft focus An effect in which sharpness of image is reduced by the use of an optical device, usually a soft-focus lens, diffusion disk, or open-weave cloth over the lens. Usually confined to close-ups. *(UFPA)* Also used to indicate an image or parts of an image which are slightly out of focus. *UFA*

solarization, color solarization A process (either chemical or electronic) that reverses or shifts color values in color film. The image appears somewhat like a color negative.

sound bridge A segment of sound track (dialogue, music, effects) that continues from one shot into another quite different shot, that is, time, space, or characters change radically enough for the two shots to be part of two separate scenes. The sound track thus acts as a unifier, a bridge, between the two and the transition is less abrupt.

sound effects, SFX Any sound from any source other than synchronized dialogue, narration, or music.

sound-on-disk, sound-on-record   The first commercially used sound process, which was then superseded by the more efficient and economical sound-on-film (or optical sound) process. Sound on phonograph records was synchronized to the projector, and thus image and sound synchronization on the screen was achieved.

sound-on-film   See **optical sound.**

sound perspective, aural perspective   The impression of distance in sound. *UFA*

sound track, track   The portion of the length of film reserved for the sound record, of any recording so located. Also, any length of film bearing sound only. *UFA (UFPA)*

Soviet Social Realism   A film movement in postrevolutionary Russia that joined ideology and aesthetics to celebrate the new Soviet Union cinematically. The emphasis was on documentary realism illuminated by artistic and purposeful editing and camera technique. The movement lost all its imagination and energy after Stalin came to power and saw its earlier practitioners as too elite and formalist.

special effects   Shots unobtainable by straightforward motion picture shooting techniques. In this category fall shots requiring contour matting, multiple image montages, split screens, vignetting, models, and the like. *(UFPA)* Term also applies to explosions, ballistics effects, and mechanical effects. *UFA*

Spieler, der (German and Yiddish, literally "the player")   A term applied to the person who told the story and read the title cards during the exhibition of silent movies so that non-English-speaking immigrants and illiterates could follow the plot.

splice   The act of joining two pieces of film by any of several methods — by cementing, butt-welding, taping, or, for processing, by staples or grommets. Also, the resulting lapped or joined portions of film. *UFA (UFPA)*

split screen effect, split screen, split screen shot   The division of the film frame into two or more separate nonoverlapping images, done either in the camera or in an optical printer. *UFA*

spotlight, spot   A luminaire in which light from a contained source is directed by means of a reflector and lens into a relatively narrow beam. *UFA (UFPA)*

sprockets, sprocket roller, sprocket wheel   A roller having teeth that engage the perforations of a film in order to pull the film along. *UFA*

star system   The system of developing audience appeal through publicity stressing a leading performer rather than other elements of a film. Begun in the second decade of this century with such stars as Mary Pickford and Charlie Chaplin, the system allows star actors to command extremely high salaries. *UFA*

Steadicam   Trade name for a camera support attached to the operator's body. A movement-dampening mechanism holds the camera steady, and the outfit uses a small television monitor as a viewfinder. *UFA*

stereophonic sound   Sound that was recorded through two or more microphones each of which has its own track, and is played back in two or more corresponding loud speakers in order to achieve a 3–D effect. *UFA*

stock shots, stock footage, SS   Film footage of scenery and action catalogued and stored for possible future use. *UFA*

storyboard   A pictorial outline of a film presentation, with sketches or photographs representing shots, and usually having in writing the speech, music, and sound effects that are to go with each shot. *UFA*

straight cut   Descriptive of two shots butted together with no optical effects. *UFA*

structural film, perceptual film   Films using slow or fast camera movements, repeated loops, extended zooms, flickers, or images photographed from the screen on which they are projected in order to explore the structures of the medium.

structuralism   The study of how human institutions and art forms are structured on basic notions of conflict and opposition (for example, light and dark, good and evil) and how those structures are repetitive and archetypal.

subjective camera, subjective viewpoint   A situation in which the audience involvement with a scene is intensified through identification with the camera point-of-view. In some dramatic films, the camera has taken the place of an actor, with other actors looking directly at the lens. *UFA (UFPA)*

subjective time   The time experienced or felt by a character in a film, as revealed through camera movement and editing, for example, a fearful character climbs a flight of stairs to find out what is making a noise and the climb is prolonged to match his terror, or a character dreams and time has no meaning.

subtitle, subtitling   A title superimposed over action, usually at the bottom of the frame, used to translate foreign language, or to identify the scene. *UFA (UFPA)*

sun screens   Screens made out of mesh or gauze used to diffuse sunlight during exterior shooting.

superimpose, superimposition, super   To place a smaller image over another image by double exposure, double printing, or other technique. *UFA*

surrealism   An art movement of the 1920s that attempted to tap the world of dreams and the unconscious for its sources. Incongruity, shock, and a rejection of causality were its major characteristics. Because of its ability to move instantaneously in time and space, film greatly interested surrealist artists.

synchronization   Achieving a precise match between picture and sound. *UFA*

synchronous sound   Sound whose source is apparent in the picture, and which matches the action. *UFA*

T

take   A shot. Also, a term used to indicate the number of times a given shot has been made. Takes are usually numbered sequentially and identified in picture by slate and in track by voice. *UFA (UFPA)*

telephoto lens, telephoto shot   An extremely long lens able to bring far distant objects into close view, acting as a magnifier. It has a very narrow angle of view and therefore tends to foreshorten and flatten its distant subject matter. It also makes motion toward the camera appear extremely slow, creating a treadmill effect.

theme   The story subject matter from which the general value or idea forming the intellectual background for a film is evolved. *UFA (UFPA)*

360-degree pan   A pan shot that makes a complete circle. *UFA*

title, title card   The name or designation of a film. Also, any inscription contained in a film for the purpose of conveying information about the film, its message, or its story to the viewer. *UFA (UFPA)*

tone   The mood or atmosphere of a film (for example, ironic, comic, nostalgic, romantic) created as the sum of the film's cinematic techniques.

tracking shot, traveling shot, trucking shot   A shot made while the camera and its entire support are moving. *UFA*

tragedy   A work of literature or drama that focuses on the downfall of an admirable character whose defeat (physical or moral) usually is brought about through a flaw in an otherwise noble nature.

travelogue   A short, nondramatic film showing events in distant places or foreign countries. *UFA*

treatment, treatment outline   A short summary of a proposed film, giving information about the kind of production and describing the main sequences to be developed. *UFA (UFPA)*

trucking shot   See **tracking shot.**

typecasting, typage   The selecting or casting of actors because of their looks or type rather than for their acting experience. *UFA*

U

uncontrolled documentary   See **direct cinema.**

underground cinema   A term often used synonymously with independent film, avant-garde film and experimental film. It also, however, connotes films that deal with shocking subject matter, or are purposefully anti-traditional.

universal time   Time created through imagery (often edited in a montage sequence) that abstracts its subject matter from a specific temporal or spatial context. The actions perceived could occur, therefore, anywhere and at any time, and the experiences on the screen are universalized.

V

viewer's script, cutting continuity script   Often published after the critical and commercial success of a film, this script is a recording in dialogue or frames of the film as it appears on the screen in its final release. It may differ quite a bit from the actual shooting script.

viewpoint   The apparent distance and angle from which the camera views and records the subject. Not to be confused with point-of-view shots or subjective camera shots.

voice-over, VO   *1)* A sound and picture relationship in which a narrator's voice accompanies picture action. *2)* Any off-screen voice. *3)* A narration job. *UFA*

W

wide-angle lens, wide-angle shot.   A short lens able to capture a broad field of action. It appears to create depth and, in its extreme forms (such as the fisheye), distorts linear perspective so that the edges of the image may appear bowed.

wild   Descriptive of any device or process not susceptible to precise control. Either picture or sound, shot without synchronous relationship to the other.

wipe   An optical effect used to join one shot to another. In its commonest form, scene *A* appears to be wiped off the screen by the progressive revelation of scene *B* as a vertical dividing line separating the two advances across the screen from left to right. Many modifications of this basic form have been used, such as vertical, diagonal, iris, spiral, and even "atomic bomb" wipes. *UFA (UFPA)*

work print   Any positive duplicate picture, sound track print, or magnetic duplicate intended for use in the editing process to establish through a series of trial cuttings the finished version of a film. The purpose is to preserve the original intact and undamaged until the cutting points have been established. *UFA (UFPA)*

writer's script   The screenplay for a motion picture conceived by the writer and recorded to best represent the story and characters to potential commercial backers. Such a script will have a minimum of camera direction, lighting information, or technical specificity, but will attempt instead to convey mood, tone, plot, and characterization.

Z

zoom lens, varifocal lens, variable-focal-length lens   A lens with effective focal length continuously variable within a limited range. Changing the focal length of such a lens as a shot progresses simulates the effect of movement of the camera toward or away from the subject. *UFA (UFPA)*

INDEX